Sources and Methods in Indigenous Studies

Sources and Methods in Indigenous Studies is a synthesis of changes and innovations in methodologies in Indigenous Studies, focusing on sources over a broad chronological and geographical range. Written by a group of highly respected Indigenous Studies scholars from across an array of disciplines, this collection offers insight into the methodological approaches contributors take to research, and how these methods have developed in recent years.

The book has a two-part structure that looks, firstly, at the theoretical and disciplinary movement of Indigenous Studies within history, literature, anthropology, and the social sciences. Chapters in this section reveal that, while engaging with other disciplines, Indigenous Studies has forged its own intellectual path by borrowing and innovating from other fields. In the second part, the book examines the many different areas with which sources for Indigenous history have been engaged, including the importance of family, gender, feminism, and sexuality, as well as various elements of expressive culture such as material culture, literature, and museums. Together, the chapters offer readers an overview of the dynamic state of the field in Indigenous Studies.

This book shines a spotlight on the ways in which scholarship is transforming Indigenous Studies in methodologically innovative and exciting ways, and will be essential reading for students and scholars in the field.

Chris Andersen (Michif) is Professor and Interim Dean of the Faculty of Native Studies at the University of Alberta. He is the author of *"Métis": Race, Recognition and the Struggle for Indigenous Peoplehood* (2014).

Jean M. O'Brien (White Earth Ojibwe) is Distinguished McKnight University Professor of History at the University of Minnesota. She has authored five books, including *Firsting and Lasting: Writing Indians Out of Existence in New England* (2010).

The Routledge Guides to Using Historical Sources

How does the historian approach primary sources? How do interpretations differ? How can such sources be used to write history?

The *Routledge Guides to Using Historical Sources* series introduces students to different sources and illustrates how historians use them. Titles in the series offer a broad spectrum of primary sources and, using specific examples, examine the historical context of these sources and the different approaches that can be used to interpret them.

Reading Primary Sources
Miriam Dobson and Benjamin Ziemann

History Beyond the Text
Sarah Barber and Corinna Penniston-Bird

History and Material Culture
Karen Harvey

Understanding Medieval Primary Sources
Joel Rosenthal

Memory and History
Understanding Memory as Source and Subject
Joan Tumblety

Understanding Early Modern Primary Sources
Laura Sangha and Jonathan Willis

Sources and Methods in Indigenous Studies

Edited by Chris Andersen and Jean M. O'Brien

Routledge
Taylor & Francis Group

LONDON AND NEW YORK

First published 2017
by Routledge
2 Park Square, Milton Park, Abingdon, Oxon OX14 4RN

and by Routledge
711 Third Avenue, New York, NY 10017

Routledge is an imprint of the Taylor & Francis Group, an informa business

© 2017 selection and editorial matter, Chris Andersen and Jean M. O'Brien; individual chapters, the contributors

British Library Cataloguing in Publication Data
A catalogue record for this book is available from the British Library

Library of Congress Cataloging in Publication Data
Names: Andersen, Chris, 1973- editor. | O'Brien, Jean M., editor.
Title: Sources and methods in indigenous studies / edited by Chris Andersen and Jean M. O'Brien.
Description: Abingdon, Oxon ; New York, NY : Routledge, 2017. | Includes bibliographical references and index.
Identifiers: LCCN 2016007801| ISBN 9781138823600 (hardback : alk. paper) | ISBN 9781138823617 (pbk. : alk. paper) | ISBN 9781315528854 (ebook)
Subjects: LCSH: Indigenous peoples--Research--Methodology. | Applied anthropology. | Ethnology--Methodology.
Classification: LCC GN380 .S68 2017 | DDC 305.8/001--dc23
LC record available at https://lccn.loc.gov/2016007801

ISBN: 978-1-138-82360-0 (hbk)
ISBN: 978-1-138-82361-7 (pbk)
ISBN: 978-1-315-52885-4 (ebk)

Typeset in Times New Roman
by Saxon Graphics Ltd, Derby

Contents

Contributors

Chris Andersen (Michif) is a professor and current Interim Dean of the Faculty of Native Studies at the University of Alberta. He is the author of *"Métis": Race, Recognition and the Struggle for Indigenous Peoplehood* (UBC Press, 2014) and was recently named to the Royal Society of Canada's College of New Scholars, Artists and Scientists.

William Bauer, Jr. (Wailacki and Concow of the Round Valley Indian Tribes) is an associate professor in the Department of History at the University of Nevada – Las Vegas. He is the author of *California Through Native Eyes: Reclaiming History* (University of Washington Press, 2016) and *"We Were All Like Migrant Workers Here": Work, Community, and Memory on California's Round Valley Reservation, 1850–1941* (University of North Carolina Press, 2009).

Emilio del Valle Escalante (K'iche' Maya, Iximulew) teaches at the University of North Carolina at Chapel Hill. He is the author of *Maya Nationalisms and Postcolonial Challenges in Guatemala* (SAR Press, 2009), and various articles related to Indigenous peoples in [southern] Mexico and Central America.

Amy E. Den Ouden is Associate Professor of Women's and Gender Studies at the University of Massachusetts Boston. She is the author of *Beyond Conquest: Native Peoples and the Struggle for History in New England* and co-editor of *Recognition, Sovereignty Struggles, and Indigenous Rights in the U.S.* She has worked as a researcher and writer for tribal nation federal acknowledgment projects since 1991.

Vicente M. Diaz (Pohnpeian/Filipino) teaches American Indian Studies at the University of Minnesota. His work includes *Repositioning the Missionary: Rewriting the Histories of Colonialism, Native Catholicism, and Indigeneity in Guam* (University of Hawai'i, 2010) and *Sacred Vessels: Navigating Tradition and Identity in Micronesia* (VHS, 1997).

Sherry Farrell Racette teaches at the University of Manitoba. Recent contributions include essays in *Rethinking Canada* (2016), *The Cultural Work*

Of Photography in Canada (2012), and art installations *From Here: Story Gatherings* for the Gabriel Dumont Institute and *We Are Not Birds: Métis Rights*, for the Canadian Museum for Human Rights.

Mishuana Goeman, Tonawanda Band of Seneca, is an Associate Professor of Gender Studies and American Indian Studies at UCLA. She is the author of *Mark My Words: Native Women Mapping Our Nations*. She is also a co-PI for *Mapping Indigenous L.A.*, a community-oriented digital story project that seeks to decolonize the LA landscape.

Aroha Harris belongs to the iwi (tribes) Te Rarawa and Ngāpuhi. She is a senior lecturer in history at the University of Auckland, and member of the Waitangi Tribunal. Her most recent book was a collaboration with Emeritus Professor Atholl Anderson and the late Dame Professor Judith Binney, *Tangata Whenua: An Illustrated History* (2014), a history of Māori from the ancient past until the present.

Brendan Hokowhitu is Ngāti Pukenga from Aotearoa/New Zealand and is Dean and Professor of Te Pua Wānanga ki te Ao, The School of Māori & Pacific Development at the University of Waikato. Hokowhitu was lead editor of *The Fourth Eye: Māori Media in Aotearoa New Zealand* (University of Minnesota Press, 2013).

Robert Alexander Innes is a member of Cowessess First Nation and an assistant professor in the department of Indigenous Studies at the University of Saskatchewan. He is the author of *Elder Brother and the Law of People: Contemporary Kinship and Cowessess First Nations* and with Kim Anderson co-edited *Indigenous Men and Masculinities: Legacies, Identities, Regeneration* (both published by the University of Manitoba Press).

Margaret D. Jacobs is the Chancellor's Professor of History at the University of Nebraska-Lincoln. She is the author of *White Mother to a Dark Race: Settler Colonialism, Maternalism, and the Removal of Indigenous Children in the American West and Australia, 1880–1940*, and *A Generation Removed: The Fostering and Adoption of Indigenous Children in the Postwar World*.

Daniel Heath Justice (Cherokee Nation) holds the Canada Research Chair in Indigenous Literature and Expressive Culture at the University of British Columbia, where he is Professor of First Nations and Indigenous Studies and English. His publications include *Our Fire Survives the Storm: A Cherokee Literary History* and the co-edited *Oxford Handbook of Indigenous American Literature*.

Tahu Kukutai (Waikato-Maniapoto, Te Aupōuri) is Associate Professor at the National Institute of Demographic and Economic Analysis, Aotearoa/New

Zealand. She has published extensively on Māori and Indigenous demography and state practices of ethnic-racial classification.

Sheryl R. Lightfoot (Anishinaabe) is Canada Research Chair in Global Indigenous Rights and Politics at the University of British Columbia. She is the author of *Global Indigenous Politics: A Subtle Revolution* (Routledge, 2016) and has published articles in *Native American Indigenous Studies, The International Journal of Human Rights*, *Political Science*, and *Alternatives*.

K. Tsianina Lomawaima (Mvskoke/Creek Nation), Arizona State University, interdisciplinary scholar of Indigenous Studies, education, history, and political science, studies the federal "footprint" of policy and practice in Indian country, including debates over the status of Native citizens and nations. Author of *"To Remain an Indian": Lessons in Democracy from a Century of Native American Education* (Teachers College Press, 2006).

Mary Jane Logan McCallum is an Associate Professor in the Department of History at the University of Winnipeg. She writes on Indigenous modern histories especially in the areas of health, education, and labor. Her book is entitled *Indigenous Women, Work and History, 1940–1980*. She is a member of the Munsee-Delaware Nation.

Kelly S. McDonough (White Earth Ojibwe Heritage) is Assistant Professor in the Department of Spanish and Portuguese at the University of Texas at Austin. She is the author of *The Learned Ones: Nahua Intellectuals in Postconquest Mexico* (2014), and articles on Indigenous literacies, inter-Indigenous class conflict, and Mexican Indigenous literatures.

Brenda Macdougall, Chair of Métis Research University of Ottawa, has been researching Métis community histories for many years. She is the author of *One of the Family: Métis Culture in Nineteenth Century Northwestern Saskatchewan* (2010) and numerous articles including "Speaking of Métis: Reading Family Life into Colonial Records" (2014).

Distinguished Professor **Aileen Moreton-Robinson** is Dean of the Indigenous Research and Engagement Unit and Director of the National Indigenous Research and Knowledges network at the Queensland University of Technology. She is a Goenpul scholar, Quandamooka First Nation. Her most recent book is entitled *The White Possessive: Land, Power and Indigenous Sovereignty* (Minnesota Press, 2015).

Jean M. O'Brien (White Earth Ojibwe) is Distinguished McKnight University Professor at the University of Minnesota. Her five books include *Firsting and Lasting: Writing Indians Out of Existence in New England* and *Why You Can't*

Teach United States History Without American Indians. O'Brien is co-founder and past president of the Native American and Indigenous Studies Association.

May-Britt Öhman is Lule/Forest Sámi of Lule River valley, the Swedish side of Sábme, and Ph.D. in History of Science and Technology (2007). Since 2008, she has been a researcher at the Centre for Gender Research, Uppsala University. Her newest edited volume is *RE: Mindings: Co-Constituting Indigenous / Academic / Artistic Knowledges* (HVC, 2014).

Jeffrey Ostler is Beekman Professor of Northwest and Pacific History at the University of Oregon. He is the author of "'Just and Lawful War' as Genocidal War in the (United States) Northwest Ordinance and Northwest Territory, 1787–1832," *Journal of Genocide Research* 18:1 (2016).

Michelle Raheja is an Associate Professor of English at the University of California, Riverside, Director of the California Center for Native Nations, and author of *Reservation Reelism: Redfacing, Visual Sovereignty and Representations of Native Americans* and a forthcoming monograph on Indigenous futurities. She is a Seneca descendant living in Tongva territory.

Jacki Thompson Rand (citizen, Choctaw Nation of Oklahoma) is an associate professor at the University of Iowa Department of History and co-coordinator of the American Indian and Native Studies program. She is author of *Kiowa Humanity and the Invasion of the State* and several articles. Her current research focuses on violence against Native women and a collaborative digital mapping project on the Indigenous Midwest.

Mark Rifkin is Director of Women's and Gender Studies and Professor of English at the University of North Carolina at Greensboro. He is the author of four books, including most recently *Settler Common Sense: Queerness and Everyday Colonialism in the American Renaissance* and the award-winning *When Did Indians Become Straight? Kinship, the History of Sexuality and Native Sovereignty*. He has also served as the president of the Native American and Indigenous Studies Association.

Noenoe K. Silva (Kanaka Hawaiʻi) serves as professor of Indigenous Politics and Hawaiian Language at the University of Hawaiʻi at Mānoa. She is the author of *Aloha Betrayed: Native Hawaiian Resistance to American Colonialism* and the forthcoming *The Power of the Steel-Tipped Pen: Reconstructing Native Hawaiian Intellectual History*.

Shannon Speed (Chickasaw) is Director of American Indian Studies and Associate Professor of Gender Studies and Anthropology at UCLA. Her publications include *Rights in Rebellion: Human Rights and Indigenous Struggle in Chiapas, Human*

Rights in the Maya Region: Global Politics, Moral Engagements, and Cultural Contentions, and *Dissident Women: Gender and Cultural Politics in Chiapas*.

Heidi Kiiwetinepinesiik Stark (Turtle Mountain Ojibwe) is an assistant professor of political science at the University of Victoria. She is the co-editor of *Centering Anishinaabeg Studies: Understanding the World Through Stories*, with Jill Doerfler and Niigaanwewidam Sinclair, and the co-author of *American Indian Politics and the American Political System*, 3rd edn, with David E. Wilkins.

Nicole St-Onge is Professor of History and Director of the Institute of Canadian and Aboriginal Studies, University of Ottawa (Canada). Her research focuses on Great Lake fur trade communities and Plains Métis hunters. A recent article is "Familial Foes?: French-Sioux Families and Plains Métis Brigades in the Nineteenth Century," *The American Indian Quarterly* 39:3 (2015), 302–337.

Pauline Turner Strong is Professor of Anthropology and Director of the Humanities Institute at the University of Texas at Austin, where she is also affiliated with Native American and Indigenous Studies. Her publications include *American Indians and the American Imaginary*; *Captive Selves, Captivating Others*; and *New Perspectives on Native North America*.

Kim TallBear, author of *Native American DNA: Tribal Belonging and the False Promise of Genetic Science,* is Associate Professor, Faculty of Native Studies, University of Alberta. Dr. TallBear is a citizen of the Sisseton-Wahpeton Oyate in South Dakota. She blogs on Indigeneity and Technoscience at www. kimtallbear.com.

Gabrielle Tayac, enrolled in the Piscataway Indian Nation, serves hemispheric Indigenous communities and a diverse public as a historian at the Smithsonian National Museum of the American Indian. She holds an A.M. and Ph.D. in Sociology from Harvard University and a B.S. in Social Work and American Indian Studies from Cornell University.

Alice Te Punga Somerville (Te Āti Awa, Taranaki) writes and teaches at the intersections of Indigenous, Pacific, literary and cultural studies. Her first book was *Once Were Pacific: Māori Connections to Oceania* (Minnesota, 2012); she also writes the occasional poem.

Coll Thrush is Associate Professor of History at the University of British Columbia in Vancouver, on the unceded territory of the Musqueam Nation. He is the author of *Native Seattle: Histories from the Crossing-Over Place* (2007) and co-editor of *Phantom Past, Indigenous Presence: Native Ghosts in North American History and Culture* (2011). His next book, *Indigenous London: Native Travellers at the Heart of Empire*, will be published in late 2016.

Robert Warrior (Osage) is the author, co-author, or editor of six books, including most recently the edited volume *The World of Indigenous North America* (Routledge). He was the founding president of the Native American and Indigenous Studies Association and is the 2016–17 president of the American Studies Association.

Introduction

Indigenous Studies: An appeal for methodological promiscuity

Chris Andersen and Jean M. O'Brien

What *isn't* Indigenous Studies? A question such as this, its grammatical irregularity notwithstanding, tends to bedevil most new or emerging fields, especially those that seek the lofty status of discipline. More than fifty years of thinking, writing, presenting and publishing by committed scholars on Indigenous Studies have tended to focus not so much on what it is or is not, but rather on what it should aspire to be. Emerging from the social and intellectual flux of the 1960s, early Indigenous Studies scholarship initially ruminated on the importance of new theoretical or methodological frameworks and Indigenous Studies' relationship to Indigenous sovereignty. Despite the formulation of journals purporting to speak to Indigenous Studies that began to publish scholarship under its aegis, little sustained effort has been exerted to reflect on the field's origins, boundaries or current trajectories.

Were we to understand Indigenous Studies in all its various iterations – Native American studies, American Indian studies, Native studies, and so forth – as a discipline (by no means a foregone conclusion), what does that mean in practice? That is to say, what elements are important or even central to rendering otherwise diverse fields of interest and knowledge production, well, disciplinary? Much of the literature on disciplines in the academy focuses on them as a constitutive and governing force in producing bodies of knowledge. Bryan Turner (2006: 183) argues, for example, that "[*d*]*isciplina* were instructions to disciples, and hence a branch of instruction or department of knowledge. This religious context provided the modern educational notion of a 'body of knowledge', or a discipline such as sociology or economics."

As bodies of knowledge, disciplines thus possess important epistemological prescriptions. Tony Becher (1981), for example, argues that disciplinary boundaries are based on different intellectual clusters that include debates about distinctive concepts, methods and fundamental aims. More specifically, he suggests that since "research is a rule governed system of inquiry", disciplines produce and govern particular rules for debate and analysis (Bridges 2006). Following Krishnan's (2009) discussion, we might then present a number of defining characteristics of the intellectual aspect of disciplines: they focus on a specific object of research that, over time, produces an accumulated body of specialized knowledge through distinctive theories, concepts, terminologies and, of particular relevance here, methodologies. We delve into the importance of this volume as a methodological contribution in further detail below. We wish to flag here, however, the fact that as Indigenous Studies continues to emerge, it continues to draw on a huge array of disciplines and methodological debates to inform our perspectives and work, and it has tended to do so in a context with little collective strategy or long-term planning – hence our use of "promiscuity" in the title (referring to its original Latin use, meaning "mixed, indiscriminate, in common, without discussion") to modify "methodology".

Perhaps more than any other national context, US-based Native American or American Indian Studies scholars have reflected on the state of Indigenous Studies as a discipline. For example, a number of "state-of-the-discipline" pieces written under the auspices of a flagship journal of American-based Indigenous Studies – *American Indian Quarterly* – touch on various elements central to this endeavour. We will briefly discuss aspects of these arguments because we believe that the marketplace of ideas at play in an American context possesses significant resonance outside of its geo-political context. In her state-of-the-discipline piece, scholar Clara Sue Kidwell (White Earth Ojibwe and Choctaw) argues for American Indian studies as a "legitimate field of intellectual inquiry" with five central components: the central relationship between Indigenous culture and land (or place); that historical relations between Indigenous societies and settler communities were just that – relational – and as such, have to be told from both sides (which includes according agency to Indigenous history); that sovereignty is an inherent right of Indian nations; that language is the essential key to understanding culture and that therefore requires preservation; and finally, that "contemporary Indian music, dance, art, and literature express long-standing values of tribal cultures while adapting them to modern media" (Kidwell 2009: 4).

Similarly, Indigenous Studies doyen Jace Weaver (2007) argues that debates in Indigenous Studies have tended to produce more heat than light. In this context, he suggests a number of intellectual features to which the discipline should aspire: interdisciplinarity; comparativity; privileging an Indigenous perspective; demonstrating a commitment to Native American community; employing a "borderless" discourse that seeks to link the local with national and international Indigenous issues and peoples. In his state-of-the-discipline piece, Duane Champagne argued that

> American Indian cultural emphasis on retaining culture, identity, self-government, and stewardship of land and resulting contestations with the U.S. government and society forms a body of empirical social action that constitutes the subject matter of American Indian studies as an academic discipline.
>
> (2007: 353)

Champagne notes that American Indian studies can be extended internationally in the form of Indigenous Studies. We note here that Weaver and Champagne are less hopeful than Kidwell. Weaver characterized current American Indigenous

Studies as "a mess", while Champagne suggested that "relatively little conceptual progress has been made toward defining American Indian Studies as a discipline and toward developing theory and research that presents a coherent theoretical and methodological approach to the study of indigenous peoples" (2007: 354).

Elizabeth Cook-Lynn argues that part of the mandate of Indigenous Studies (what she terms "Indian Studies") lies in "exposing the lies of the self-serving colonial academic institutions of America, bolster[ing] the rights and obligation to disobedience, and resist[ing] the tyranny of the U.S. fantasies concerning history and justice and morality" (Cook-Lynn 1999: 16) – in other words, the hard work of decolonization. In this context, she suggests the importance of Indian Studies scholars engaging wide and public audiences and doing so in the context of our tribal nations and territories (1999: 20). More specifically, she argues that we work not for our students, our faculties or our universities, but in the interests of creating "a mechanism in defense of the Indigenous principles of sovereignty and nationhood" (1999: 20), and one that is undertaken in an explicitly endogamous fashion (1997: 11).

Despite the sophistication of these scholars' labours, relatively little space has been set aside for exploring the *methodological* prescriptions of Indigenous Studies. We should pause here to note that our understanding of Indigenous Studies methodologies is that, although they might include these, they are not (necessarily) the same as the manner in which Indigenous methodologies have been framed academically, a growing subfield of inquiry arguably most widely associated with Linda Tuhiwai Smith's *Decolonizing Methodologies* (1999). Nor, as we will explain below, is Indigenous Studies necessarily the same thing as Indigenous knowledge – at least, as it is normally conceived. Instead, our understanding underscores the importance of the approach of Innes (2010), who has contributed a chapter to this volume). In his introduction to a special issue of *American Indian Culture and Research Journal*, Innes (2010: 3) presents three central intellectual goals for Indigenous Studies: to access, understand and convey Native cultural perspective(s); to conduct research that benefits Native people and/or communities; *and to employ research methods and theories that will achieve these goals*.

Finally, Innes argues that Indigenous Studies must practice methodological diversity. He suggests that Native studies ought to be broadly multi-disciplinary insofar as the issues we examine should dictate the methods and theories used. For Innes, the *ethical* relationship to the community with whom the research problem is being formulated, rather than the specific theories and methods used, is part of what distinguishes Native studies from other disciplines: "Developing an ethical research relationship is more important than how the data is collected" (Innes 2010: 6). The central importance of methodological diversity – or, without putting too fine a point on it, interdisciplinary – has also been pointed to by scholar Jace Weaver, who makes a compelling case for the necessity of interdisciplinarity in both pedagogical and scholarly knowledge generation contexts.

One of the complications that arises from this principle, Innes suggests, is the realization that Native studies is not the same thing as Indigenous knowledge, although in any given instance it may incorporate Indigenous knowledge as part of its explanatory framework. Distinguishing between the two and not losing sight of their key differences is, we suggest, important to building the legitimacy of Indigenous Studies in the academy *and* in Indigenous communities, both theoretically and, more importantly here, methodologically. Indigenous Studies entered into academic histories under particular conditions and these early conditions have since shaped the kind of training its progenitors undertook and the kind of knowledge it produced. This means that Indigenous Studies is different from – but in certain cases and under the right conditions can be broadly allied with – Indigenous knowledge, particularly as situated and practised outside of the academy. Acknowledging their difference without pronouncing their ontological discreteness is far more effective than swallowing traditional pieties offered by academics with little respect given to the complexity of the social relations that animate them. Nowhere is the successful negotiation of this creative tension more apparent than the recent and overwhelming achievement of NAISA, the Native American and Indigenous Studies Association.

Begun in the spring of 2007, with the first organizing meeting held at the University of Oklahoma, NAISA has grown into the largest Indigenous Studies association in the world, now regularly attracting more than a thousand scholars – most of them Indigenous – to locales across the United States and Canada. A perusal of any of the programmes over its past near-decade of existence evidences the astounding range of methodological approaches employed by scholars who, through their participation in the annual meetings, shore up and build on the intellectual richness of Indigenous Studies. While various scholars have noted the limitations and boundaries of NAISA's knowledge-production tendencies (see TallBear, forthcoming), it nevertheless constitutes a crucial fork in the road of Indigenous Studies' growth as/into a discipline. And its methodological richness and diversity are equally undeniable.

It is within this animus of acknowledging our methodological complexity that this current volume, *Sources and Methods in Indigenous Studies*, took shape. We have, through our own long-standing networks, brought together a disciplinarily extensive and geographically expansive group of Indigenous Studies scholars who have, regardless of their formal disciplinary affiliation and training, signalled a commitment to Indigenous Studies as a growing field – perhaps – discipline. Our invitation to participate made clear that participation would not require a "toeing the line" in terms of what we wanted the contribution to look like. Instead, we left the shape of the argument nearly solely up to the authors, limited only by word count (about 4,000 words) and animated by a single question: "What is your methodological approach to the way you undertake research, and how does it differ from past research in your field or discipline?"

As you will see, contributors responded with an astonishing array of sophisticated, subtle and above all *useful* chapters that offer academics at all levels – from Master's-level students to senior scholars – much grist for the mill as they undertake research in their varied fields of inquiry. One of the reasons for this approach is that "literature review" essays – while invaluable – have a quality that fixes them in time and, almost by definition, dates them, given production schedules and the passing of time. Given the vibrancy of Indigenous Studies at this moment, we wanted to capture a hybrid approach that both looks back at important touchstones for the field and looks to the exciting work being undertaken now and aimed for in the future.

The volume has been organized into two major parts ("Emerging from the past" and "Alternative sources and methodological reorientations"), the second of which comprises five main sections: Reframing Indigenous Studies; All in the family; Feminism, gender and sexuality; Indigenous literature and expressive culture; and Indigenous peoples in and beyond the state. Part I, "Emerging from the past", is meant to take on the various ways in which, while engaging with more venerable disciplines, Indigenous Studies scholarship has harnessed its central concepts, but also moved beyond them. White Earth Ojibwe scholar Jean M. O'Brien begins with a discussion of historical sources and methodologies, laying out how American Indian history in particular has fared within those methodological boundaries, then moving to a discussion of what Indigenous Studies' historical methods looks like. Then, Daniel Heath Justice (Cherokee Nation) reflects on and explores the intersection of Indigenous Studies with English literature, in particular focusing on the complex rise of "Indigenous literary nationalism" through a consideration of three works considered central to that subfield.

Following Justice's piece, Pauline Turner Strong speaks to the roots of Indigenous Studies in history and anthropology, tracing its genealogy through the emergence, in the postwar period, of ethnohistory, and the interdisciplinary manner in which Indigenous Studies builds upon those complex roots. Finally, Michif (Métis) scholar Chris Andersen and Maori scholar Tahu Kukutai speak to the ways that quantitative information, particularly through official data like the census, has constructed Indigenous communities statistically, the manner in which this has produced simplistic and stereotypical depictions, and how Indigenous Studies scholars have more recently made creative use of official datasets to "speak back" against these conversations.

As mentioned above, Part II contains five sections, the first of which is titled "Reframing Indigenous Studies". This section's first chapter, by Kelly McDonough (White Earth Ojibwe descent), uses a case study of the Nahuas to outline how and why Indigenous intellectualism and alphabetic writing have been obscured and ignored by scholars until relatively recently. It documents current efforts to recover both the memory and textual evidence of nearly 500 years of Nahua knowledge production and dissemination as it relates to the written word. The myriad ways in which Nahuas have engaged the world and the word through a diverse array of written forms and genres are discussed, as are the cultural and linguistic revitalization projects that aim to reconnect Nahuas today with these recovered writings. Following McDonough, Mvskoke/Creek Nation scholar K. Tsianina Lomawaima offers an affective understanding of historical methodology based in Deloria's principle of relativity, asking us to think broadly not only about what historical subjects might have written (or had written about them), but about how they thought, did and felt, and the affective relationship of those elements to archival contents.

Then, Goenpul scholar Aileen Moreton-Robinson's chapter presents *relationality* as an Indigenous research paradigm that can shape Indigenous social research. She explores how this paradigm sits in marked contrast to Western methodologies, which operationalize being disconnected from the world as a presupposition of its application. She illustrates the value and utility of this paradigm through an analysis of the research methodologies literature produced by Indigenous scholars in Canada, the United States, Hawaii, Australia and New Zealand.

Following Moreton-Robinson, Kim TallBear (Sisseton-Wahpeton Oyate and Cheyenne & Arapaho Tribes of Oklahoma) explores how the reciprocity or "giving back" that forms the basis of critical research communities is actually predicated on a binary between those who inquire and those whose lives are studied. In this chapter and in the specific context of science and technology studies, she instead articulates overlapping intellectual, ethical and institution-building projects – to share goals while staying engaged in critical conversation through which new knowledge and insights are articulated together.

Next, Pohnpeian-Filipino Vicente Diaz's chapter is based around a provocative question of method: "Just how do we smell our histories?" In an invitation to think through what a possible answer to this question might look like, Diaz considers olfaction's ontologies and their epistemological possibilities, that is, olfaction's various states of being in the interest of studying their analytical (and other) possibilities in general, and in the context of Indigenous pasts in particular. Methodologically, Diaz encourages us to embrace total bodily immersion in the most visceral of activities that are central to projects of political and cultural reclamation and nation re-building.

Following Diaz, Osage scholar Robert Warrior argues that intellectual history has played a large role in the development of Indigenous Studies over the past two decades, and he offers two contexts for understanding the relationship between the two: 1) the articulation of traditional Indigenous knowledges in the academic field; and 2) the integration of theorizing and knowledge creation created in antagonistic social and cultural concepts of Euro-American intellectual practices. Warrior explores some of the methodological tensions in writing Indigenous intellectual histories in the midst of these two tensions and offers methodological insights that Indigenous intellectual history makes available in our attempts to grapple with these tensions.

Next, Kanaka Maoli scholar Noenoe K. Silva reviews the advent and development of critical Hawaiian studies from the 1980s to the present day. She focuses mainly on the work of Kanaka scholars who broke the ground (or cleared the path) for Kanaka-centred study, making use of the large and long-standing archives of writing in ʻōlelo Hawaiʻi (the Hawaiian language). Finally, Coll Thrush's chapter argues that although urban and Indigenous histories are often framed as though they are mutually exclusive, treating them instead as mutually constitutive offers opportunities for new research and writing at the intersection of those two fields of history. Focusing on the United States, Canada, New Zealand and Australia, Thrush offers three lenses of urban Indigenous history: the presence of local peoples in whose territories settler cities have been built; the migration of diverse Indigenous peoples to urban places; and the use of Indigenous images in the urban imaginary.

The second section of Part II, "All in the family", contains chapters by Indigenous authors who speak to the central importance of family in the construction of their scholarly methodologies. We start with Maori scholar Alice Te Punga Somerville, who explodes our notions of what is – or counts as – an archive, and within that context, makes use of two Pacific texts relating to the interconnectedness across time and space, and makes an appeal to understanding geographical disparity in terms of presence rather than absence. Next, Maori scholar Aroha Harris speaks to the complexity of oral history and its relationship to Maori tellings of their own histories. More specifically, she addresses questions about subjectivity and ethics, and provides an example of oral life histories as illuminating source, well-suited to reading with and against the archives and manuscripts on which historians typically depend.

Following Harris, Cree scholar Robert Innes explores how researchers have begun to employ stories as theoretical frameworks to explain Indigenous peoples' views, thoughts and motivations to gain a better understanding of their historic and contemporary realities. His chapter outlines how traditional stories such as "Elder Brother" can assist in exploring the connection between the beliefs, insights, concepts, ideals, values, attitudes and codes of conduct and the interactions of contemporary members of First Nations. Next, Amy Den Ouden explores ways to understand and engage in histories with communities. Her chapters offers insights into the process of community-based historical production, and discusses examples of Indigenous historical knowledges that illuminate the complexities, and transformational possibilities, of history-making as an intellectual, social and political endeavour.

Following Den Ouden, Sweden-based Sámi scholar May-Britt Öhman presents what she refers to as a "supradisciplinary methodology", through which she addresses her scholarly work in the context of Sámi history and present time from her own perspective, that of a Forest Sámi of the Lule River Valley. Within the (colonial) academic context, she makes personal use of supradisciplinary methodology to assist in recovering her own personal hidden Sámi history, but also, more broadly, to fight the amnesia regarding Sámi history in general, and then more particularly in her work with allies to promote Sámi rights to lands and waters, defending and struggling for the survival of diverse Sámi cultures within an aggressively colonial Sweden.

Finally, William Bauer (Wailacki and Concow of the Round Valley Indian Tribes) explores the complex importance of oral histories to Indigenous Studies. He argues that oral histories are vital for understanding American Indian history because they provide information on the everyday experiences of American Indian people (women in particular), and stitch together a collective memory of the American Indian past. Most importantly, Bauer argues, oral histories allow us to express our sovereignty.

In the third section of Part II, the volume turns to dynamics relating to feminism, gender and sexuality in Indigenous Studies. Jacki Thompson Rand (Choctaw

Nation of Oklahoma) argues that scholars ought to actively reconsider their reliance on the "status" of women as an analytical frame, subject to criticism as inconsistent with Indigenous perspectives, and consider sustainability as a way to capture women's economic, social and political roles in modern tribal communities and the challenges women face from without and from within. Scholars of native women's studies work with limited primary sources, making the collection of oral histories and their careful analysis crucial to the field, conducive to community collaboration, and amenable to public humanities platforms. Then, Chickasaw Nation scholar Shannon Speed explores the issues involved in telling the stories of Indigenous women migrants from Mexico and Central America. She unpacks some of the ethical and practical issues involved in an Indigenous feminist anthropologist retelling of stories marked by extreme violence. She argues that while the dilemmas and contradictions of anthropological representation are never fully resolvable, using Indigenous feminist oral history practice allows both for sustained attention to the avoidance of perpetuating further violence through the representational process, and potentially for representations that challenge hegemonic hierarchies of knowledge and truth in the colonized world.

Following Speed, Tonawanda Band of Seneca scholar Mishuana Goeman's chapter examines feminism and its relationship to colonialism, social justice and Indigenous Studies. The chapter first explores and critiques the historic approach to feminism, then presents an alternative genealogy, breaking down the problems with the three waves of feminism, and presenting Indigenous women's engagement and relationship to mainstream and women-of-color feminism. Indigenous feminism's goals support self-determination, sovereignty, healthy Indigenous communities and a thriving planet. Next, Maori scholar Brendan Hokowhitu explores how, unlike the typical ahistorical treatment of masculinity within the general field, Indigenous masculinity scholarship is linked to the tenets of Indigenous Studies more broadly. That is, a common method that has developed within this nexus has characteristically been "genealogical" in nature in that most scholars have tended to locate the production of contemporary Indigenous male bodies within the broader frames of settler colonialism and colonial history.

Finally, Mark Rifkin explains how, as a concept, "Indigenous" provides a means of challenging settler political and social norms. He goes on to explain, however, that it can also allow certain formulations of indigeneity to become the norm through which the concept implicitly is defined. Rifkin suggests that although similar tension operates within the term *queer*, queer studies' unpacking and tracing of the implicit normalizations enacted through its use can aid Indigenous Studies in thinking about what is at stake in the ways the notion of Indigenous/indigeneity circulates.

Following a discussion of these dynamics, the fourth section of Part II focuses on Indigenous Studies practitioners' engagement with various elements of expressive culture. In K'iche' Maya Emilio del Valle Escalante's chapter, he uses literary text to explore the "poetics of survival" through which displaced Mayan survivors of massacres by the Guatemalan state narrate experiences of violence, pain and chaos not only to disclose the operations of settler colonialism, but also to "re-member" the Maya social body by confronting the past. In doing so, he rewrites or re-rights history in order to inscribe the historical memory of Maya survivors of the armed conflict. Sherry Farrell Racette (Timiskaming First Nation) then explores material culture considerations of objects as witnesses, archival documents, storytellers and teachers. Beginning with a brief historical context of the relationship between Indigenous peoples and museums, she reflects on twenty years of museum- and community-based research centred on objects, archives and story. She shares a conversation initiated with two fellow scholars, asking the basic question, "Is there something fundamentally different about the way Indigenous scholars engage with material culture?"

Resonating with Farrell Racette's work, Piscataway Gabrielle Tayac's chapter presents a concept for curatorial practice that inscribes the place of museums and exhibits as sites of indigenized three-dimensional authorship. Museum-based sources are situated to overturn colonial legacies. Indigenous Studies students and scholars are encouraged to exercise three-dimensional authorship as a complement to publication. Museum-based scholarship and curation should be elevated to parity with published products across fields beyond fine arts disciplines. The National Museum of the American Indian provides a current example of work that utilizes three-dimensional authorship. Finally, we turn to film, through the chapter of Michelle Raheja (Seneca heritage), which analyzes Indigenous film history through the lens of settler colonialism, arguing that, since film's inception, motion picture companies have participated in a "logic of elimination" (Wolfe 2006) designed to erase Indigenous people visually. The chapter contrasts these desires by demonstrating the success of contemporary Indigenous science fiction filmmakers in drawing from both Indigenous speculative oral narrative as well as colonial literary and visual culture representations of "first contact" to institute new modes of thinking about Indigenous futurity.

The fifth section of Part II is titled "Indigenous peoples in and beyond the state". The section begins with Turtle Mountain Anishinaabe scholar Heidi Kiiwetinepinesiik Stark, who makes the methodological argument that understanding story as law not only unearths a rich body of Indigenous thought, it also dispels the notion of the inviolability of the law, demonstrating that law is likewise a set of stories. In examining the creation stories of the state, she explores how Western law took form and functions to legitimate the settler nation-state through Indigenous dispossession. The study of Indigenous law, in presenting alternative frameworks for the restoration of Indigenous–state relations, not only contains the potential to produce new methodological approaches, but may also unearth alternate methods for living together differently. Following Stark, Métis scholars Brenda Macdougall and Nicole St-Onge examine how the 49th parallel effectively created a historical myth by attributing American and Canadian national identities to Indigenous populations. They argue, however, that designating Indigenous populations as either Canadian or American has obscured the historical reality that the Northern Plains was an Indigenous space shaped by these populations' diplomatic protocols and internal frameworks for belonging. During this era, the Métis in particular used the borderland to advance their own sense of rights and ownership as they operationalized networks, connections and webs of exchange via the systems of mobility necessitated by their trade economy.

Next, Margaret Jacobs explores how the study of Indigenous education challenges the progressive narratives of education in American history and adds new dimensions to studies of colonialism worldwide. The sources that scholars use to examine Indigenous education have influenced their approaches and interpretations. Those using government records and the papers of missionary and reform groups have emphasized the oppressive nature of Indigenous education as a weapon of colonialism. Scholars who prioritize the use of Indigenous-authored sources have given more weight to the ambivalent experiences of Indigenous survivors and how Indigenous communities have sought to gain control of education as a key means of asserting sovereignty.

Following Jacobs, Mary Jane Logan McCallum discusses some of the procedures historians undergo when researching modern institutional records pertaining to Indigenous people – in particular, medical records to which public access is restricted because they contain personal health information. After describing the records and some early encounters with them, she discuss the complicated nexus of ethics codes and the research agreement that has come to regulate her research, and she delineates some of the methods used to research Indigenous institutional archives both in the presence and in the absence of such regulations.

Following McCallum, Jeffrey Ostler draws on recent trends in the overlapping fields of settler colonial and genocide studies to propose possibilities for the development of an alternative approach to the study of the history of genocide in North America. Taking examples from recent literature, the chapter discusses new approaches to disease and its intersection with other forces of destruction, patterns of violence, state policy toward Indigenous people, and demography. Throughout, the chapter emphasizes the methodological importance of a sustained analysis of native agency and survival.

Finally, Anishinaabe scholar Sheryl Lightfoot (Lake Superior Band/Keweenaw Bay Indian Community) positions the importance of Indigenous Studies in the context of the recent spate of reconciliation projects engaged in by various nation-states. Such projects are charged with improving relationships between Indigenous peoples and the governments that have caused them harm. This chapter argues that scholarship and political activism can be effectively and ethically bridged through research that engages active Indigenous–state reconciliation projects in three "R" ways: Revealing, Reporting and Reflecting – the "past–present–future" concept of researching social change.

It is our hope that this volume will provide readers with a sense of this particularly dynamic moment in the emergence of Indigenous Studies. Following more than five decades of scholarship tilling new fields and searching for approaches to capture Indigenous perspectives on the long history of settler colonialism globally, Indigenous Studies seems to have arrived at a moment of incredible synergy and unprecedented engagement on a global stage. We hope this volume shines a spotlight on some of the ways in which scholarship is transforming Indigenous Studies in innovative and exciting ways.

References

Becher, Tony. 1981. "Towards a definition of disciplinary cultures". *Studies in Higher Education*, 6(2): 109–122.

Bridges, David. 2006. "The discipline and disciplines of educational research". *Journal of Philosophy of Education*, 40(2): 259–272.

Champagne, Duane. 2007. "In search of theory and method in American Indian studies". *American Indian Quarterly*, 31(3): 353–372.

Cook-Lynn, Elizabeth. 1991. "The radical conscience in Native American studies". *Wicazo Sa Review*, 7(2): 9–13.

Cook-Lynn, Elizabeth. 1997. "Who stole Native American studies?" *Wicazo Sa Review*, 12(1): 9–28.

Cook-Lynn, Elizabeth. 1999. "American Indian studies: an overview". *Wicazo Sa Review*, 14(2): 14–24.

Innes, Robert. 2010. "Introduction: Native Studies and Native cultural preservation, revitalization, and persistence". *American Indian Culture and Research Journal*, 34(2): 1–9.

Kidwell, Clara Sue. 2009. "American Indian Studies: intellectual navel gazing or academic discipline?" *American Indian Quarterly*, 33(1): 1–17.

Krishnan, Armin. 2009. "What are academic disciplines: some observations on the disciplinarity vs. interdisciplinarity debate". *NCRM Working Paper series*. University of Southampton: ESRC National Centre for Research Methods, pp. 1–57.

Smith, Linda Tuhiwai. 1999. *Decolonizing Methodologies: Research and Indigenous Peoples*. London and New York: Zed Books.

TallBear, Kim. Forthcoming, 2016. "Dear Indigenous studies, it's not me, it's you: why I left and what needs to change". In Aileen Moreton-Robinson, ed. *Critical Indigenous Studies: Engagements in First World Locations*. Tucson: University of Arizona Press.

Turner, Brian. 2006. "Discipline". *Theory Culture Society*, 23(2–3): 183–197.

Weaver, Jace. 2007. "More heat than light: the current state of Native American studies". *American Indian Quarterly*, 31(2): 233–255.

Wolfe, Patrick. 2006. "Settler colonialism and the elimination of the native". *Journal of Genocide Research*, 8(4): 387–409.

Part I

Emerging from the past

1 Historical sources and methods in Indigenous Studies

Touching on the past, looking to the future

Jean M. O'Brien

Indigenous histories have always existed. Indigenous notions of the past that connect people to places, events, peoples, and memories help Indigenous peoples define their place in the created world and explain its shape, wonders, and human relations (like other kinds of history). Indigenous peoples have their own ways of reckoning and remembering histories, including over the past several decades incorporating historical methodologies associated with western European traditions (Nabokov 2002). Even though Indigenous peoples have always understood their place within the created world according to narratives (many rooted in oral transmission supplemented with other memory technologies, such as winter counts, wampum belts, memory piles, pictographs, and more), Indigenous voices and agency in producing historical narratives have rarely been accorded a place of legitimacy in the formal discipline of history and have instead been dismissed as "myth," "legend," "folklore," or "saga" (Nabokov 2002; Basso 1996).

Philip Deloria periodizes ways of thinking about the history of American Indian history into four broad approaches: (1) Frontier imaginings, characterized by spatial reckonings of encounters that moved from conflict to conquest (beginning in the "contact" era); (2) Racial/developmental hierarchies as a way of accounting for peoples, encounters, and difference (dating from the late eighteenth century); (3) Modernist approaches that focused on the notion of fixed social boundaries between peoples, but also the possibility of their transcendence (beginning in the late nineteenth century); and (4) Postmodern/postcolonial ways of thinking about Indian history, which focus on "the tension between the liberating discussion of boundaries and the constant reshaping of them as political memories of the colonial past" (roughly World War II to the present) (Deloria 2002).

Deloria's synthesis is remarkable in what it captures, including the easily overlooked fact that certain traces (or even larger elements) of each of these approaches continue to shape narratives about Indigenous peoples. Monographs continue to promote a narrative arc of an epic clash between Euro-American and Indigenous foes, which ends in the defeat of the admirable Indigenous nations, their struggles ultimately futile as they inevitably fade into insignificance, with no acknowledgment of the continuation of their political existence. The historical literature continues its fixation on "mixed bloods" as somehow racially and culturally "deficient" compared to their supposedly "pure" forebears, frequently purporting to "measure" the degree of "assimilation." In these formulations, "racial" change via "mixing" with other races (via discredited nineteenth-century notions of racial science predicated on "pure," distinct races) or cultural change supposedly diminishes the indigeneity of the person/peoples, and greases the slide into "assimilation." These deeply held and often unconscious assumptions presume that Indigenous peoples can only be the victims of change, never its agents. Indigenous peoples, then, can never be a part of modernity, but instead stand in as modernity's polar opposite, thus robbing them of the possibility of being historical actors and peoples (O'Brien 2010).

Part of the problem for proponents of Indigenous history is that the discipline of history is deeply wedded to national narratives as the infrastructure that channels analysis and interpretation in particular directions to the exclusion of others. The logical outcome is the rise and triumph of the nation-state in the face of internal and external foes. In the case of the United States and its Indigenous peoples, the standard plot line follows the long history of Indigenous displacement (often figured as "territorial expansion" or "territorial acquisition") that secures the land base of the nation, a process that in Indigenous Studies is understood as "settler colonialism." In Patrick Wolfe's classic formulation, "settler colonialism is an inclusive, land-centred project that coordinates a comprehensive range of agencies, from the metropolitan centre to the frontier encampment, with a view to eliminating indigenous societies" (Wolfe 2006).

A standard means of framing the United States as a nation might begin with "pre-contact" Native North America, then proceed through "exploration," "discovery," the claiming of Indigenous lands for European nations, and the contest among European nations for mastery of the hemisphere. As Michael Witgen has shown, claims to imperial mastery of Indigenous peoples existed in their own fantasies rather than in actual power relations throughout the upper Great Lakes region into the nineteenth century, depending on where in Native North America you stood (Witgen 2007, 2012). In Latin America, Patricia Seed has demonstrated convincingly the degree to which Spaniards engaged in mere "ceremonies of possession" rather than claims to conquest that could be plausibly defended (Seed 1995). In the case of the United States, a long period of "colonial" history follows these claims of possession (however illusory), with the American Revolution rendered as *the* "post-colonial" moment of the nation (meaning shedding the shackles of English colonialism for the free development of a democratic republic, the United States). After the American Revolution, the nation fends off internal and external threats to become *the* world power. With these framings, the outcome is predetermined (the triumph of the nation), and plot lines lead to "declension narratives" for Indigenous peoples. Many make the leap from "declension" to the "extinction" of Indigenous peoples.

The fundamental problem in national narratives of the United States is that they cannot possibly account for the existence of more than 560 federally recognized tribal nations engaged in continuing nation-to-nation relationships with the US federal government, and they cannot adequately represent even a fraction of

Indigenous historical and contemporary experiences (which include far more complexity than even the basic fact of federally recognized tribal nations standing in diplomatic relationships to the United States, including state-recognized tribes as well as tribal peoples unrecognized by any external political body) (Wilkins and Stark 2011). Accounts that fail to acknowledge the political dimension of Indigenous nationhood typically elect to reckon Indigenous people as racial or ethnic minorities, which cannot capture the unique status of First Peoples in the United States (and elsewhere). Too often, narratives about Indigenous peoples founder when they train their focus too tightly on Indigenous "culture(s)" without probing, for example, the power and prerogative Indigenous nations possess to defend their cultural practices on the political and legal level. Framing Indigenous histories within the rubric of "multiculturalism" distorts their place within the settler colonial state. Indigenous Studies cannot settle for the idea that Indigenous peoples have *culture* in the absence of *politics*.

Published accounts produced by non-Indigenous people until well into the twentieth century followed two basic trajectories. The first was that which plotted the Wars for the West, the military history that eventually dispossessed Indigenous peoples in the service of casting the United States as a national power. The second concerned the proto-ethnology and then anthropology emerging largely from the mid-nineteenth century onward that purported to create a science of man, including Indigenous North Americans, as part of a racial hierarchy and then as a culturally distinct mosaic of peoples whose ways of life faced constant threats in the face of modernity; this was figured as "salvage anthropology", aimed at producing snapshots of cultures in supposed eclipse.

The tide seemed to turn for Indigenous history at the very end of the 1960s and into the 1970s. No book can claim the massive influence in the United States of Vine Deloria, Jr.'s *Custer Died for Your Sins: An Indian Manifesto* (1969), which boldly called out mainstream America for its treatment of Indian people and Indian history, and signalled a dramatically new direction that many of us trace as the touchstone for the development of Indigenous Studies as a field. This book appeared amidst the Red Power movement, and the emergence of "ethnic studies" units and programs, as well as departments of American Indian Studies. Robert Berkhofer's 1971 call for a New Indian history looked to interdisciplinarity (especially between history and anthropology, or the emergent approach of ethnohistory) to write dynamic Indian histories that imagined Indians as part of the national "present," and took Indians seriously as political actors (Berkhofer 1971). Over time, the "New Indian History" took on the notion of placing Indians themselves at the centre of historical analyses.

Indigenous history methodologies

At one time, many mainstream historians regarded Indigenous history as marginal on the basis that rich and thorough archives were sparse or non-existent: What to do in the absence of "real archives" or "reliable documentation" as typically figured by the discipline? How does one confront the demands of the discipline of history regarding particular kinds of written documentation, and the continued marginalization of particular kinds of sources – oral histories, for example? Who gets to decide what history matters, and what counts as reliable evidence? How does one narrate histories in the absence of documents historians routinely demand? What makes the sources of Indigenous history different (and what *doesn't* make them different)? What kinds of sources *do* exist that are core to the discipline, as traditionally composed? These are crucial questions for the field, and areas of robust critical engagement for scholars of Indigenous history.

In fact, as recent scholarship has amply demonstrated, Indigenous peoples have been producing written documentation of and about their lives for hundreds of years, even if the standard is writing in European languages (let alone the ancient writing technologies in rich evidence across the Americas that pre-date the presence of Europeans in this hemisphere) (see for example Deloria 2002; Jaskoski 1996; O'Connell 1992; Warrior 2005; Round 2010). Beginning with the first Native scholars in the Indian College at Harvard in the 1660s, Indigenous peoples have been writing and publishing at an accelerating rate into the present (Deloria 2002).

The long-standing marginality of the field has produced a situation of rich possibilities for transforming Indigenous histories, and, if there is the will, national narratives as well. An active embrace of the many and diverse archives of Indigenous history, and openness to the methodologies of Indigenous approaches that have been marginalized or disdained, promise the transformation of the field in fruitful directions (as outlined in this volume). From the perspective of Indigenous histories, a couple of overarching notions are vital to bear in mind: First, there is an abundance of documentation to support the pursuit of Indigenous history. No longer can it be claimed that the sources just don't exist to do justice to that history. There are also "unexpected" archives that have been underutilized and unappreciated, many of them stemming directly from the relationship of tribal peoples within settler colonialism. And second, these archives – those longer known and those now being uncovered – must be appreciated from Indigenous perspectives, which have overturned older understandings in countless instances.

Indigenous Studies, Indigenous history, and, increasingly, a move toward global approaches to Indigenous Studies and Indigenous history subsume an expansive embrace of different perspectives on historical actors and events, imaginative approaches to identifying and using source materials, creativity in developing rigorous analytical frames that can transform Indigenous histories and their interventions, and an almost seamless interdisciplinarity that seeks to illuminate historical experiences that have been kept on the margins. Indigenous Studies as currently practised draws on many scholarly traditions, but no one volume captures the preoccupations, ethics, and fundamentally distinct research methodologies better than Linda Tuhiwai Smith's path-breaking book *Decolonizing Methodologies: Research and Indigenous Peoples* (1999). Indigenous Studies requires the acknowledgment of two fundamental commitments in order to gain legitimacy in the view of other practitioners and of the peoples, communities, and/or nations involved: an acknowledgment of the positionality of the researcher/writer in relation to the peoples, communities, and/or nations involved, and an acknowledgment of the accountability of the research/writer in relation to the peoples, communities, and/or nations. Smith's eloquent study contains a wealth of insights stemming from these ethics and a thorough genealogy of the problem of Western knowledge systems for Indigenous peoples. Indigenous Studies pertains to living, breathing peoples, and what is written carries real consequences for the subjects of the research/writing. These relationships read very differently from the notion of "objectivity" formerly elevated to such heights in the discipline but now understood by most to be a problematic notion at best (Novick 1988).

In the space remaining, I'd like to take account of some of the possible "archives" for Indigenous history (by no means exhaustive), and some of the methodologies already in use in fruitful and promising ways in Indigenous Studies and Indigenous histories.

First and foremost, the obsession (in the case of the United States) of English colonialism with the legalities of land ownership (broadly including the resources on and underneath the land), inherited by the United States, has resulted in the production of massive, complex archives. These archives are far from perfect, and settler colonial claims to "proper" transfer of Indigenous homelands to the colonial state by no means followed the espoused protocols whereby the United States claimed the mantra of "expansion with honour" toward Indigenous peoples. Still, the stated imperative to follow protocols regarding landownership resulted in the accumulation of rich materials for Indigenous history.

The "New Social History" that emerged in the 1960s and 1970s embraced interdisciplinarity as an approach, including quantitative methods. Indigenous Studies has been somewhat slower to take up this approach (but see Chapter 4 in this volume). Yet abundant material is available for particular Indigenous peoples at times. Such documentation is an outgrowth of the apparatus of settler colonialism, with the built-in mandate of surveillance of Indigenous subjects, "assimilationist" programs, and the bureaucracy of Indian affairs. In some cases, the state apparatus provides *more* abundant documentation for Indigenous people than non-Indigenous. For example, the Bureau of Indian Affairs (BIA) mandated an *annual* census on many Indian reservations in the United States in the late nineteenth and early twentieth centuries. While not unproblematic, they are rich and underutilized sources nonetheless. As well, assimilation mandates resulted in photographic and ethnographic studies of countless reservation communities, also underused and rich for analysis (Parker 2015).

Many tribes maintain their own archives, archivists, and museums, which vary considerably in their composition (Roy et al. 2011; Sleeper-Smith 2009; Lonetree 2012). The movement to organize, maintain, and protect archival material has been a strong one in Indian Country for decades. These are important sites for portraying Indigenous histories and the contemporary world – an important element in exercising sovereignty for tribal nations.

Material culture studies are of deep significance to Indigenous Studies. Understanding the study of objects as a window into the complexity of Indigenous cultural practices and the meanings objects are imbued with constitutes a methodological approach that deepens Indigenous history. Moving long past nineteenth-century museum practices that fixed objects in cases to signify entire cultures, dynamic approaches to the cultural complexes surrounding objects can provide insights into Indigenous aesthetics, worldviews, technologies, and more (Cruikshank 1998). In the United States, the passage of the Native American Graves Protection and Repatriation Act (1978 and subsequently amended) has provided a way for many tribes to reclaim cultural material and skeletal remains seized from them through dubious means over a long history, though for many the struggles for repatriation remain mired in contention and confrontation.

Family history is central to any reckoning of Indigenous history, and many of the same archives used for non-Indigenous histories and genealogies contain rich materials. Ancestry.com, a boon for professional and amateur genealogists alike, contains a wealth of relatively easily accessible source material for Indigenous history, including BIA annual censuses, land records, allotment records, and military records, in addition to the vital records that are at the heart of genealogical approaches.

Particular Indigenous communities contain their own wealth of stories about their histories, and, in this sense, the communities themselves constitute "archives". Conducting oral histories in communities (through proper protocols) promises to shed light on the longer history of their compositions, the intrusion of the state, and the activism of community members in asserting their nationhood. Indigenous peoples frequently retain deep-seated suspicions about "researchers," which requires building relationships, establishing protocols, and working out how accountability will be assured. Communities themselves frequently create their own boundaries around knowledge to be shared and that to be keep private, including what kinds of historical narratives are appropriate for distribution versus those narratives that ought not to be made public.

Language is a deeply rooted archive of a particular sort, accessible only to those willing to dedicate themselves to the learning of Indigenous languages. Languages contain vital knowledge about worldviews, cultures, and perspectives that lend particular insights into Indigenous communities and their histories. Language preservation and revitalization is a major initiative in a great many Indigenous communities, and language research generally contributes to these efforts in important ways. Language studies have transformed certain areas of Indigenous Studies, such as in Hawaiian studies (see Chapter 11 by Noenoe Silva in this volume). Silva's own work in uncovering rich, deep archives in the language have absolutely transformed our understanding of Native Hawai`i.

As a final example, Indigenous methods of reckoning place – through place names, mapping practices, and oral stories about the characteristics and meanings of physical features of the landscape – are related to language usage and the ways Indigenous people understood and understand their place in the created world (Basso 1996; Cruikshank 2005). Important work has been done to understand the sophistication and precision of Indigenous mapping practices (Barr 2011; Witgen 2007), and even the ways in which Indigenous land usage involved complex understandings of the intricacies of ecosystems (Cronon 1983), and the manipulation of land usage for geopolitical purposes (Hamalainen 2010). The imposition of Western cartography on Indigenous systems of understanding place has created gross distortions and bolstered false claims to Indigenous landscapes (Barr 2011; Hamalainen 2010; Jortner 2015).

In sum, Indigenous history – in particular because of its attachment to the broader methodologies of Indigenous Studies beyond the discipline of history – is a vibrant and dynamic field that is poised to re-write narratives of all sorts.

References

Barr, Juliana. 2011. "Geographies of power: Mapping Indian borders in the 'borderlands' of the early southwest". *William and Mary Quarterly*, 68: 5–46.

Basso, Keith H. 1996. *Wisdom Sits in Places: Landscape and Language among the Western Apache*. Albuquerque: University of New Mexico Press.

Berkhofer, Jr., Robert F. 1971. "The political context of a new Indian history". *Pacific Historical Review*, 40: 357–382.

Cronon, William. 1983. *Changes in the Land: Indians, Colonists, and the Ecology of New England*. New York: Hill and Wang.

Cruikshank, Julie. 1998. *The Social Life of Stories: Narrative and Knowledge in the Yukon Territory*. Lincoln: University of Nebraska Press.

Cruikshank, Julie. 2005. *Do Glaciers Listen? Local Knowledge, Colonial Encounters, and Social Imagination*. Vancouver: University of British Columbia Press.

Deloria, Philip J. 2002. "Historiography". In Philip J. Deloria and Neal Salisbury, eds. *A Companion to American Indian History*. Malden, MA: Blackwell Publishing, pp. 6–24.

Deloria, Jr., Vine. 1969. *Custer Died for Your Sins: An Indian Manifesto*. New York: Macmillan.

Hamalainen, Pekka. 2010. "The politics of grass: European expansion, ecological change, and Indigenous power in the southwest borderlands". *William and Mary Quarterly*, 67: 173–208.

Jaskoski, Helen, ed. 1996. *Early Native American Writing: New Critical Essays*. New York: Cambridge University Press.

Jortner, Adam. 2015. "The empty continent: Cartography, pedagogy, and Native American history". In Susan Sleeper-Smith, Juliana Barr, Jean M. O'Brien, Nancy Shoemaker and Scott Manning Stevens, eds. *Why You Can't Teach United States History Without American Indians*. Chapel Hill: University of North Carolina Press, pp. 71–86.

Lonetree, Amy. 2012. *Decolonizing Museums: Representing Native America in National and Tribal Museums*. Chapel Hill: University of North Carolina Press.

Nabokov, Peter. 2002. *A Forest of Time: American Indian Ways of History*. New York: Cambridge University Press.

Novick, Peter. 1988. *That Noble Dream: The "Objectivity Question" and the Historical Profession*. New York: Cambridge University Press.

O'Brien, Jean M. 2010. *Firsting and Lasting: Writing Indians Out of Existence in New England*. Minneapolis: University of Minnesota Press.

O'Connell, Barry, ed. 1992. *On Our Own Ground: The Complete Writings of William Apess, A Pequot*. Amherst: University of Massachusetts Press.

Parker, Angela. 2015. "Photographing the Places of Citizenship: The 1922 Crow Industrial Survey". *Native American and Indigenous Studies*, 2: 57–86.

Round, Phillip H. 2010. *Removable Type: Histories of the Book in Indian Country, 1663–1880*. Chapel Hill: University of North Carolina Press.

Roy, Loriene, Anjali Bhasin, and Sarah K. Arriaga, eds. 2011. *Tribal Libraries, Archives, Museums: Preserving Out Language, Memory, and Lifeways*. Lanham: Scarecrow Press.

Seed, Patricia. 1995. *Ceremonies of Possession in Europe's Conquest of the New World, 1492–1640*. New York: Cambridge University Press.

Sleeper-Smith, Susan. 2009. *Contesting Knowledge: Museums and Indigenous Perspectives*. Lincoln: University of Nebraska Press.

Sleeper-Smith, Susan, Juliana Barr, Jean M. O'Brien, Nancy Shoemaker, and Scott Manning Stevens, eds. 2015. *Why You Can't Teach United States History Without American Indians*. Chapel Hill: University of North Carolina Press.

Smith, Linda Tuhiwai. 1999. *Decolonizing Methodologies: Research and Indigenous Peoples*. Dunedin: University of Otago Press.

Warrior, Robert. 2005. *The People and the Word: Reading Native Nonfiction*. Minneapolis: University of Minnesota Press.

Wilkins, David E., and Heidi Kiiwetinepinesiik Stark. 2011. *American Indian Politics and the American Political System*. Lanham: Rowman & Littlefield.

Witgen, Michael. 2007. "The rituals of possession: Native identity and the invention of empire in seventeenth-century western North America". *Ethnohistory*, 54: 639–668.

Witgen, Michael. 2012. *An Infinity of Nations: How the Native New World Shaped Early North America*. Philadelphia: University of Pennsylvania Press.

Wolfe, Patrick. 2006. "Settler colonialism and the elimination of the native". *Journal of Genocide Research*, 8: 387–409.

2 Reflections on Indigenous literary nationalism

On home grounds, singing hogs, and cranky critics

Daniel Heath Justice

The year 2014 marked the fifteenth publishing anniversary of Craig Womack's *Red on Red: Native American Literary Separatism* and its affirmation of Muskogee Creek-specific literary history; 2015 was the twentieth anniversary of "intellectual sovereignty" from Robert Warrior's *Tribal Secrets: Recovering American Indian Intellectual Traditions*, with Jace Weaver's *That the People Might Live: Native American Literatures and Native American Community* and its notion of "communitism" celebrating its own twentieth anniversary in 2017. Although none of these is the first or last work in the critical mode now known as "Indigenous literary nationalism," they arguably stand as the most prominent in both critical regard and controversy. This brief chapter considers the conversation around literary nationalism between these and other interpretive projects in the field, with attention to their continuing importance to the intellectual and ethical concerns of Indigenous literary studies.

By way of full disclosure, I look to all of these works as central to my own scholarly development, with Womack's *Red on Red* being the most immediately transformative. I read it shortly after its publication, when I was a first-year Ph.D. student at the University of Nebraska-Lincoln, and it was a revelatory experience, especially Womack's reading of Creek literature through Muskogee political history and cultural expression, not the crossblood criticism or French Continental theory in vogue at the time. Indeed, my coming-of-age as a scholar can quite readily be divided into two chapters, pre- and post-*Red on Red*, and while other works up until that point and after were incredibly significant, including those of Weaver and Warrior noted above, Louis Owens's *Mixedblood Messages*, and Elizabeth Cook-Lynn's varied essays, for me it was Womack's book that had the most electrifying scope of possibility.

Earlier literary criticism of the 1990s focused on hybridity and poststructuralist play, the dynamic trickster mixedbloods and crossbloods of Owens (Choctaw/Cherokee), Gerald Vizenor (Anishinaabe), Diane Glancy (Cherokee), and others. Worthy and important works, but over that decade (and after) the scholarship in response was increasingly distanced from the lands and politics of Indigenous nations and generally more focused on identity, pan-Native urbanity, and movement over rootedness and grounded memory. (As an example, Vizenor's consistent aesthetic and intellectual concerns with land and reimagining of

Indigenous sovereignty outside of the limiting rhetorics of colonization are far less prominent in the scholarship about his work from this period, which is heavily oriented toward identity and trickster play.[1]) For those of us hungering to understand our work within their intellectual and tribal genealogies – and for whom the concept of tribal sovereignty was more than metaphorical or symbolic, but actually involved real relationships to land, history, and political continuity – *Red on Red* opened up other possibilities for literary scholarship. Abenaki scholar Lisa Brooks reflects in her own experience of Womack's book: "I remember how reading *Red on Red* suddenly made my own project seem more possible, more achievable, more acceptable in what I perceived to be a somewhat hostile academic argument … In short, his work gave me hope" (Brooks 2006: 234).

So this is a personal as well as professional reflection. I locate my emergence as a scholar in the immediate aftermath of *Red on Red* and other literary nationalist texts, along with their contested legacy of ideas, questions, and provocations, but I'm far from the only one; there is an entire generation of scholars for whom this movement has been substantive to our intellectual and political awakening. And for all of us in the increasingly transnational field, whether located in the United States, Canada, Europe, Oceania, or elsewhere in the Indigenous world, these debates and conversations have irrevocably changed the *how* and *why* of what we do, but in a way that connects us to something more immediate, more relational. They remind us that the point is to be part of a community – or a network of communities – and that we have responsibilities to one another, and to the arguments and ideas we engage as scholars.

An imprecise definition

What, then, is Indigenous literary nationalism, and why does it matter? The term is admittedly imprecise, and it encompasses constelled approaches, methods, and perspectives. For some scholars, the term is shorthand for the diverse, community-based and historically contextualized focus of Indigenous scholars like Womack, Weaver, Warrior, Brooks, Cook-Lynn, and non-Indigenous scholars like James Cox, Sam McKegney, and Keavy Martin.[2] Here literary nationalism is a broad category for a diverse set of connected ideas about the role that Indigenous perspectives and experiences play in the interpretation of Indigenous literary productions – not unlike the defiant announcement in disability activism of the 1990s, "nothing about us without us."

Literary nationalism is about the specificity of orientation: very simply, to understand Indigenous literatures it is both intellectually and ethically imperative to know something about the meaningful contexts from which those literatures emerge *and* with which those literatures are engaged. It argues for the centrality of Indigenous perspectives, and sees cultural expressions and politics as having as substantive a significance to literary concerns as aesthetics. It considers the collective, the local, the specific – in a word, the national – in the idea of distinctive peoples and the creative and interpretive relationships they have with the specificities of their particular place and time. It doesn't presume uniformity or singularity in the national – there's no single Cherokee or Creek or Inuit or Anishinaabe national identity, but rather wide spectra of identifications and affiliations within each national framework. It doesn't insist on insularity or exclusivity, as any thoughtful reader/critic can engage these contexts in meaningful ways. And of course the national is *always* engaged with the political, especially for Indigenous peoples, for whom affirmations of distinctiveness are vital to sovereignty, self-determination, and even survival as peoples – and which have consistently been targeted for destruction by assimilative settler-colonial policy and social practice.

Although Acoma Pueblo poet Simon Ortiz is rightly credited as a forefather of the mode with the publication of his 1981 essay "Towards a National Indian Literature: Cultural Authenticity in Nationalism," he was not the first Indigenous intellectual to call for a literary lens that privileged Indigenous imaginations and aesthetics; indeed, in their various writings E. Pauline Johnson (Mohawk), Charles Alexander Eastman (Dakota Sioux), Zitkala-Ša/Gertrude Bonnin (Dakota Sioux), Arthur C. Parker (Seneca), and others were making proto-literary nationalist arguments in the late nineteenth and early twentieth centuries. This was in part a response to the domination of the settler-colonial press and publishing establishment, which insisted on literary noble savages divorced from the devastating material and political realities of Indigenous peoples. Yet it was also the recognition that Native writers had important things to say to the world *and with one another*. In his supportive 1911 correspondence with sociologist Fayette Avery McKenzie, who wanted to create a four-year Indian university that would enable graduates to successfully transfer to an advanced college of their choice, Parker was supportive, noting that:

> I should like to see a school of this sort foster an Indian literature, not necessarily the old, but also the new. The poems of Pauline Johnson, Alex Posey, the writings of Eastman, Simon Pokagon, Zitkalasa [*sic*] and others might be rescued from oblivion or popularized still further.[3]
>
> (Maddox 2005: 99)

The school never materialized, but Parker's commitment to the visible intellectual production of Indigenous peoples within a curriculum that also engaged the broader world is one that remains provocative over 100 years later.[4]

As Weaver et al. affirm in the preface to *American Indian Literary Nationalism* (2006: xv):

> Nationalism is a term on a short list, one that also includes sovereignty, culture, self-determination, experience, and history, that is central to understanding the relationship between the creative expression of Native American literature and the social and historical realities that such expression embodies.

This is to say that it *matters* when we affirm these contexts, as they represent the ongoing creative vibrancy of Indigenous peoples. It's an affirmation of commitment to Indigenous communities, peoples, and relations, of the continuing relevance of Indigenous imaginations and intellectual works to ensure our collective continuities into the future. When decontextualized, the general categories of "Native" or "Indigenous" can be an evacuation of meaning; they can readily flatten out the profound expressive, aesthetic, political, and ideological distinctions that best articulate the complexities of our shared humanity. As such, literary nationalism is as much an *ethical* approach and commitment as an intellectual one, and as with any area of ethics, it's one that challenges its practitioners and interlocutors by its very affirmation.

A nationalist approach doesn't presume that one must be Indigenous or, if Indigenous, affiliated with the community under discussion. A nationalist approach does, however, insist that there's a meaningful interpretive relationship between specific writers, their specific communities on specific lands shaped by specific social, cultural, and political histories. It's also a direct intervention in a representational history that has consistently and aggressively denied Indigenous peoples the right to be heard or even recognized as having any sort of authority over our own ideas and expressions. Given the diverse ways of approaching these diverse intellectual, political, and theoretical concerns, there's clearly no singular or universal approach. There are many ways of doing this, and doing it well.

This is one way of understanding the term as articulated by its practitioners, and one to which I'll return. Yet another way it's been represented is as its supposed opposite, what's come to be known as "cosmopolitanism," another broad term for theoretical modes that argue for de-emphasizing these specificities and considering literary productions more broadly in terms of artistic and intellectual dialogue and exchange, especially with non-Indigenous contexts and influences. Here nationalisms are treated with skepticism if not suspicion, and often for good cause, as nation-state nationalism and even many ethnic nationalisms have left the carnage of genocide, dispossession, alienation, and multi-generational trauma in their wake. Cosmopolitanism affirms a dissolution of boundaries, a blending of subjectivities, a full or at least partial collapse of the meaningful distinctions between cultures. It is, to some degree, a universalizing approach that sees the specificities of history and place – and therefore any interpretive method privileging those specificities – as necessarily incomplete, partial, arbitrary, compromised, even dangerous. As Elvira Pulitano provocatively insists in *Toward a Native American Critical Theory* (2003: 131), "whether we like it or not, Native American authors are already implicated within the dominant discourse of the metropolitan center. Any appeal to a pure or authentic Native American theory is utopian and absurd."

The result is some degree of decoupling literature from its tribal contexts – or at least not privileging those contexts over others. Hybridity, mixedbloodedness, syncretism are central to this mode, whereby non-Indigenous contexts are as important as Indigenous ones – indeed, the idea of Indigenous literature itself is conceptualized as inherently a product of exchange and cross-cultural interaction. Accordingly, at its best literary nationalism represents exclusivism and naive cultural chauvinism, at its worst parochial and bigoted sentiments that presume that only Indigenous people can talk about Indigenous literature. Literary nationalists have gone through great pains to be (as Weaver memorably put it) "coruscatingly clear" about the inclusivity at the heart of literary nationalism, and

Warrior declared as early as 1995 that "the struggle for sovereignty is not a struggle to be free from the influence of anything outside ourselves, but a process of asserting the power we possess as communities and individuals to make decisions that affect our lives" (Warrior 1995: 124). Even so, some scholars – notably Pulitano, Kenneth Lincoln, and Scott Andrews – have criticized literary nationalism and its practitioners as being everything from isolationist, reductionist, and anti-intellectual to outright xenophobic and racist.[5]

So which is it? Is literary nationalism a thoughtful affirmation of the specificity of Indigenous perspectives, histories, and intellectual contexts and their interpretive applicability to Indigenous writing, or is it an essentially reactionary mode that limits Indigenous literature to being little more than ethnographic reportage or a cliquey, self-referential club for Indians only?

One passage in *Red on Red* captures this dilemma and, I think, offers a useful example of why this very question is part of the problem. Interspersed throughout the literary analysis is the running commentary of Jim Chibbo and Hotgun, fictional Creek observers whose narrative purpose is to puncture academic pretensions, to bring community voices directly into dialogue with the interpretations, and to leaven the ponderous academic tone with humor. In the book's introduction, Womack-as-narrator insists on the necessity of Native people engaging one another without focusing on non-Native readers as the central concern. This is the driving impetus of *Red on Red*, to center Indigenous criticism on Indigenous perspectives within Indigenous writing. Womack (and Hotgun) then make the following argument:

> If we take a look at the nineteenth century, we might note two facts: lots of whites spoke on behalf of Indians, and when Indians did author their own books, they had to address a white audience, since they were writing in English, and their people, for the most part, couldn't read them. Those days are over. Educating white folks about Indians can only be taken so far. Hotgun claims it's like teaching hogs to sing: it wastes your time and only frustrates the hog. Now it's time to direct our literary efforts toward our own folks.
>
> (Womack 1999: 21)

If the devastating history of settler-colonialism in North America teaches us anything, it's that educating non-Indigenous people has only limited efficacy in ensuring our sovereignty and protecting what remains of our nations' land bases, ceremonial practices, languages, and identities.

But limited isn't the same as non-existent. Since the earliest days of colonization Indigenous writers and intellectuals have made the profound moral, intellectual, spiritual, legal, and political case for our shared humanity, socio-political distinctiveness, and attachments to land – this is nothing new, and it continues. But focusing our energies on that process of external validation is only a partial victory at best if we don't *also* engage our own families and communities in these questions and concerns, too. Not all writers will want to privilege a community readership, and that's entirely fine, but those who do shouldn't then be pathologized or dismissed for making that conscientious decision to attend first to home. And it's worth noting that even in this case, Womack isn't rejecting the possibility of change – instead, he's arguing for *different registers of possibility*. Womack-the-scholar is self-consciously and openly exploring these issues in an academic book published by a major university press with a commercial mandate for an expansive readership; Hotgun-the-character reminds us that there are other audiences of significance, and it's high time they get some attention. It's a nuanced and provocative argument, but one that goes beyond simple identity binaries.

The problem here is, of course, that the debate has so often been figured in precisely these reductive ways. "Nationalist" and "cosmopolitanist" have become a kind of shorthand that clarifies nothing by diminishing diverse and complicated ideas and reasoned debate to points of caricature. But thoughtful nationalists have always engaged cosmopolitanist concerns – to argue for Indigenous sovereignty as realized by distinctive tribal nations is to *necessarily* acknowledge other sovereignties and the engagements that such acknowledgments require. It's not only a reality of contemporary jurisprudence: it's a historical reality of Indigenous trade, diplomacy, and ideological, material, linguistic, and biological exchange. And to acknowledge the problems of particular forms of nationalism isn't to dismiss its clear importance to Indigenous resistance and resurgence; rather, it's to insist on more nuanced, complicated, and inclusive understandings of "the nation" that attend to the actual complexities of our histories as peoples.

Similarly, some scholars identified as cosmopolitanists have looked to the specific as the meaningful jumping-off or returning point for their analysis, such as Arnold Krupat's 2009 collection of essays, *All that Remains: Varieties of Indigenous Expression*. Other scholars' work is actively situated outside the nationalist/cosmpolitanist divide, offering Indigenous-grounded global interpretive strategies, such as the trans-hemispheric and alliance-based analyses of Shari Huhndorf (Yup'ik), the global "trans-Indigenous" readings of Chadwick Allen (Chickasaw), and the Pacific relationalities of Te Ātiawa Māori critic Alice Te Punga Somerville. These scholars carefully engage specificity *and* exchange, locatedness *and* movement, nationalism *and* cosmopolitanism without a necessary hierarchy of value between the varied categories (Huhndorf 2009; Allen 2012; Te Punga Somerville 2012). As Joseph Bauerkemper notes:

> A critical framework founded on the interdependence, rather than opposition, of nationhood and transnationalism reveals the intensely relational nature of sovereignty, a practical and conceptual fundamental too often neglected. The emergent mood within American Indian literary studies that is cautiously making its own uses of the transnational turn while continuing to tend to the ethical imperatives elaborated by the nationalist turn holds great promise for the ongoing growth of the field.
>
> (2014: 400)

This field-specific understanding of the "transnational turn" in Indigenous literary studies, then, offers a potential gathering grounds where some of the complicated realities of contemporary Indigenous experience and expression can be understood in respectful, nuanced, and productive ways.

And it's worth noting, too, that although they remain grounded in the intellectual concerns of their earlier works, most scholars on every side of the nationalist/ cosmopolitanist binary have moved to other discussions that destabilize the narrow categories to which they've been consigned (Weaver's work on the "Red Atlantic" is an important case in point). Like all organisms, scholars evolve, or we (and our ideas) die. We don't all agree, nor should we; the health of the field depends on sound and reasoned debate, and the continuing adaptability of our ideas to changing circumstances and conversations.

Closing thoughts

Indigenous literary nationalism has never been about shutting down our possibilities or narrowing our imaginations. It's never been about cutting people out of the conversation, or saying that only certain people with a certain identity credential should take part. It's been about centering our experience within our stories, and coming to them on our own terms, not those of arbitrary authorities. The scholarship emerging from this approach has given so many of us a language for the questions we need to ask, questions that have only grown with time: about being and belonging, about our obligations to our communities and to the larger world of which we are a part, and how literature can be a part of those processes.

Most of all, it's been about finding out who we are and where we belong – individually and collectively – in our own ways, in our home grounds or in the classroom, hearing one another's voices and witnessing our own possibilities, as we face this richly varied world in all its wildness and wonder.

Notes

1   Regarding sovereignty, Vizenor's role in drafting the White Earth constitution is a clear extension of his previous work, not a departure, and more recent scholarship is taking up his more complicated network of concerns and commitments. See for example *Studies in American Indian Literatures* 23.4 (Winter 2011), a special issue dedicated to "constitutional criticism."
2   See, for example, Cox (2006), McKegney (2007) and Martin (2012). Of the three, Martin's book most fully articulates literary nationalism in its structure and approach, but all three scholars discuss the significance of the movement to their scholarship.
3   Thanks to Michael Taylor for bringing this reference to my attention in his paper, "Moving beyond Modernism: Recovering Terminological Sovereignty at the Turn of the Twentieth Century," presented at the Native American and Indigenous Studies Association conference in Austin, Texas.
4   Although Parker remains a complex figure who supported policies we might now read as both assimilationist and subversive, his insistence on placing Indigenous peoples at the centre of Indigenous conversation is worth highlighting when discussing the genealogy of literary nationalism and Indigenous Studies as a whole. See Colwell-Chanthaphonh (2009).
5   For the criticism of literary nationalism, see Pulitano (2003, esp. Ch. 2), Lincoln (2007: A3) and Lyons (2010: 146–160).

References

Allen, Chadwick. 2012. *Trans-Indigenous: Methodologies for Global Native Literary Studies*. Minneapolis: University of Minnesota Press.

Bauerkemper, Joseph. 2014. "Indigenous trans/nationalism and the ethics of theory in Native literary studies". In James H. Cox and Daniel Heath Justice, eds. *The Oxford Handbook of Indigenous American Literature*. New York: Oxford University Press.

Brooks, Lisa. 2006. "Afterword: At the gathering place". In Jace Weaver, Craig S. Womack and Robert Warrior. *American Indian Literary Nationalism*. Albuquerque: University of New Mexico Press.

Colwell-Chanthaphonh, Chip. 2009. *Inheriting the Past: The Making of Arthur C. Parker and Indigenous Archaeology*. Tucson: University of Arizona Press.

Cox, James. 2006. *Muting White Noise: Native American and European American Novel Traditions*. Norman: University of Oklahoma Press.

Huhndorf, Shari M. 2009. *Mapping the Americas: The Transnational Politics of Contemporary Native Culture*. Ithaca, NY: Cornell University Press.

Lincoln, Kenneth. 2007. "Red stick lit crit". *Indian Country Today*, 26(44).

Lyons, Scott Richard. 2010. *X-Marks: Native Signatures of Assent*. Minneapolis: University of Minnesota Press.

McKegney, Sam. 2007. *Magic Weapons: Aboriginal Writers Remaking Community after Residential School*. Winnipeg: University of Manitoba Press.

Maddox, Lucy. 2005. *Citizen Indians: Native American Intellectuals, Race, and Reform*. Ithaca, NY: Cornell University Press.

Martin, Keavy. 2012. *Stories in a New Skin: Approaches to Inuit Literature*. Winnipeg: University of Manitoba Press.

Pulitano, Elivira. 2003. *Toward a Native American Critical Theory*. Lincoln: University of Nebraska Press.

Te Punga Somerville, Alice. 2012. *Once Were Pacific: Māori Connections to Oceania*. Minneapolis: University of Minnesota Press.

Warrior, Robert Allen. 1995. *Tribal Secrets: Recovering American Indian Intellectual Traditions*. Minneapolis: University of Minnesota Press.

Weaver, Jace, Craig Womack, and Robert Warrior. 2006. *American Indian Literary Nationalism*. Albuquerque: University of New Mexico Press.

Womack, Craig S. 1999. *Red on Red: Native American Literary Separatism*. Minneapolis: University of Minnesota Press.

3 History, anthropology, Indigenous Studies

Pauline Turner Strong

Introduction

The relationship between history and anthropology is both productive and fraught. Prior to the emergence of Indigenous Studies as a multidisciplinary enterprise, history and anthropology were intertwined in a number of forms, including cultural, social, and oral history; historical anthropology and archaeology; subaltern and colonial studies; and ethnohistory. The last field is most significant for Indigenous Studies: ethnohistory has focused squarely on the experiences of Indigenous peoples (if often through colonial lenses) and there is a direct line of scholarship connecting ethnohistory to Indigenous Studies. While it is tempting to propose that Indigenous Studies may become a "successor discipline" to ethnohistory (Haraway 1988), both of these multidisciplinary formations are currently thriving, with a significant number of scholars actively participating in both.

Ethnohistory is a multidisciplinary approach to Indigenous, colonial, and postcolonial history that developed in North America in the 1950s. Combining the approaches of history, cultural anthropology, and archaeology, ethnohistory centres on the history of non-European peoples, including their experiences of colonization, resistance, and cultural change. Ethnohistory began as an applied field, as historians and anthropologists collaborated on US tribal land claims cases, and soon became institutionalized in the organization now known as the American Society for Ethnohistory (Harkin 2010). The discipline expanded unevenly into other regional contexts, with the Americas remaining at its core. Most ethnohistorians are trained primarily as anthropologists, historians, or archaeologists, making ethnohistory a complex interdisciplinary pursuit.

Over seven decades ethnohistory has both integrated and revealed tensions among historical, anthropological, and Indigenous perspectives on cultural and historical processes (Krech 1991). These tensions have influenced the development of Indigenous Studies, in which Indigenous sources, perspectives, and methodologies are of paramount importance.

A genealogy of Ethnohistory

Following the enactment in the United States of the Indian Claims Commission Act (1946), anthropologists and historians served as expert witnesses in court cases adjudicating tribal claims to territory. This development was influenced by an important Supreme Court decision that defined the basis of Indigenous land claims as evidence of occupancy from "time immemorial" (McMillen 2007). Conducting research for both sides (Indian tribes and the Justice Department), expert witnesses relied on colonial documents, oral histories, and ethnographic research to delineate Indigenous beliefs about territory and resources; Indigenous patterns of land use; Indigenous and colonial understandings of treaty rights; the history of appropriation of land and resources from Indigenous communities; and cultural continuities and changes among Indigenous populations. After 1978, when the Indian Claims Commission issued its final report, anthropologists and historians, by then often identified as ethnohistorians, continued to serve as expert witnesses in other contexts, including tribal recognition cases.

By 1978, however, ethnohistorians were conducting research that went well beyond the testimonial. Ethnohistory consolidated a previously marginalized focus on Indian history within the field of history, while providing a corrective to the synchronic nature of traditional ethnographic research, in which Indigenous peoples were often treated as timeless (Wolf 1982). The neglect of history among anthropologists should not be overemphasized, however, as Mooney's work on the Ghost Dance in the late nineteenth century demonstrates. In the early twentieth century, anthropologists such as Swanton, Speck, Steward, and Fenton used historical methods to reconstruct Indigenous culture. The acculturation studies of Redfield, Herskovits, Lewis, and others in the 1930s also constituted a move toward analyzing cultural change. Meanwhile, Evans-Pritchard moved British anthropology away from the synchronicity of structural-functionalism, describing social anthropology as "a kind of historiography" (1950: 123).

Ethnohistorians have produced numerous collections of primary documents, including documents in Indigenous languages, as well as cultural histories of particular Indigenous peoples. These are important for providing fine-grained, diachronic perspectives on Indigenous experiences. Wallace (1969), for example, drew on archival and ethnographic research to analyze the development of the Handsome Lake religion among the Senecas in the eighteenth century. Wallace has influenced subsequent analyses of cultural revitalization, including Harkin's (2004) collection, which shows the comparative power of Wallace's approach by considering Pacific cargo cults, the Ghost Dance movement on the US Plains, and contemporary social movements. Ethnohistorians have also considered revitalization in the context of Indigenous schools, cultural centres, language programs, and economic development efforts.

Research on the politics, economics, ideologies, and social relations of the "colonial situation" (Cohn 1987) is central to ethnohistorical research. Ethnohistorians have analyzed the political economy of colonial empires, the impact of epidemics on Indigenous populations, the nature of imperial bureaucracies, the acculturation of Indigenous children in boarding schools, Indigenous strategies of survival and resistance, and Christian evangelization and Indigenous responses, among other topics. Studies of the gendered nature of the colonial situation, and especially changes in gender roles under colonialism and Christianity, led to the development of feminist ethnohistory (Strong 1996). Leacock conducted important early work in this area, researching the impact of the fur trade on gender roles among the Innu. Etienne and Leacock (1980) offer a historical materialist explanation of gender inequality, emphasizing how together the allied forces of capitalism, colonialism, and Christianity led to the degradation of women's status. Studies inspired by Leacock show that the impact of capitalism and Christianity on gender roles is extremely complex, varying according to Indigenous gender relations as well as the way Indigenous economies articulated with capitalist economies. More recently, the ethnohistory of sexuality has emerged in the work of scholars such as Gutierrez (1991), Roscoe (1998), and Stoler (1995), all interested in the dynamics of race, class, and sexuality in colonial systems of inequality.

In political economy and environmental history the research of White has been particularly significant. Beginning with a monograph on the colonial production of dependence among the Choctaws, Pawnees, and Navajos, White (1983) developed an ethnohistorical approach that focuses on changing modes of production, social relationships, and environmental relationships. He and others have chronicled the impact of the fur trade, farming, mining, and other European interventions on Indigenous ecologies and economies, analyzing the various forms of dependence and innovation that these interventions engendered. Brooks (2002) offers another approach to political economy, analyzing the transformation of Indigenous Southwestern forms of captivity, servitude, and adoption under colonialism. Subsequently, Miles (2005) presented an intimate portrayal of Cherokee slavery and family life.

White is also known for the influential concept of the "middle ground" (1991), which refers to social and cultural patterns that develop under sustained culture contact. Sahlins (1981) developed a somewhat similar concept, "structures of the conjuncture," in his analysis of the early history of Hawaii. Both scholars offer ways of conceptualizing the hybrid sociocultural forms that develop over the course of intercultural encounters. Sahlins's earlier work on foraging economies has also been influential on ethnohistories like Brightman's (1993) that focus on Indigenous economies and cultural logics.

Relations between Indigenous peoples and the colonizing state have been a recurring concern of ethnohistory. In his scholarship on India, Cohn (1987) developed the concept of "rule by records," which has inspired many important studies of colonial rule as an exercise of knowledge and power (Axel 2002). Dirks (2001), for example, historicizes the notion of "caste," analyzing it as a product of Indigenous culture, colonialism, and resistance. In the North American context, many studies of the colonial state center on treaties and sovereignty issues (Wilkins and Lomawaima 2001).

An especially productive arena of ethnohistorical research is the study of colonial missions and Indigenous responses. Clendinnen (2003) considers missionary work and resistance among sixteenth-century Yucatan Mayans, while Jean Comaroff (1985) analyzes the Church of Zion among the Tshidi of southern Africa as a form of Indigenous agency. Among the many studies of religious change in North America, Spicer's work on the Southwest (1962) stands out for its scope, while works by Axtell (1986), Salisbury (1982), Kan (1989) and others consider other regions.

Ethnohistorians have offered important contributions to the understanding of "ethnogenesis" – the formation of social groups through historical processes of culture contact. Studies of the Métis of Canada, the Seminoles of the US Southeast, the Garifuna of the Caribbean, and the Yoruba of Africa, among others, have employed this concept productively. Hill (1996) considers the development of new cultural identities among Indigenous American and African American groups, tying the emergence of new identities to global processes of domination, resistance, and exchange.

Silverstein (1997) has promoted the ethnohistory of "languages of encounter," which concerns the reciprocal transformation of linguistic forms and linguistic communities. In this vein, Collins (1998) analyzes the relationship between discourses of place and the expropriation of land among the Tolowa.

Notable recent ethnohistorical works abandon "ethnographic authority" or authoritative history (Clifford 1988) for collaborative, polyphonic, and reflexive modes of research and representation. For example, Ferguson and Colwell-Chanthaphonh (2006) interweave perspectives of Tohono-O'odham, Hopi, Zuni, and San Carlos Apache collaborators. Reflexive ethnohistorical scholarship critically examines the role of history and anthropology in producing and circulating hegemonic representations of Indigenous people. Wilmsen (1989), for example, examines ideological constructions of the San of southwestern Africa as "primitive" rather than as a displaced and excluded underclass. O'Brien (2010) analyzes the discursive extinction of Indian peoples in New England through the "last of his tribe" trope, while Deloria's works (1988, 2004) offer wide-ranging critiques of historical, ethnographic, and popular representation. Coming full circle to the beginnings of ethnohistory, Campisi (1991) has reflected critically on his experience as an expert witness in the Mashpee tribal recognition case.

Sources and methodologies

A recurrent theme in ethnohistory has been the tension between the methodologies of anthropology and history, tensions aptly captured in Brown's (1991) metaphor of "strange bedfellows, kindred spirits." Historians have relied primarily on the critical analysis of colonial and state documents, while anthropologists have pursued oral history and "upstreaming," as Fenton (2009) called informed speculation about the past based on more recent cultural practices. Anthropologists have also emphasized comparative analysis and Indigenous conceptions of history, leading Fogelson (1989) to advocate for "ethno-ethnohistory."

As Fogelson's ironic term suggests, there has been some debate over the very name of the field. To what does the "ethno" in "ethnohistory" refer? For some it refers substantively to Indigenous and other ethnic groups, making ethnohistory the history of these groups. For others, it has methodological significance, and refers to an ethnological or ethnographic approach to history. For still others, "ethnohistory" refers to ethnic and Indigenous groups' conceptions of their own pasts. All of these endeavours have taken place under the rubric of "ethnohistory", sometimes in the very same works. In light of these difficulties some scholars, especially those conducting research outside of the Americas, avoid the term altogether, referring instead to "historical anthropology" or "anthropological history." Yet the term "ethnohistory" persists, as does the scholarly tradition and community that has grown up around it.

Ethnohistorians typically rely on multiple forms of data, all of which must be utilized with considerable care. These include:

- Colonial and other institutional documents, including travel journals and memoirs; policy statements; and missionary, administrative, judicial, and treaty records. In interpreting primary documents the ethnohistorian attempts to distinguish official categories, prejudices, and misapprehensions from Indigenous beliefs and practices, putting the documents within the larger context of governmentality. The ethnohistorian must also be aware of the selective and contingent nature of archiving (Dirks 2002; Galloway 2006).
- Written records in Indigenous languages. Particularly significant for literate cultures, these may exist for oral cultures in transcriptions. They also may exist in written form for Indigenous peoples like the Cherokee who developed a written form of their language after contact, or those, like the Lakota, who learned to read and write in their native language from missionaries. Regarding his work with Euro-American and Lakota documents, DeMallie writes, "in a fundamental sense they represent conflicting realities, rooted in radically different epistemologies. The challenge of ethnohistory is to bring these two types of historical data together to construct a fuller picture of the past" (1993: 516).
- Archaeological evidence, which offers a significantly lengthier diachronic dimension than historical and ethnographic evidence. Rogers and Wilson (1993: 7) describe ethnohistorical and archaeological sources as "complementary investigative routes" into cultural change, with archaeology particularly valuable for information on demography and geography, settlement and land use patterns, travel routes, and ethnic relationships.
- Collections, including maps, illustrations, photographs, and artifacts. Much ethnohistorical research occurs in museum collections, which must be understood as subject to the same processes of selection, appropriation, misinterpretation, reinterpretation, and loss as historical archives (Galloway 2006).
- Oral traditions, including oral histories, genealogies, folk tales, and place names. Like institutional documents, oral traditions must be contextualized

within contemporary social structures and projects. As Vansina (1985) emphasizes, oral traditions represent the viewpoints of particularly situated actors and often shift over time.

- Ethnographic research, including systematic participant-observation, aimed at finding traces of, or attitudes toward, the past in the present. For some, ethnographic fieldwork is what differentiates the ethnohistorian from the historian; for others, the difference resides in a more general "anthropological orientation" toward culture (Cohn 1968). Regardless, the results of ethnographic research must always be understood as situated within a particular moment and particular ethnographic encounter. Ethnographic research produces its own archive, and ethnohistorians typically rely on the ethnographic research of previous generations as well as their own. Brown's (2009) ethnohistorical works on the Ojibwa, using materials from Hallowell's fieldwork in the 1930s, exemplify work with an ethnographic archive.

Given the range of data, and the different training that historians, anthropologists, and archeologists bring to their research, it is unsurprising that methodological disputes arise frequently in ethnohistory. These concern, for example:

- The contingency and partiality of documentary sources. Galloway (2006) notes the significance of material not noticed by or not available to European observers; material misinterpreted by European observers; and material that has been lost. Ethnohistory requires a methodology of suspicion and convergence, in which documentary sources are viewed as compromised and explanations are strengthened by the convergence of several lines of evidence.
- The role of oral history, tribal history, and living memory as supplements or correctives to written documents, which usually represent colonial perspectives. Vansina (1985) offers a methodology for the interpretation of oral history, including a way of distinguishing among ecological, genealogical, sociological, and extraordinary time. Anthropologists including Cruikshank (1998) have emphasized the importance of prophecy and other Indigenous orientations to time, which contrast sharply with linear time.
- The problem of "mixed epistemologies," with history, cultural anthropology, and archaeology each relying on different modes of explanation and validation. Wilson contrasts an archeological approach focused on long-term and large-scale processes with historical approaches more concerned with small-scale, shorter-term processes. This difference in temporal scale poses "the challenge of integrating macroprocesses and microprocesses of culture change into a coherent analysis" (Rogers and Wilson 1993: 21, 23).
- Differences between Western and Indigenous epistemologies, which dwarf the differences between disciplinary epistemologies highlighted by Wilson. Taking Indigenous epistemologies seriously is a hallmark of Indigenous Studies (Smith 2012; Denzin et al. 2008).
- The ability of ethnohistory to deal adequately with plural interpretations, including tensions between (and within) archaeological, documentary, and

oral histories. Hoxie argues for an ethnohistory that aims "to describe community lives in their own terms," producing "stories that allow for an open vision – one that is coherent but attends to several layers of meaning and many co-existing interpretations" (1997: 606, 610). Fogelson (1989: 141) enumerates the difficulties posed to ethnohistorians by "multicultural frames of reference," by "different modes of discourse, by documentation that cannot always be limited to written manuscripts, and by recognition of different conceptions of reality."

- The role of theoretical concepts in the field (e.g., Sahlins's structuralism and Wolf's use of world systems theory). Hoxie (1997), for example, counterpoises the pluralistic ethnohistory he advocates against Wolf's (1982) influential attempt to locate tribal histories within a global system. And Sahlins's (1981, 1995) influential structural history has drawn vigorous opposition as a misinterpretation of Indigenous beliefs and actions (Obeyesekere 1997).

Cohn (1987) mediated wisely between "anthropologyland" and "historyland," noting that history and anthropology have a common subject matter, "otherness"; a common project, translation; and a common interest in studying social transformation. He called for an "anthropological history" in which the colonial situation presents a unified analytic field for the study of the construction and representation of culture – Indigenous, colonial, and postcolonial culture alike. Requiring a working experience of both the field and the archive, this endeavour must be highly reflexive and attuned to the ways in which current scholarly concepts (e.g., "culture," "race," "tribe") are often remnants of colonial forms of rule. Even the division between history and anthropology is a remnant of colonial notions of the timeless "primitive"; in overcoming this disciplinary divide, then, ethnohistory offers a way of moving beyond colonial ideologies.

Ethnohistory and Indigenous Studies

The newer field of Indigenous Studies builds upon, critiques, and reframes ethnohistory. In formative methodological works (Wilson and Yellow Bird 2005; Smith 2012), Indigenous scholars critique colonizing knowledges; articulate Indigenous knowledges and methodologies; foreground Indigenous experience and agency; and argue for activist research agendas. Blackhawk (2006) exemplifies this approach, productively coupling his account of imperial violence during Anglo-American expansion into the Great Basin with an account of Indigenous agency.

Also characteristic of Indigenous Studies is a global comparative perspective, which contrasts with the particularism of much ethnohistorical work. A particularly significant comparative framework for Indigenous Studies is settler colonialism (Wolfe 1999; Veracini 2011), which emphasizes commonalities in the project of eliminating and excluding Indigenous peoples found across settler states. Simpson (2014) illustrates the transformative potential of the framework of settler colonialism, explicitly countering the ethnohistorical tradition of Wallace, Fenton, and others in emphasizing Iroquois sovereignty and resistance over traditionalism and revitalization.

There are no sharp lines between ethnohistory and Indigenous Studies, however. Blackhawk's book has been acclaimed across history, ethnohistory, and Indigenous Studies. But Indigenous Studies has broadened the meaning of interdisciplinary scholarship, expanded the scope of comparison, and focused productively on Indigenous experience, knowledge, and agency. History, ethnohistory, and Indigenous Studies are together forging productive discussions on how the historical and cultural dimensions of Indigenous experience are related to other dimensions – the philosophical, the textual, the political, the economic, the geographical, the artistic, the psychological – and how these can best be researched and represented.

References

Axel, B., ed. 2002. *From the Margins*. Durham, NC: Duke University Press.

Axtell, J. 1986. *The Invasion Within*. New York: Oxford University Press.

Blackhawk, N. 2006. *Violence Over the Land*. Cambridge, MA: Harvard University Press.

Brightman, R. 1993. *Grateful Prey*. Berkeley: University of California Press.

Brooks, J.F. 2002. *Captives and Cousins*. Chapel Hill: University of North Carolina Press.

Brown, J.S.H. 1991. "Ethnohistorians: Strange bedfellows, kindred spirits". *Ethnohistory*, 38(2): 113–123.

Brown, J.S.H. 2009. *Memories, Myths, and Dreams of an Ojibwe Leader*. Montreal: McGill-Queen's University Press.

Campisi, J. 1991. *The Mashpee Indians*. Syracuse: Syracuse University Press.

Clendinnen, I. 2003. *Ambivalent Conquests*. 2nd edn. Cambridge: Cambridge University Press.

Clifford, J. 1988. *The Predicament of Culture*. Cambridge, MA: Harvard University Press.

Cohn, B.S. 1968. "Ethnohistory". In *International Encyclopedia of the Social Sciences*, 6: 441–448. New York: Macmillan/Free Press.

Cohn, B.S. 1987. *An Anthropologist among the Historians and Other Essays*. Delhi and New York: Oxford University Press.

Collins, J. 1998. *Understanding Tolowa Histories*. New York: Routledge.

Comaroff, J. 1985. *Body of Power, Spirits of Resistance*. Chicago: University of Chicago Press.

Cruikshank J. 1998. *The Social Life of Stories*. Lincoln: University of Nebraska Press.

Deloria, P.J. 1988. *Playing Indian*. New Haven: Yale University Press.

Deloria, P.J. 2004. *Indians in Unexpected Places*. Lawrence: University of Kansas Press.

DeMallie, R.J. 1993. "'These have no ears': Narrative and the ethnohistorical method". *Ethnohistory*, 40(4): 515–538.

Denzin, N.K., Y.S. Lincoln, and L.T. Smith. 2008. *Handbook of Critical and Indigenous Methodologies*. Los Angeles: Sage.

Dirks, N.B. 2001. *Castes of Mind*. Princeton: Princeton University Press.

Dirks, N.B. 2002. "Annals of the archive: Ethnographic notes on the sources of history". In B. Axel, ed. *From the Margins*. Durham, NC: Duke University Press, pp. 47–65.

Etienne, M. and E. Leacock. 1980. *Women and Colonization*. New York: Praeger.

Evans-Pritchard, E.E. 1950. "Social anthropology: Past and present". *Man*, 50(198): 118–174.

Fenton, W. 2009. *William Fenton: Selected Writings*. Ed. W.A. Starna and J. Campisi. Lincoln: University of Nebraska Press.

Ferguson, T.J. and J.S. Colwell-Chanthaphonh. 2006. *History is in the Land*. Tucson: University of Arizona Press.

Fogelson, R.D. 1989. "The ethnohistory of events and nonevents". *Ethnohistory*, 36(2): 133–147.

Galloway, P. 2006. *Practicing Ethnohistory*. Lincoln: University of Nebraska Press.

Gutierrez, R. 1991. *When Jesus Came, the Corn Mothers Went Away*. Palo Alto: Stanford University Press.

Haraway, D. 1988. "Situated knowledges". *Feminist Studies*, 14(3): 575–599.

Harkin, M.E., ed. 2004. *Reassessing Revitalization Movements*. Norman: University of Nebraska Press.

Harkin, M.E. 2010. "Ethnohistory's ethnohistory: Creating a discipline from the ground up". *Social Science History*, 34(2): 113–128.

Hill, J.E., ed. 1996. *History, Power, and Identity*. Iowa City: University of Iowa Press.

Hoxie, F. 1997. "Ethnohistory for a tribal world". *Ethnohistory*, 44(4): 595–615.

Kan, S. 1989. *Memory Eternal*. Seattle: University of Washington Press.

Krech, Shepard, III. 1991. "The state of ethnohistory". *Annual Reviews in Anthropology*, 20: 345–375.

McMillen, C. 2007. *Making Indian Law*. New Haven: Yale University Press.

Miles, T. 2005. *Ties that Bind*. Berkeley: University of California Press.

Obeyesekere, G. 1997. *The Apotheosis of Captain Cook*. 2nd edn. Princeton: Princeton University Press.

O'Brien, J. 2010. *Firsting and Lasting*. Minneapolis: University of Minnesota Press.

Rogers, J.D. and S.M. Wilson, eds. 1993. *Ethnohistory and Archaeology*. New York and London: Plenum.

Roscoe, W. 1998. *Changing Ones*. New York: St. Martin's.

Sahlins, M. 1981. *Historical Metaphors and Mythical Realities*. Ann Arbor: University of Michigan Press.

Sahlins, M. 1995. *How "Natives" Think*. Chicago: University of Chicago Press.

Salisbury, N. 1982. *Manitou and Providence*. New York: Oxford University Press.

Silverstein, M. 1997. "Encountering language and languages of encounter in North American ethnohistory". *Journal of Linguistic Anthropology*, 6(2): 126–144.

Simpson, A. 2014. *Mohawk Interruptus*. Durham, NC: Duke University Press.

Smith, L.T. 2012. *Decolonizing Methodologies*. London and New York: Zed Books.

Spicer, E. 1962. *Cycles of Conquest*. Tucson: University of Arizona Press.

Stoler, A. 1995. *Race and the Education of Desire*. Durham, NC: Duke University Press.

Strong, P.T. 1996. "Feminist theory and the invasion of the heart in North America". *Ethnohistory*, 43: 683–712.

Vansina, J. 1985. *Oral Tradition as History*. Madison: University of Wisconsin Press.

Veracini, L. 2011. "Introducing settler colonial studies". *Settler Colonial Studies*, 1(1): 1–12.

Wallace, A.F.C. 1969. *The Death and Rebirth of the Seneca*. New York: Knopf.

White, R. 1983. *The Roots of Dependency*. Lincoln: University of Nebraska Press.

White, R. 1991. *The Middle Ground*. New York: Cambridge University Press.

Wilkins, D.E. and T. Lomawaima. 2001. *Uneven Ground*. Norman: University of Oklahoma Press.

Wilmsen, E.N. 1989. *A Political Economy of the Kalahari*. Chicago: University of Chicago Press.

Wilson, W.A. and M. Yellow Bird. 2005. *For Indigenous Eyes Only*. Santa Fe, NM: SAR Press.

Wolf, E. 1982. *Europe and the People Without History*. Berkeley: University of California Press.

Wolfe, P. 1999. *Settler Colonialism and the Transformation of Anthropology*. London: Cassell.

4 Reclaiming the statistical "native"

Quantitative historical research beyond the pale

Chris Andersen and Tahu Kukutai

This chapter examines the ways in which quantitative research approaches and statistical sources have constructed Indigenous peoples and Indigenous histories, often to negative effect, and gives voice to the efforts of Indigenous scholars and communities to transform those practices. There are three sections. The first section describes the practice of quantitative history in relation to Indigenous peoples, with a particular focus on demographic history. We identify key critiques of the field and discuss some of the broader methodological challenges of using quantitative methods to tell Indigenous histories. The second section focuses on the statistical sources used to inform historical representations of Indigenous peoples, with an emphasis on the national population census. In the third section we explore changes to the statistical field from one in which Indigenous peoples had no say to one in which it is becoming increasingly difficult to envision large-scale data collection being carried out without the consent and active participation of Indigenous experts and communities. We argue that while there have been changes in terms of statistical coverage that will inform future history-telling, this has yet to translate fully into Indigenous agency in telling of our histories in that quantitative space, and this is where attention remains most needed.

Quantitative history – "in the absence" of

In contrast to an earlier reliance on textual records and archival research, quantitative historical analysis today relies heavily on the use of large (and now digitized) databases of economic and demographic data drawn from statistical sources such as the population census, births, deaths and marriage registers, parish, taxation, military and hospital records, ship logs and voting rolls. These forms of numerical data are typically collated and arranged by researchers into time-series datasets to fit their own analytical purposes, but increasingly, researchers also have recourse to large volumes of digitized historical data centralized in a single repository.

Quantitative approaches to Indigenous histories most often take the form of demographic histories focused on issues of past population change (see, for example, Cook 1976; Cook and Borah 1979; Dobyns 1983; Pool 1991, 2015; Thornton 1987, 2000). Population histories draw heavily on the use of mathematical models and are often animated by the goal of estimating the size of pre- and post-contact populations with the aim of quantifying the timing and magnitude of population decline. Earlier works were primarily histories of disease epidemiology focused on the mechanisms and rate of disease diffusion and subsequent changes in mortality, fertility, and population size and structure. Later works broadened the focus to consider the indirect social determinant effects of epidemic disease, such as disrupted relationships, social disorganization, malnutrition, and starvation, on post-epidemic mortality and fertility. At the risk of oversimplifying, the tone and focus of most population histories have been in the vein of dispassionate, independent, apparently objective observers whose primary goal is to get the numbers "right." There have been noteworthy exceptions. In his seminal book *American Indian Holocaust and Survival*, for example, Cherokee scholar Russell Thornton confronted narratives about the benign nature of colonization and of American Indian population decline as an "unfortunate concomitant of Manifest Destiny."

Subsequent works, such as Stannard's demographic history of Hawai'i, *Before the Horror*, married classic demographic techniques with literary criticism and textual analysis, archaeology and epidemiology, to argue that previous estimates underestimated the pre-colonization Hawai'ian population and thus in turn seriously underestimated the numbers of who died following contact. For him, the revision of population estimates was not just an academic exercise, but offered a compelling context to "the rewriting of island history" for those "who have suffered so terribly and in so many ways as the victims of ... western avarice" (1989: 143).

The dominance of historical demography within the broader ambit of quantitative Indigenous history reflects, to some extent, the obsession of colonists with documenting what they saw as the inevitable demise of native peoples in the face of conquest, disease, and "civilization" (see, for example, Newman 1882 and Walsh 1908; for a Māori response see Hiroa 1924). In Aotearoa New Zealand, for example, the first official Māori census of 1857/8 contained lengthy observations on the likely causes of Māori population decline and their future viability as a race (Fenton 1859). The situation for Māori in New Zealand, for example, was seen as part of a wider threat facing native peoples across the colonies where population decline had banished the "necessity for caution and respect" toward them. The "ultimate result," if left unchecked, would be the "speedy obliteration of the colored race from the list of peoples" (Fenton 1859: 29).

The preoccupation with technical issues of measurement – to the perceived detriment of "deeper" meaning – has rendered quantitative history vulnerable to charges of reductionism. While critiques of quantitative history were most vocal in its heyday of the 1970s, there remains a level of skepticism over claims to "scientific" veracity given the reliance on numerical data that are fragmentary, inconsistent, and – in the context of Indigenous population histories – almost universally filtered through a colonial lens (Anderson 2007). Notwithstanding the considerable diversity that exists within the demography discipline, it is fair to say that most demographers are neither inclined nor equipped to read historical sources "against the grain." Sources are interrogated primarily with the aim of identifying logical flaws and potential biases in relation to the numbers rather than probing the underlying motivations and embedded racial biases in the sources from which the data are drawn. The drive to produce "social facts" from numerical data also reflects the value accorded to precise quantification and the minimization of error (Caldwell 1996).

For the Indigenous "subjects" of these population histories, academic debates about models and measurement serve to alienate us further from our own stories as the terms of the debate are elevated to a level of techno-speak from which we are largely absent. More poignantly, reducing the conversation to estimates and errors decontextualizes the numbers from the trauma of colonialism and the loss of sovereignty, land, knowledge, and lifeways. Perhaps not surprisingly, Indigenous methodologies scholars have argued that statistical research sits in fundamental tension with "Indigenous ways of knowing" (Kovach 2009; Smith 2012). This argument is usually laid out along something like the following lines. Colonial regimes the world over have devalued Indigenous ways of being and knowing. Part of this devaluation has included their overlay and erasure by Western paradigms of knowledge. Quantitative research methodologies are part and parcel of the *positivism* that characterizes Western knowledge (and scientific inquiry more specifically). As such, positivism, with its reliance on "external evidence, testing and universal laws of generalizability … contradict[s] a more integrated, holistic and contextualized Indigenous approach to knowledge" (Kovach 2009: 78). Hence the devaluation and dismissal of "Indigenous ways of knowing."

While it is certainly true that quantitative research methodologies that focus solely on aggregate patterns do abstract from local context, we argue that this is neither inevitably a bad thing, nor is it the only contemporary research methodology that does so (see Walter and Andersen 2013: 19). The issue is not so much that simple abstraction from local (Indigenous) milieus has led to the production and legitimation of stereotypes about Indigenous communities. Rather, we argue, it is the historical contexts within which this abstraction occurred: namely, in the stark absence of any collaboration with the Indigenous communities and peoples who provided this information. We turn to a discussion of sources now.

Narrow sources, no collaboration

As scholars have argued (Curtis 2001; Woolf 1989), statistics and their study have been integral to the development of the modern state and modern society. Far from representing the social world in a neutral way, statistics instead constitute a form of social power that allows for the selection of specific aspects of information about our collective selves that then come to stand in for the whole. The national population census has long occupied a central position in the state architecture of official statistics. Despite appeals to the objective and scientific nature of the census, the context and motivations underpinning census-taking activities have always been tied to the exercise of power. The expansion of colonial powers into "new" lands reshaped the census as a mechanism for the control and subjugation of Indigenous peoples as colonial subjects. State imperatives to dominate and exclude local peoples clearly influenced decisions about who, how and what to count. In these contexts, ideas about race were used to justify colonial dominance and to disqualify the full participation of Indigenous populations in economic and political life (Ittmann et al. 2010). The complexity of Indigenous and local groupings posed a major challenge for imperial governance and the development of classificatory grids of race and ethnicity. Rarely did these simplified and compressed categories reflect local understandings of human difference.

In Aotearoa New Zealand, the historical legacy of Indigenous statistics is one of population data collected in service of evolving state efforts to civilize, assimilate, and integrate Māori. In the late nineteenth and early twentieth centuries the statistical interest in Māori–European "half-castes" was clearly linked to colonial policies of racial amalgamation whereby the increasing ratio of half-castes to Māori "full-bloods" served as an important indicator of "success" (Kukutai 2012). In Australia the interest in blood quantum was also tied to the social expectation that Aboriginal peoples would disappear as a consequence of inexorable and excess mortality among so-called "full-blood" Indigenous people, as well as via the social reclassification of those considered "half-caste" under a deliberate policy of cultural assimilation into mainstream society up until the 1960s (Smith 1980). In the nineteenth-century Canadian context, initially shaky official enumeration practices were shaped by numerous enumerative difficulties that rendered the entire enterprise expensive, time-consuming, and frustrating (Curtis 2001; Hamilton 2008; Inwood and Hamilton 2011; Ruppert 2009).

Since at least the early part of the twentieth century, quantitative data have come to sit at the centre of most strategies and policies for governing Indigenous populations and communities. One might argue with very little hyperbole that most non-Indigenous people (and even a surprising number of Indigenous people) form opinions about Indigenous life – and its apparent "lag" relative to that of non-Indigenous communities – from conclusions drawn from quantitative research and reported to the media. To the extent that modern governance is based on the rhetoric of evidence-based policy making, nation-states conceive of and act on the governance of Indigenous communities – as with all communities – through the extensive use of quantitative research. However, although many of us largely take for granted the kinds of summaries we see in statistical form, this becomes an acute problem when communities get little or no say in the interpretation of the information or in the forms in which it gets collected. In an Indigenous context in particular, Walter and Andersen (2013: 14) argue that the growing volume of research has itself come to stand in for the underlying complexity that it seeks to draw information from (also see Taylor 2011).

Perhaps the defining characteristic of historical quantitative research involving Indigenous individuals and communities is that quantitative researchers engaged in virtually no collaboration with Indigenous peoples with respect to the categories used to organize the information they proposed to collect, the specific questions asked, the communities from which the information was drawn and the eventual interpretations derived from these efforts. That is, Indigenous peoples were completely absent from the entirety of the "statistical cycle" (Walter and Andersen 2013: 40) and as such, our lack of expertise or "statistical literacy" resulted in little place for our thoughts or concerns in the creation, collection, and analysis of the data.

The sum total of this has meant, at least in recent years, a growing critique of the quantitative collection of information on Indigenous peoples, and the policies and programs for which they are putatively used to provide evidence (Kukutai and Walter 2015; Nobles 2000; Perlmann and Waters 2002). Initially the stance was one of resistance and dismissal. In more recent years, however, a cadre of Indigenous researchers has emerged who have argued for the usefulness of indigenizing official statistics. Few Indigenous communities are in a position to dismiss the power of statistical interventions, not least because of the policies that make use of their data. The critiques of historical quantitative research notwithstanding, valuable information can be gleaned from undertaking respectful and collaborative quantitative research with Indigenous communities. As we will argue in the chapter's final part, more contemporary quantitative research regarding Indigenous communities differs – in positive and even hopeful ways – from previous research relations and results. We turn to that now.

Contemporary practices: toward more respectful and collaborative relations

It is fair to suggest that although current Indigenous state-based quantitative practices still leave much to be desired, they are more equitable than past relationships. Indeed, a century or even five decades ago, imagining Indigenous communities holding *any* power in quantitative relationships with official actors would be as difficult to imagine as these communities holding *no* power today. This is not to suggest that more equitable statistical relationships immediately or even necessarily translate to more equitable policy or outcomes for Indigenous communities; the complexity of modern nation-states is such that a number of "articulations" have to happen between the relations that produce the statistics and the various contexts within which they are (or are not) taken up in order for that to be so. Nonetheless, bad statistics rarely assist in producing more just relations elsewhere, and failing to heed Indigenous voices and expertise produces bad statistics (Kukutai and Walter 2015).

Several structural features have played a role in producing more equitable statistical relationships between Indigenous communities and policy actors and state-based ones. First, they must be understood as part of a broader restructuring of relationships between Indigenous peoples and nation-states in general. Beginning in the post-World War II period and gathering steam in the 1960s, new eras ushered in new civil rights and protections that, in concert with demographic shifts in Indigenous populations, produced more vocal Indigenous political voices but also what liberal philosopher James Tully (2005) termed a "listening state." Part of the incorporation of Indigenous thoughts, experiences, and desires into the framework of a broad spectrum of policies that impact Indigenous communities has included discussions about how to produce statistics more meaningful to Indigenous communities. In turn, while this has assumed a number of different trajectories, the idea that we as Indigenous peoples should be involved in the creation, interpretation, and dissemination of information about us has slowly seeped its way into the inner workings of official statistical institutions and practices.

To the extent that Indigenous peoples have been able to exploit macro-level changes to influence some degree of change in the official statistics system, this might be viewed as "top-down" change in which the control still remains largely vested in the state. However, Indigenous polities have also responded by generating their own surveys, demographic profiles, and social indicators as a form of community governance. Examples of this "bottom-up" form of engagement with statistics includes the Māori Plan for Tamaki Makaurau in Aotearoa New Zealand; the Yawuru survey in Australia (Kukutai and Taylor 2012); and the health surveys carried out by the First Nations Information Governance Centre in Canada (FNIGC 2012).

While some headway has thus been made in the collection and utilization of contemporary statistics about and for Indigenous peoples and communities, this has yet to translate into Indigenous agency in the telling of our histories in quantitative spaces, and this is where attention is most needed. While some (typically non-Indigenous quantitative researchers) might attribute the absence of Indigenous scholars in the field to a dearth of those with statistical capability, more substantive critiques demonstrate a deep distrust of quantitative methods and their methodologies in the field of academia and in the community. While these critiques are somewhat simplistic, their authors raise an important point, which is that, ultimately, Indigenous engagement with quantitative research remains a double-edged sword. On the one hand, Indigenous scholars can deploy numbers strategically to "talk back" on our own terms. And indeed, we have done so successfully in ways that have benefitted our communities. On the other hand, in order to do so, we must necessarily invest some level of legitimacy in the numbers, warts and all. As one Indigenous Australian scholar argues:

> if we, as Indigenous researchers, do not undertake the quantitative research in the areas of pressing concern for Indigenous Australians, we can be very sure that others will. And it will be their questions that will be posed, their interpretation of the analysis that will have the influence, and their prioritisation of what is important that will drive the research and policy agenda.

> (Walter 2005)

References

Anderson, M. 2007. "Quantitative history". In W. Outhwaite and S. Turner, eds. *The Sage Handbook of Social Science Methodology*. London: Sage, pp. 246–264.

Caldwell, J.C. 1996. "Demography and social science". *Population Studies*, 50(3): 305–333.

Cook, S. 1976. *The Population of the California Indians*. Berkeley: University of California Press.

Cook, S. and W. Borah. 1979. *Essays in Population History: Mexico and California*. Berkeley: University of California Press.

Curtis, B. 2001. *The Politics of Population: State Formation, Statistics and the Census of Canada*. Toronto: University of Toronto Press.

Dobyns, H. 1983. *Their Number Become Thinned: Native American Population Dynamics in Eastern North America*. Knoxville: University of Tennessee Press.

Fenton, F. 1859. *Observations on the State of the Aboriginal Inhabitants of New Zealand*. Wellington: New Zealand Government.

First Nations Information Governance Centre (FNIGC). 2012. *First Nations Regional Health Survey (RHS) 2008/10: National Report on Adults, Youth and Children Living in First Nations Communities*. Ottawa: FNIGC.

Hamilton, Michelle. 2008. "'Anyone not on the list might as well be dead': First Nations and enumeration in Canada, 1851–1901". *Journal of the Canadian Historical Association*, 19: 57–79.

Hiroa, T.R. 1924. "The passing of the Maori". *Transactions and Proceedings of the New Zealand Institute*, LVII: 362–375.

Inwood, Chris and Michelle Hamilton. 2011. "The Aboriginal population and the 1891 Census of Canada". In P. Axelsson and P. Sköld, eds. *Indigenous Peoples and Demography: The Complex Relation Between Identity and Statistics*. New York: Berghahn Books, pp. 95–116.

Ittmann, K., D.D. Cordell, and G.H. Maddox. 2010. *The Demographics of Empire: The Colonial Order and the Creation of Knowledge*. Athens: Ohio University Press.

Kovach, M. 2009. *Indigenous Methodologies: Characteristics, Conversations and Contexts*. Toronto: University of Toronto Press.

Kukutai, T. 2012. "Quantum Māori, Māori quantum: Representations of Māori identities in the census, 1857/8–2006". In R. McClean, B. Patterson, and D. Swain, eds. *Counting Stories, Moving Ethnicities: Studies from Aotearoa New Zealand*. Hamilton: University of Waikato, pp. 27–51.

Kukutai, T. and J. Taylor. 2012. "Postcolonial profiling of Indigenous populations: Limitations and responses in Australia and Aotearoa New Zealand". Special issue on indigenous demography. *Espace, Populations, Sociétiés*: 13–27.

Kukutai, T. and M. Walter. 2015. "Recognition and indigenizing official statistics: Reflections from Aotearoa New Zealand and Australia". *Statistical Journal of the IAOS*, 31: 317–326.

Moreton-Robinson, A. and M. Walter. 2009. "Indigenous methodologies in social research". In M. Walter, ed. *Social Research Methods: An Australian Perspective*. 2nd edn. Melbourne: Oxford University Press, pp. 1–18.

Newman, A. 1882. "A study of the causes leading to the extinction of the Maori". *Transactions and Proceedings of the New Zealand Institute*, XV: 459–477.

Nobles, M. 2000. *Shades of Citizenship: Race and the Census in Modern Times*. Redwood City: Stanford University Press.

Perlmann, J. and M. Waters. 2002. *The New Race Question: How the Census Counts Multiracial Individuals*. Washington, DC: Brookings Institution Press.

Pool, I. 1991. *Te Iwi Maori: A Population Past, Present and Future*. Auckland: Auckland University Press.

Pool, I. 2015. *Colonization and Development in New Zealand between 1769 and 1900: The Seeds of Rangiatea*. Zurich: Springer.

Ruppert, Evelyn. 2009. "Becoming peoples: 'Counting heads in northern wilds'". *Journal of Cultural Economy*, 2(1/2): 11–31.

Smith, Len. 1980. *The Aboriginal Population of Australia*. Canberra: Australian National University.

Smith, L. 2012. *Decolonizing Methodologies: Research and Indigenous Peoples*. London and New York: Zed Books.

Stannard, D. 1989. *Before the Horror: The Population of Hawai'i on the Eve of Western Contact*. Honolulu: University of Hawai'i.

Taylor, J. 2011. "Beyond the pale: Measures of mobility in postcolonial Australia". *Law, Text Culture*, 15(1): 72–99.

Thornton, R. 1987. *American Indian Holocaust and Survival: A Population History since 1492*. Norman: University of Oklahoma Press.

Thornton, R. 2000. "Population of native North Americans". In M. Haines and R. Steckel, eds. *A Population History of North America*. Cambridge: Cambridge University Press, pp. 9–50.

Tully, J. 2005. *Strange Multiplicity: Constitutionalism in an Age of Diversity*. Cambridge: Cambridge University Press.

Walsh, P. 1908. "The passing of the Maori". *Transactions and Proceedings of the New Zealand Institute*, XL: 154–175.

Walter, M. 2005. "Using the 'power of the data' within Indigenous research contexts". *Australian Aboriginal Studies*, 2: 27–34.

Walter, M. and C. Andersen. 2013. *Indigenous Statistics: A Quantitative Methodology*. Thousand Oaks: Left Coast Press.

Woolf, S. 1989. "Statistics and the modern state". *Comparative Studies in Society and History*, 31(3): 588–604.

Part II

Alternative sources and methodological reorientations

I. Reframing Indigenous Studies

5 Recovering, restorying, and returning Nahua writing in Mexico

Kelly S. McDonough

Nahuatl, the common language of the so-called Aztec Empire and native language of some 1.5 million people today, is one of the most of the widely spoken and best-documented Indigenous languages in the Americas.[1] This robust number of speakers and written corpus, however, does not translate to language or cultural vitality. Similar to other Indigenous peoples across the world, over the past five centuries Nahuas have been subject to systematic discrimination, displacement, dispossession, and deprivation of their cultural resources, particularly their language (UN Division of Economic and Social Affairs 2009: 1). Today fewer and fewer Nahua children learn their maternal language at home. Add to this that language, reading, and writing skills in Nahuatl are rarely taught beyond the second grade, if at all, in public schools in Nahua communities. It is common for Nahuas to deny that they speak an Indigenous language or to refuse to speak it in public, having long endured intense discrimination based on their indigeneity (McDonough 2014: 60–61). Deemed inferior to Spanish, Indigenous languages in Mexico such as Nahuatl are at risk of extinction.[2]

Along with the very real issue of language disappearance, variations of the "disappearing Indian" trope often seen north of the Rio Grande circulates widely in Mexico as well, including the disappearing *good* Indian. Public monuments, grade school primers, social and political programming, and until recently even academic studies, have contributed to a storyline of the gradual deterioration of Nahua culture. Representations of glorious Aztecs of the past stand in stark contrast with those of today's Nahuas depicted as withered vestiges of a once-great people. Indeed, one of the more widely circulating texts providing a much-needed Indigenous counterpoint to European versions of Mexican conquest has the unfortunate title of *Visión de los vencidos* or *Vision of the Vanquished* (León Portilla 1959, 1962). Notwithstanding the fact that the editor of that volume, Miguel León-Portilla, has done more for Nahuatl Studies than anyone else in his generation, the "vision" is presented unwittingly as one of defeats and endings.

An especially harmful manifestation of this stereotype has been the insistence upon the radical incompatibility of notions of indigeneity, intellectualism, and writing. Many will cede that pre-Hispanic Nahuas had rich oral, pictographic, and other material practices of producing, recording, and transmitting knowledge. These activities, however, are generally thought to have ceased or decreased dramatically since conquest in the early sixteenth century. As is common with minoritized cultures in the context of conquest and colonialism, the existence and persistence of Indigenous intellectual work, especially alphabetic writing thought to be the realm of superior Europeans, has been suppressed or obscured by dominant culture. The result is that today, along with the general public and the majority of the academic community, Nahuas themselves are unaware of the existence of the enduring and dynamic trajectory of their people's engagement with the Roman alphabet – in Nahuatl, Spanish, Latin, and other Indigenous languages – since the early sixteenth century. That is, Nahuas have been denied access to the myriad ways in which their people have engaged the world and the word through a diverse array of written forms and genres, including dictionaries, grammars, religious texts, epistolary, mundane legal documents, formal and informal community histories, political speeches, personal testimony, prose, poetry, ethnographies, and drama to name just a few. But this is changing, and for the better.

Today academics and Indigenous peoples (not necessarily mutually exclusive categories) are working together to recover the physical documentation and memory of Nahua writing since the early sixteenth century through the present day in order to "restory" the narrative of Nahua culture and that of Mexico at large with these long-silenced perspectives.[3] Aimed at shifting public perceptions and academic conversations, this is also a project of repatriation. Ideally, with access to their own cultural patrimony, Nahuas can better understand the continuities and innovations of their language and culture over the centuries. The remainder of this chapter consists of examples of Nahua writing from the colonial period through the present that depict a broad spectrum of Indigenous experience, disrupting time-worn notions of Indigenous peoples as non-thinking beings, frozen in time, and averse to change. I also comment briefly on the process of return, of reading these texts with present-day Nahua researchers and colleagues.

The colonial period is especially rich in epistolary, religious, linguistic, historical, and legal documents produced by Nahuas. These texts were often, but not always, written in the Nahuatl language since for nearly 300 years Nahuatl served as a semi-official administrative language in New Spain. That said, some notable texts written by Nahuas in languages other than Nahuatl include four letters written to King Philip II in Latin by Nahua noble and nephew of Moctezuma II, don Pablo Nazareo de Xaltocan. Surely it was not the intention of the Catholic priests who had taught don Pablo how to write in Latin that he would go on to use these skills to demand restitution of lands that had been wrongfully taken from his family during conquest. We might also consider the multilingual grammar and linguistic treatise (Spanish–Nahuatl–Latin) written by the Jesuit priest Antonio del Rincón, descended from a noble line of Texcoco. His late sixteenth-century *Arte mexicana* is one of the first Indigenous-language grammars in the Americas written by a native speaker, and the first to articulate the highly complex aspects of Nahuatl contrastive vowel length and pronunciation that had previously eluded non-native grammarians (Rincón 1595; McDonough 2014: 52–54). Much can be gleaned from colonial Nahuatl-language historical annals regarding Indigenous views of colonial cultures in contact. Domingo Francisco de San Antón Muñón

Chimalpahin Quauhtlehuanitzin (often referred to simply as "Chimalpahin"), arguably the most important and prolific Indigenous writer of colonial Mexico, observed the arrival of delegates from Japan to Mexico City in 1610. With an ethnographic gaze, he wrote of his own perception of the Japanese: "yuquin aquen momamamati. amo yocoxcatlaca. amo mocnomatcatlaca. çan iuhquin quaquahti" / "They seem bold, not gentle and meek people, going about like eagles" (Chimalpahin 2006: 170–171). Charting mounting racial tensions, in 1609 he writes that rumors were circulating of a black rebellion being planned in Mexico City. Whereas the insurgency never transpired, he does remark that the alleged conspirators were arrested and publicly executed (Chimalpahin 2006: 154–155). Another prominent annalist, seventeenth-century Tlaxcalan noble and statesmen don Juan Buenaventura Zapata y Mendoza, wrote extensively of the interactions between the Tlaxcalan cabildo (municipal council), Indigenous commoners, and Spanish government authorities. His text is abundant in rare descriptions of the elaborate religious and political processions orchestrated by the Indigenous cabildo members in order to establish and confirm their place in the colonial order (McDonough 2014: 63–82). Such manuscripts also provide valuable evidence of the transformations of Nahua methods of recording social memory. The structure of the annals shows a continuation of the pre-Hispanic *xiuhpohualli*, a year-count method of recording *altepetl* (city/state) histories, while at the same time the use of alphabetic writing demonstrate Nahua people's creative appropriation and adaptation of new cultural practices and technologies (Lockhart 1992: 376–392).

Not all Nahua histories followed the year-count structure of the annals. Seventeenth- and eighteenth-century primordial titles or "informal community histories" can be best described as a collages of alphabetic and pictographic stories that served to teach the people of their common past and to protect their landholdings from usurpers, Indigenous and non-Indigenous alike. The heroic deeds of ancestors, acts of possession, and inter-ethnic pacts join descriptions of the landscape and borders of the territory in question. Primordial titles are quite rare in comparison to the copious cache of mundane Nahuatl documents from the colonial period such as testaments; land documents; census, parish, and *cofradía* (guild) records; municipal council minutes; petitions; election reports; and tax collection records (Horn and Lockhart 2007). These types of documents shed light on, among many other topics, the varied ways in which Indigenous people in colonial Mexico utilized the Spanish court system to their benefit, how certain Nahuas adopted and adapted the Catholic religion, and transformations of Nahua societal structures and gender relations.

The Nahua scriptural trace becomes faint beginning in the early nineteenth century, but this does not mean that Nahuas ceased writing. Instead, due to the fact that Mexico claimed Spanish as its unifying official tongue with its declaration of independence from Spain, Nahuatl was no longer a viable vehicle for administrative business. Nahua participation in politics – what we might call "Indigenous politics," even though all ethnic identities were legally erased in exchange for a blanket-term of "citizen" with independence in 1821 – demanded the use of Spanish, and Nahuas were up to the task. A cache of Spanish-language documents in the Archivo General de la Nación in Mexico City from the late 1820s and 1830s exemplifies how Nahuas wrote in the Spanish language as the means to shape and respond to the ever-changing world. Protesting the fact that outside forces were imposing a non-Indigenous candidate for the rectorship of the Colegio de San Gregorio, a traditionally Indigenous and at one time Jesuit school in Mexico City, Francisco Mendoza y Moctezuma filed petition after petition brimming with trenchant criticism of the 300 years of misery and discrimination suffered by Indigenous people in Mexico, and their present right to justice. At the very least, according to Mendoza y Moctezuma and the scores of Nahua men who signed in support, they deserved to control their beloved school and the properties and lands that supported it.[4] Employing the double discourse of "miserable Indians" and "free citizens," Mendoza y Moctezuma asks the president of Mexico to intervene. Did the president wish to continue to treat its citizens in the same manner as the vilified Spaniards? Or, he asks, would he end the tyranny and truly invest Indigenous peoples with the rights and freedom promised with full citizenship? In another nineteenth-century document, one of the signees of the above-mentioned petitions, Faustino Galicia Chimalpopoca, penned what appears to have been a draft of a public speech in Spanish. He laments the suppression of Nahuatl in the nineteenth century and argues for a reconsideration of the policies and practices that are contributing to the denigration and disappearance of his language and the knowledges it encapsulates.[5] Far ahead of his times, his declaration that Indigenous languages hold certain knowledges and ways of relating to the world, and that they should therefore be celebrated not stigmatized, continues to be one of the major arguments of those who work to protect, promote, and revitalize Indigenous languages today. Although they wrote in Spanish, these nineteenth-century multilingual Indigenous citizens of Mexico show themselves to be agents of their own discourses. They also demonstrate that issues of language and cultural survival have long figured in the intellectual agenda of their people. With access to these documents, contemporary Nahuas can see that they are joining an ongoing struggle to protect and promote their cultural heritage.[6]

Moving into the twentieth century, written and oral Indigenous testimony and short stories as recorded by anthropologists and linguists are relatively untapped sources for understanding Nahua thought and experience. These types of texts are especially ripe for use in revitalization curricula in that they bear witness to lifeways and knowledges that have been erased from the consciousness of many present-day Nahuas due to assimilative processes. While we cannot ignore the role of the academic interlocutor (and editor) in the collection and compilation of the words of the so-called informants, without a doubt Nahuas chose carefully what they would and would not share. We can look to the case of Doña Luz Jiménez, who, up until Nahua Yolanda Matías Garcías's bilingual collection of poetry (*Tonalxochimej*) in 2013, was the only published Nahua female. In *De Porfirio Díaz a Emiliano Zapata: Memoria Náhuatl de Milpa Alta* (1968) doña Luz collaborated with Mexican anthropologist Fernando Horcasitas in writing the memories of her experiences of forced assimilative education and the violence and displacement wrought by the Mexican Revolution (Jiménez 1968).[7] In a separate posthumously published project, *Los cuentos en náhuatl de doña Luz Jiménez* (1979), doña Luz shared stories related to the origins of man, ceremony, local lore, moralizing/didactic stories, and comedic tales. The generative potential of returning Nahua writing to Nahuas is especially evident in the case of doña Luz's work. In Miguel León-Portilla's legendary Seminario de Cultura Náhuatl during the 1980s, several native speakers found in doña Luz's words a spark that would inspire a resurgence of poetry, prose, and drama in the Nahuatl language. León-Portilla maintains that doña Luz's stories became akin to a Bible for these Indigenous readers: her words were a place in which to "revivir la memoria de lo que fue su pueblo ... Es – así lo dicen – como ver en un espejo algo de uno mismo y reencontrarse" ("revive the memory of who they had been as a people ... It is – they say – like looking into a mirror and finding, or seeing, themselves once again"). Similarly, several native speakers reported similar revelations during our readings of doña Luz's work in what we called Reading Circles: sitting together, reading Nahuatl texts out loud, and discussing them.[8] Our conversations did not focus solely on content. The collaborative nature of doña Luz's writing drew the group to a discussion of unequal relationships influenced by ethnicity, class, and gender. The extractive nature of academic research as well as its potential to create spaces for Indigenous voices to be heard was also a much-debated topic.

We closed our 2011 Reading Circles with a study of Nahua playwright, painter, and teacher Ildefonso Maya Hernández's play *Ixtlamatinij* (*The Learned Ones* 1987). Taking on the issue of bilingual-bicultural education for Indigenous peoples in Mexico, Maya's open-air drama was performed in the Huasteca region of the states of Hidalgo and Veracruz during the 1980s and 1990s. Focusing on the co-optation of Indigenous peoples to become agents of the assimilation of their own people to dominant culture norms, Maya's play struck a nerve for the Reading Circle participants. On the one hand, they found the representations of the physical and epistemological violence of the educational process to be quite accurate, one that they had experienced first-hand. On the other, the participants were disappointed with the way that the play ended; they wanted to know what happened the next day, and the next. They already knew what the problems were; they wanted examples of solutions. They wanted to know what kinds of actions the characters in the play would have taken once they clearly understood – and rejected – the forced disappearance of their language and culture. They wanted to know what they should they do in their own communities. This was Maya's plan after all, to provoke a sense of urgency and to stimulate dialogue and action once the play ended. *Ixtlamatinij*, then, is less an overtly didactic text than it is an open-ended thinking device for creating Indigenous theories and practices.

The texts I mention above are the tip of the iceberg in terms of Nahua writing and intellectual work throughout the past five centuries, and their potential contributions to revitalization projects. We must, of course, approach these kinds of sources critically, taking into consideration the factors that influenced who did – and did not – have access to alphabetic writing, particularly women and the poorest members of Nahua societies. That doña Luz stands alone, even today, as the only published female Nahua writer for nearly 500 years should give us pause.

The historical contextualization of these texts is also key in that Nahua writing was inscribed in a grid of filters that both obscured and revealed what could and could not be said (and what was said anyway), intended audiences and anticipated outcomes, aesthetic innovations, and political emergencies. Attention to these factors can in and of themselves be quite instructive as we continue to recover, restory, and return Nahua written sources. Reflecting the creative ways in which Nahuas have taken up the pen to reflect upon and change the world around them, these texts are signs of survival in the face of insurmountable challenges. They are stories of past ideas and actions, which Nahuas – and others – today can dialogue with, emulate, and critique as they create new ones in the twenty-first century.

Notes

1   "Aztecs," it should be noted, were but one group of Mesoamerican peoples that spoke the Nahuatl language. See recent government census data on Indigenous languages in Mexico at www.inegi.org.mx. Many believe there are substantially more native speakers who decline to identify themselves as such to census takers due to the stigma associated with Indigenous languages. According to current studies, there are 68 Indigenous languages and 362 or more dialects of Indigenous languages in Mexico today.
2   Approximately two-thirds of Nahuatl's 30+ variants are considered to be at "very high risk," "high risk," or "medium risk" of disappearing (Embriz Osorio and Zamora Alarcón 2012).
3   I take the concept of "restorying" from Regan (2010: 6).
4   Archivo General de la Nación (Mexico City) *Justicia e Instrucción Pública*, vol. 1, exp. 49.
5   Archivo Histórico of the Biblioteca Nacional de Antropología e Historia (Mexico City) Colección Antigua, no. 254.
6   Access alone can be challenging since these types of colonial and independence-era documents often lie uncatalogued in archives both within and beyond Mexican borders. See Lockhart (1992: 614–615) and Schwaller (2001) for censuses, although not exhaustive, of holdings in major international and national archives. A sampling of recently digitalized colonial Nahuatl manuscripts can be viewed at http://amoxcalli. org.mx/.
7   Doña Luz spoke in Nahuatl as Horcasitas transcribed her words. He would then read the text back to her; she would make any adjustments necessary, and then provided her own version in Spanish. Horcasitas later published the Nahuatl portion of *De Porfirio Diaz* with his own English translations entitled *Life and Death in Milpa Alta: A Nahuatl Chronicle of Diaz and Zapata* (Jiménez 1972).
8   Doña Luz Jiménez's and Ildefonso Maya Hernández's writing were workshopped with Nahuas in Reading Circles in 2008, 2009, and 2011. See McDonough (2014: 144–153).

References

Chimalpahin Cuauhtlehuanitzin, Domingo Francisco de San Antón Muñón. 2006. *Annals of His Time: Don Domingo de San Antón Muñón Chimalpahin Quauhtlehuanitzin*. Ed. Doris Namala, Susan Schroeder, and James Lockhart. Stanford: Stanford University Press.

Embriz Osorio, Arnulfo, and Oscar Zamora Alarcón. 2012. *México: Lenguas indígenas nacionales en riesgo de desaparición*. Mexico City: INALI.

Horn, Rebecca and James Lockhart. 2007. "Mundane documents in Nahuatl". In James Lockhart, Lisa Sousa, and Stephanie Wood, eds. *Sources and Methods for the Study of Mesoamerican Ethnohistory*, 1–22. http://whp.uoregon.edu/lockhart/HaskettTitulos.pdf.

Instituto Nacional de Estadística y Geografía (INEGI). 2010. "Censo de población y vivienda 2010". INEGI. www.inegi.org.mx

Jiménez, Luz. 1968. *De Porfirio Díaz a Zapata: Memoria náhuatl de Milpa Alta*. México D.F.: UNAM, IIH.

Jiménez, Luz. 1972. *Life and Death in Milpa Alta: A Nahuatl Chronicle of Díaz and Zapata*. Civilization of the American Indian Series, v. 117. Norman: University of Oklahoma Press.

León Portilla, Miguel. 1959. *Visión de los vencidos: Relaciones indígenas de la Conquista*. Mexico City: UNAM.

León Portilla, Miguel. 1962. *The Broken Spears: The Aztec Account of the Conquest of Mexico*. Boston: Beacon Press.

Lockhart, James. 1992. *The Nahuas after the Conquest: A Social and Cultural History of the Indians of Central Mexico, Sixteenth through Eighteenth Centuries*. Stanford: Stanford University Press.

McDonough, Kelly. 2014. *The Learned Ones: Nahua Intellectuals in Postconquest Mexico*. First Peoples: New Directions in Indigenous Studies. Tucson: University of Arizona Press.

Maya Hernández, Ildefonso. 1987. "Ixtlamatinij/The Learned Ones". In Carlos Montemayor and Donald Frischmann, eds. *Words of the True Peoples/Palabras de los seres verdaderos: Anthology of Contemporary Mexican Indigenous-Language Writers. Theater/Teatro*. Austin: University of Texas Press, 3, pp. 230–281.

Regan, Paulette. 2010. *Unsettling the Settler Within: Indian Residential Schools, Truth Telling, and Reconciliation in Canada*. Vancouver: University of British Columbia Press.

Rincón, Antonio del. 1595. *Arte mexicana; Compvesta por el Padre Antonio del Rincon de la Compañia de Iesus*. En México: en casa Pedro Balli.

Schwaller, John Frederick. 2001. *A Guide to Nahuatl Language Manuscripts Held in United States Repositories*. Publications of the Academy of American Franciscan History. Franciscan Publications in Nahuatl Series, vol. 1. Berkeley: Academy of American Franciscan History.

UN Division of Economic and Social Affairs. 2009. "State of the world's Indigenous peoples". The United Nations.

Zapata y Mendoza, Juan Buenaventura, Andrea Martínez Baracs, and Luis Reyes García. 1995. *Historia cronológica de la noble ciudad de Tlaxcala*. Colección Historia. Tlaxcala: Universidad Autónoma de Tlaxcala, CIESAS.

6 Mind, heart, hands

Thinking, feeling, and doing in Indigenous history methodology

K. Tsianina Lomawaima

In 2013, Thomas King wrote that:

> [i]f there is any methodology in my approach … it draws more on storytelling techniques than historiography. A good historian would have tried to keep biases under control. A good historian would have tried to keep personal anecdotes in check. A good historian would have provided footnotes. I have not.
>
> (2013: xii)

A good historian also tells a good story, but King teases scholarly gravitas. King is funny, and with humour opens up serious questions for Indigenous history. What do we think about in Indigenous history? How do we feel about it? How do we do it? What did our subjects think and feel and do? How do *thinking*, *feeling*, and *doing* interact to produce Indigenous histories? To tackle these questions I hew to Vine Deloria, Jr.'s principle of relativity:

> "We are all relatives" when taken as a methodological tool for obtaining knowledge means that we observe the natural world by looking for relationships between various things in it … This concept is simply the relativity concept as applied to a universe that people experience as alive and not as dead or inert.
>
> (Deloria 1999: 34)

Following Deloria, I search for relationships among *thinking*, *feeling*, and *doing*. Examples from the archive, scholarship, and teaching embody the interpretive and methodological potential of an Indigenous principle of relativity.

Thinking

> Personally, I'd want to hear a creation story, a story that recounts how the world was formed, how things came to be, for contained within creation stories are *relationships* that help to define the nature of the universe and how cultures understand the world in which they exist.
>
> (King 2003: 20, emphasis added)

Creation stories transmit theories explaining the world and its history. The discipline of History debates its relationship with theory but churns out anthologies explaining the worlds of Indigenous history. Scanning edited volumes surveying Native North American history is one way to get at *what we think*, but most readers are likely well-acquainted with the literature. I will sacrifice a literature review to concentrate on thinking, feeling, and doing in other arenas, with an aside – read *Reflections on American Indian History* (Hurtado 2008). Calloway, Edmunds, Hauptman, Iverson, and Child appreciated relativity within Indigenous lives.

Feeling

Emotions connect scholars, subjects, and Indigenous communities through expansive Indigenous theories of kinship, including biological descent, adoption, marriage, and clan affiliation. We rarely experience a cut-and-dried status, though, as insider or outsider. Indigenous identities are complicated and generate a continuum for judging: Insider? Outsider? The cross-examining analytic of relativity contextualizes two impassioned letters from the National Archives, written by Native employees of the Office of Indian Affairs (OIA) in a matrix of insider/outsider identity, emotion, and the work we do.

We may view the OIA as monolithically oppressive, but Indians have always worked there. They valued a steady paycheck; wished to serve Indian communities with their talents and skills learned in school; and aspired to get ahead (Cahill 2011). The OIA was never an easy place for an Indian to work, simultaneously insider and outsider. Carlos Montezuma felt any Indian working for the OIA was a traitor to the race. Employees – Charles Dagenett, Gertrude Bonnin – spiritedly defended their service to Indian communities. Navigating tribal, pan-Indian, and professional OIA identity was tough. The following letters attest to that toughness.

Ruth Muskrat Bronson (Cherokee teacher at Haskell Indian School) wrote the editor of the *Good Housekeeping* magazine on March 7, 1929 to protest articles titled "The Cry of a Broken People." On March 10, 1932 Henry Roe Cloud (Winnebago, OIA Field Representative) wrote to a Native employee at the Rosebud Agency, where Roe Cloud had investigated a complaint. Typed, paginated, and carbon copied, the letters were official and public. Spectacularly long (17+ pages), each is packed with emotion: outrage, self-certainty, wounded pride, grief. Each letter emanated from the writer's job, was intensely personal, and expressed "insider" Native identity. Relativity guides us to examine their content for braided strands of thinking, feeling, and doing.

"As an Indian": Ruth Muskrat Bronson

A folder in the Haskell records is labeled "Charges against Indian Service in 'Good Housekeeping' 1929" (National Archives and Records Administration/ NARA, Kansas City, 1929). Letters from OIA officials and "friends of the Indian" to the magazine's editor protested the "scandalous" attacks on the OIA made by Vera L. Connelly (NARA, Kansas City, 1929). They accused Connelly of ventriloquizing the "propaganda" of the Indian Defense Association and John Collier. Bronson's letter stands out for its length, its defensiveness, and an emotional argument rooted in a Native employee's pride in her work.

Beginning "As an Indian I am impelled to protest," Bronson repeatedly invoked her identity:

> According to Miss Connelly it would be something unusual for an Indian woman to be so bold as to rise up and speak out in meeting, but I happen to come from a tribe whose women ... selected the tribal rulers. Therefore I dare to speak.
>
> (NARA, Kansas City, 1929)

Bronson also stressed her loyalty to the Service and its employees: "in justice to my own people and in loyalty to those who have served us so nobly and so well I cannot ... remain silent" (NARA, Kansas City, 1929). She responded to Connelly's picture of agents as "brutal, over-bearing, despotic, greedy, [and] indifferent" with her own experience as a teenaged assistant to an agent – also Cherokee – who encouraged her to attend college, counseled her on jobs, and devoted his life to service to his people and to the OIA. Bronson admitted to "blunders – oh yes, a great many" but denied rampant viciousness and abuse (NARA, Kansas City, 1929). Connelly's critique of boarding schools brought the importance of Bronson's *doing* to the foreground.

If Connelly were correct, Bronson wrote, Native teachers at Haskell "would refuse to stay on the pay roll of such an institution. For we are not rascals, any of us ... We have come to the Government Boarding School because we believe it to be the best medium for the thing we wish to do" (NARA, Kansas City, 1929). Given the boarding school abuses and deficiencies documented by the Institute for Government Research one year earlier (Meriam et al. 1928), Bronson's unflagging defense seems unrealistic. *Good Housekeeping*'s editor was amazed that "anyone as intelligent as you are should be so ignorant of the conditions that exist among your people" (NARA, Kansas City, 1929). Bronson was indeed intelligent. I do not read her letter as a knee-jerk defense by a co-opted assimilationist. She wrote from the centre of where she thought, and felt, and worked as a Native woman, dedicated to her people, within a bureaucracy employing others who shared her ideals and commitment to the work, "the thing we wish to do."

"We Who Are Indians": Henry Roe Cloud

Henry Roe Cloud's 1932 letter spoke to similar issues – pride as a government employee, frustration with "unfair" critiques, commitment to "his people" – but Roe Cloud vented his outrage against an agent who fit the image painted by Connelly, not Bronson. Like Bronson, Roe Cloud's outrage was rooted in life experience, in his case the tragic loss of his young son. In 1932, as a Field Representative, Roe Cloud investigated a complaint against the Rosebud Agent; afterward he corresponded with a Native employee who supported the Agent. Roe

Cloud excoriated agency personnel for their unfeeling treatment of Indians, especially Clark Little Thunder, who lost his young son to tuberculosis. It was not long after that that three-year-old Henry Roe Cloud, Jr. passed away after a brief illness. Clearly Roe Cloud's grief connected him to Little Thunder, but his outrage also sprang from his work as a Native person to make the OIA bureaucracy more just and humane.

The letter began with accusations of local incompetence, continuing: "[W]hat is worse … [is your] attack [on] the one friend [Roe Cloud] who came there to assist your administration" (NARA, Seattle, 1932). Roe Cloud, like Bronson, took his job personally. He filled 14 pages with the facts of the case. On page 15 he came to "Little Thunder and his boy Ellis." On his first examination of Ellis the agency doctor reported his emaciation, with "affection of the knee joints of some seven months standing": his knees were locked. "Great Caesar's Ghost!" wrote Roe Cloud. "What was he and the Superintendent doing during these seven long months! Had the father become a ten per center [a complainer]? Does the ten per center lose even the claims of humanity?" (NARA, Seattle, 1932). Roe Cloud recounted the "heart rending" tale of the father who searched unsuccessfully for a job, carrying his son on a pallet in the back of his wagon. When he reached the clinic, the doctor noted Little Thunder gave his son a "multicolored silk handkerchief and some other worthless stuff" (NARA, Seattle, 1932). Roe Cloud's comment devastates:

> We who are Indians have all passed through the "silk handkerchief" stage. There was a time when a silk handkerchief meant more to us than anything in the world. This father found he could not do any more for the body so wracked with disease, but he could do something for the spirit, the immortal part of us, to build up, if he could, in the fast closing days, the morale of his son by giving to him what he knew he most desired. Let me say to you that in like manner, to my own dying little son, I gave a pretty pair of moccasins. He fondled them for a little while for only one day, and left me the next day. What father in this world will not do anything, give all he has of wordly goods if only to save his son?
>
> (NARA, Seattle, 1932)

A few paragraphs later, Roe Cloud closed:

> I have many faults, and these worry me often, but I have not yet proved traitor to the cause of our great government for the amelioration, justice and civilization of our Indian people.
>
> (NARA, Seattle, 1932)

Decades later, Roe Cloud's emotion explodes from the archive. We cannot hope to understand this episode absent the context of grief over his son, but it would be equally impoverishing to lift the "emotional" content of this letter out of the context of Roe Cloud's commitment – among "we who are Indians" – to his work and the work "of our great government." Roe Cloud's emotion interlaced with commitment to family, community, and Indian peoples; his professional pride; his self-identification as Winnebago; and his loyalty in 1932 to an Indian Office where he believed justice might be possible.

Searching for relationships among thinking, feeling, and doing while reading the two letters together makes more visible the key importance of doing, of day-to-day, year-to-year striving to effect change. Bronson and Roe Cloud believed in what they were *doing*.

Doing

When working from archives, what documents should we leave on the shelf? In a provocatively brief article, Laura Terrance shared two stories of "resistance to colonial education": the anonymous autograph journal of "a young woman who attended a residential boarding school in the early twentieth century" (Terrance 2011: 621), and Zitkala-Ša's published autobiographical account of her schooling (Zitkala-Ša 2003). Terrance refused to use the journal because it was produced within the boarding school, an examplar colonial "state apparatus" that disciplined and denigrated Indian people (Terrance 2011: 622). Terrance admitted the journal's seductions, though:

> I projected my interpretation-as-meaning into each of the entries, gradually coming to feel like I "knew" these students. I came to like them, to respect them, to feel a connectedness to them.
>
> (2011: 622)

Resisting the feeling of "connectedness" and questioning "methodologies of knowledge production," Terrance implemented an archival version of Audra Simpson's ethnographic refusal (2007).

Terrance questioned if archival sources should be used when the author did not make a conscious effort to publish. Her archival refusal resonates through Indigenous Studies; much of our evidence is unpublished, and ethical and moral research issues pervade the field. Archives (like boarding schools) nest like Russian dolls within layers of colonial state apparatuses that have silenced countless Native people who never heard of or negotiated the publishing opportunities pursued by Zitkala-Ša. Hundreds of thousands of archived documents are saturated with Indian voices. They were in some sense "published" – in federal superintendents' annual reports or independent investigative committee transcripts, for example – but not usually with Indian intent or consent. Indian-authored letters to superintendents, field inspectors, commissioners of Indian Affairs, and elected officials were stored without Indian intent or consent.

Do we refuse them all? Is the resultant silence colonial, or anti-colonial, or just a can of worms bouncing down a slippery slope? Archival refusal may not be appropriate for all sources, but it raises demanding questions: What and where are our archives? Whom and what might we refuse, and why? Where do we owe affection, respect, connectedness, and responsibility for scholarly diligence? How do we conscientiously carry out those responsibilities?

Thinking–feeling–doing: a principle of relativity

"Come home now!" A Yavapai perspective on history

Maurice Crandall (Yavapai-Apache Nation of Clarkdale, Arizona) visited the Newberry Library in Chicago, which holds the papers of Carlos Montezuma, early twentieth-century Yavapai physician and Red Progressive. Crandall thought biographers had done Montezuma justice, but reading the papers convinced him that a Yavapai perspective could yield "an alternate narrative" of Montezuma's life (Crandall 2013: 2). Crandall pushes beyond the trope that Montezuma "reconnected" with Yavapai late in life; Montezuma "actively searched for his family from a young age," and most importantly, his relatives never forgot him (2013: 2). Crandall's story exemplifies the principle of relativity, pursuing relationships among thinking, feeling, and doing: an intellectual's search for new meaning in a well-combed archive, the affections binding families, and the historian's responsibility to represent Montezuma's life enmeshed in horrific violence. The result is a rebalanced narrative. Crandall puts Montezuma's 1871 capture and enslavement at the centre of his life story, and importantly, recognizes what Montezuma *does* for the Yavapai-Apache Nation today:

> Carlos Montezuma connects us to an ephemeral past, one that was full of horror and violence, and one from which a young boy eventually returned, showing us that we can always go home.
>
> (2013: 12)

Hearing voices: relationships with Abalone

Abalone Tales, co-produced by ten authors and the Cultural Committee of the Yurok Tribe, is sub-titled *Collaborative Explorations of Sovereignty and Identity in Native California* (Field et al. 2008). *Tales* respectfully elucidates Native relationships with Abalone herself. Possessed of lustrous beauty, reflecting (fire) light, Abalone also speaks. When regalia enlivened with Abalone is danced in ceremony, movement enables Abalone's voice. Intellect and emotion connect Abalone, regalia, dancers, artists, community, and all who hear Abalone's voice as Native Californians come together to fix the world, the ultimate *doing* for others. Mind, heart, and hands pull together.

> I kind of picture the regalia as children, because it's my responsibility to house them, to make sure they're maintained ... And then it's my responsibility to run that regalia all over, wherever the dances are going on ... it's my responsibility to make sure it gets to that place ... It's a life, it's a spirit, it's a living being, and we don't own other living beings ... But in the process of, I

guess you could say, giving birth to the regalia, all of my emotions, all of my feelings – my essence, in short – is going in to create that piece of regalia. Bradley Marshall.

(Field et al. 2008: 124)

Connections clicked: relativity in the classroom

Fall semester, 2013: Twice a week, 250 students enrolled in *Many Nations of Native America* met for 50 minutes in a big square classroom. We began in late August. On December 2, I tried to represent the genocide of Native Californians in the Gold Rush era. Two days later this email arrived:

> Professor Lomawaima,
>
> After class on Monday, I felt the topic we discussed was still bothering me. I sat and talked with my mom ... and we both felt very disturbed by it ... Personally, I have had a hard time feeling connected and concerned with the many topics we have discussed ... I know they are important, but I have unfortunately found myself asking why does it matter so much, why is it so important to them? After Monday's lesson, I knew. As my mind wandered after class, connections with so many past lessons clicked and I felt like I really cared about what had happened ... Just a little feedback, I hope it helps in some way.
>
> Best,
> Student

This student thought things over; talked things over with Mom; made connections; and let me know. The student thought, and felt, and did. The doing made the lesson real. Why did the connections click for this one student? I will never know, but I hope that 14 weeks of effort to attest to relationships helped: among thinking–feeling–doing; among diverse sets of US citizens; among past, present, and future Native experiences; among faculty, TAs, and students. On December 2, 2013, the principle of relativity made a difference and the connections clicked.

Conclusion: What is at stake in doing Indigenous history?

In *Indians in Unexpected Places*, Philip Deloria (2004) roots his work in time spent with his grandparents.

> The memories and emotions contained in those encounters led me to start thinking more seriously about Indian athletes and drivers and about the inclination within American culture to insist on the separation of categories like *Indian, sports, automobiles,* and *New York.*

(2004: ix)

Memories and emotions are powerful engines, as is the courage of Deloria's choice of his first chapter's title and topic: violence. In 1903 on Lightning Creek, within steps of the gates in the fence marking the Pine Ridge reservation, shots rang out. Deloria tells a powerful story about the violence that enveloped Peter White Elk, Hope Clear, Charlie Smith, and their relatives and friends. Violence has defined too much Indigenous history, taken too many Indigenous lives, and scarred too many survivors.

Terrance refused the archive because of the violence embodied by the boarding school where the journal was written. Connelly criticized the violence done to a people whom she called "broken," while Bronson protested the violence done by Connelly to *her* people (and herself), whom she knew to be alive and kicking, and working for a better chance. Roe Cloud bitterly decried the violence of rampant unemployment, malnutrition, substandard health care, and bureaucratic disregard for the humanity of the so-called ten-percenters in Indian Country. My student grappled to assimilate all that violence students have never heard of that contradicts almost everything they have been taught their entire lives to be true about the United States.

Violence is a noxious miasma that motivates and chokes, inspires and shrouds *doing* Indigenous history. How do we *do* violence justice? What a thought. The keenest writers and thinkers – Will Rogers, Vine Deloria, Jr., Paul Chaat Smith, Thomas King – disembowel the monster of violence with a weapon of fiercely sardonic humor. Humor is not necessarily disrespectful of tragedy; laughter can be a medicinal thread that stitches together thinking, feeling, and doing. Laughter fixes the world, even as we struggle with violence.

References

Cahill, C.D. 2011. *Federal Fathers and Mothers: A Social History of the United States Indian Service, 1869–1933*. Chapel Hill: University of North Carolina Press.

Crandall, M. 2013. "Wassaja comes home: A Yavapai perspective on Carlos Montezuma's search for identity". *The Journal of Arizona History*, 54(1): 1–26.

Deloria, P.J. 2004. *Indians in Unexpected Places*. Lawrence: University Press of Kansas.

Deloria, V., Jr. 1999. "Relativity, relatedness, and reality". In B. Deloria, K. Foehner, and S. Scinta, eds. *Spirit and Reason: The Vine Deloria, Jr. Reader*. Golden: Fulcrum Publishing, pp. 32–39.

Field, L.W., C. Seidner, J. Lang, R. Cambra, F. Silva, V. Hailstone, D. Marshall, B. Marshall, C. Lara, M. George, Sr., and the Cultural Committee of the Yurok Tribe. 2008. *Abalone Tales: Collaborative Explorations of Sovereignty and Identity in Native California*. Durham, NC: Duke University Press.

Hurtado, A.L., ed.. 2008. *Reflections on American Indian History: Honoring the Past, Building a Future*. Norman: University of Oklahoma Press.

King, T. 2003. *The Truth about Stories: A Native Narrative*. Minneapolis: University of Minnesota Press.

King, T. 2013. *The Inconvenient Indian: A Curious Account of Native People in North America*. Minneapolis: University of Minnesota Press.

Meriam, L., R.A. Brown, H.R. Cloud, E.E. Dale, E. Duke, H.R. Edwards, F.A. McKenzie, M.L. Mark, W.C. Ryan, Jr., and W.J. Spillman. 1928. *The Problem of Indian*

Administration. Baltimore: Johns Hopkins Press for the Institute for Government Research.

National Archives and Records Administration (NARA), Kansas City, Kansas. 1929. "Charges against Indian service in 'Good Housekeeping' 1929". Record Group 75. Haskell Indian School Records. Box 32. Decimal Correspondence File, 1917–1959. Folder 3.

National Archives and Records Administration (NARA), Seattle, Washington. 1932. March 10, 1932 Henry Roe Cloud to Charles Brooks. Record Group 75. Rosebud Agency Records, Box 14.

Simpson, A. 2007. "On ethnographic refusal: Indigeneity, 'voice,' and colonial citizenship". *Junctures*, 9: 67–80.

Terrance, L.L. 2011. "Resisting colonial education: Zitkala-Sa and Native feminist archival refusal". *International Journal of Qualitative Studies in Education*, 24(5): 621–626.

Zitkala-Ša. 2003. "The school days of an Indian girl". In her *American Indian Stories, Legends, and other Writings*. New York: Penguin Books, pp. 87–103.

7 Relationality

A key presupposition of an Indigenous social research paradigm

Aileen Moreton-Robinson

As an expression of Indigenous sovereignty most Indigenous researchers adhere to a research agenda informed by our respective cultural knowledges, ethics and protocols. In operationalizing this agenda we are creating a new social research paradigm requiring rigorous and heavy intellectual work. Over the past three decades Indigenous scholars have built this paradigm, and our efforts have drawn attention. Usually this takes the form of a question: If there is an Indigenous social research paradigm, what are its core components? An interesting question given that there are competing definitions of what constitutes a non-Indigenous paradigm, and some argue it is the very nature of a paradigm to avoid the specificities of definition, while others tacitly agree that core components are evidenced by the standards that shape how research is operationalized within the social sciences and humanities. In this chapter I do not define the general laws, standards and methodological principles of an Indigenous social research paradigm. Instead, my aim is to demonstrate a key presupposition of the paradigm: Relationality is the interpretive and epistemic scaffolding shaping and supporting Indigenous social research and its standards are culturally specific and nuanced to the Indigenous researcher's standpoint and the cultural context of the research. This presupposition is revealed through an examination of Indigenous research methodologies literature produced in Canada, the United States, Hawaii, Australia and New Zealand.

I acknowledge that the United Nations has defined 'Indigenous' as including those who self-identify as Indigenous peoples at the individual level and are accepted by the community as its members; have a historical continuity with pre-colonial and/or pre-settler societies; have a strong link to territories and surrounding natural resources; have distinct social, economic or political systems; have distinct language, culture and beliefs; form non-dominant groups in society; and resolve to maintain and reproduce their ancestral environments and systems as distinctive peoples and communities (UNPFII 2015). Māori, Métis, First Nations, Native Americans and Aborigines all share these attributes with other Indigenous peoples. However, our lands are occupied by first-world Western states on the basis of an alien form of judicial sovereignty and a shared genealogy of predominantly British colonization. Our legal status, marked respectively by the signifiers Native American, Māori, First Nation, Métis, Native Hawaiian and Aborigine, is not shared with other citizens. Though there are other Indigenous scholars who have produced research methodologies, the emergence of an Indigenous research discourse flourished in first-world countries in the latter part of the twentieth century (Rigney 1997; Battiste 1998; Smith 1999a, 1999b; Moreton-Robinson 2000, Weber-Pillwax 2001; Steinhauer 2002; Kahakalau 2004; Porsanger 2004; Graham 2005; Estrada 2005; Wilson 2005, 2008; Martin 2008; Nakata 2008; Tipa et al. 2009).

Indigenous peoples conducted research, though in our languages it is not the word used to describe our ancestors' and creators' processes for producing knowledge. Over thousands of years our existence and survival depended on flexible knowledge systems, and they exist in different forms in the present. We developed new forms of knowledge in making sense of, and interpreting, alien colonizing knowledges. Like all researchers, Indigenous scholars operationalize our respective knowledges within the research process to produce new methodologies, and we draw on our disciplinary training. As I have argued elsewhere:

> Even when we are developing Indigenous methodologies we are influenced by discourses that presuppose our existence as scholars within academia. To recognise our disciplinary knowledges and academic training as part of our [research] ... is not a case of being either Indigenous or academic but of recognising the epistemological, ontological and axiological complexity of being an Indigenous researcher that is politically challenging, intellectually creative and rigorous.
>
> (Moreton-Robinson 2013: 339)

Thus the actualities of our living, knowing and disciplinary training provide the epistemological grounds for understanding and critiquing domination as well as theorizing and researching our modernity; we share privileged epistemic positions that are culturally dense and divergent (Andersen 2009). Feminists have mounted a similar argument about epistemic advantage in relation to the production of gendered knowledge by beginning inquiry from the perspective of women's experiences and knowledges forged through sites of political struggle including bedrooms, kitchens, board rooms and universities.

Feminist Sandra Harding argues that traditional social science methodologies have

> unconsciously followed a "logic of discovery" which we could formulate in the following way: Ask only those questions about nature and social life which (white, Western, bourgeois) men want answered ... white men's experiences leads to partial and even perverse understandings of social life.
>
> (Harding 1987: 6–7)

Feminists argue that gendered cultural beliefs and behaviours influence all research, but within traditional social science research the researcher's standpoint is hidden and suppressed by the patriarchal social construction of objectivity, which is predicated on a mind/body split and a logic of discovery (Haraway 1988; Collins 1990; Harding 1993; Hartsock 1998; Smith 1999). Feminist critique of patriarchal knowledge production's claims to objectivity is insightful but it is rationalized within a human-centred paradigm. The detached knowing subject, observing from a neutral position following a logic of discovery, does not just rely on a mind/body split to portend to its way of knowing; it also requires being disconnected from the living earth. This discursive separation from the living earth privileges the disconnected human-centred knowing subject and the logic of discovery within non-Indigenous research methodologies. This positioning is different from researching within an Indigenous social research paradigm.

Relationality

Relationality, as the core presupposition of the Indigenous social research paradigm, finds expression within culturally specific and gendered axiologies, ontologies and epistemologies that are connected to the earth (Porsanger 2004; Wilson 2008; Martin 2008; Edosdi 2008). I use the term "social" to qualify Indigenous research because the social is relational, involving the inter-connectedness of what people are doing and experiencing as the outcome of actions in the actualities of their lives and lands (Smith 1999: 7). The social is constituted by our histories, our culturally embodied knowledges and life force that connect us to our respective lands, our creators, all living entities and our ancestors (Moreton-Robinson 2000; Wilson 2008; Martin 2008). By privileging and following the logic of our cultural knowledges, we come to know who we are and who we claim to be, as well as who claims us and how we are connected to our lands. This is a matter of ontology, our being – not a matter of identity – and how relationality informs an Indigenous social research paradigm.

As a presupposition of an Indigenous social research paradigm relationality is a historically enduring discursive formation that gives rise to distinct forms of thought, often unconscious, which inform the intellectual work and research of Indigenous scholars. It provides a network of ideas for perception within which thought, communication and action occur in research. Relationality forms the conditions of possibility for coming to know and producing knowledge through research in a given time, place and land.

Relationality is grounded in a holistic conception of the inter-connectedness and inter-substantiation between and among all living things and the earth, which is inhabited by a world of ancestors and creator beings. It informs our epistemological and ethical premise that social research should begin with an awareness of our proper relationships with the world we inhabit, and is conducted with respect, responsibility, generosity, obligation, and reciprocity. In different forms these values are shared and are evident within the existing Indigenous research literature written by first world Indigenous scholars. Relationality is an inextricable part of our sovereign knowledges, informing our scholarship to produce innovative social research. As a presupposition it shapes ways of knowing, being, and doing; to be connected is to know, and knowing is embodied in and connected to country, but not all knowledge is accessible. As always within our knowledge systems, there are rules that are enmeshed in social relations and bloodline to country, determined by ancestors and creator beings that guide who can be a knower and of what knowledges.

Relationality as a distinct Indigenous social research presupposition within academia shapes Indigenous scholars' research. Within New Zealand, Kaupapa Māori operationalizes Whakapapa, which holds several relational principles. These consist of:

> [A] way of thinking, a way of learning, a way of storing knowledge, and a way of debating knowledge ... *te reo* the centring of Māori language ... *Tikanga Māori* customary practices, obligations, and behaviours, or the principles that govern social practices ... *Rangatirataga* the goal of control over one's own life and cultural well being ... *Whanau* the principle of extended family.
>
> (Smith 1999b: 12)

Relationality informs Māori cultural ethics involving respect, generosity of spirit, hospitality and humility (Smith 1999b: 13).

Relationality is also evidenced in the work of Kanaka Maoli scholar Kau Kahakalau (2004), who developed and deployed a Native Hawaiian Heuristic Action methodology in researching what constitutes a quality Kindergarten to Year 12 model of Hawaiian education. Embedded within Kahakalau's question is the necessity to bring about positive change for Indigenous people. Kahakalau was immersed in her community and, while her research was designed for the benefit of that community, she also required the support of the community. Kahakalau was attuned to her *mana*, that is her personal power, and her *na'au*, her heart. She abided by Hawaiian cultural protocols and relations involving herself, elders, and her family and community, as well as the school community. In this way Kahakalau's research is integrally connected to others as an expression of self. Over a period of two years, Kahakalau's cultural and immediate kin relationships enabled and enhanced the quality of data gathering and contributed to her interpretation understandings within formal and informal educational spaces.

The premise that inter-substantiated and proper relations inform Indigenous research is also evidenced in the work of Margaret Kovach, a Cree scholar who developed *Nehiyaw Kiskeyihtamowin*, a relational methodology. Her methodology involves being grounded in tribal epistemology, having a decolonizing and ethical aim, with researcher preparations incorporating cultural protocols and standard research design to make meaning of knowledges gathered and in giving back. Kovach argues that:

> Relational responsibilities exist between the Indigenous researcher and the Indigenous community; the Indigenous community and the researcher; the Indigenous researcher and the Indigenous academic community; non

Indigenous researchers and the Indigenous community; and between the academic community and Indigenous methodologies. Specific responsibilities will depend upon the particular relationship. They may include guidance, direction, and evaluation. They may include conversation, support, and collegiality. Responsibility implies knowledge and action. It seeks to genuinely serve others, and is inseparable from respect and reciprocity.

(Kovach 2009: 178)

As is evidenced in the work of Smith (1999b), Kahakalau (2004), and Kovach (2009), who are from different cultures and geographical locations, relationality shapes Indigenous research methodologies, informing the way research is conceived, interpreted, designed, conducted, analyzed, and presented. Cree scholar Shawn Wilson (2008) argues that Indigenous research is the ceremony of maintaining accountability to our relationships. Hawaiian researcher Mahulani Meyer (2008) focuses on the use of body, mind and spirit to triangulate the Hawaiian way of meaning and relating. The work of Australian Indigenous scholar Lester-Irabinna Rigney (1997) demonstrates that an Indigenist research agenda emphasizes being connected to others while pushing boundaries "in order to make intellectual space for Indigenous cultural knowledge systems that were denied in the past." These scholars argue in different but similar ways that knowledge systems are grounded in relations to land, place, entities, ancestors, creators and people. Cherokee scholar Laurie Eldridge, in defining an Indigenous research methodology in art education, argues that interconnectedness also requires responsibility in research. She notes that:

Interconnectedness is the traditional Native American belief that human beings are made of an intertwining of spirit, mind, emotions and body ... it means that all living beings in this world including the earth are connected and that one's actions have far reaching consequences.

(Eldridge 2008: 1)

Russell Bishop (2008) uses Māori metaphors and repositions researchers within Māori sense-making contexts, with a focus on the centrality of relations with others and Māori epistemologies. This scholarship may have emerged from these different cultural contexts, but in common they accentuate the importance of the relational within Indigenous research. As Sioux scholar Vine Deloria Jr. argues:

We are all relatives when taken as a methodological tool for obtaining knowledge means that we observe the natural world by looking for relationships between various things in it. That is to say, everything in the natural world has relationships with every other thing and the total set of relationships makes up the natural world as we experience it. This concept is simply the relativity concept as applied to a universe that people experience as alive and not as dead or inert.

(Deloria 1999: 34)

Methodology: a few definitional problems

As I mentioned rather briefly at the beginning of this chapter, heavy intellectual lifting is required to sustain an Indigenous social research paradigm, requiring us to define our key concepts and to engage with and critique Western knowledge-making. Two cosmological frames of knowledge-making in modern Western history, theology and philosophy/science, despite being in competition with each other, will join forces when the need arises to discredit forms of knowledge that exist outside these frames (Mignolo 2009: 164). We are engaged in an epistemic battle that requires more than defining our research methodologies and conducting research with and for our communities. We have to sustain an Indigenous social research paradigm with its own standards, rules of engagement and epistemological field. Part of the battle involves exposing the epistemic privilege of the first world and how it continues to hinder our modernity by being epistemically disobedient within the learned academy (Mignolo 2009).

Indigenous methodologies and race

There is resistance within the academy to embracing Indigenous research methodologies and a separate Indigenous social research paradigm. Critique of Indigenous research methodologies is usually made on the grounds that they are considered to be metaphysical and, by implication, lacking rationality. Yet Western methodologies also have metaphysical origins in Greek mythology and Judeo-Christian beliefs, which privilege human hierarchical centredness and disconnection through otherworldliness. This metaphysical thinking was operating during the Enlightenment, informing Western research methodologies and their pre-conceptual schemata of differentiation, categorization, and classification. Classification in particular was the key scientific epistemological driver (Goldberg and Saucier 1996: 49). It became a fundament of scientific methodology. "With its catalogues, indices and inventories" classification enables an ordering of data and structures observation, "but it also claims to reflect the natural order of things" (Goldberg and Saucier 1996: 49). Classification is central to scientific methodology and its methods, which have long been taken as the ideal model of rationality. In turn, rational capacity became the measure of humanness and was operationalized to produce a hierarchy of races. This racial ordering was tied to white human behavioural expectations (Goldberg and Saucier 1996: 50). Goldberg argues that the conceptual schemata constituted by and of racialized discourse are:

> classification, order, value and hierarchy; differentiation and identity, discrimination and identification; exclusion, domination, subjection, and subjugation as well as entitlement and restriction.
>
> (Goldberg and Saucier 1996: 49)

Possession is also a part of these schemata for in the process of classifying and identifying one is producing epistemological possessions by bringing into consciousness and naming the previously unknown: Aborigines/Indians/Natives. This racialized knowledge operates discursively within disciplines, moderating what can be known, who can know, and what constitutes valid knowledge enabled by claims to objectivity. Through this way of knowing, the "God trick" is deployed; it is simultaneously the view from everywhere and nowhere and is the arbiter of everything. Thus the distinct metaphysical origins embedded within Western social research paradigms predispose Western researchers to particular ways of understanding and interpreting the world. Native American scholar Clayton Dumont argues:

> Think about this. "Objective reality": they cannot find it. "Objective Research": they cannot do it. Nonetheless, they continue to insist that, despite being beyond their reach, both are real. How can we understand this as other than a faith-based, inherited, and institutionalized pursuit of a metaphysical ideal?
>
> (Dumont 2008: 52)

The metaphysical basis of objectivity within social science and humanities methodologies disavows embodiment, rendering race and gender invisible enablers in the production of knowledge. Social sciences and the humanities are concerned primarily with the "scientific" study of human action and meaning, which are operationalized to present a particular race- and gender-blind worldview of the social and cultural construction of thought and behaviour. Through racialized discourse Indigenous peoples and our knowledges have been deemed lacking and this has influenced the disciplines and the kind of research methodologies that are considered acceptable.

Conclusion

Through the deployment of the "God trick", Western methodologies are designed to obfuscate the metaphysical origins of disconnectedness and claims to objectivity and rationality. Within these methodologies the embodiment of knowledge is disavowed because there is no relation between the body and the mind. Yet Indigenous and feminist research demonstrates that bodies do matter in research and knowledge production and that these processes embody specific orientations towards the social. It is as valid and appropriate to approach the world on this basis as it is to make a metaphysical argument that one is disconnected from the living earth.

Methodologically, an Indigenous social research paradigm offers new approaches to collaborative and participatory research by seeking to make visible our connectedness with the earth and with each other. The challenge for Indigenous research is undoing the Western methodological presupposition of nature as servant to humanity and humanity as master of nature. As such, we require new Indigenous ways to understand and research the complexity of our relations with our mother the living earth. For humans are worth no more or no less than all living things.

References

Andersen, C. 2009. "Critical Indigenous studies: From difference to density". *Cultural Studies Review*, 15(2): 80–100.

Battiste, M. 1998. "Enabling the autumn seed: Toward a decolonized approach toward Aboriginal knowledge, language and education". *Canadian Journal of Native Education*, 22(1): 16–27.

Bishop, R. 2008. "Te Kotah: Kaupapa Māori in mainstream classrooms". In N.K. Denzin, Y.S. Lincoln, and L.T. Smith, eds. *Handbook of Critical and Indigenous Methodologies*. Thousand Oaks: Sage Publications.

Collins, Hill P. 1990. *Black Feminist Thought*. Boston: Unwin Hyman.

Deloria, V. 1999. *Spirit & Reason*. Colorado: Fulcrum Publishing.

Dumont, Jr., C.W. 2008. *The Promise of Poststructuralist Sociology: Marginalized Peoples and the Problem of Knowledge*. Albany: State of New York Press.

Edosdi, Thompson J.C. 2008. "Hede kehe hotzi kahidi: My journey to a Tahltan research paradigm". *Canadian Journal of Native Education*, 31(1): 24–40.

Eldridge, L. 2008. "Indigenous research methodologies in art education". *Journal of Cultural Research in Art Education* 26.

Estrada, V.M. 2005. "The tree of life as a research methodology". *Australian Journal of Indigenous Education*, 34: 44–52.

Goldberg, L.R. and G. Saucier. 1996. "The language of personality: Lexical perspectives on the five-factor model". In J.S. Wiggins, ed. *The Five-Factor Model of Personality: Perspectives*. New York: Guilford.

Graham, J. 2005. "He Apiti Hono, He Tatai Hono: That which is joined remains an unbroken line: Using Whakapapa (genealogy) as the basis for an Indigenous research framework". *Australian Journal of Indigenous Education*, 34: 86–95.

Haraway, D. 1988. "Situated knowledges: The science question in feminism and the privilege of partial perspective". *Feminist Studies*, 14(3): 575–599.

Harding, S. 1987. *Feminism and Methodology*. Bloomington: Indiana University Press.

Harding, S. 1993. "Rethinking standpoint epistemology: What is 'strong objectivity'?" In Linda Alcoff and Elizabeth Potter, eds. *Feminist Epistemologies*. New York: Routledge.

Hartsock, N. 1998. *The Feminist Standpoint Revisited and Other Essays*. Colorado: Westview Press.

Kahakalau, K. 2004. "Indigenous heuristic action research: Bridging Western and Indigenous research methodologies". *Hulili: Multidisciplinary Research on Hawaiian Well-Being*, 1(1): 91–103.

Kovach, M. 2009. *Indigenous Methodologies: Characteristics, Conversations, and Contexts*. Toronto: University of Toronto Press.

Martin, K.L. 2008. *Please Knock Before You Enter: Aboriginal Regulation of Outsiders and the Implications for Research*. Tenerife: Post Pressed.

Meyer, M. 2008. "Indigenous and authentic: Hawaiian epistemology and the triangulation of meaning". In N.K. Denzin, Y.S. Lincoln, and L.T. Smith, eds. *Handbook of Critical and Indigenous Methodologies*. Thousand Oaks: Sage Publications.

Mignolo, W. 2009. "Epistemic disobedience, independent thought and decolonial freedom". *Theory, Culture & Society*, 26(7–8): 159–181.

Moreton-Robinson, A. 2000. *Talkin Up to the White Woman: Indigenous Women and Feminism*. St Lucia: Queensland University Press.

Moreton-Robinson, A. 2013. "Towards an Australian Indigenous women's standpoint theory". *Australian Feminist Studies*, 28(78).

Nakata, M. 2008. *Disciplining the Savages: Savaging the Disciplines*. Canberra: Aboriginal Studies Press.

Porsanger, J. 2004. "An essay about Indigenous methodology". Accessed 13 August 2008, http://uit.no/getfile.php?PageId=977%FileId=188.

Rigney, L.I. 1997. "Internationalisation of an Indigenous anti-colonial cultural critique of research methodologies: A guide to Indigenist research methodology and its principles". *Journal for Native American Studies, WICAZO sa Review*, 14(2): 109–121.

Smith, D.E. 1999. *Writing the Social: Critique, Theory, and Investigations*. Toronto: University of Toronto Press.

Smith, Tuhiwai L. 1999a. *Decolonizing Methodologies: Research and Indigenous People*. London: Zed Books.

Smith, Tuhiwai L. 1999b. "Kaupapa Maori methodology: Our power to define ourselves". Accessed 28 September 2009, www.hauora.com/RESEARCH/PUBLISHED/KaupapaMaoriMethodology/tabi.

Steinhauer, E. 2002. "Thoughts on an Indigenous research methodology". *Canadian Journal of Education*, 26(2): 69–81.

Tipa, G., R. Panelli, and Moeraki Stream Team. 2009. "Beyond 'some else's agenda': An example of indigenous/academic research collaboration". *New Zealand Geographer*, 65(95): 95–106.

UNPFII. 2015. UNPFII History of Indigenous Peoples and the International System. Accessed 20 June 2015, www.un.org/development/desa/indigenouspeoples/about-us/unpfii-history.html.

Weber-Pillwax, C. 2001. "What is Indigenous research?" *Canadian Journal of Native Education*, 25(2): 166–174.

Wilson, S. 2005. "What is an Indigenous research methodology?" *Canadian Journal of Native Education*, 25(2): 175–179.

Wilson, S. 2008. *Research is Ceremony: Indigenous Research Methods*. Halifax and Winnipeg: Fernwood Publishing.

8 Standing with and speaking as faith

A feminist-Indigenous approach to inquiry

Kim TallBear

I inquire in concert with diverse thinkers and communities implicated in knowledge constituted at the intersections of technoscience and Indigenous governance. I am part anthropologist of science and technology (technoscience), but with an ethical and methodological inheritance from a previous career as a tribal environmental planner. The intersectional knowledges that I help articulate involve communities of scientists, some of whom are Indigenous. I also work with science educators, science policy experts, and Native American and other Indigenous community members. (I am allergic to the term "informant.") I converse with thinkers who resist, monitor, regulate, collaborate in and sometimes reconfigure scientific research to serve Indigenous communities. I engage with technoscience in the service of Indigenous self-governance and livelihoods.

Reciprocity and jargon

Among social justice-minded researchers, there is an emphasis on reciprocity with research subjects and communities. This is evident in the 2014 special issue of the *Journal of Research Practice* subtitled "Giving Back in Field Research," in which an earlier version of this chapter first appeared. Feminist political ecologists Clare Gupta and Alice Bridget Kelly edited the volume. They wrote in the introduction:

> [During fieldwork in sub-Saharan Africa] both researchers faced the difficult question of "giving back" to the communities in which, and with whom, they worked – communities that were often far less privileged than the researchers were in terms of wealth, mobility, education, and access to health care. Returning from their field sites, both researchers felt a combination of guilt and frustration that they had not done enough or had not done things right.
>
> (Gupta and Kelly 2014)

Likewise, Indigenous researchers or "native anthropologists" – working as "insiders," although we acknowledge that insiderness is always complicated (Chipps 2004; Jacobs-Huey 2002; Innes 2009; Medicine 2001; Narayan 1993; Ohnuki-Tierney 1984; Simpson 2007; Todorova-Pirgova 1999) – sometimes struggle with our academic privilege. While we sometimes foreground *reciprocity*, Indigenous researchers are also likely to emphasize caring for our relations with home communities when we do research there. Sometimes those relationships can feel undermined by the protocols and foundational assumptions of academic research: informed consent forms, interview techniques, recording technologies, implicit hierarchies and presumed distance between researcher and researched, knower and known.

To lessen that divide, we desire to make complex ideas accessible. It is not uncommon to see discomfort with theoretical language, "jargon" as it is disparagingly called, which is portrayed as disingenuous. Shawn Wilson in *Research is Ceremony* (2008) writes:

> It may be necessary for me to use some pretty big and daunting words. I try hard not to use these words in everyday conversations, because I think that too many people use big language as a way of belittling others. However, some of the ideas I want you to understand require these words, as they are able to get across a lot of meaning.

> (Wilson 2008: 13)

I want to trouble – as I have elsewhere – this assertion that specialized academic terminology (social theory usually, with "hard" science terminology exempted) is elitist and meant to obscure (TallBear 2013: 121–122). This charge is also conditioned by a presumed separation and hierarchy between researcher and researched. It seems less objectionable when non-academics or Indigenous or other marginalized researchers who feel historically objectified and disempowered by the dominant gaze critique complex theoretical language. But paradoxically, speakers of highly complex scientific languages, e.g., genome terminology, made intelligible (as with any language) only through years of study, sometimes share a defensive and even anti-intellectual streak regarding complex social-theoretical language. For example, I have witnessed scientific thinkers charge social theorists with being "silly, self-indulgent, and caught up in a diminutive subculture" when the person trained in genomics does not immediately understand, say, a philosopher of science. I counter that we need precise languages to talk about precise ideas that have derived from specific histories of work, from the development of theories and methods. Specialists of all persuasions wield dense specialty languages, from medical professionals to attorneys, electricians, and hairdressers to information technology (IT) professionals. My allergy to thinking about "informants" extends to the concept of a "field" that is somehow out there, while the hallowed halls of the academy are "in here." This includes challenging the idea that specialty languages are necessarily indicative of hierarchy. I am especially concerned that Indigenous Studies scholars committed to Indigenous self-determination and to maintaining relations with communities become adept at switching between academic specialty languages and the languages of home. We should acknowledge that different ideas can be robustly analyzed within different languages. We must find some level of comfort with imperfect translations.

As an Indigenous thinker concerned with staying in relation, I find the notion of reciprocity or "giving back" inadequate. I and other researchers do not, in simpler terms, exchange data for aid or service to the communities we study. Most Indigenous researchers study topics that include Indigenous people, cultures, practices, and/or lands. In thinking about the ethics of accountability in research (whose lives, lands and bodies are inquired into and what do they get out of it?), the goal of "giving back" to research subjects seems to target a key symptom of a major disease in knowledge production, but not the crippling disease itself. That is the binary between researcher and researched – between knowing inquirer and those who are considered to be the resources or grounds for knowledge production. This is a fundamental condition of our academic body politic that has only recently been problematized, and still not by everyone. If what we want is democratic knowledge production that serves not only those who inquire and their institutions, but also those who are inquired upon, we must soften that boundary erected long ago between those who know and those from whom the raw materials of knowledge production are extracted. Part of doing this is broadening the conceptual field – thinking more expansively about what counts as risk (ontological harms?) and rightful benefit (institution building and community development?) in the course of building knowledge. It is also helpful to think about the research process as a relationship-building process – a professional networking process with colleagues (not "subjects"), as an opportunity for conversation and sharing of knowledge, not simply data gathering. Research must then be conceived in less-linear ways without necessarily knowable goals at the outset. For the institutions that employ and fund us, we will articulate specific goals as guideposts. A researcher who "stands with" a community of subjects is willing to be altered, to revise her stakes in the knowledge to be produced.

"Giving back," however, sounds akin to standing on two sides of a boundary that parties view as pretty much set. We well-intentioned liberals in the broader imperialistic academy negotiate treaties – with individual subjects and sometimes with collectives – across that boundary. We do this in good faith, and we figure out ways to do service or help build capacity in the communities in which we work. Over the past decade I have been trying to figure out incrementally how to articulate research questions, conceive of subject populations, and approach knowledge production from shared conceptual ground. I want to circumvent the dualistic relationships – even if they are not easily read as hierarchical – that more typically characterize academic research and that the concept of *reciprocity* implies. I offer some insights that have helped me articulate shared conceptual ground and shared stakes with those with whom I build knowledge.

I often study non-Indigenous people (i.e., bioscientists), but I do this in the service of Indigenous self-determination. I advocate that Indigenous peoples engage explicitly with technoscience in order to make sure it serves their/our interests rather than undermining us. The ethic of maintaining relations is one I feel compelled to carry into my work with *non*-Indigenous communities too – those bioscientists, genetic genealogists and other scientific thinkers whose work has important implications for Indigenous lives. First with Indigenous communities and thinkers and later with scientific communities and thinkers I seek out and try to articulate overlapping respective intellectual, ethical and institution-building projects. I articulate shared goals and desires while staying engaged in critical conversation and knowledge production.

Indigenous and feminist standpoint and care for the subject

My preoccupation with democratizing academic knowledge production began 40 years ago when I encountered Vine Deloria, Jr.'s (1969) ideas about the role of anthropology in the colonial project, but simultaneously the promise of intellectualism in helping us to resist colonialism. My mother, LeeAnn TallBear, exposed me to Deloria's thinking before I could read, when she was an undergraduate student at Northern State College in Aberdeen, South Dakota in the politically turbulent early 1970s. She demonstrated every day for her four children that change and hope for our people involve constituting our own narratives from our own lives and histories. She always had alternative history books in the house and shared with us oral historical narratives of our Dakota people to counteract the dominant colonial histories we received in public schools.

About 15 years ago, I encountered feminist theorists Donna Haraway and Sandra Harding, who challenge standard notions of objectivity that conflate it with neutrality. Rather, they advocate *situated knowledges* (Haraway 1991) from the "standpoint" of women, traditional cultures, and other marginalized subjects. This means that hypotheses, research questions, methods and valued outputs – including historical accounts, sociological analyses and textual interpretations – must begin from the lives, experiences and interpretations of marginalized subjects (Harding 1991, 2008). If we promiscuously account for standpoints, objectivity will be strengthened. Their language made quick sense to me precisely because Deloria and TallBear had paved the intellectual path.

I am also indebted to feminists who analyze and critique in a manner that "cares for the subject" (Schuurman and Pratt 2002). They write of the intellectual and ethical benefits of being invested in the knowledges and technologies one critiques, and the shortcomings of critique for critique's sake. Haraway provided me with a conceptual and pragmatic framework that helps guide me in how to engage critically in high-stakes problems as both an intellectual and an invested moral agent. She does not simply study, but lives in dog worlds. She engages in everyday technical conversations. She and her companion dogs do agility sports together. She cares for, challenges, critiques and is generous with her human and nonhuman companions. She inhabits that material and virtual world. "Fieldwork" would be a misnomer. Likewise, I do not simply study Indigenous communities. I inhabit them, both locally and globally, within and outside of the academy. I am family, friend, and/or colleague to a stunningly diverse set of Indigenous actors. I participate daily in their – our – conversations related to Indigenous governance, science, technology, economies and cultures. I work for Indigenous flourishing. I also critique toward that end. I have been figuring out how to do this work since I was five years old, and also in a previous career as a planner. Haraway and Harding gave additional intellectual language beyond what Vine Deloria, Jr. and my mother gave me to describe my approach and ethos.

Standing with and speaking as faith

The writing of another feminist intellectual has recently offered me additional conceptual language for enacting the ethical orientation I have come to refer to as "standing with" in inquiry. Neferti Tadiar's articulation of *sampalataya*, Tagalog for "act of faith," helps address the outsider/insider angst that results from attending too much to a non-feminist *politics of objectivity* and too little to the politics of research for change within communities (Tadiar 2002). Tadiar explains *sampalataya* as referring in part to being "already caught up in the claims that others act out," which is different from speaking on behalf of (Tadiar 2002, 736). Rather, one speaks as an individual "in concert with," not silenced by one's inability to represent one's people fully. I read this to be a sort of co-constitution of one's own claims and the claims and acts of the people(s) who one speaks in concert with. *Sampalataya* involves speaking as faith – as furthering a people's claims while refusing to be excised from that people by an imperialistic, naive notion of perfect representation.

Sampalataya guides me in inquiry from out of my commitments to, and experiences among, my fellow Native Americans and other Indigenous people. It helps me articulate experiences among certain bioscientists whose projects I decide to care for. I transfer an ethic of standing with other Indigenous people – to inquire in concert with their intellectual projects in the service of Indigenous sovereignty – for example, with (Indigenous) bioscientists in the service of shared causes. That is, I work with them in ways that support their success in scientific endeavours, and simultaneously the development of their critical lenses that may help democratize science from within. Initially, I viewed this as "studying across," a term I adapt from Berkeley anthropologist Laura Nader's groundbreaking call for anthropologists to "study up."

Several years after Vine Deloria, Jr. lambasted anthropology for its colonialism, Nader admonished anthropologists to study "the colonizers rather than the colonized, the culture of power rather than the culture of the powerless, the culture of affluence rather than the culture of poverty" (Nader 1972: 284, 289). I took this to heart in my study of biological and other physical scientists and their extractive practices of Native American bones, blood, saliva and hair. Instead of studying Indigenous "perspectives" on genetics, which federal agencies love to fund, I decided to return the gaze – to study scientists. The bulk of my research has been to study the histories and politics of genetic research practices as they impact Indigenous bodies, representations and governance.

However, methodologically and ethically, I found that studying up was not easier than the traditional act of "studying down." My book, *Native American DNA: Tribal Belonging and the False Promise of Genetic Science* (TallBear 2013), is critical of the colonial practices that have made the concept of Native American DNA possible. While the science is fascinating, I had little positive investment in the particular intellectual projects of the non-Indigenous human genome diversity researchers whose work I studied. I could not adequately "care" for them as my subjects, which felt like bad feminist practice (Schuurman and Pratt 2002). I was in a bind. In addition to enacting an oppositional politics of returning the gaze, I had chosen to study scientists in order to avoid the social challenges of doing anthropology at home. In studying up, I found another sort of discomfort. I could not disown that feminist ethical imperative to study a community in whose projects I can be invested. I had to find a way to study bioscientists (whose work has profound implications for Indigenous peoples) in a way in which I could stand more within their community.

Taking ethics as the starting point, I began to interview and do participant observation with other Native American PhDs – that is, biological scientists. I am interested in their potential roles in the democratization of science and in the development of Indigenous science policy. Emphasizing participant observation, I find myself moving, in Tadiar's language, toward faithful knowledges – toward co-constituting knowledge in concert with the acts and claims of those among whom I inquire. I have become invested in the careers of the young Indigenous scientists with whom I work – in their development as good scientists in a world historically dominated by White men. Indeed, because I care for them, I have come to engage more productively in their fields. I serve as an ethics advisor for the annual Summer internship for INdigenous peoples in Genomics (SING) for Indigenous students and community members who want to learn genetics. I help teach them about the politicized history of the field and explain the links between collaborative research and Indigenous regulation and sovereignty. Young scientists teach me how someone coming from Indigenous communities and landscapes becomes passionate about bioscience. They help facilitate my growing curiosity about and knowledge of the science. It is as an act of faith in the groundbreaking work that they will do as Indigenous scientists that I continue to network with and professionally mentor SING graduates as they become professional scientists, social scientists, or go back to positions in their communities where they will help review and regulate scientific research in their communities. We quickly become colleagues.

Accordingly, I also write and speak in venues that are not obviously fitting for a social scientist's career advancement. I frequent bioscientific venues, and I try to write and speak accessibly. I do this to encourage their more democratic vision of what the biosciences can be. The more I network, the more I am a useful resource for Indigenous scientists. I work in small ways to enact the change that I and other critics envision for the sciences. I attended and blogged a critical but supportive review of an annual meeting of the Society for the Advancement of Native Americans and Chicanos in Science (SACNAS).[1] SACNAS's biannual news magazine editor quickly asked me to serve on the editorial board as an advisor on Native American issues. I blog to prompt conversation. In this case, I cultivated an opportunity to help shape scientific ethics and policy content in the organization's regular publication. I served on the editorial board because I was asked to serve. It is a sign of recognition that I was a valuable resource in the community. It is also a case of the organization deciding how I should "give back." The board also enabled me to help build discourse collaboratively about what constitutes more democratic scientific research and education. I expect that change will come more profoundly from inside bioscientific fields rather than from critical social science and humanities analyses alone. I could not do this work if I held fast to the misguided ship of distanced objectivity with my research subjects. I work with bioscientists in ways that demonstrate feminist and Indigenous concepts of objectivity in action. In the meantime, my blogs – posted to my website, *Indigeneity and Technoscience* – often serve as rough drafts of academic pieces. They highlight my expertise in a unique multidisciplinary world that I help create by naming it.

Some may find my insights and methods insufficiently replicable, although I see them as pragmatic. Not all researchers will be situated as I am – a second-career academic with training as a community planner, and an Indigenous ("insider"?) scholar who circulates regionally, nationally and internationally. I find it doable to combine theory with practice for institutional change. Perhaps a take-home point that will appeal to a wider array of readers is that feminist objectivity – that is, inquiring not at a distance, but based on the lives and knowledge priorities of subjects, reinforced by an Indigenous ethic of staying in relation – helps open up one's mind to working in non-standard ways. It may take you to new and surprising places.

Note

1   "SACNAS: Beyond 'diversity and inclusion,' making science more multicultural and democratic," Indigeneity and Technoscience Blog, November 10, 2011, www. kimtallbear.com/homeblog/sacnas-beyond-diversity-and-inclusion-making-science-more-multicultural-and-democratic.

References

Chipps, Pakki. 2004. "Family first". *Native Studies Review*, 15: 103–105.

Deloria, Jr., Vine. 1969. *Custer Died for Your Sins: An Indian Manifesto*. Norman: University of Oklahoma Press.

Gupta, Clare and Alice B. Kelly. 2014. "The social relations of fieldwork: Giving back in a research setting". *Journal of Research Practice*, 10. Retrieved from http://jrp.icaap. org/index.php/jrp/article/view/423/352.

Haraway, Donna. 1991. *Simians, Cyborgs, and Women: The Reinvention of Nature*. New York: Routledge.

Harding, Sandra. 1991. *Whose Science? Whose Knowledge? Thinking from Women's Lives*. Ithaca, NY: Cornell University Press.

Harding, Sandra. 2008. *Sciences from Below: Feminisms, Postcolonialities, and Modernities*. Durham, NC: Duke University Press.

Innes, Robert Alexander. 2009. "'Wait a second. Who are you anyways?': The insider/outsider debate and American Indian studies". *The American Indian Quarterly*, 33: 440–461.

Jacobs-Huey, Lanita. 2002. "Exchange across difference: The production of ethnographic knowledge. The natives are gazing and talking back: Reviewing the problematics of positionality, voice, and accountability among 'native' anthropologists". *American Anthropologist*, 104: 791–804.

Medicine, Beatrice. 2001. *Learning to Be an Anthropologist and Remaining "Native"*. Urbana: University of Illinois Press.

Nader, Laura. 1972. "Up the anthropologist: Perspectives gained from studying up". In Dell Hymes, ed. *Reinventing Anthropology*. New York: Vintage, pp. 284–311.

Narayan, Kirin. 1993. "How native is a 'native' anthropologist". *American Anthropologist*, 95: 671–686.

Ohnuki-Tierney, Emiko. 1984. "'Native' anthropologists". *American Ethnologist*, 11: 584–586.

Schuurman, Nadine and Geraldine Pratt. 2002. "Care of the subject: Feminism and critiques of GIS". *Gender, Place and Culture*, 9: 291–299.

Simpson, Audra. 2007. "On ethnographic refusal: Indigeneity, 'voice' and colonial citizenship". *Junctures*: 67–80.

Tadiar, Neferti X.M. 2002. "*Himala* (miracle): The heretical potential of Nora Aunor's star power". *Signs: Journal of Women in Culture and Society*, 27: 61–76.

TallBear, Kim. 2013. *Native American DNA: Tribal Belonging and the False Promise of Genetic Science*. Minneapolis: University of Minnesota Press.

TallBear, Kim. 2014. "Standing with and speaking as faith: A feminist-indigenous approach to inquiry [research note]". *Journal of Research Practice*, 10. Retrieved from http://jrp.icaap.org/index.php/jrp/article/view/405/371.

Todorova-Pirgova, Iveta. 1999. "'Native' anthropologist: On the bridge or at the border". *Anthropological Journal on European Cultures*, 8: 171–190.

Wilson, Shawn. 2008. *Research is Ceremony: Indigenous Research Methods*. Winnipeg: Fernwood Publishing.

9 Stepping in it

How to smell the fullness of Indigenous histories[1]

Vicente M. Diaz

Epigraph: an old joke

Three guys are walking on a sidewalk and come upon a pile of dog shit. They stop and take turns dropping to the ground to check it out in their own way. The first touches it, the second smells it, and the third tastes it. Agreeing that it is in fact dog shit, they proceed, cautiously stepping over it in order not to step into it.

Having stepped in it

A few years ago I published an essay, "Sniffing Oceania's Behind" (Diaz 2012), that urged historians of Oceania to smell our histories. As have "sensory" historians (Classen 2012; Jenner 2011; Smith 2014), I lamented how modernist modes of knowledge production have privileged visuality and literacy at the expense of olfaction, rendering olfaction exemplary of the debased status of the total sensate in that historically unequal relationship.[2] And because native peoples themselves have been analogously marginalized in colonial discourses, as if they were supposedly governed by the "lower senses" (as olfaction was classified), I thought it usefully subversive to focus on olfaction and its related embodiments, and to look sacrilegiously to the most vile of these as archives for source "documents." Thus the first half of the essay focused on the figure of the anus in Epeli Hau'ofa's (1995) novel, *Kisses in the Nederends*, offering an inventory of sniffing and associated fuller sensory activities connected specifically with the anus, while its second half sampled traditional olfactory practices in the Pacific for whiffs of Pacific pasts. A visionary in our field, Hau'ofa was Tongan born, but raised in Papua New Guinea by missionary parents. He was a trained cultural anthropologist who grew disillusioned with academia and post-independence "development" politics and its conceptual underpinnings (Hau'ofa 2008, esp. "Our Sea of Islands"). Hau'ofa was among Oceania's first postcolonial critics, and he turned to fiction and the fine arts as his preferred modes of critical analyses. *Nederends* is political satire, in the vein of the absurdist and picaresque. In my read, the anus, scene of an acute fistulae, is its central protagonist, its setting, and its principal narratological engine all rolled into one complex agent. Teresia Teaiwa (1999) credits *Nederends* with offering a radical counter to eroticist/ exoticist conventions of "the Polynesian body," made famous by European artists like Gauguin. Thus it was with Hau'ofian tongue-in-cheek(i)ness that I found in the visceral performances around the anus the material to resist conventions of respectability and normativity that order colonial discourses about natives and that inform "highbrow" academic practice.

The aim of this chapter is now to ask and answer the question of method that follows logically from that earlier publication: Just *how do we smell* our histories? The answer is remarkably but deceptively simple, and can be stated in terms of the opening joke, which, at the risk of snuffing out humour with analysis, can be said to subordinate visuality and common sense to fuller sensory perception as it is both opened and climaxed by the olfactory twins of dubious social stature: smell and taste. Just how do we smell Indigenous history? Simple: just smell it. After all, it is *in the doing* that we truly begin to learn method.

Would that it were so simple (or that an academic essay could end so quickly). For even a cursory consideration of what it means to smell something in general opens up a host of matters involving meaning, modality, subjectivity, and protocol. For example, as timing is to historians and location is to anthropologists, time and place also matter in the effort to smell the right things properly. Because scents are miasmic, temporary, and transient – though they can also have remarkable staying power, a point to which I'll return later – the person who knows what to nose for will also recognize the need to be at the right place at the right time. In fact, the visceral practice of smelling necessitates conceptual legwork, as shaped and conditioned by olfaction's properties. In what follows, I consider olfaction's ontologies – its states of being – and their epistemological possibilities, and illustrate these abstractions with material from Oceania.

Snorting Coke: meanings and modalities

What, exactly, does it mean to smell something? In his study of Coca-Cola's penetration into Papua New Guinean (PNG) society Robert Foster (2002) explained that the company's efforts to "teach" the islanders "how to drink Coke" consisted not of a literal teaching of how to put bottle to lips and swallow, but instead how to *value* the beverage. For Foster, the bid for new valuation was a corporate strategy to establish new wants and needs, to forge new social relations around Coca-Cola's bubbly product, in the presence of persisting Indigenous Papua New Guinean socialities between self and object. The Kanaka Maoli scholar Emalani Case (2015) extends Foster's social analyses in her self-reflexive interrogation of the company's "Share a Coke" campaign in Hawai'i. But on her blog page on Hawaiian food sovereignty, Case queries just what, exactly, it is that we are supposed to "share" with one another by placing herself firmly in the muck and confessing a prior "deep addiction" to Diet Coke, her "crav[ing] the fizzing and popping, [the] running down my throat, [the] enlivening [of] my senses" caused by the bubbly beverage. While Foster correctly analyzes the competing structurations between external and Indigenous valuations involved in globalization in PNG, Case is awash in the mess of embodied literalities as a way to begin to question the marketing strategies in her backyard/body. Following her, but also friendly to Foster's critique, I've come to *feel differently* about that familiar tickling of our tongues and throats, which I would now describe as the shocking into submission of our palates, the better to have us kill ourselves so sweetly. So much for bubbly vitality. The question, following Case, is not only whether, following Foster, there is something more going on in Coca-Cola's antics than learning how to put bottle to lip and swallow, but also whether *that which is* going on through the gesture can also open up radical insight if we direct our fullest sensory perception to the matter at hand. How might the visceral nature of drinking inform our bid to understand what's going on differently? The critical point is that, per Foster, the coca-colization of PNG is fed by asymmetrical forces from without and within, it involves transforming and sustaining systems of valuation, and that such insidious forces are also highly embodied processes that also inform rather than simply invite critical analyses and transformative practice. The beverage company may not, in fact, have taught the natives how to drink per se, but we also can't dismiss as irrelevant what that embodied literality can teach us as matters of analytic method for emancipatory purposes. So let's counter the deadly fizz and pop with the sizzle of rage and sweet aftertaste of recovery rather than leave them as misguided and blinded consumerist gulp. And if it be bubbles we crave, let us produce them as we spray back a collective refusal of Coke's status as "the real thing," the jingle that Coca-Cola once used for my generation. Or better yet, as the next section will show, let us expel the gaseous aftereffects through the orifices at the other ends of our bodies. For if the literal putting of bottle to lips and swallowing is at once simple and usefully complicating for rethinking questions of agency and identity, the question of *how to* smell also merits further consideration for the project of methodological and political transformation. To *this end*, much as how the science of flatology – the serious study of what farts tell about our bodies (Sciencedump n.d.; Olson 2014) – has demonstrated in its findings, a critical occupation with farts can also deliver new social and historical understanding. And so to farts we turn.

Ontology in the full company of the sensate

Contrary to popular opinion, the really unfortunate thing about the equally popular adage "he who smelt it first, dealt it" is not its unreliability for the purposes of positive identification, but its demonization of the subject position. The smeller, like the deed, gets a bum rap. In fact, quite literally, and perhaps disturbingly, the line that separates our farts from ourselves and any other person with whom we come into close proximity is, well, *fine*. In fact, among all humans there is a dust cloud of bodily particles – those made up of excretory material are called "farticles." Well-known is how smell in general is a powerful trigger of the past. Less-known is how olfaction is in fact constituted in complex relationship to the full sensate and not just to taste, and that this complex co-constitution approximates that of the interrelationship between the aura of farts and supposed boundaries, territorialities, of where our bodies begin and end. According to *Science Daily* (2014), olfaction's connection to memory, and therefore to subjectivity, is what gives our nose the ability to guide us. And still, though none of the five to nineteen senses operates autonomously, olfaction – once regarded in the West as the "lowest" of the human faculties – may even turn out to be the portal into worlds – past and present – we've yet to imagine. Let me return to more modest claims for what olfaction in particular can offer us by turning to a true story of how I came to revalue flatulence, and life, and the doing of history – by having had to smell really bad farts.

In the summer of 1996 my eldest brother Carl was diagnosed with advanced colon cancer. He had been dissertating in clinical psychology at the Ateneo University de Manila, on a method of treatment called genograms, which basically used family histories to identify flashpoint events and the behaviours and habits around them. Practitioners of the method believe that certain behaviors and conditions, especially involving trauma and high stress, in one generation can snowball in subsequent generations if not checked and managed properly. A tendency toward habitual suspiciousness might reappear a generation or two later as certified paranoid schizophrenia. At the Ateneo, Carl was influenced by *Sikolohiyan Pilipino* Philippine psychology, a nationalist movement that embraced culturally appropriate practices (Pe-Pua and Marcelino 2000). His mentor was Fr. Jaime Bulatao S.J., a reputed mystic who mixed hypnotherapy, folk practices, and the Ignatian Spiritual Exercises, a rigorous form of meditation and bodily discipline that melded the power of prayer with total sensory "exercises." Bulatao and his students also used breathing and visualization exercises, including astral traveling, the ability to occupy two distant places physically and simultaneously.

Carl in fact drew from this transdisciplinary and transcultural theory and method to oust the invasive cancer. One evening, he gathered the extended family for a healing session that began with prayer, then a powerful soliloquy through which he implored each of us, as a preliminary step in his healing protocol, to face the pain and hurt inside ourselves, especially those that involved other family members. A pond of tears filled the living room that night, tears of sorrow and pain overflowing from a (once) dammed river of historical denial. Then Carl commenced the next phase, which employed visualization and astral traveling. Thus did he evenly distribute the forty-some members of the family present (ages ranging from five to seventy-eight) into a fleet of canoes, shrink then navigate us into his body, through his mouth, down the throat, and onwards into the small and then large intestines. Some of us, quick to realize what was transpiring, expressed relief at the use of the oral rather than the other (faster and more direct) route. Once we were in the colon, Carl instructed us to help him oust the invasive tumor in whatever ways we so chose. But none worked. Nor did surgery and chemo treatment in the Philippines, Hawai'i, and California. Nor desperate juicing, at treatment centres (outlawed in the United States) in Mexico. He passed on a mere five months after the diagnosis. But how Carl taught us to embrace pain convinces me that he/we won the battle that raged inside and outside his body, for since then, we've drawn from lessons learnt about the kind of healing power that is unleashed when come crumbling down the walls that separate self from other, past from present, inside from outside, enemy from friend, death from life, science from superstition, reason from passion, and method from madness. The confirmation of this assessment came from how we learned to love his farts, and this is no smoke up the proverbial ass: on account of surgery gone awry, there developed a condition in which gas remained trapped in a sutured pocket in Carl's colon and could only be released after a long and voluminous build up. The interim was excruciating pain. Hence, any release of the entrapped gas, often in the most explosive and wrenching of farts, also brought some of the loudest cheers and most hysterical laughter. To this day, often in the presence of the most silent and deadliest of the matter, I am instantly transported to a time in the past when farts came to signal not just the temporary release from pain and suffering, but bigger lessons of life and living learnt through the ordeal of surviving Carl's cancer, meanings that would carry me through the equally temporary adversities that life would subsequently throw my way in the future.

Indigeneity: a matter of life and method

Unlike "traditional" sensory historians who still peddle in conventionally defined archives and written sources, there is already a new generation of scholars/artists (Bolozan 2015; Garchik 2014; Metcalfe 2014; Westlake 2015) who actually experiment with the use of olfaction and other fuller sensory methods and technologies *to do* their work. In Native Pacific Studies we also have a growing body of scholarship that engages with olfaction, indeed, that embraces total bodily immersion in the most visceral of activities that are central to projects of political and cultural reclamation and nation re-building. These projects center on foodways, traditional knowledge and technologies, performing and expressive arts, martial arts, religion and spirituality, health and wellbeing, to name the broad categories in which Indigenous Pacific Islanders are connecting scholarship to the broader needs of their communities' struggles to endure as Indigenous peoples. These projects have become the materiality for the doing of Indigenous Pacific Islander scholarship today. But my task here is not so much to survey the literature as to identify the key considerations that shape the successful doing of any of these full-bodied practices. At the core of such considerations is the conviction that indigeneity matters, by which I mean the claims and conditions of aboriginal belonging to ancestral places, the demands that come with them, and their analytical implications and possibilities as articulated by those communities. Indigenous matters include the ethical, historical, cultural, and political reasons for which such claims ought to be genuinely considered in research pertaining to those communities. Let me elaborate, with a nose to questions of timing and location.

Because indigeneity matters thus, there are at least three possible subject positions in regards to participating in the full sensate of Indigenous reclamation for analytical purposes: 1) when one is a non-native person, which would basically mean keeping one's nose out of where it doesn't belong, certainly desisting from leadership positions, unless one heeds Indigenously oriented research protocol (Smith 1999); 2) when one is native, but not of the people whose histories one wishes to research, for which one had better foreground that status of non-belonging, had better clarify the terms of relative involvement, and finally, find one's appropriate place; and finally, 3) when the researcher is a member of the community in question, a status which presents the most difficult task given the obligations and responsibilities expected of members of the group *even while* specific membership in a particular family, clan, or tribe might *constrain* his or her speech and action with respect to the larger body. For Maori in Aotearoa, for example, the term tangata whenua/people of the land, does not simply apply to all Indigenous Maori but to those who have bona fide lineal kinship and primary accountability to a specific community of a specific locale or region in question.

Because indigeneity matters in our histories, it matters in our studies. And for this, the mattering of indigeneity to matters of sniffing as a method means that to sniff Indigenous histories is to ensure that one knows one's proper place, and that one understands and follows through with the responsibilities and obligations that come with how one is positioned to the matter. In terms of timing, knowing one's place and one's responsibility also signals to everyone when one knows that one's nose is ready. Then, as they say, the fun really begins.

Into the shit

From these considerations of olfaction's ontological and epistemological conditions we are now ready to return to the deceptively simple answer to our key question: so, just *how do we* go about smelling native histories? The answer lies in the joke, and the joke is in, on, and about us. How do we smell native pasts? Get down to the ground, where natives are said (or made) to dwell, and stick your nose into the pile. Better yet, pick up a piece of it and feel it. Squeeze it between your fingers. Or pop it in your mouth and taste what it has to offer (after all, you've already smelt it). Best of all, throw yourself entirely into it. Roll in it. Savor the traces of the past of which it reeks, and follow the trail of its aroma. But whatever you do, just don't step over or around in order to avoid the shit.

Notes

1   Kalangan yan Saina Ma'ase to Jean O'Brien and Chris Andersen for inviting me to contribute to this anthology. Also to Christine Taitano DeLisle and Teresia Teaiwa for critical feedback. I would like to dedicate this chapter to my late brother, Carlos Diaz (1947–1997), whose unconventional scholarship and farts from a cancer-ridden colon inspire this chapter.
2   Modern science identifies nine to nineteen senses (Fox n.d.; Wikipedia n.d.).

References

Bolozan, Catalina. 2015. "The science of smelling stories". *1984BoldIdeas*. Accessed 28 July 2015, http://1984boldideas.com/science-smelling-stories/.

Case, Emalani. 2015. "Share a Coke: A complex gesture.". *He Māʻona Moku: Decolonizing Our Diets, One Mouthful at a Time*. Blog. August 18. Accessed 20 August 2015, https://maonamoku.wordpress.com.

Classen, Constance. 2012. *The Deepest Sense: A Cultural History of Touch*. Champaign: University of Illinois.

Diaz, Vicente M. 2002. "'Fight Boys till the Last': Football and the Remasculinization of Indigeneity in Guam". In Paul Spickard, Joanne Rondilla and Deborah Hippolite-Wright, eds. *Pacific Diaspora: Island Peoples in the United States and the Pacific*. Honolulu: University of Hawaiʻi Press, 167–194.

Diaz, Vicente M. 2007. "The 'Man's Thing': The Testicularization of Traditional Micronesian Seafaring". Paper presented at the panel 'Native Men on Native Masculinities', Native American and Indigenous Studies Meeting, University of Oklahoma May 3–5.

Diaz, Vicente M. 2011. "Tackling Pacific Hegemonic Formations on the American Gridiron." *Amerasia Journal* 37(3): 2–25.

Diaz, Vicente M. 2012. "Sniffing Oceania's behind". *The Contemporary Pacific*, 24(2): 323–344.

Foster, Robert. 2002. *Materializing the Nation: Commodities, Consumption, and Mass Media in Papua New Guinea*. Bloomington: Indiana University Press.

Fox, Kate. n.d. *The Smell Report: An Overview of Facts and Findings*. Social Research Issues Centre. Accessed 20 July 2015,www.sirc.org/publik/smell_culture.html.

Garchik, Leah. 2014. "Smelling history and sniffing Mission Street". February 21. Accessed 28 August 2015, www.sfgate.com/entertainment/garchik/article/Smelling-history-and-sniffing-Mission-Street-5253161.php.

Hau'ofa, Epeli. 1995. *Kisses in the Nederends*. Honolulu: University of Hawai'i Press.

Hau'ofa, Epeli. 2008. *We Are the Ocean: Selected Works*. Honolulu: University of Hawai'i Press.

Jenner, Mark S.R. 2011. "Follow your nose? Smell, smelling, and their histories". AHR Forum. Accessed 28 August 2015, https://urbanheritages.files.wordpress.com/2011/11/follow-your-nose.pdf.

Metcalfe, John. 2014. "Now you can experience the nasty stench of cities throughout history". CityLab, February 12, 2014. Accessed 27 August 2015, www.citylab.com/design/2014/02/perfumers-recreate-nasty-stench-cities/8375/.

Olson, Samantha. 2014. "Our favorite fart smells are protecting our bodies from diseases". *Medical Daily*, November 11. Accessed 25 September 2015, www.medicaldaily.com/pulse/our-favorite-fart-smells-are-protecting-our-bodies-possible-disease-310216.

Pe-Pua, Rogelia and Elizabeth Protacio Marcelino. 2000. "Sikolohiyang Pilipino (Filipino psychology): A legacy of Virgilio G. Enriquez". *Asian Journal of Social Psychology*, 3: 49–71.

Science Daily. 2014. "How smells stick to your memories." April 16. Accessed 28 August 2015, www.sciencedaily.com/releases/2014/04/140416133341.htm#.VeM7Nlawu-c. email.

Sciencedump. n.d. "Facts about your fart" (Infographic). Accessed 28 August 2015, www.sciencedump.com/content/facts-about-your-farts-infographic.

Smith, Linda Tuhiwai. 1999. *Decolonizing Methodologies: Research and Indigenous Peoples*. London: Zed Books and Dunedin: University of Otago Press.

Smith, Mark M. 2014. *The Smell of Battle, the Taste of Siege: A Sensory History of the Civil War*. Oxford: Oxford University Press.

Teaiwa, Teresia. 1999. "Reading Paul Gauguin's Noa Noa with Epeli Hau'ofa's Nederends: Militourism, feminism and the 'Polynesian' body". In Vilsoni Hereniko and Rob Wilson, eds. *Inside Out: Literature, Cultural Politics, and Identity in the New Pacific*. Boulder: Rowman & Littlefield, pp. 249–264.

Westlake, Ben. 2015. "Smelly telling: The rise of the olfactory story. New technology is allowing storytellers to experiment with the coupling of smell and narrative". *1984BoldStory*. Accessed 27 August 2015, http://1984boldideas.com/smelly-telling-the-rise-of-the-olfactory-story/.

Wikipedia. n.d. "List of common misperceptions". 2011. Accessed 5 May 2011,http://en.wikipedia.org/wiki/List_of_common_misconceptions.

10 Intellectual history and Indigenous methodology

Robert Warrior

Intellectual history has played an outsize role in versions of Native and Indigenous studies that have developed over the past two decades, and here I will argue specifically for the centrality of a focus on histories of Indigenous intellectual work as mediations between important, but opposed, critical projects.[1] The first of those projects is the academic articulation of traditional Indigenous knowledge, a project that has taken many forms but that has by and large consistently run into the same conceptual and practical barriers across different areas of inquiry and interest – most tellingly, a lack of some of the features of contemporary academic knowledge-making that are necessary to establishing scholarly credibility, including identifiable canons of rigour, blind peer scrutiny, and scholarly independence.[2]

The second project seeks to integrate various forms of theorizing and knowledge creation that originate not just outside Indigenous contexts, but from within the antagonistic social and cultural context of Euro-American intellectual practice, into the process of creating new knowledge about, for, and by Native and Indigenous people. This project has altogether different challenges. The very act of academic writing like I am doing here may very well be chief among these challenges, one that demonstrates the built-in slant toward forms derived from non-Indigenous practices that is seemingly inherent in this second project. This inherent bias in favour of the conventions of academic writing is exacerbated by the simple fact that Indigenous knowledge-making has historically had its most productive context inside Indigenous communal settings. What happens when the place from which knowledge is enunciated shifts to a more strictly academic setting?

This chapter does not work through all of these challenges, but I hope it demonstrates the importance of a self-reflexive mode of inquiry that is a common thread between these two broad intellectual projects. Self-reflexive intellectual historical work provides a generative undergirding to scholarly attempts to grapple with some of the most basic issues that proliferate in contemporary Native studies practice.

In the conclusion of this methodological chapter, I will make what I hope is a clear case for intellectual history playing a central role in the continuing development of Indigenous studies. This is, I will argue, not just for those who are historically minded, but for a broad spectrum of scholars in the field. I will base that conclusion on a discussion of two examples that highlight some different aspects of what falls under the rubric of Indigenous intellectual history. Taken together, these examples provide what I hope is a compelling case for regarding intellectual history as synonymous, or at least largely so, with Native studies method.

Example: Approximately ten years ago, I had the opportunity to witness the scrutinization of a potential new wa-zhe-pah, or crier, for the Osage in-losh-ka dance. The annual three weekends of the in-losh-ka are the primary cultural events for Osages as a people.[3]

The wa-zhe-pah does many things during the dances, but most prominently sits under the large arena-like "arbour" where we dance and ceremoniously stands up to call out the Osage names of those who request it. The wa-zhe-pah's chair sits in the dance space between the center of the arbor, where the drum, male singer/drummers, and women who sing (or lady singers) sit, and the benches where the men who dance (the in-losh-ka is a men's society) sit between songs and during water breaks. The wah-zhe-pah leads new dancers and their families into the arbour when they first present themselves publicly to come into the dance.

For two extended periods of several years, the in-losh-ka had no wah-zhe-pah, which is one of several things that make this position unusual among the many in our dance. A tail dancer, waterboy, or even head committeeman might be absent for a day, but those positions are always held by someone. Further, the wah-zhe-pah is not, as far as I know, asked to be part of the dance committees in the three districts, like the head cook or head singer. He is an assumed part of each district's committee.

I have been involved in the in-losh-ka for over twenty-five years, and being a dancer has become a primary way in which I think about myself as a person and as an Osage. I think about our dances literally every day, and during June when the three weekends of our dances take place, I often find myself thinking about our dance society and what it means to us as Osage people, including while I am dancing.

For all that, though, I have only written about the in-losh-ka once in an extended way, and that effort was more sociological than philosophical or cultural.[4] While I consider myself knowledgeable about our dance and have been fortunate enough to be able to consider it from some incredibly rich angles, I am not someone who can speak with authority about the deep structures and complex meanings of the various aspects of the in-losh-ka dance.

All that is to say that when I write about the wah-zhe-pah, I do so not as someone who has gained the right and respect to represent our dance, nor am I trying to work through in writing the deeper levels of meaning that take place as part of it. Which brings me back to watching the process of the advisors to the in-losh-ka choosing a new person to fill that role.

What I recall hearing and then witnessing in that process was that someone had been identified who could take on the responsibilities of the position and that the last step in the process was a gathering at the Grayhorse Village dance arbour to reach a final decision on whether or not the candidate could become the new wa-zhe-pah.

I learned at the start of the gathering that the small group of advisers charged with making the decision had no immediate idea as to how they should come to their decision. So, for a long time, the advisers huddled in conversation. I didn't hear any of what they said, but learned from those who had access to the process that much of the conversation was about what to do when you find yourself in their position, and that among the small group they could piece together memories that showed them how to proceed. What was remarkable, though, was that none of those advisers had direct memories to guide them, but instead figured things out based on memories of listening to accounts from people who had been present decades before for this same selection process or something close to it.

The advisers agreed on the process, which was primarily an audition in which the candidate had to demonstrate that his voice was strong enough to perform the wa-zhe-pah's role and that he could pronounce Osage names. Not long after, we not only had a new wa-zhe-pah, but also a clear path to follow a few years later when once again the position was open for a time and a new candidate was ready to be selected.

For all the ways contemporary scholars try to describe traditional Indigenous knowledge and its transmission, that gathering always sticks with me as embodying something crucial that these academic discussions easily miss. Along with being much more simply articulated than academic descriptions tend to be, I have come to see what happened among those advisers at Grayhorse as a profound example of Indigenous intellectual history in practice.

I could go on at length about many of the specifics of that practice – the collaborative approach to knowledge, for instance, or the relationship between those empowered to come up with a solution and the community whose history they carry. What I want to highlight for my purpose here, however, is the powerful sense these Osage intellectual historians modeled that working with each other to come up with a process grounded in Osage memory is, in fact, satisfying in and of itself. They didn't, that is, huddle with each other then tell us that they didn't know exactly what to do but had come up with a reasonable process that would get us from point A to point B.

Instead, we participated in a deliberative process that demonstrated that the space between the two points is every bit as important as arriving at point B. Importantly, these were men and women who became advisers after a lifetime of not just being exposed to the unfolding history of a cultural tradition, but who for whatever reason had come decades before to understand that unfolding history was important to learn and remember. They also provided living proof that Osage answers remain available to Osage questions, meaning the specificity of who we are and who we are becoming is sufficiently distinct and discrete to be identifiable. I will return to these points in concluding this chapter.

Example:
The history of modern Indigenous writing provides a much different kind of living proof. Whereas my account of Osage advisers is one of the recovery of an answer to a question that had not been asked for many years, modern Native writing is more like an answer that has only ever at brief moments been confident of the question (or questions) to which it corresponds.

That is to say, Indigenous writing under the sign of modernity is an aporia, an act of Indigenous agency that seems to pave the inroads of colonization even if and when its intent is to resist their encroachment.[5] Such has been the case in every history of the colonization of Indigenous peoples I know of, though the history of writing I know best is the one of what has come to be Anglophone North America. From the seventeenth century, when Caleb Cheeshahteaumuck and other New England Indian students attended the Indian College at Harvard in Massachusetts, to the twenty-first century proliferation of Native American and First Nations intellectuals writing in every form imaginable (and increasingly in Indigenous languages), the technology of Western writing has marked a separation, or at least the threat of it, between Indigenous people and their communities.[6]

Samson Occom, the Mohegan man who in his youth went to mission school, learned to read and write, and eventually traveled throughout New England and Britain as a celebrated convert, has become for many of us who study Anglophone Native intellectual history a figure who both exemplifies that separation and also the complexity that becomes easy to miss in the simplistic binaries of conversion, assimilation, and capitulation versus resistance (Brooks 2006). Occom was devout, pious, and moralistic in his Christian beliefs, but he also worked tirelessly for the political rights of Native people in New England, had extensive Mohegan knowledge of botany, and demonstrably kept the well-being of other Native people foremost in his work.

His writing, both in his time and in our own, has made him a celebrated figure among Native people and others. And yet his writing (or perhaps more accurately his Christian faith in the power of written words) drew distinctions that divided the people he was dedicated to serving. The Brothertown settlement, where he spent his last years, was founded by a group of Christian Indians who believed they could withstand the devastation of colonialism by withdrawing into their own space away from whites, but also away from Natives who did not share their Christian faith.[7] It was self-consciously a movement of Christian Indians.

That may sound like an indictment or a judgment, but in fact it is a direct statement of fact. The Brothertown experiment was many things, including a profound attempt to find a way forward against the crushing tide of white settlement and the establishment of a settler nation in New England. One doesn't have to blame Christian Indians or assert that Christianity is only a vehicle of Native oppression to comprehend the gulf that Occom and others chose in separating themselves from the unconverted.

Something similar is true across the history of Native writing, a history now available in a way it wasn't three decades ago. That history highlights not just the deeply conflicted and ambiguous witness of figures like Occom, but also the more clearly heroic (if flawed) witness of William Apess or John Ross.[8] Through it all, however, writing merely as resistance is hard to find in non-ambiguous ways.

Rather than attempting to trace the contours of that history, what is important for my purposes here is what arises through being a student of that Indigenous intellectual history of writing. Namely, engagement with the archive of Native writing provides an opportunity to come to an understanding of the stakes of academic discourse that is not, in fact, nearly so clearly derived from seeking to understand the intellectual histories that the Osage advisers from my first example continue to access and participate in.

This is much more practical, even starkly and existentially so, than philosophically or critically differentiating between orality and alphabetic literacy.[9] That is, when I read Occom, Apess, or other figures from this history of Native writing, I gain a chance to get perspective on what I am doing and why when I seek to make Indigenous knowledge (or make knowledge Indigenous) through a form like this one. Thus, while writing about traditional Indigenous knowledge-making may demonstrate just how different Native and Western forms of knowledge are, studying written Native intellectual history is, in and of itself, a platform upon which a self-reflexive critique of writing can take place.

One of my favorite examples of this point comes from teaching Native writing, especially to Native students. Writers who succeed in modeling traditional knowledge draw students into a way of seeing the world that is not readily available on a college campus. Students, Native and non-Native, who have not experienced those ways of knowing gain insight, perhaps for the first time, into the stakes of Indigenous persistence. Writers who use forms and provide accounts of their lives that highlight separation from those ways of knowing, including figures like Charles Eastman, Carlos Montezuma, or Gertrude Bonnin, often turn students off.[10]

What turns them off, to use Eastman as an example, are books like *From the Deep Woods to Civilization*, which is the title of Eastman's most widely read work. Native students (and others) come to class hungry for the deep woods – those places where an alternative to what Eastman calls civilization comes from and persists. Eastman himself, in fact, shares that hunger insofar as his account of his professional and political life finds him later in life seeking a way back in some form to the life he left behind when he left for boarding school.

Sometimes the dislike by Native students of accounts like Eastman's is especially severe. I have had students make it clear that they think *From the Deep Woods* doesn't belong on a reading list of an introductory Native studies course, which they think ought to be reserved for writings that are a celebration of traditional Native ways of life. The great irony, of course, is that a contemporary Native student who has come to college to pursue a degree seemingly to open opportunities for professional advancement can become so exercised by Eastman's account of how he went to school then college then medical school to open opportunities for professional advancement.

Those strong reactions, though I should add that they are far from the most common ones among Native students in my classes, vindicate Eastman's place on the syllabus better than anything else could. For this chapter, what I want to highlight is the self-reflexivity of Eastman's narrative and how that invites Native readers to be similarly self-reflexive. Any reader, further, gains the opportunity to consider along with Eastman what it means to exercise modern Indigenous agency.

Many of the accounts of traditional Indigenous knowledge have important modern dimensions – one way to read the development of the Osage in-losh-ka dance, for instance, is as a response to modernity. What differentiates these approaches, though, is the self-aware highlighting of those dimensions of modernity. I can illustrate this with one of Eastman's most noted quotations, which appears at the very end of *From the Deep Woods*:

> I am an Indian; and while I have learned much from civilization, for which I am grateful, I have never lost my Indian sense of right and justice. I am for development and progress along social and spiritual lines, rather than those of commerce, nationalism, or efficiency. Nevertheless, so long as I live, I am an American.
>
> (Eastman 1916: 195)

This is a profound statement of Eastman's identity as an exemplary American Indian Progressive, critical of American progressivism even as he articulates his interpellation in it. As such, it is a statement that I contend would not appear in an account of the intellectual history embedded in the process of finding a new wa-zhe-pah or similar writings. Indeed, I would go so far as to suggest that we can also read this famous Eastman quote as a statement of historical method.

These two examples highlight different way of thinking about Indigenous intellectual history and how and where we can look for it. To conclude, I want to return to those points offered in each example in order to see what we gain by being explicit about the role of the intellect in our shared work.

Both examples are elaborations, of course, of tensions that have been discussed many times and in many ways before. We could declare the development of their opposition as two positions in a dialectical relationship out of which we hope to find generative space for discussion. But we would then too easily miss just how already interpellated these positions are. Why focus on the dialectic, in other words, if the search for a new wa-zhe-pah and the consideration of the history of Indigenous writing are much more commensurate than we thought?

Yet, for all the generative space for understanding Indigenous intellectual history bounded inside the area marked by these varieties of intellectual experiences, I come back in the end to a strong sense of needing to highlight the written history. This is not because writing can lay claim to being more important or a better vehicle than other forms. Rather, what is inescapable is that the history of writing is the history I am contributing to when I do what I have done here.

This brings me back to Eastman's statement at the end of *From the Deep Woods* and my claiming of it as a statement of method and methodology. Eastman provides a concentrated set of questions to ask as we write historically with Indigenous agency at the centre. Is it too much to expect, after all, that Native agents in their own histories emerge with the same sort of complexity and ambiguity Eastman articulates? Of course not, and it's that sort of synchronicity that makes me confident that Indigenous intellectual history deserves a central place in Indigenous studies. Even more important, though, and worth stressing to everyone who puts Indigenous persons at the centre of their scholarly work, is that Indigenous agents of history express their agency through their ideas. Persistence is thus, and always will be, an intellectual act.

Notes

1 Some of the more prominent examples of work focused specifically on Native intellectual history are Silva (2004); Justice (2006); and Monture (2014); L. Brooks (2008). See also Warrior (1995, 2006, 2013).
2 For some recent work in scholarly articulation of traditional knowledge, see Gonzales (2012) and Gaudet (2014).
3 Little quality scholarship on the Osage in-losh-ka exists. My descriptions and comments about it derive primarily from my direct participation.
4 The article in which I use examples from the in-losh-ka is "The Subaltern Can Dance, and So, Sometimes, Can the Intellectual" (2011).
5 Justice (2006) and L. Brooks (2008) provide excellent readings of these dynamics in the history of Native writing.
6 Though now dated, see Hochbruck (1992).
7 My reading of Occom's relationship to the Brothertown movement comes primarily from correspondence in J. Brooks (2006).
8 See the writings of Cherokee John Ross (Dale 1939; Ross 1985), and for the published works of William Apess see O'Connell (1992).
9 An excellent reading of orality/literacy debates with a compelling alternative is Teuton (2010).
10 For an up-to-date bibliography on critical work on Eastman, Montezuma, Bonnin, and others, see Vigil (2015).

References

Apess, William. 1992. *On Our Own Ground: The Complete Writings of William Apess, a Pequot.* Amherst: University of Massachusetts Press.
Brooks, Joanna, ed. 2006. *The Collected Writings of Samson Occom, Mohegan: Leadership and Literature in Eighteenth-Century Native America.* Oxford: Oxford University Press.
Brooks, Lisa. 2008. *The Common Pot: The Recovery of Native Space in the Northeast.* Minneapolis: University of Minnesota Press.
Dale, Edwards Everett. 1985. *Cherokee Cavaliers: Forty Years of Cherokee History as Told in the Correspondence of the Ridge-Watie-Boudinot Family.* Norman: University of Oklahoma Press.
Eastman, Charles Alexander (Ohiyesa). 1916. *From the Deep Woods to Civilization: Chapters in the Autobiography of an Indian.* Boston: Little, Brown.
Gaudet, Janice Cindy. 2014. "Rethinking participatory research with Indigenous peoples". *NAIS*, 1(2): 69–88.
Gonzales, Patrisia. 2012. *Red Medicine: Traditional Indigenous Rites of Birthing and Healing.* Tucson: University of Arizona Press.
Hochbruck, Wolfgang. 1992. "'Honoratissimi Benefactores': Native American students and two seventeenth-century texts in the university tradition". *Studies in American Indian Literatures: The Journal of the Association for the Study of American Indian Literatures* (SAIL), 4(2–3): 35–47.
Justice, Daniel. 2006. *Our Fires Survive the Storm.* Minneapolis: University of Minnesota Press.
Monture, Rick. 2014. *We Share Our Matters: Two Centuries of Writing and Resistance at Six Nations of the Grand River.* Winnipeg: University of Manitoba Press.
O'Connell, Barry, ed. 1992. *On Our Own Ground: The Complete Writings of William Apess, a Pequot.* Amherst: University of Massachusetts Press.

Ross, John. 1985. *The Papers of Chief John Ross*. Ed. Gary Moulton, 2 vols. Norman: University of Oklahoma Press.

Silva, Noenoe. 2004. *Aloha Betrayed: Native Hawaiian Resistance to American Colonialism*. Durham, NC: Duke University Press.

Teuton, Christopher. 2010. *Deep Waters: The Textual Continuum in American Indian Literature*. Lincoln: University of Nebraska Press.

Vigil, Kiara. 2015. *Indigenous Intellectuals: Sovereignty, Citizenship, and the American Imagination, 1880–1930*. Cambridge: Cambridge University Press.

Warrior, Robert. 1995. *Tribal Secrets: Recovering American Indian Intellectual Traditions*. Minnesota: University of Minnesota Press.

Warrior, Robert. 2006. *The People and the Word: Reading Native Nonfiction*. Minnesota: University of Minnesota Press.

Warrior, Robert. 2011. "The subaltern can dance, and so, sometimes, can the intellectual". *interventions*, 13(1): 85–94.

Warrior, Robert. 2013. "The SAI [Society of American Indians] and the end(s) of intellectual history". In Chadwick Allen and Beth Piatote, eds. Special issue of *Studies of American Indian Literatures* 25(2) and *American Indian Quarterly* 37(3): 221–235.

11 A genealogy of critical Hawaiian studies, late twentieth to early twenty-first century

Noenoe K. Silva

In this chapter I review the advent and development of critical Hawaiian studies from the 1980s to the present day. I choose to focus mainly on the work of Kanaka scholars who broke the ground (or cleared the path) for Kanaka-centred study, using the rich and vast archive of writing in 'ōlelo Hawai'i. The last part of this genealogy gets the most attention, as the critical academic works by Kanaka scholars building on the previous generations now pour forth. Readers should also understand that it is not possible to document and analyze all the works in the broad, interdisciplinary field that I am calling Hawaiian studies, and that much more work that I cannot detail here has been and continues to be done in other books, journal articles, theses, and dissertations.

The first generation: 1980s to mid-1990s

The first academic generation was related to the Hawaiian renaissance, during which pride and interest in Hawaiian culture, language, and history broke through the floodgates of oppression and shame at being Kanaka that characterized the twentieth century. Activists worked successfully to institute a Hawaiian studies program at UH Mānoa. Simultaneously, the Hawaiian language revitalization movement gathered thousands of students into study from preschool through university. Language activists started immersion preschools called Pūnana Leo, modeled after Aotearoa/New Zealand Māori Kōhanga Reo. They also successfully established immersion K-12 education in the state Department of Education. Other activists created Hawaiian-centred charter schools that allowed them more freedom in the curriculum. At the University of Hawai'i in both Mānoa and Hilo, thousands of people, Hawaiian and non-Hawaiian, took up advanced language study at the undergraduate level. Some majored in the language or in Hawaiian studies or both.

Haunani-Kay Trask and Lilikalā Kame'eleihiwa each published a critical (in both senses of the word) text: Trask's *From a Native Daughter* has educated many thousands of people, in and outside of university settings, on colonialism in Hawai'i and the necessity of engaging in native-centred study in politics and history, as well as political activism (Trask 1993, 1999). Kame'eleihiwa's *Native Land and Foreign Desires* was the first text in Hawaiian history to centre its narrative and analysis using Hawaiian epistemology (Kame'eleihiwa 1992).[1]

Both Kameʻeleihiwa and Trask joined the faculty of the Hawaiian Studies department and worked tirelessly to expand the numbers of majors, and its curriculum, and to reach into the core of the university. That program now teaches hundreds, perhaps thousands, of undergraduates each year in core courses.

The second generation: late 1990s to early 2000s

Two Kanaka historians follow Kameʻeleihiwa and Trask, both men who also joined the faculty of Hawaiian Studies at Mānoa: Kanalu Young published *Rethinking the Native Hawaiian Past* in 1998, which insisted on research into Hawaiian language archives, and focused on the history of kaukau aliʻi, or lesser-ranked aliʻi (Young 1998). In 2002, Jonathan Kamakawiwoʻole Osorio published *Dismembering Lāhui*, a book that rewrote the history of the loss of Hawaiian sovereignty by tracing the evolution of constitutions and laws throughout the Hawaiian Kingdom era, roughly 1840–1887 (Osorio 2002). Osorio also emphasized use of Hawaiian language sources.

This period also saw the 1998 dissertation of Manulani Aluli Meyer, which presented the case for taking seriously Hawaiian epistemology (Meyer 1998, 2003). Meyer presents this idea, grounded in our ancestral knowledge, as living on in contemporary narratives. The promotion of the term "epistemology" in connection with Kanaka ideas about the nature of the world has had a lasting impact on Hawaiian studies.

Although it feels uncomfortable to do so, I feel I also have to mention my own book *Aloha Betrayed: Native Hawaiian Resistance to American Colonialism*, published in 2004. This book made the case that we cannot understand our own Indigenous histories without reading what our ancestors wrote, and in the case of Hawaiian history, they wrote in Hawaiian. Thus a knowledge of our native language is necessary for any future historical work on our people and our nation.

The third generation: late 2000s

This important period includes groundbreaking works in Hawaiian historiography and ethnography: specifically J. Kēhaulani Kauanui's *Hawaiian Blood: Colonialism and the Politics of Sovereignty and Indigeneity*, which provides much-needed analysis of the role of blood quantum institutional requirements in the fracturing of Hawaiian communities, and Ty P. Kāwika Tengan's *Native Men Remade: Gender and Nation in Contemporary Hawaiʻi*, a model for Indigenous participant-observer ethnography (Kauanui 2008; Tengan 2008). Both of these were published by Duke University Press.

The latest generation: the 2010s

Here I focus more deeply on six recent books among a cascade of Hawaiian academic texts that all draw, to a greater or lesser degree, on Hawaiian language sources or document their importance.[2] Several of the scholars have been supported by the Mellon-Hawai'i postdoctoral fellowship; four of the books were published through the First Peoples: New Directions in Indigenous Studies initiative, one published by Duke University Press, and another by Oregon State University Press. These kinds of support are crucial to our ability to produce publishable works.

In 2012, Hokulani K. Aikau's *A Chosen People, a Promised Land* was published by the University of Minnesota Press; this was a groundbreaking work that has encouraged that press to build a substantial offering in Hawaiian and Pacific Studies. In this critical and original work, Aikau combines her family history and personal engagement and struggle with the Church of Latter Day Saints (Mormonism) with archival and ethnographic research to illuminate several difficult questions. Aikau goes far beyond the usual analysis of the role of churches in colonialism. She gives us the background of the establishment of the church in Hawai'i, the origins of how Polynesians became the titular Chosen People. Why do some native peoples become the ardent faithful of foreign religions? Aikau offers Hawaiians a well-researched and brilliantly analyzed story that will assist individuals in searching out their own answers to that question. For example, she connects for us the Māhele, which privatized land tenure and resulted in the loss of both land and crucial social and community relationships (Osorio 2002; Kame'eleihiwa 1992), to the establishment of the Lā'ie church community as a pu'uhonua (site of refuge) for Hawaiians that both fit neatly and conflicted with the church's gathering principle. Aikau writes, "Whereas Native Hawaiian Latter-Day Saints saw gathering as a way to live the gospel principles, it also allowed them an opportunity to reconnect with 'āina – land as the source of physical and spiritual nourishment" (2012: 57).

The heart of the book, for me, is two chapters in which Aikau delves deeply into the experiences of Hawaiians and other Polynesians who flocked to Lā'ie, Hawai'i, and to Utah, as enthusiastic and faithful members of their church. The church brought them together, but these settlements were also opportunities for the church to exploit the members' labour, and for Polynesians to experience the racism in the Utah church. In the chapter titled "Called to Serve," Aikau gives us the history of the call to members to travel and work in Lā'ie to build permanent structures that would become Brigham Young University Hawai'i and the Polynesian Cultural Center. In addition to the analysis of these ventures as colonial capitalism, Aikau gives us an opportunity to hear the stories of the member-workers themselves and learn what our Hawaiian and Polynesian people went through and thought/think about those experiences. Aikau's following chapter is a stunning work of Indigenous ethnography about the workers who built and first worked at the Polynesian Cultural Center. Many of them viewed their experiences as opportunities to practice and demonstrate their native arts with pride. These were also opportunities for community and sharing knowledge across cultures. For some, this was a place in which to learn their native culture for the first time. One of Aikau's interviewees said, "I learned more about Māori culture than I did in 17 years in New Zealand" (2012: 134).

One of the major achievements of this book, a ha'awina (lesson and gift) for the rest of us, is how Aikau is able to critique the Mormon church seriously for its acts of settler colonial capitalism and racism, and very seriously and honestly honour the members of the church, including her beloved father who has passed, and current members of her close extended family.

The year 2013 brought Noelani Goodyear-Kaʻōpua's *The Seeds We Planted: Portraits of a Native Hawaiian Charter School* (Goodyear-Kaʻōpua 2013). The title of this book is somewhat misleading in two ways: the cover photo shows children planting not seeds, but huli of the kalo (taro) plant. The word "huli" refers not only to the plantable stalk of the kalo, but also to overturning and changing. The subtitle implies that the book is a history or ethnography of a charter school, but the overarching argument and analysis in the book is that schools are primary sites for Hawaiian movements to recover land and sovereignty, as well as to provide Hawaiian-centered education. The introduction to the book is called "Indigenous Education, Settler Colonialism, and Aloha ʻĀina". There Goodyear-Kaʻōpua writes:

> This book follows the work of educators reclaiming public K-12 education as a form of Hawaiian self-determination and sovereign practice in the first decade of the twenty-first century. After a century of assimilationist schooling, Kanaka Maoli communities seized the opportunity to assert a limited measure of autonomy in the settler state's public education system by starting charter schools that made Hawaiian culture, including ʻāina-based knowledge and language, the foundation of their educational programs.
>
> (2013: 5)

A bit farther on she explains, "I chart connections between Hālau Kū Māna [charter school] and broader Hawaiian struggles for cultural persistence, political power, and land" (2013: 7). She goes on to describe and analyze Hawaiʻi's schools as part of the fabric of settler colonialism. She notes, "the Hawaiʻi state public education system is the only [one] in the United States in which Indigenous students comprise the largest proportion" (2013: 7). The middle and upper classes in Hawaiʻi send their children to private schools. Goodyear-Kaʻōpua makes a convincing case that Kanaka taking over schooling presents opportunities for "realizing their own power" (2013: 10). Her introduction also presents a new view of the history of education in Hawaiʻi, which was previously assumed to be controlled by white elites. Her research into the schools of the Hawaiian Kingdom, in which the language was Hawaiian until the late nineteenth century, demonstrates that the vast majority of teachers were Hawaiian, who modified the curriculum taken from American-oriented texts to include Hawaiian knowledge. She also traces the development of the settler state through the history of schooling (2013: 14–23). After giving an analysis of Hawaiʻi as a settler colonial state, Goodyear-Kaʻōpua writes that this book "explores one community's efforts to enact epistemic self-determination and to articulate sovereign pedagogies, working within settler state structures but also trying to imagine and create futures beyond those structures" (2013: 29). In this introduction, she also presents the idea of aloha ʻāina as "a multiplicity of land-centered literacies", and in that section the fullest and most elaborated study of this most important of Kanaka concepts that we have seen up to this point (2013: 31–9). In describing just one of these multiplicities, she writes: "Aloha 'āina centers the cultivation and protection of the relationship of all Kānaka to all elements of our natural world" (2013: 35). This book is a marvelous example of Indigenous participant-observer ethnography honed with situated political analysis.

A Nation Rising: Hawaiian Movements for Life, Land, and Sovereignty, published in 2014, is an edited volume comprised of essays by many actors in these various movements, including the Hawaiian language movement, which, while not specified in the subtitle, is assumed within the text as part of the movements for life, land, and sovereignty (Goodyear-Ka'ōpua et al. 2014). The above-mentioned Noelani Goodyear-Ka'ōpua is one of the editors, joined by non-academic Ikaika Hussey, and Erin Kahunawaika'ala Wright, then-director (at that time) of Native Hawaiian Student Services at UH Mānoa. The volume brings together the photography of Ed Greevy, who documented Hawaiian movements from the late 1960s to the 1990s, with essays by activists and academics, many of whom fill both roles. One of the brilliant achievements of this first-ever book on Hawaiian movements is the ability of these young editors to pull together essays by people of radically different political views, who have clashed in the past both politically and personally.

The introduction by Goodyear-Ka'ōpua is a tour de force framing how these disparate views fit together to forward Kanaka 'Ōiwi goals of cultural, political, and linguistic resurgence. Her research and deep understanding of our language serve as a basis for a section on the Hawaiian term "ea":

> The word "ea" has several meanings. As … Leilani Basham argues, each utterance of the word carries all these meanings at once… Ea refers to political independence and is often translated as "sovereignty." It … carries the meanings "life" and "breath," among other things. A shared characteristic in each of these translations is that ea is an active state of being. Like breathing, ea cannot be achieved or possessed; it requires constant action day after day, generation after generation.
>
> (2014: 3–4)

Ea also means to rise, and was a framing concept for the volume while it was being written and edited, and inspiration for the title. Each of the authors (including me) uses ea and the related concept of aloha 'āina in our chapters. Included in this volume are articles on the struggles over land and water rights, Hawaiian history, the department of Ethnic Studies at UH Mānoa, the US military in Hawai'i, Kanaka student activism at UH, and the recent development of the movement for political independence of Hawai'i.

In 2014, Kamehameha Publishing, associated with the Kamehameha schools, published Kamanamaikalani Beamer's *No Mākou ka Mana: Liberating the Nation*, a work of Kanaka-centered history and geography (Beamer 2014). Beamer uses his training in geography and Hawaiian language to recast the history of the

Hawaiian Kingdom (1840–1893). He convincingly argues that Hawaiian aliʻi were the agents of change in the development of the Kingdom's government, constitutions, laws, and land policies. In addition to combing the Hawaiian language archives here in Honolulu, he traveled to London to study the correspondence between Kanaka monarchs and their emissaries with the British crown government. He presents an Indigenous Hawaiian geographical analysis of land boundaries in that period, using a concept he calls palena, from the word for boundary in Hawaiian. One of the arguments that threads through the book is that the Hawaiian Kingdom period should not be considered a time of colonialism. Rather, the aliʻi selectively appropriated various Western institutions and ways for their own purposes and to benefit their people. Beamer presents the view that the United States is an occupier of Hawaiʻi, rather than a colonizer.[3]

The chapter titles accurately describe the scope of this work: "Ōiwi Agency", "Indigenous Hawaiian Statecraft", "Aliʻi Diplomacy on the World Stage", "Emergence of the Hawaiian State", "Aliʻi Education and Governance", and "Beyond the Occupation".

A student in an undergraduate class of mine said that this work is "a breath of fresh air". Another student found the book refreshing because Beamer's style so closely reflects his upbringing in Hawaiʻi. The book is beautifully illustrated with photographs of important documents, including some of the correspondence between monarchs, maps drawn in the Kingdom period, and works of Hawaiian knowledge reclamation in the Kalākaua period.

Following closely after Beamer is Kapā Oliveira's work of geography, *Ancestral Places: Understanding Kanaka Geographies*, also published in 2014 (Oliveira 2014). This work is firmly rooted in Oliveira's Hawaiian language and geography training. She brings together the important ideas and practices of genealogy, both cosmic and familial, kinship and political structures prior to the formation of the Western-style government, performance cartography, and sensual geography. In each chapter, Oliveira carefully presents and explains both terminology and practice of land use and boundary-making, and their relationships to political structures and to Hawaiian epistemology. The book is satisfyingly drenched in ʻōlelo noʻeau, which she translates as "wise poetic sayings" (2014: xviii). Those sayings feature and Oliveira celebrates the inherent ambiguity and opportunities for kaona ("concealed meanings") so prized by our ancestors. This book is an excellent introduction to Kanaka geography that demonstrates the close connectedness of our language, land, and genealogies.

Finally, another groundbreaking book is kuʻualoha hoʻomanawanui's *Voices of Fire: Reweaving the Literary Lei of Pele and Hiʻiaka* (hoʻomanawanui 2014). The terms Pele and Hiʻiaka literature refers to the many works in Hawaiian about Pele, the volcano deity, and her sister, Hiʻiaka, who takes a coming-of-age epic journey across the island archipelago. This is the first book of criticism and analysis of Hawaiian language literature. Hoʻomanawanui frames each chapter with her autobiographical accounts that link her to the ʻāina and to this genre of Kanaka literature, which is itself a reflection of our and our ancestors' close connection to and identification with our ʻāina. She begins and titles each chapter with a mele (song, poem, etc.) from this literature, artistically using the chants to frame the analysis in each chapter. Hoʻomanawanui uses the idea of genealogy to show how the various texts in this genre are related to each other. Further, she highlights the idea of intellectual history and genealogy in the book. Graphics in the text help the reader to see her mapping of these genealogies. It is important to note here, too, that she frames this book as an analogue to several other works in Indigenous literary studies, naming works by Lisa Brooks, Daniel Heath Justice, Robert Warrior, Jace Weaver, and Craig Womack, among others, "adding a Kanaka ʻŌiwi voice to the ongoing conversation" (2014: xxix).

Readers will find extended interpretations of various episodes and mele in this book, along with clear explanations and revelations of the literary devices used in Hawaiian language literature. Very unlike some discussions of Hawaiian language literature, hoʻomanawanui's book carefully contextualizes each of the texts historically and politically. In doing so, she reveals the colonialist nature of some of the translations in earlier times. By the end, the reader is fully prepared to join with hoʻomanawanui in considering "Pele and Hiʻiaka moʻolelo as a foundation of Hawaiian literary nationalism today, and [understanding] how it continues to inspire Kanaka nationalism via the continuity of our literary and performative arts" (2014: xxxiii).

Conclusions

I have presented here a genealogy of Hawaiian scholarship, roughly dividing works into generations. Each generation draws on the works of the previous generations, overturning some ideas, taking Kanaka concepts further, using the works written by our kūpuna in more thorough ways, each knowing that it is like another stream restored to bring much-needed water to the ʻāina and to the greater sea of our resurgence as Kanaka ʻŌiwi. This is a time for celebrating breakthroughs in both Kanaka thought and intellectual history. My somewhat arbitrary designation of works into generations is in part defined by my sense of whose works build on whose, along with some knowledge of who sat on whose dissertation committees.

The books that I highlighted in the final section on scholarship in 2012–2014 have been written and published, not only as a result of activism and previous scholarship and tutelage by Kānaka, but also within the milieu of global Indigenous academic work. The authors have connections with Indigenous scholars and programs throughout Oceania, as well as Australia, Aotearoa/New Zealand, Okinawa, and the Americas. They attend conferences such as the Native American and Indigenous Studies annual meeting, the Native American Literary Studies annual conference, the World Indigenous Peoples' Conference on Education, and many others that bring us together with Indigenous scholars, both academy- and community-based. The books themselves also reach to non-academic communities, in Hawaiʻi nei, and around the world.

The reader will notice, too, that every one of these works details our aloha ʻāina, our love of and identification with our land. This is characteristic of

Hawaiian-language literature and missing from many works about rather than by Kanaka authors. Our scholarship, our artistic productions, and our daily lives reflect our deep, familial love for our ʻāina.

These texts are but a few of the important works by Kanaka scholars in recent decades and I am delighted to report that many more could have been included, and many, many more are in the works.

Notes

1   Kameʻeleihiwa uses several "metaphors" to describe aliʻi worldview and behavior during the nineteenth century.
2   Other important books were published by Kanaka authors in this era and not mentioned here because I want to focus on those that use the Hawaiian language archive (with one exception).
3   It is important to note, however, as Goodyear-Kaʻōpua does in *A Nation Rising*: "In the last ten years, some scholarship utilizing occupation theory to analyze Hawaiian sovereignty has proposed throwing out the language of colonialism altogether … one might consider that a prolonged U.S. occupation of Hawaiʻi enables the ongoing hegemony of a settler society – settler colonialism" (Goodyear-Kaʻōpua et al. 2014: 19).

References

Aikau, Hokulani K. 2012. *A Chosen People, a Promised Land: Mormonism and Race in Hawaiʻi*. First Peoples: New Directions in Indigenous Studies. Minneapolis: University of Minnesota Press.

Beamer, Kamanamaikalani. 2014. *No Mākou Ka Mana: Liberating the Nation*. Honolulu: Kamehameha Schools Press.

Goodyear-Kaʻōpua, Noelani. 2013. *The Seeds We Planted: Portraits of a Native Hawaiian Charter School*. First Peoples: New Directions in Indigenous Studies. Minneapolis: University of Minnesota Press.

Goodyear-Kaʻōpua, Noelani, Ikaika Hussey, and Erin Kahunawaikaʻala Wright, eds. 2014. *A Nation Rising: Hawaiian Movements for Life, Land, and Sovereignty*. Narrating Native Histories. Durham, NC: Duke University Press.

hoʻomanawanui, kuʻualoha. 2014. *Voices of Fire: Reweaving the Literary Lei of Pele and Hiʻiaka*. Minneapolis: University of Minnesota Press.

Kameʻeleihiwa, Lilikalā. 1992. *Native Land and Foreign Desires: How Shall We Live in Harmony (Ko Hawaiʻi ʻĀina a Me Nā Koi Puʻumake a Ka Poʻe Haole: Pehea Lā E Pono Ai?)*. Honolulu: Bishop Museum Press.

Kauanui, J. Kēhaulani. 2008. *Hawaiian Blood: Colonialism and the Politics of Sovereignty and Indigeneity*. Durham, NC: Duke University Press.

Meyer, Manulani Aluli. 1998. "Native Hawaiian epistemology: Contemporary narratives". Ed.D. diss. Harvard University.

Meyer, Manulani Aluli. 2003. *Hoʻoulu: Our Time of Becoming: Collected Early Writings of Manulani Meyer*. Honolulu: ʻAi Pōhaku Press.

Oliveira, Katrina-Ann R. Kapāʻanaokalāokeola Nākoa. 2014. *Ancestral Places: Understanding Kanaka Geographies*. First Peoples: New Directions in Indigenous Studies. Corvalis: Oregon State University Press.

Osorio, Jonathan Kay Kamakawiwoʻole. 2002. *Dismembering Lāhui: A History of the Hawaiian Nation to 1887*. Honolulu: University of Hawaii Press.

Tengan, Ty P. Kāwika. 2008. *Native Men Remade: Gender and Nation in Contemporary Hawai'i*. Durham, NC: Duke University Press.

Trask, Haunani-Kay. 1993. *From a Native Daughter: Colonialism and Sovereignty in Hawai'i*. Monroe, ME: Common Courage Press.

Trask, Haunani-Kay. 1999. *From a Native Daughter: Colonialism and Sovereignty in Hawai'i*. Rev. edn. Honolulu: University of Hawai'i Press.

Young, Kanalu G. Terry. 1998. *Rethinking the Native Hawaiian Past*. New York: Garland.

12 Placing the city

Crafting urban Indigenous histories

Coll Thrush

Canada Day in Vancouver. Leafy neighbourhoods are noisy with block parties and barbecues, the banks are closed but the bars open, and the grey sand beaches are full of partiers, waiting for the fireworks that will fill the sky with thunderous explosions tonight. The harbour is full of freighters, black and red hulls anchored in deep blue water. Downtown seems of two parts: gleaming white and aquamarine glass high rises in one half, the deep green of Stanley Park's forests in the other. In the background, the mountains of the North Shore rise steeply above Burrard Inlet, all blue-green and stone grey under a clear July sky. Few cities are as beautiful in the summer as Vancouver, few have higher real estate prices, and few so regularly make *The Economist*'s list of most livable cities. Vancouver, in the eyes of many, is an urban paradise.

It is also Indigenous territory. At least three Indigenous First Nations – the Musqueam, the Sḵwx̱wú7mesh, and the Tsleil-Waututh, all related Coast Salish peoples – claim part or all of the city as their traditional territory. This is unceded territory, too; no treaties have been signed between these three peoples and the government of Canada, a fact recently, formally, and unanimously acknowledged by Vancouver's city council. The urban landscape is rich with their historical presence, perhaps best illustrated by their names on the land. One of the best views in the city – one that starts from one of those grey-sand beaches and takes in the harbour and the city and Stanley Park and the mountains – is from a place called Jericho Beach by most Vancouver residents, but which is also known to the Musqueam as ɁiɁálməxʷ, a name meaning either Good Place or Good Spring Water.[1] It was the site of a village until at least the late eighteenth century, when George Vancouver, the first European to explore the region, arrived (Suttles 2004: 571).Visiting Jericho Beach, there is little evidence of ɁiɁálməxʷ, but even – and perhaps especially – on a day of national(ist) celebration like Canada Day, then, there is clearly a deeper story at work here, built into the very landscape of the city itself: urban and Indigenous histories in the same place.

Urban Indigenous people and communities are perhaps the most "unexpected" of "Indians," to borrow Philip J. Deloria's famous turn of phrase (Deloria 2004). Similarly, cities seem unlikely places to find rich, complex, and robust Indigenous histories more generally. The city, as the ultimate expression of colonial modernity, seems to offer little space for Indigenous presence. This has been replicated in both popular culture and most academic studies, in which urban Indigenous people, if they are acknowledged at all, are often portrayed as little more than the collateral damage of settler colonialism: as husks, shells, ghosts, and otherwise inauthentic manifestations of some lost past. These sorts of narratives not only relegate "real" Indigenous people to the pre-urban past; they also elide and negate present-day claims, whether legal or simply social, to urban spaces while also ignoring that fact that in places like North America, Australia, and New Zealand, the majority of Indigenous people now live in places defined by census agencies and other administrative entities as urban. Towns and cities are now at the centre of Indigenous life in these countries, and our urban stories have yet to catch up with this fact.

This chapter is an attempt to challenge the narrative estrangement that renders urban and Indigenous realities as somehow mutually exclusive, arguing instead that the two kinds of past and present are in fact connected, and at times even mutually constitutive. It does so by emphasizing three kinds of Indigenous history in urban places: the presence of local Indigenous peoples in whose traditional (and at times, as in the cases of Vancouver or Australian cities such as Sydney, unceded) territories cities were founded and constructed; the migration of diverse Indigenous peoples to urban places; and the use of Indigenous imagery in the urban imaginary. Along the way, it discusses the kinds of sources that can be useful in limning these kinds of histories. Focusing primarily on the United States, Canada, New Zealand, and Australia, it argues that city-making is a crucial element of settler colonialism and needs to be brought to the centre of the larger stories we tell.

First, however, it is important to note that every city's history will be unique. Most of the cities discussed here are ones that were founded in the nineteenth century, when a certain kind of urban industrial capitalism was ascendant. Despite their local differences, such histories share common ideological, technological, and cultural elements that also make their stories look a lot like each other. Cities with much earlier or later founding dates – for example, Boston in the seventeenth century, in the homeland of the Massachusett people, or the suburbs of Minneapolis-St. Paul in the second half of the twentieth century, amid the territories of the Dakota and Anishinaabeg and the spaces of the Dakota War – will necessarily have significantly different valences and characteristics. The simple fact remains that we have rarely asked the question.

As I have argued elsewhere, every city in a place like the United States or Aotearoa/New Zealand is, by definition, built in Indigenous territory, and the place-stories we tell are implicated in this process (Thrush 2007). Recovering this local Indigenous territoriality often means moving into the ethnographic literature of the peoples and nations in whose territory the city in question was founded. Collections of "folklore" and "mythology," in a place like the San Francisco Bay or Auckland, along with place names that remain on the land in sites like Honolulu or the urban Gold Coast in Australia, can serve as clues to Indigenous worldviews and inhabitance in places where such things seem at first to be masked or even erased. Indeed, "informants" sharing such knowledge with anthropologists and local historians were often speaking to their own people's presence on the land in ways that can be understood as political acts. In the case of ongoing land disputes, for example, such "data" can be critical to documenting and legitimating contemporary Indigenous claims to territory. These kinds of sources can reanimate urban spaces as Indigenous places.

The transformation of these landscapes, however, is at the heart of the urban story. Such transformations – the remaking of watersheds, the emplacement and enforcement of Cartesian grids, and the legal or extralegal expulsion of Indigenous communities – had (and continue to have) profound effects on Indigenous peoples and nationhood. Again, these histories can look much the same across diverse urban spaces; places as far-ranging as Seattle, Victoria, and Vancouver in Coast Salish territories or Melbourne in the homelands of the Kulin Alliance can bear striking resemblances to each other, with their Victorian regulations of morality or their Progressive Era emphases on hygiene and high modernity (Thrush 2006; Keddie 2004; Barman 2007; Stanger-Ross 2008; Edmonds 2010). Often, though, Indigenous people are entirely absent from the engineering documents, city planners' records, or archives related to the development of urban parks; it is exactly this absence, however, that speaks to the larger silencing of Indigenous people and presence in urban spaces. As the aphorism goes, the absence of evidence is not evidence of absence.

At the same time, conflicts over urban sites can attest to the persistence of local Indigenous peoples while drawing attention to the specific urban practices of transformation. Protests over development of midden sites in the East Bay of California, calls for the safeguarding of Indigenous burials at a historic Spanish mission in Los Angeles, or vigils at an ancestral village site threated with condominium development in Vancouver each speak to the ongoing relevance and vitality of "earlier" periods of urbanization. Meanwhile, "supernatural" entities in the urban landscape – urban legends of Indigenous ghosts and hauntings in Seattle, accounts of non-human spirit powers in Perth, or assertions of the presence of ancestors at a downtown church in Honolulu – speak to the continued agency of Indigenous communities and the survival of Indigenous ontologies, embodied in the very spaces and places from which they are believed by many outsiders to be absent.

A second kind of urban history has to do with the in-migration of Indigenous people from territories beyond the city. In the case of the United States, such movements are relatively well-documented. In particular, the federal relocation programs of the 1950s have received a great deal of attention (see, for example, Blackhawk 1995; Fixico 1986; Philip 1985). Such programs often inspired sociological and other studies of urban Indigenous communities; while such works often suffer from a pathologizing emphasis on notions of "acculturation," "alienation," "success," or "failure," they can also be crucial sources for documenting where and when Indigenous communities began to coalesce and organize themselves in urban spaces (see, for example, Ablon 1964, 1965; Chadwick and Strauss 1975; Graves 1970; Gundlach and Roberts 1978; Wagner 1976).[2] Beginning in the 1980s, accounts of urban Native life and community that were based on first-hand accounts began to appear, drawing attention to the challenges of the urban context while also articulating a sense of shared vitality, cultural empowerment, and broadening political and economic engagement. This trend has continued, with works now available on Native communities in quite a few of the nation's large cities, most emerging either out of the community itself or through first-hand relationships between communities and academic researchers (see, for example, Carpio 2011; Danziger 1991; Rosenthal 2012). Often, these studies focus on well-being rather than pathology, while also drawing attention to the broader processes of colonialism that are still faced by urban Indigenous people, with particular attention to the maintenance and sharing of cultural traditions and practices, the development of community institutions, and questions of policy and social justice.[3]

Together, these works support Canadian Métis scholar Chris Andersen's efforts to define the particular characteristics of urban Indigenous communities: economic marginalization; a growing middle and professional class; the experience of social exclusion and outright racism; cultural and legal status diversity, including what he calls "status blindness," produced by the complexities of colonial bureaucracies; the rise of urban Indigenous institutions such as friendship centres; a distinct policy ethos; informal networks of support; continued connections to non-urban communities; struggles over political representation; and the centrality of women (Andersen 2013). Cities, then – to use Renya Ramirez's term – are hubs for Indigenous people and the centre of a powerful form of Indigeneity that links often-distant communities to urban places through migration, kinship, and community organizing (Ramirez 2006).

Urban symbolism, meanwhile, can be crucial to crafting an urban Indigenous history. While towns and cities, in the creation of a story for themselves, often engage in the process that Ojibwe historian Jean O'Brien has called "firsting and lasting," a simultaneous emphasis on colonial origin stories and on identifying the "last Indian" as part of a narrative of Indigenous extinction (O'Brien 2010). But events such the reenactment of a town founding or the anniversary of a massacre or treaty, often lavishly documented in local newspapers, can be crucial to telling the Indigenous story of a city, not least because they often include at least nominal Indigenous participation. Similarly, the use of Indigenous images in creating civic identities, such as the use of totem poles as urban symbols in a place like Seattle, can help us make sense of the ways in which settlers understood a sense of their own engagement with Indigenous peoples. And urban mega-events such as the Olympic Games, whether in Sydney or Vancouver, can speak to the appropriation of Indigenous "heritage" while also highlighting the ways in which living Indigenous people have participated, even if only marginally or as tokens, in such happenings.

The territoriality of local Indigenous peoples, Indigenous migration, and the deployments of Indigenous imagery: when combined, these three kinds of Indigenous history can dramatically alter our understandings of a city's past and present. Whether in the continued claims of several iwi to an ancestral island in Auckland Harbour, the postwar development of a diverse urban Aboriginal community in Sydney's Redfern neighborhood, or the installation of "Native American" statuary at the Capitol in Washington, DC, these kinds of urban history can also dramatically transform the way we think about the Indigenous past and present (and future). We might even take such Indigenous studies practices to the centre of empire. In my own and others' work on Indigenous history in Europe and Great Britain, the story of Indigenous travelers to imperial centres over the past five centuries, along with the accounting of the ways in which the processes and practices of settler colonialism emanated from places like London, can offer up a new kind of globalized Indigenous narrative that challenges the broader shape of world history, which, like urban history more generally, places Indigenous people firmly in the past or uses them as anti-modern metaphors (see, for example, Feest 1999; Vaughan 2008; Flint 2008; Kroes 2014; Thrush 2016).

Lastly, it cannot be overestimated how important it is to engage directly with urban places and spaces in our research. Like the kinds of ethical research with and for Indigenous communities called for by scholars like Linda Tuhiwai Smith, directly encountering the civic landscape offers opportunities that traditional archives do not. Such approaches work particularly well as pedagogy. Asking students to ask questions about the differences between Jericho Beach and ʔiʔálməxʷ, for example – between the site of cedar longhouses and Vancouver Parks Board outbuildings; between clam harvesting and kite flying; between ancient, blurry boundaries between forest and sea and the hard lines that modern environmental practice so often demands – can bring students into a place of deep questioning not only about what happened in that particular place but also about the larger story of settler colonialism.

All told, this set of scholarly approaches and practices, whether based in the archives or in the community and urban landscape, has the capacity to reorient the way we think about both urban and Indigenous pasts and presents (and again, futures). These approaches challenge the narrative estrangement that denies urban Indigenous realities and that keeps the two kinds of history from engaging each other in meaningful ways. Together, they both document and affirm Indigenous presence in the city, while also witnessing and confronting the urban aspects of settler colonialism that have shaped and continue to shape Indigenous lives. Deepening the work of crafting urban Indigenous histories, then, has the potential to enrich our understanding of both Indigenous experience(s) and the nature(s) of empire.

Winter Solstice in Vancouver. The Vancouver Art Gallery sits at the heart of the city. No surprise there: before its role as one of Vancouver's most important cultural venues, it was British Columbia's provincial courthouse. As such, it was also a prime site of Canadian colonialism – it was here that the ban on the potlatch was enforced for nearly seven decades, and the carved words "Land Office" above one side entrance speak to another, not unrelated, kind of expropriation.

It is also, however, a site of contestation; the open courtyard along Georgia Street on the north side of the gallery is Vancouver's leading site of public protest. In midwinter of 2012, it saw hundreds gather as part of the grassroots movement called Idle No More, which had formed only a few weeks earlier, starting in Saskatoon and quickly spreading across the country and attracting solidarity from Indigenous communities and allies around the world. We were there to protest many aspects of Canada's continued assault on Indigenous rights and peoplehood: not just the new bills that had been proposed that fall by the Harper government, all of which impinged on Indigenous sovereignty, but also the tar sands development that threatened to destroy vast swaths of Indigenous territory and the hundreds of missing and murdered Indigenous women whose cases lay fallow across the country. The demonstrators who gathered that day were also there to protest local issues: the ways in which British Columbia continued to stall on the question of Indigenous land title and serve the interests of corporations; the ongoing gentrification of parts of the city where Indigenous people lived; and the continued struggle of Indigenous men, women, and children in places like the Downtown Eastside, where poverty, addiction, and homelessness remained seemingly, but not necessarily inevitably, intractable. In Musqueam songs, Nisga'a prayers, and speeches by Indigenous and allied activists of many ancestries, the Idle No More protests gave the lie to the notion that Indigenous history does not – cannot – exist in urban places. In Vancouver that day, such estrangements fell apart entirely, and scholars would do well to follow their lead.

Notes

1   ʔiʔálməxʷ is pronounced, roughly, "ee-AHL-muh-hw."
2   Similar framings are strongly implied in Kent McKenzie's 1961 semi-documentary film *The Exiles*, set in 1960s Los Angeles.
3   For examples from North America, see Baird-Olson and Ward (2000), Cheshire (2001), Deer (2010), Jackson (2002), Jojola (2000), Krouse (2001), Lobo (1998), Lucero (2010), Newhouse et al. (2012), Sanderson and Howard-Bobiwash (1997) and Lawrence (2004). For an example from Aotearoa/New Zealand, see Gagné (2013).

References

Ablon, Joan. 1964. "Relocated American Indians in the San Francisco Bay Area: Social interaction and Indian identity". *Human Organization*, 23(4): 296–304.

Ablon, Joan. 1965. "American Indian relocation: Problems of dependency and management in the city". *Phylon*, 26(4): 362–371.

Andersen, Chris. 2013. "Urban Aboriginality as a distinctive identity, in twelve parts". In Evelyn Peters and Chris Andersen, eds. *Indigenous in the City: Contemporary Identities and Cultural Innovation*. Vancouver: UBC Press, pp. 51–63.

Baird-Olson, Karren and Carol C. Ward. 2000. "Recovery and resistance: The renewal of traditional spirituality among American Indian women". *American Indian Culture & Research Journal*, 24(4): 1–35.

Barman, Jean M. 2007. "Erasing Indigenous indigeneity in Vancouver". *BC Studies*, 155: 3–30.

Blackhawk, Ned. 1995. "'I can carry on from here': The relocation of American Indians to Los Angeles". *Wicazo Sa Review*, 11(2): 16–30.

Carpio, Myla Vicente. 2011. *Indigenous Albuquerque*. Lubbock: Texas Tech University Press.

Chadwick, B.A. and J.M. Strauss. 1975. "The assimilation of American Indians into urban society: The Seattle case". *Human Organization*, 34(4): 359–369.

Cheshire, T.C. 2001. "Cultural transmission in Urban American Indian families". *American Behavioral Scientist*, 44(9): 1528–1535.

Danziger, Edmund J. 1991. *Survival and Regeneration: Detroit's American Indian Community*. Detroit: Wayne State University Press.

Deer, Sarah. 2010. "Relocation revisited: Sex trafficking of Native women in the United States". *William Mitchell Law Review*, 36(2): 621–683.

Deloria, Philip J. 2004. *Indians in Unexpected Places*. Lawrence: University Press of Kansas.

Edmonds, Penelope. 2010. *Urbanizing Frontiers: Indigenous People and Settlers in Nineteenth-Century Pacific Rim Cities*. Vancouver: UBC Press.

Feest, Christian F. 1999. *Indians and Europe: An Interdisciplinary Collection of Essays*. Lincoln: University of Nebraska Press.

Fixico, Donald L. 1986. *Termination and Relocation: Federal Indian Policy, 1945–1960*. Albuquerque: University of New Mexico Press.

Flint, Kate. 2008. *The Transatlantic Indian, 1776–1930*. Princeton: Princeton University Press.

Gagné, Natacha. 2013. *Being Maori in the City: Indigenous Everyday Life in Auckland*. Toronto: University of Toronto Press.

Graves, T.D. 1970. "The personal adjustment of Navajo Indian migrants to Denver". *American Anthropologist*, 72(1): 35–54.

Gundlach, J.H. and A.E. Roberts. 1978. "Native American Indian migration and relocation: Success or failure". *The Pacific Sociological Review*, 21(1): 117–128.

Jackson, Deborah Davis. 2002. *Our Elders Lived It: American Indian Identity in the City*. Dekalb: Northern Illinois University Press.

Jojola, Theodore S. 2000. *Urban Indians in Albuquerque, New Mexico: A Study for the Department of Family and Human Services*. Albuquerque: University of New Mexico Press.

Keddie, Grant. 2004. *Songhees Pictorial: A History of the Songhess People as Seen by Outsiders*. Victoria: Royal British Columbia Museum.

Kroes, Rob. 2012. *Buffalo Bill in Bologna: The Americanization of the World, 1869–1922*. Chicago: University of Chicago Press.

Krouse, Susan Applegate. 2001. "Traditional Iroquois socials: Maintaining identity in the city". *American Indian Quarterly*, 25(3): 400–408.

Lawrence, Bonita. 2004. *"Real" Indians and Others: Mixed-Blood Urban Native Peoples and Indigenous Nationhood*. Vancouver: UBC Press.

Lobo, Susan. 1998. "Is urban a person or a place? Characteristics of urban Indian country". *American Indian Culture & Research Journal*, 22(4): 89–102.

Lucero, Nancy M. 2010. "Making meaning of urban American Indian identity: A multistage integrative process". *Social Work*, 55(4): 285–305.

Newhouse, David, Kevin FitzMaurice, Tricia McGuire-Adams, and Daniel Jetté, eds. 2012. *Well-Being in the Urban Aboriginal Community: Fostering Biimaadiziwin, a National Research Conference on Urban Aboriginal Peoples*. Toronto: Thompson Educational Publishing, Inc.

O'Brien, Jean M. 2010. *Firsting and Lasting: Writing Indians out of Existence in New England*. Minneapolis: University of Minnesota Press.

Philip, Kenneth R. 1985. "Stride toward freedom: The relocation of Indians to cities, 1952–1960". *Western Historical Quarterly*, 16(2): 175–190.

Ramirez, Renya. 2006. *Native Hubs: Culture, Community, and Belonging in Silicon Valley and Beyond*. Durham, NC: Duke University Press.

Rosenthal, Nicolas G. 2012. *Reimagining Indian Country: Native American Migration and Identity in Twentieth-Century Los Angeles*. Chapel Hill: University of North Carolina Press.

Sanderson, Frances and Heather Howard-Bobiwash, eds. 1997. *The Meeting Place: Aboriginal Life in Toronto*. Toronto: Native Canadian Centre of Toronto.

Stanger-Ross, Jordan. 2008. "Municipal colonialism in Vancouver: City planning and the conflict over Indian reserves, 1928–1950s". *Canadian Historical Review* 89(4): 541–580.

Suttles, Wayne. 2004. *Musqueam Reference Grammar*. Vancouver: UBC Press.

Thrush, Coll. 2006. "City of the changers: Indigenous people and the transformation of Seattle's watersheds". *Pacific Historical Review*, 75(1): 89–117.

Thrush, Coll. 2007. *Native Seattle: Histories from the Crossing-Over Place*. Seattle: University of Washington Press.

Thrush, Coll. 2014. "The iceberg and the cathedral: Place, power, and encounter in Inuit London". *Journal of British Studies*, 53(1): 59–79.

Thrush, Coll. 2016. *Indigenous London: Native Travellers at the Heart of Empire*. New Haven: Yale University Press.

Vaughan, Alden T. 2008. *Transatlantic Encounters: American Indians in Britain, 1500–1776*. Cambridge: Cambridge University Press.

Wagner, J. 1976. "The role of intermarriage in the acculturation of selected urban American Indian women". *Anthropologica*, 18(2): 215–229.

II. All in the family

13 "I do still have a letter"

Our sea of archives

Alice Te Punga Somerville

> My father Albert Joseph Rzoska used to correspond with your [great-]grandfather Hamuera … I do still have a letter written by Hamuera to my father when the family was contesting the sale of shares in Palmerston North.
>
> (Email to author, 2015)

There are as many stories about archives as there are stories kept inside them. What long string of coincidences and near-misses meant certain bits of paper, photos and other items found their way here? Who visits, and for what? What hours is the archive open, and why? Who has quietly slipped what into pockets? What do the cleaners and security people think of the place they look after? We collectively constitute archives. We create them and tend them through our engagements with specific sources alongside each other. Some archives claim to be exhaustive or at least representative. Archives New Zealand, for example, describes itself as "Keeper of the Public Record – the Memory of Government" as if there are no other memories (and no other governments) than those you find housed in its lovely glass and steel structure. Some archives are not housed in a place with the word "archive" painted on the front door. An archive in my line of work is just as likely to be in a wardrobe, cupboard or meetinghouse; Indigenous texts might be carved, oral, written, sung, woven, danced and so on. Archives are places where things, people and ideas come together. In this chapter I engage two texts from the Pacific – an essay by Epeli Hauʻofa and poem by Evelyn Patuawa-Nathan – that argue for assuming Indigenous presence and proximity rather than focusing on distance and loss. I then turn to my own research in order to elaborate how this approach can lead not only to different archives but to different understandings of what one might find there.

Our sea of archives: Indigenous worlds

The Tongan scholar, writer and artist Epeli Hauʻofa tipped the way we think about the Pacific region on its head in his 1993 essay "Our Sea of Islands." The minimization of Indigenous worlds has been central to the colonial project and Hauʻofa suggests that in the Pacific this colonial shrinking has been literal: islands (land) are understood as unsustainably microscopic, remote and disconnected specks in a giant nothingness (sea). However, "the idea of smallness is relative; it depends on what is included or excluded in any calculation of size" (Hauʻofa 1993: 6). Foregrounding traditional perspectives of (and practices in) the region, and migrations through and beyond it, Hauʻofa demonstrates that Pacific people do not experience the region in such limiting terms. In Indigenous understandings of the ocean – sea as presence rather than absence – the region is writ large rather than little. In this context, nations and individual islands are secondary to complex networks of mobility as well as deities and other ancestral giants. Hauʻofa's inversion is often shorthanded as seeing Oceania not as "islands in a far-flung sea" but as "our sea of islands."

Certainly, archives are never complete repositories: archival work can feel scattered. We hope the things we are looking for will be in the places we are looking, but items go missing, were never collected, or are not clearly catalogued. Sometimes you throw a hook over the side hoping for a snapper and get nothing; other days you get a kahawai that turns out to be more interesting than the snapper you thought you were looking for. Some days you pull in a shark and sit there, astonished, wondering how on earth you can deal with a shark, especially when your current frying pan can only fit a much smaller fish. Some days you lose your hook by catching the wharf or a rock, and on those days you just feel thankful you didn't snap your rod (unless you did). Many days you sit there, waiting. Then eat your lunch. Then sit there again, waiting, then go home.

Things can feel even more far-flung when there are so many kinds of archives. Despite the impulse to stay close to home when thinking about where memories reside, oral histories can be as globally scattered as the paper ones. It seems obvious to discuss the early twentieth-century Māori scholar and politician Te Rangihiroa with tribal historians, but after being introduced by a Tuscarora friend working at Yale I enjoyed a conversation with Hal Conklin, an elderly anthropology professor emeritus. One summer day in 1951, Hal (then a PhD student) walked into his advisor's office and was asked to accompany someone around campus so he would be in the right places at the right times to receive an honorary doctorate. At the Bishop Museum in Honolulu, waiting for the archives to open so I could look through Te Rangihiroa's papers there, I chatted with two old women with a punnet of cherries. One of the women, it turned out, started her first job at the museum just before the then-director's passing in 1951; as we snacked, she shared specific memories of talking with him all those years ago. Yes, in both cases this man (in Connecticut, in Honolulu) was Te Rangihiroa.

Hauʻofa suggests that when we think about islands – or, I suggest, archives – as "scattered" and tiny we risk *not* noticing the many forms of connection between them. Describing a friend who travels between Fiji, Honolulu and the United States to exchange goods and nurture relationships, Hauʻofa argues that the actual mobility of Pacific islanders directly undermines outsider assumptions about separation and smallness. This kind of deliberate and reflective noticing is what enabled Hauʻofa to see the region differently. If I have one tip about archival work it relates to note-taking: taking notes about archives – not just about items but about your experience of the archive – makes you more aware of connections. When I'm on the road doing archival research I'm a taker of reflective notes. Mostly these are written in coffee shops, pubs and library cafes; others in planes, bedrooms, kitchens. Usually my notes are in diary form, sometimes they are poems. One year I kept a blog. The actual texts you find are only as good as the notes you take about them, the things you think to record about where they are, and the reliability of your own system that denotes which notes go with which photocopies or photographs. It is immensely valuable to record whatever occurs to you in the space of the archive: associations you make upon engaging with material (which, I assure you, you will not recall later even if they feel unforgettable); impressions, feelings, things you notice about proximity and distance. If you believe in coincidences, archives are full of them. If you don't believe in coincidence, as I happen not to, archives are full of interactions, messages, connections.

"Reach among comments": Indigenous presence

It is possible to engage an archive differently when your focus is on tracing genealogies rather than sketching master narratives. In "Education Week," a short poem included in her 1979 collection *Opening Doors*, Sydney-based Māori poet Evelyn Patuawa-Nathan describes her Aboriginal students reaching for names of relatives written on the walls of the local jail (Patuawa-Nathan 1979). The teacher's initial expectation is that the specific space is empty. The only single-word line in the poem – "bare" – describes the cell in which the teacher stands with her students: jail, after all, is supposed to separate, isolate, singularize. Claims of "bare[ness]" have particular implications in Indigenous contexts, as in places where stories about "vanishing Indians" abound, where "real Natives" are presumed to be physically elsewhere and/or culturally nowhere, and where islands are impossibly microscopic. In Australia, where the poem was written and where it is set, the existence of that settler nation has depended (legally but also rhetorically) on an assumption of *terra nullius*; that the land itself is "bare."

Rather than focusing on bareness and separation, however, Patuawa-Nathan's poem foregrounds the possibility that hope and expectation – and specifically writing – can reframe a context. The "cell / bare / but for the humour of wall graffitti [*sic*]" becomes a space of unexpected reconnection. The "Aboriginal students" can see the same graffiti as the teacher but see it as something else: they "reach among comments for names / of cousins / and brothers / and fathers." Significantly, the students have both desire and ability to differentiate between "comments" and "names" even though the teacher's (governing, powerful, narrating) perspective that the room is "bare" is underpinned by being unable (perhaps undesiring) to see these "comments" and "names" as anything but a generalized "wall graffitti [*sic*]." Without "names" it follows there can be no (genealogical, Indigenous) presence. For the students, the wall is a palimpsest on which layers of writing co-exist; their ability to distinguish between the "comments" and "names" echoes, perhaps, Hau'ofa's distinguishing between the European-imagined "Pacific" and the Indigenous-imagined "Oceania."

Patuawa-Nathan provides a way for us to think about archives: in spaces that are presented to us as "bare" we have the capacity (the responsibility, and ultimately the opportunity) to insist there are "names of cousins and brothers and fathers" there too; and we need to do the time-consuming and risky unbalancing work of "reach[ing] among comments" (in the archives but also in the stories we tell ourselves). Interestingly, "reach[ing] among comments for names" doesn't guarantee the names are there on the wall. However, this is somehow secondary to the act of reaching – and thus reframing – by the powerless. What's interesting about this poem *to me* as a literary scholar is that the kids' act of faith depends not just on prior presence (ancestors and relatives were there) but on prior writerly presence (ancestors and relatives wrote there). The kids reach for an act of writing – and if the writing is there, theirs are not the first hands to have "reach[ed]" for these specific walls. Having "reach[ed] among comments," they have repopulated the space genealogically (cousins, brothers, fathers) and repeated/echoed the prior acts of reaching by their ancestors. The space is one of presence, relationship and fullness rather than absence, isolation and "bare[ness]."

I do not turn to this poem in order to suggest simplistically that all Indigenous people have the ability to see all things because of some kind of intellectual birthright. Instead, I believe this poem reminds us that we all see what we expect, and those expectations are shaped by all kinds of experiences and contexts. Indigenous scholars may not have superpowers but we might bring different questions and assumptions to our work. Abenaki scholar Lisa Brooks, reflecting on her work on early Indigenous writing in the US Northeast, recalls:

> When I first began, I was told that looking for writing by Indians would be like looking for needles in a haystack. But I figured if you knew the names of the needles and the places they are from, it might be easier to find them.
>
> (Brooks 2008: xxxv)

For those of us who are Indigenous scholars we find ourselves sometimes being like the teacher; other times we might identify with the students' desire to seek "names" on walls declared bare. There is no pure location: all of us (Indigenous and non-Indigenous) see certain places as "bare" and all of us struggle sometimes to tell the difference between "comments" and "names" – and all of us benefit from deliberately seeking and cultivating ways of recognizing and reaching for names. How differently might histories – might academia – look if we all always assumed Indigenous presence?

A world of Māori letters

I first read "Education Week" while standing next to a bookshelf in the library at BYU-Hawai'i which has a smaller Pacific collection than the one at University of Hawai'i-Manoa on the same island but stores it on open shelves rather than in a separate room. As a visiting doctoral student, I reached for their copy of Vernice Wineera's *Mahanga* (the first collection of poetry in English by a Māori woman which had been published on that campus in 1978) (Wineera 1978) and as I pulled it out another very slim volume fell out ("māhanga" means twin/s). When I picked up the fallen book, I saw its title was *Opening Doors*. I had never heard of it. After all, Patuawa-Nathan wrote in Sydney and published in Fiji; no story of Māori writing I knew allowed me to imagine her book existed.

I am a Māori literary scholar – and primarily a scholar of Māori literature – and although there is enough published and easily accessible Māori-written literature to keep me busy for the rest of my life, I spend a lot of time in archives. Partly this is because my research has been under the influence of the "historical turn" in Indigenous literary studies. But I also came to the archives because like Hauʻofa, who writes in the early moments of "Our sea of islands" that it was his students at USP who forced him to rethink the story of the Pacific he was telling them, "the faces of my students continued to haunt me mercilessly" (Hauʻofa 1993: 5). I wanted to tell my students a more expansive Māori literary history than I was reciting in lectures. Responding to Penny van Toorn who, in the context of Australian literary studies, asks what we notice when we consider Indigenous "cultures of reading and writing" (van Toorn 2006) I reframed my focus on what I came to call "Māori acts of writing." For the sake of my students in Wellington, the place where my tribe has lived – and written – for many years, I started "reach[ing] among comments for names." My work has become, at its heart, about the world of Māori letters where "letters" is understood in three ways: the uses to which Māori people have put alphabetic writing; the body of writing produced by Māori people; and written Māori correspondence.

In May 1816 Mowhee, a Northerner about whom I've written elsewhere (Te Punga Somerville 2014), who had moved to Norfolk Island as a child and relocated to Australia as a teenager before returning home to New Zealand, arrived in London. The Church Missionary Society (CMS) had recently commenced regular meetings about foreign missions, including the primary mission to the Māori people via Samuel Marsden who was chaplain of the NSW colony based in Parramatta (near Sydney), but had anticipated a one-way flow of people between "home" and missions. However, they accepted responsibility for this young man who had stayed with Marsden in Parramatta; under the care of the CMS Mowhee continued his education and even taught in London before perishing from disease there later in the year. Before his passing, Mowhee was asked to write a memoir which was posthumously published as a religious tract in several forms.

I first read Mowhee's memoir in Hawai'i after the Bishop Museum archive, where I was researching Te Rangihiroa and eating cherries, had closed for the day. Friends had suggested I visit another small archive in Honolulu; one had heard of some Māori writing at the Mission Houses Museum. (No name, no place. A needle in a haystack.) I later, hopefully but unsuccessfully, searched for an original (in Mowhee's hand?) at the University of Birmingham where the official CMS archive is held. When I asked an archivist there about the paucity of Māori materials she explained that everything relating to that mission had moved to New Zealand so people could visit the archive more easily. While this makes a kind of sense, this repatriation implied the rest of the CMS archive was now "bare"; surely all Māori material was tied to the New Zealand mission? Māori experiences always extend beyond geographic or institutional bounds; as long as we assume that Māori engagements with the CMS all happened in New Zealand, logically Mowhee (like Patuawa-Nathan) can't exist.

As I remade my "Māori literature" powerpoint each year, adding and extending as I conducted more archival research, I found that genre boundaries collapsed, and new time periods and places of active Māori writing became visible. A story that used to start with specific publications in New Zealand in 1972, then 1951, now starts with a writer in London in 1816. My search for writing (by Te Rangihiroa) took me to place (Honolulu), which took me to writing (by Mowhee), which took me to place (Sydney, London). I do not aim to revise a canon of Māori literature to a new full authorized state of completeness. Instead, I ask how our worlds might look when we imagine (even assume) that our stories about ourselves (including comfortable stories that have been useful to us) could be closing us off to fully seeing our pasts, our presents and our futures.

The world of a Māori letter

There is an old black and white photo I love. The composition is beautiful: it's all angles and light and shade. At the center of the scene is a man at a desk engaged in the task of writing as I know it. Leather-bound books sit in a curtained bookcase over his shoulder. Pens and a typewriter are not the only instruments in the room: a piano, metronome and sheets of music are behind his back. He is making use of natural light coming through the window, reading something that's been typed, holding a pen in one hand, quietly enjoying the opportunity to sit with and among words. The original photo is at my aunty's house because the man is my great-grandfather, Hamuera Hautu Irirangi Te Punga. It was taken at Concordia Lutheran seminary in Springfield, Illinois, where he was training to be a pastor, which means it dates from sometime between August 1906 and November 1912. We could see this image of an Indigenous man in a starkly European (Euroamerican) scene as an anachronistic juxtaposition, like the woman in regalia having her nails done in Deloria's *Indians in Unexpected Places* (2004), but I just see my relative in a room, writing.

Hamuera was a prolific writer, and his letters (like his descendants) are everywhere. Because the Lutheran Church in New Zealand, which Hamuera served for the rest of his life, is part of the Lutheran Church of Australia, in 2011 I asked the Adelaide-based LCA archives if they had files for past pastors. An archivist replied that they had a slim file for Pastor Te Punga. Because I was on sabbatical and already in Australia, I made the trip. In Adelaide I found documents, photographs and correspondence, including two letters Hamuera had written from Springfield – perhaps at that desk in the photo – in 1906 and 1907 (Te Punga Somerville 2013). The first letter is in Māori (his first language); in 1907 he wrote in English (his second). Both letters are addressed to Blaess, the German pastor based in Taranaki where we come from, and in both Hamuera writes about the difficulty of all classes being taught in German (his third); this made learning Latin (his fourth language) particularly difficult. The archivist explained that one of Pastor Blaess's sons later served as seminary principal and archivist in Australia;

the Blaess family is thus especially well represented and, guilty by association, so is Hamuera. Since then, I've found his letters at several archives in New Zealand as well as in Illinois, Missouri and Indiana. Hamuera married a German American woman, my great-grandmother Lydia, and in 2012 my parents and I spent a memorable two days with relatives in Charlotte, NC, where we laughed and cried our way through letters he'd sent to their parents.

My favorite of Hamuera's letters is the one from 1906: it is the first example of writing in the Māori language I have seen by a direct ancestor, although I know there will be more when I look for them. Because of the way Māori history has turned out, with the exception of a short telegram sent by Hamuera's eldest son in his role as an officer in the Māori Battalion during World War II, it is also the last. Or it was until my nephew Matiu started to write at his Māori immersion school. The 1906 letter can be read by itself, on its own terms, but it is richer – and indeed it is only visible – when considered within the world of the photo, the other letters, the telegram, the Lutheran archive and the great-granddaughter who only has the ability to write in English.

As for me and my writing, I started writing this chapter a million times, and almost gave up (and I'm sure the editors of this volume almost gave up on me). Then one morning, when I was about to send an email to apologize profusely and withdraw from the project, I received an email from a mutual descendant of my great-great-grandmother Ripeka Karena. He wrote to make contact; to connect. He was exploring the broader links between the various descendant lines of this fascinating ancestor we share, and held some correspondence between two cousins: Albert Rzoska and Hamuera Te Punga. The email, which explicitly links letters with land and family, nudged me to keep writing. Like Patuawa-Nathan's students, I find myself reaching among comments for Hamuera's name. As I do so, I become aware of the vast – the oceanic – world of Māori letters, and the many, many more letters yet to come.

References

Brooks, Lisa. 2008. *The Common Pot: The Recovery of Native Space in the Northeast.* Minneapolis: University of Minnesota Press.

Deloria, Philip. 2004. *Indians in Unexpected Places.* Lawrence: University Press of Kansas.

Hau'ofa, Epeli. 1993. "Our sea of islands". In Vijay Naidu, Epeli Hau'ofa and Eric Waddell. *A New Oceania: Rediscovering Our Sea of Islands.* Suva: The University of the South Pacific, pp. 2–16.

Patuawa-Nathan, Evelyn. 1979. *Opening Doors.* Suva: South Pacific Creative Arts Society.

Te Punga Somerville, Alice. 2013. "'My words shall not come back void': Pastor Hamuera Te Punga, multilingualism, and the archive". *Journal of Friends of Lutheran Archives*, 23.

Te Punga Somerville, Alice. 2014. "Living on New Zealand street: Maori presence in Parramatta". *Ethnohistory*, 61(4): 655–669.

van Toorn, Penny. 2006. *Writing Never Arrives Naked: Early Aboriginal Cultures of Writing in Australia.* Canberra: Aboriginal Studies Press.

Wineera, Vernice. 1978. *Mahanga.* La'ie: BYU Hawai'i/Polynesian Cultural Center.

14 History with Nana

Family, life, and the spoken source

Aroha Harris

My nana – my paternal grandmother Violet Otene Harris (1922–2004) – had a recurring role in my research for many years. She lent her skill as a composer of *waiata* (songs) to my high-school speechmaking, and her recounting of tribal traditions wove its way into my undergraduate Māori Studies essays. She was my go-to source of *hapū* (tribal kinship group) history. In the 1990s, Nana became a key interview contributor, alongside several others, who indulged my interrogation of their lives for the sake of multi-year post-graduate research projects. This chapter pauses on a particular set of life history interviews with her, spoken sources that hold their own amid the myriad written sources that fuel historical writing.[1] While Nana's interviews anchor this chapter, the questions it addresses are raised well beyond the recorded narrations of her memories and experiences. What historical light do they shed? And how ought they be read, or listened to, in relation to the other sources, textual sources, on which historians are so quick to rely? These questions seek to understand the value of life histories as both source and method in Māori history, and perhaps Indigenous history more generally.

Context is everything

In history, context is everything. And in doing history with Nana, context abounds. First, there is Nana's context, the life history that is both the substance and the frame for her interviews. From birth till death she lived almost entirely in the settlement of Mangamuka, Hokianga, in the Far North of Aotearoa New Zealand. The tenth in a family of eight girls and seven boys, six of whom died as children, she married locally, in 1938, my grandfather, Karanga Titipa Harris (1917–1979). They established their home, raised their family, and farmed at Mangamuka.

Bringing in my context – that is, the context of interviewer, academic, researcher, and historian – I was interested in Nana's (and Grandpa's) life in the 1950s and 1960s. I wanted to know about their farming experience, particularly as it intersected with government policies on Māori land. I asked about Nana and Grandpa's roles in the migrations of their children from Mangamuka to Auckland and other cities – they would have been counted among the statistics that saw the Māori population migrate to city centers in unprecedented proportions.[2] Woven through these discussions, I was interested in Nana and Grandpa's roles at that most important of community institutions, Mangamuka Marae, including the operation of local organizations like the tribal committee and how community leadership functioned.[3]

There are other contexts to account for here: the context of our grandmother–granddaughter relationship; and the context of other interviews – interviews I undertook on the same subjects, for the same projects; and interviews Nana gave to other students and researchers, with projects of their own. I am sure Nana's agreement to be interviewed was due in large part to the love between a nana and her mokopuna (grandchild). And certainly, being her grandchild had its benefits. For example, Nana allowed me access to some of the minutes of the Mangamuka Tribal Committee. However, that access was not immediate; it had to be worked out and worked for, and came very late in the research process. Nana could never be taken for granted, even though each time she agreed, the more likely it seemed she would agree again. Nonetheless, I do not think my being her granddaughter was the only reason Nana agreed. To an extent I was merely one among a steady stream of young (and not so young) mokopuna (grandchildren), students, film-makers and seekers of whānau and hapū histories who sought her guidance and views. For sure, our family relationship probably meant I had an access to Nana that others did not. But her participation cannot be separated from the fact she was a lively, supportive, and patient contributor to many projects and a great advocate for education and te reo Māori (the Māori language), her willingness to be interviewed a practical expression of those dynamics.

Problems and ethics

The interviews at the heart of life histories can be problematic, as can any of the sources on which history relies. Though largely unstructured, they are not free-flowing narrations without purpose or design. They are undertaken entirely inside a research-based relationship, organized around questions the interviewer introduces, which the interview contributor answers in that moment. Neither interviewer nor interview contributor knows where the conversation will take them. Nor are the interviews contained in the recording alone. In a Māori context they are typically preceded by rituals of encounter, often including important questions about the current wellbeing of families. Once the recordings end, the exchange of acknowledgments follow; the sharing of food probably expected. Often a signal for children and mokopuna to re-enter the room, the post-recording component of the interviews is a useful reminder of the way that my search for oral history has interrupted continuous lives and also, as Hirini Kaa points out, the multiple demands for people's time (Kaa 2000: 18).

In these circumstances, as in all research relationships, ethics are important – and not simply those for which university ethics committees grant approval using meticulously crafted documentation, but also the ethics that reside with the interview contributors, their families and communities. Several familiar guidelines outline what these might be, such as those proposed by Linda Smith for researching among Māori – *aroha ki te tangata* (respect for people) and *kānohi kitea* (the seen face) for example (Smith 1999: 120). Several Māori I have interviewed have been distinctly indifferent toward the paperwork that accompanies research interviews, including consent forms, project outlines, and letters of introduction, and the ethical assurances they contain – but they have not been unconcerned about ethical responsibility. When the researcher and researched are connected by *whakapapa* (genealogy, blood lines), as with any nana and her mokopuna, ethical reasoning may well be infused with cultural and familial considerations. Often who the researcher *is* provides access to the *kōrero* (talk) of contributors and, as Bernadette Arapere infers, the researcher does not stand alone but stands within his or her own *whānau* (extended family). More context: who the whānau is might also influence access (Arapere 1999: 30). Furthermore, as Kaa observes, the agreement and participation of contributors ultimately rests on their "aroha and understanding" and their "trust in me ... to treat their words with due respect and care" (Kaa 2000: 18).

Thus it helps to be guided not only by disciplinary and university expectations, but also the expectations of the people among whom the interviews are conducted. When those people are also *whanaunga* (relations), it is useful to consider the ways that subjectivity occurs – whether Nana's subject position as she felt, remembered, and retold her life stories, or my subject position as her admiring mokopuna injecting her conversation with my historian's questions. For sure, subjectivity can be difficult to contend with in history writing. Yet it is practically a requirement of Māori scholarship. Danny Keenan, for example, has articulated a range of Māori customary processes and frameworks through which Māori constructed tribal knowledge of the past. He pays particular attention to "whakapapa as the primary organising device" of those histories, proposing it as the main frame for controlling and structuring Māori history (Keenan 2000). Few Maori historians would disagree, and none who share either Charles Royal's position that "there is no such thing as Maori history, only tribal history" or Joseph Pere's that only those who *whakapapa* (genealogically link) to an iwi (tribe) ought to be considered to write that iwi's history (Royal 1992: 9; Pere 1991: 45).

Doing history with Nana – among my own – fits easily with these ideas, and their implied demand for a certain level of cultural cognition from the researcher. They also open up the possibility of producing histories that are not simply about an impersonalized "other," nor even an amorphous, generic "us." Rather, it gives Māori historical subjects the "mana and identity" for which Pere has argued (1991: 30). It locates whānau, family, as the centrifugal force in history, bringing into focus the distinctive subject position – including the problems it entails – of nana and mokopuna, researched and researcher. In this way, the implicit subjectivity of the interviews can be embraced rather than avoided providing, Maori Marsden suggests, an effective opportunity to reconcile the problems with it. Marsden declares his approach as not only subjective but also "passionate." However, he also states that when "viewing attitudes from within the culture ... the writer must unmask" his or herself (Marsden 1992: 143). This unmasking includes being honest about the subjectivity (and *whakapapa*) that exists – admitting, for example, that perhaps Nana, and others, told me some things not just because of what I asked, but also because of who I am. Such an approach in no way absolves the resulting history from any inherent tensions, but it does allow for clarity about them.

Life as history

Māori life histories are grounded in the Māori world, and told with Māori voices. They provide important narratives, interested in daily life and concerned with local needs. Yet the potential of life history can been downplayed, reduced to the role of offering perspective or examples of personal experience against more dominant written sources, particularly the vast deposits of government archives. Even treating life histories as narratives to be corroborated or contradicted – which is important – can limit their potential. Certainly life histories help to counter-balance the dominance of the state's records in constructing Māori history, even when the state is integral to the history being told. They present rich and deep narratives of how (perhaps if) families and communities engaged with Māori policy and with demographic change. And they encourage the narrators to contemplate what was (and is) important about those engagements and why. The examples are plentiful, and enlightening, as the history I undertook with Nana has demonstrated.

Violet and Karanga farmed together from the late 1930s until Karanga's death in 1979, earning a modest income from running a herd of dairy cows. Like others of his generation, Karanga supplemented that income by taking waged work when it was available. The area of land they farmed was not huge – the main part comprised some seventeen hectares, and Karanga also leased some neighboring paddocks. Importantly, the land was ancestral, a tangible remnant that had survived the processes of colonization which had steadily transferred Māori land out of Māori ownership to make it available for Pākehā settlement. Karanga's mother, Erina (nee Rakena), called on him to take up responsibility for the land which had passed down the generations to her and her siblings, and which would eventually pass to Karanga and his. Like so much communally owned Māori land, it was eventually swept up in the comprehensive program of Māori land title improvement. Begun in the 1920s, title improvement aimed at reorganizing Māori land titles, ostensibly to consolidate the typically scattered interests of individual and related groups of owners. One of the aims was to reduce the number of owners in individual blocks of land to simplify the titles and make it easier therefore to include it in the state's programme of Māori land development. More generally, Māori land policy was underpinned by long-standing goals to integrate Māori people into New Zealand's mainstream. In the government's view, communal ownership of Māori land hindered not only the development of the land but also the general advancement of the Māori people and their capacity to adapt to the modern world (Harris 1997).

Violet and Karanga were farming under the Māori land development program in the 1950s when Karanga entered into a family arrangement that reorganized the land interests of the wider whānau, on his mother's side. Facilitated and effected by the Māori Land Court, the arrangement included Karanga's siblings, their aunts, uncles and cousins. The upshot was that Karanga and his siblings would become the main group of owners in the Mangamuka property, but would give up their rights in other lands in favor of their relations. Though such arrangements have long been the subject of criticism from Māori, in this case the whānau seemed quite comfortable with the process and its outcome, which effectively realigned the group of titles to reflect the way whānau members had already arranged themselves on the lands concerned. However, Karanga drew a clear line when the Department of Maori Affairs, the agency responsible for Māori land development, urged him to seek sole title to the Mangamuka property. This could be arranged, with the department's help, by having Karanga's siblings transfer their interests to him. And it would be more fitting, in the age of integration, for Karanga to have sole title given he was the one living on and farming the property, while the others had all moved away. However, according to Nana, who viewed sole ownership as providing a level of security for their growing family, Karanga was happy to carry on farming while his siblings shared the title alongside him. In his opinion, the land was their inheritance and they should all maintain their interests wherever they lived.[4] Thus, whānau context and ethos were central to the way Karanga engaged with the title improvement policies that were presented to him, an approach that is far more easily discerned in Nana's life history than the archives of the Department of Māori Affairs, which suggest Karanga was unable to encourage his siblings to agree to transfer their interests. These two narratives do not necessarily contradict each other, but nor are they corroborative. They are, as I have described elsewhere, concurrent – moving with and against each other, sometimes easily and sometimes in tension (Harris 2008).

And so Violet and Karanga continued to farm. One by one their children left home, most of them moving to the nearest city, Auckland. There they set up their new homes and gave birth to the next generation of mokopuna, taking their part in the mass migrations of Māori to the cities in the 1950s and 1960s. Histories of these migrations have tended to gloss over rural Māori homelands, regarded as in decline and becoming less and less relevant, while emphasizing urbanization as a burdensome and destructive process that has effectively defined Māori ever since. However, emerging Māori scholars such as Melissa Matutina Williams (2015) have disrupted that line of analysis and proposed a far more complicated process in which Māori both maintained responsibilities to their rural homelands *and* created tribally inspired spaces in the distant city, keeping the kainga rua, the two homes, connected in dynamic ways. The dynamics of these connections are reflected in the commentary of the era, with Revd Rua Rakena reasoning that as they moved to the unfamiliar city Māori would continue to seek each other out to "give expression to their traditional and cultural inherencies" as evidenced by plans to build extra-tribal marae at Christchurch and Auckland (Rakena 1961: 633). Leo Fowler agreed, predicting that Māori identity would become stronger not weaker as the years passed, and pointing out that Māori would continue to return to their tribal marae to "refresh the springs" of their Māori ways of being (*Te Ao Hou* 1960: 49). Home communities would thus remain relevant, charged – for example – with keeping marae alive and functioning.

These ties and connections happened in the specifics of daily life. One of the many examples available in Violet's life history concerns that most basic of needs, kai (food). When their children and mokopuna visited, she and Karanga would often provision them with food to take back to Auckland – *kūmara* (sweet potatoes) and other vegetables, home-killed beef or pork, depending on what was available at the time. If supplies were plentiful, the kai might be redistributed among family members in Auckland.[5] The provision of kai was not simply a matter of contributing to the family pantry, though that was surely an important element, particularly if families were stretched financially. "Kai from home" was a fact of city living for many Māori who hungered for the delicacies and family recipes with which they had grown up – boil-up, toheroa, and smoked mullet. But the food did more than satiate appetites. The sharing of kai was also often accompanied by social and cultural exchanges, whether by informally gathering at a relation's home to share a meal and news from home or gathering for "a good feed" at a dance or after church on Sundays.[6] Thus food holds a particular eminence in many Māori life histories of the era, identifying Māori in the city as similar to each other while also signifying connections to the individual homes (including tribal sources of food) from which Māori migrated to the cities. Kōrero about kai exemplifies a specific contribution to the much larger postwar project of putting down Māori roots in the city while retaining tribal life-ways.

Further examples from Violet's life histories, among others, could build a fuller picture of Māori lives in the 1950s and 1960s. However, the few examples summarized here are sufficient to make some worthy concluding remarks about doing history with Nana, doing history from an inherently subject position. Life histories, particularly the oral history component, are well-suited to Māori scholarly approaches to the past. They are not unproblematic, although embracing the problems, particularly the subjectivity, provides an access to dealing with them. Even with their problems, life histories still provide illuminating sources that can be read with and against the conventional archives and manuscripts on which writers of Māori history usually depend. For example, with its detail and interest in the mundane, Nana's life history sheds important light on historical understandings of Māori during a period of unprecedented change. It shows the ongoing relevance of the home community even as its population moved away, and pitches Māori as engaging intelligently with the policies and circumstances of the time in ways that gave weight to Māori ways of being. The picture it provides is fruitful and particularized, showing the unprecedented demographic change that characterized the period as complex and nuanced, and not necessarily the lineal, permanent and irreversible process that the history books usually depict.

Notes

1   Violet Otene Harris, interviewed by Aroha Harris, October 23, 1995, July 2–3, 1998, and October 8, 2000.
2   Between 1945 and 1966 the proportion of Māori living in urban centres more than doubled from 26 to 62 percent; by 1990 that proportion reached more than 80 percent (King 1992: 289; Pool 1991: 154; Harris 2008).

3   In this context *marae* means the complex of tribal community buildings and grounds
    used for a range of community gatherings, usually consisting of a meeting house,
    dining hall and ablution block and sometimes extending to include a sports ground,
    church and/or *kōhanga reo* (Māori language nest or pre-school).
4   Māori land policy and legislation has moved on considerably since the 1950s, and as
    the decades have passed the whānau of Violet and Karanga have been able to reorganize
    their interests under a trust.
5   Margaret Harris, interviewed by Aroha Harris, May 28, 1998.
6   Letty Brown, interviewed by Aroha Harris, May 24–27, 1998; Margaret Harris
    interview; Williams (2010: 128).

References

Arapere, Bernadette. 1999. "'Maku ano hei hanga i toku nei whare': Hapu dynamics in the Rangitikei area, 1830–1872". MA thesis, University of Auckland.

Harris, Aroha. 1997. "Maori land title improvement since 1945: Communal ownership and economic use". *New Zealand Journal of History*, 31(1): 132–152.

Harris, Aroha. 2008a. "Ngā Tāone Nui – Māori and the city". *Te Ara – Encyclopedia of New Zealand*. Accessed 2 September 2014, teara.govt.nz/en/nga-taone-nui-maori-and-the-city/sources.

Harris, Aroha. 2008b. "Concurrent narratives of Maori and integration in the 1950s and 60s". *Journal of New Zealand Studies*, Stout Research Centre, Victoria University of Wellington, pp. 139–155.

Keenan, Danny. 2000. "Ma Pango Ma Whero Ka Oti: Unities and fragments in Maori history". In Bronwyn Dalley and Bronwyn Labrum, eds. *Fragments: New Zealand Social Policy and Cultural History*. Auckland.

King, Michael. 1992. "Between two worlds". In Geoffrey Rice, ed. *The Oxford History of New Zealand*. 2nd edn. Auckland.

Marsden, Maori. 1992. "God, man and universe: A Maori view". In Michael King, ed. *Te Ao Hurihuri: The World Moves On*, rev. edn. New Zealand.

Pere, Joseph. 1991. "Hitori Maori". In C. Davis and P. Lineham, eds. *The Future of the Past: Themes in New Zealand History*. Palmerston North.

Pool, Ian. 1991. *Te Iwi Maori: A New Zealand Population Past, Present and Projected*. Auckland.

Rakena, Revd R.D. 1961. "Some comments on the Hunn Report on Maori affairs". *New Zealand Methodist Times*, 25 March.

Royal, Te Ahukaramu Charles. 1992. *Te Haurapa: An Introduction to Researching Tribal Histories and Traditions*. Wellington.

Smith, Linda. 1999. *Decolonizing Methodologies: Research and Indigenous Peoples*. London.

Te Ao Hou: A New World. 1960. 32: 49.

Williams, Melissa Matutina. 2010. "'Back-home' and home in the city: Māori migrations from Panguru to Auckland, 1930–1970". PhD thesis, University of Auckland.

Williams, Melissa Matutina. 2015. *Panguru and the City: Kainga Tahi, Kainga Rua: An Urban Migration History*. Wellington.

15 Elder Brother as theoretical framework

Robert Alexander Innes

Recently Indigenous Studies scholars have employed traditional stories as a means to assist them in gaining a better understanding of Indigenous people's perspectives of their historic and contemporary realities (e.g., Martin 2012; Doerfler et al. 2013). These authors demonstrate the central importance of Indigenous stories and therefore Indigenous knowledge to Indigenous Studies. What becomes apparent is that in order to better understand Indigenous people, it is crucial to become familiar with certain central Indigenous cultural concepts. Indigenous cultural knowledge can be employed as a theoretical framework as a means to explain Indigenous peoples' views, thoughts, and motivations.

This chapter explores how I utilized traditional stories of Elder Brother to explain the connection between Indigenous cultural knowledge and the interactions of contemporary members of Cowessess First Nation. The basis of this chapter is the notion that historically, traditional stories governed peoples' interactions. In my work, I applied traditional stories from Cowessess First Nation, a community located in the southeastern portion of the province of Saskatchewan, comprised primarily of Plains Cree, Saulteaux (Plains Ojibwe), Assiniboine, and Métis, as a way to explain the way in which contemporary kinship practices continue to guide interactions of Cowessess people. American anthropologist Alanson Skinner collected the Elder Brother stories I used as the basis for my study when he visited Cowessess in 1913; they were published in *American Folklore* in 1914. The contention here is that the Elder Brother stories are the basis for the kinship practices of contemporary people from Cowessess First Nation. Working toward that understanding begins with an examination of how stories worked in traditional societies.

Spiritually/supernaturally based stories such as the *Wísahkécâhk* or Elder Brother stories express certain values central to the culture.[1] In Cree, the two main categories of stories are *âtayôhkêwina* and *âcimowina*. *Âtayôhkêwina* refer to the ancient stories, while *âcimowina* are the stories of more recent times. The stories have been understood by some scholars to progress in a somewhat linear fashion from the very old stories to the more recent. As Brightman states in talking about the Rock Cree of Northern Manitoba, "events in *âcaoohkiwina* are understood as temporally antecedent to those in *âcimowina* and comprise most of what is conventionally labeled as 'myth'" (Brightman 1989: 6). Eva Mary Linklater explains for the Nelson House Cree, also from northern Manitoba, the stories within *âtayôhkêwina* are further divided into four subcategories – the beginning of time (*Mimoci Kiyahs*), ancient time (*Mawac Kiyahs*), long ago (*Kiyahs*) and more recent time (*Anohciki*). She states that the

> Cree notion of *kayahs*, a long time ago, is without calendrical years; it is a single time beyond living memory. It is a mythic time in which the creation story and subsequent history were acted on the landscape of north central Manitoba ... These stories are validated by our elders and they are witnessed on the land.
>
> (Linklater 1994: 32)

Linklater explains:

> It is said that in *Kiyahs*, that there were many beings that are different from today. The *Mimikwisihwahk* were the water people who could go through rock. Their house and canoe was located at *Wahskahihkahn awka Cimahn* and here they continue to reside. There was *Mihsihpihsew*, the water lynx and *Wasahkacahk*, the transformer. A conflict between these two beings resulted in a great flood over the land. Muskrat then brought *Wasahkacahk* a dab of dirt on his paw, and from this he recreated the earth and made it livable for Cree people. In gratitude, *Wasahkacahk* gave muskrat a special place to live, a river (*Wahcasko-sipih*) and a lake (*Wahcasko-sahkahikahn*). Muskrat's relatives continued to be found here in great numbers until inundation by Churchill River diversion. *Wasacahkacahk* then began his travels, changing the animals and the land into what they are today. In his journey, he was always hungry and continually trick other animals into becoming his meal ... Most importantly, however, as *Wasacahkacahk* continued his travels through the land, he left behind marks of his passing so future people would know of his presence ... at *Otitiskiwihnihk* he left his footprints in the cliff, giving rise to *Otitiskihwin-sahkahihkahnihk*, the Lake of the Footprints. It is on Footprint Lake that the Nelson House people have now chosen to reside.
>
> (Linklater 1994: 67–68)

She adds, "That many of these sites continue to be remembered at all, in spite of their current situation beneath several feet of water, emphasized their importance to sense of place and sense of identity for the Nelson House people" (1994: 63).

Though there is a temporal distinction between the two sets of stories, there was, however, overlap between the two. Brightman, for example, states that *âcimowina* "focus on human characters, but this is not their defining feature since humans figure also in *âcaoohkiwina*" (Brightman 1989: 7). That is *âtayôhkêwina* and *âcimowina* are not completely distinct from each other as they "are temporally situated in a kind of 'historical' time possessing continuity with the situation and narration." As Winona Wheeler points out, echoing Linklater, "*âtayôhkêwina* are sacred stories of the mystical past when the earth was shaped, animal peoples conversed, and Wisakejac transformed the world" (Wheeler 2005: 202). However, *âcimowina* also includes mythical elements (Brightman 1989: 7). Wheeler explains that:

âcimowina are stories of events that have come to pass since *Wisakejac's* corporeal beingness transformed into spirit presence, that there are many different kinds of overlapping and related *kayâs âcimowina*, stories about long ago, that are often infused with the sacred.

(Wheeler 2005: 202)

Brightman says that *âcimowina* stories can relate true events that can be old or contemporary, funny or serious, but also notes that they may not all be factual and could contain supernatural characters. According to him *kayâs âcimowina* "refers to stories which are temporally remote from the situation of narration" (Brightman 1989: 7). Therefore, *âtayôhkêwina* has influenced the way in which *âcimowina* can be told because it allows for the inclusion of spiritual components into stories of relative recent times.

Âtayôhkêwina contain many characters known as *âtahôhkanak*, the mythical beings that helped shaped the earth and its people. Neal McLeod explains that "*âtayôhkanak*, which means 'spiritual helpers,' spiritual grandfathers and grandmothers. [*Âtayôhkêwina*] are essential because they give insight into the way in which Cree people related to their ecology and the environment, and with other beings" (McLeod 2007: 17). These characters include Pine Root and Beaded Head, *mêmêkwêsiwak*, or the little people, Thunderbird, the Great Serpent/Lynx, that caused the great flood, the *Pâhahk*, the skeleton, and the *Wîhtikôw*, the cannibal that preys on human flesh, and of course *Wîsahkécâhk*, Elder Brother (Cuthand 1988: 197; Carlson 2009: 359). According to Nathan Carlson's oral historical research of Cree and Métis in Northern Alberta, *Wîhtikôw* is one character that has crossed the boundary from *âtayôhkêwina* to *kiyâs âcimowina* (Carlson 2009: 386). This opens the possibility of thinking about other *âtahôhkanak*, such as Elder Brother, who may have also made that journey. For example, McLeod notes that,

The narratives of *wîsahkêcâhk* should be seen as part of the *genre* of sacred stories, *âtayôhkêwina*. The term *âtayôhkêwina* denotes stories of *wîsahkêcâhk* (and, indeed, other beings). When we shift the paradigm to think of *âtayôhkêwina* as "spiritual narratives," we can see them as core to Cree culture and beliefs. They are key to the construction of what is meant by Cree narrative memory, and also Cree narrative imagination, which is essentially the process of expanding our narrative memory in light of new experiences. These narratives re-imagine the landscape of Cree territory, noting the place names of *wîsahkêcâhk's* travels. The narratives also point to relationships between humans and other beings, and to the possibility of radically re-imagining constructed social spaces.

(McLeod 2007: 97–98)

McLeod's notion of Cree narrative memory can be of assistance in applying concepts found within *âtayôhkêwina*, and indeed *âcimowina*, to a contemporary context.

These stories apply to Cowessess even though it is a culturally mixed community with many Plains Cree and Saulteaux people. Though some Cree and Saulteaux/ Ojibwe traditional stories have some significant differences, they are very similar in structure, form and purpose. For example, Cree and Ojibwe share many of the same mythical beings. The Ojibwe mythical beings are known as *atiso'kanak* (variously spelled) as opposed to the Cree *âtahôhkanak*. According to A. Irving Hallowell *atiso'kanak* "refers to what we would call the characters in these stories; to the Ojibwa they are living persons of an other-than-human class ... A synonym for this class of persons is 'our grandfathers'" (Hallowell 1975: 150). Many of the *âtahôhkanak* found in Cree stories, such as the Thunderbird, the great Lynx and others are also Ojibwe *atiso'kanak*. The stories of the spirit beings have a direct relationship with how Ojibwe and Cree society operate as they served to reinforce socially beneficial behavior. Theresa S. Smith provides examples from a series of Thunderbird stories to illustrate the importance *atiso'kanak* played in Ojibwe society. In these stories we learn among other things that the Thunderbirds live in communal group with a heavy emphasis on sharing, that the young Thunderbirds, due to their immaturity and their inexperience with lightning strikes, cause havoc to the environment and to humans.

According to Brightman, *wîsahkêcâhk* was the Cree cultural hero from Ontario westward, while *Nanabush* was the Ojibwe cultural hero. He notes that although these two characters have differences they share similarities. For example, Smith notes that like the Cree, some Ojibwe refer to *Nanabush* by the kinship term of Elder Brother (Smith 1995: 175). More interesting is the fact that "many attributes of the characters are similar and many stories are common to both" (Brightman 1989: 61). In fact, Brightman found the first reference to *Wîsahkêcâhk* in the historical records attributed to Ojibwe/Odawa of the Mackinac region in 1669, where a fur trader recorded the word "Ouisaketchak" referring to the great hare. Many commonly refer to *Nanabush* as the Great Hare.[2] According to Brightman numerous fur traders and anthropologists have noted some Ojibwe used the term *Wîsahkêcâhk* instead of *Nanabush* and that some Cree and Ojibwe used the term interchangeably. Edward Ahenakew from Ahtahkakoop reserve in Saskatchewan related a Plains Cree story of "Wesakaychak and the 'Startlers'" that seems to correspond to these observations:

> As he went along he came upon a nest of young prairie chickens. "Little prairie chickens," asked he, "pray, what is your name?" "That is our name you call us by," they replied. "Everything that breathes has two names," said Wesakaychak. "I myself have three: Wesakaychak, Nanaposo, and Mutchekewis. Do not tell me you have only one name." "Well, then," replied the little birds, "we are sometimes called startlers."
>
> (Ahenakew 1929: 333)

In the end, Brightman asserts that the level of similarity between the Cree and Ojibwe cultural heroes relates to the proximity of the two groups prior to European contact. Ojibwe/Saulteaux who resided in northern regions prior to contact have no cultural influence with the Cree, while those Ojibwe/Saulteaux who moved into the region after the contact period were impacted by Cree cultural influences (Brightman 1989: 64).

My research was to ascertain the basis for contemporary kinship practices among Cowessess First Nation. Even though the process of colonization had changed kinship practices enacted by Cowessess from the pre-reserve period, yet it was still different from non-Indigenous Canadians. Looking for a way to explain contemporary Cowessess kinship patterns meant recognizing that these practices did not appear out of thin air, but were grounded in historical practices guided by the culturally normative expectations that were conveyed through traditional stories. Cree and Saulteaux traditional stories, such as Elder Brother stories, though viewed simply as entertainment, or even children's stories, expressed these cultural expectations. Whether Ojibwe *atiso'kanak* or Cree *âtahôhkanak*, the spirit beings stories were central to their societies. As Wheeler states, "*Âtayôhkewina* are the foundations of Cree spirituality/religion, philosophy, and world view, and contain the laws given to the people to live by" (Wheeler 2005: 202).

The legal systems of pre-contact Indigenous peoples, as James Zion points out, "were based upon the idea of maintaining harmony in the family, the camp, and the community" (Zion 1984: 265). The failure to follow prescribed regulations could, according to what happens to Elder Brother in the stories, result in severe negative consequences. Conversely, adhering to the positive Elder Brother behavior was seen as the ideal that all should attain. The stories also provide insight into contemporary peoples' ability to maintain certain aspects of their kinship roles and responsibilities.

Traditionally, stories acted to impart the philosophical ideals upon which Indigenous societies should function. As Robert Williams Jr. notes, "The stories socialized children and reminded adults of their roles and place within the universe … Indians have long practiced the belief that stories have the power to sustain the many important connections of tribal life" (Williams 1990: 84). The telling of stories, such as those of Elder Brother, conveyed Indigenous philosophical meanings to the people. The stories show Elder Brother as generous and kind, yet he can also be selfish and cruel. In a story, if he was kind, he usually met with success; if he was cruel, he often met a disastrous and sometimes humorous end. His adventures and misadventures guided the peoples' social interactions, and therefore he is highly regarded. As Basil Johnston states about the esteem the Ojibwe have for Nanabush:

> For his attributes, strong and weak, the Anishnabeg came to love and understand Nanabush. They saw in him themselves. In his conduct was reflected the characters of men and women, young and old. From Nanabush, although he was a paradox, physical and spirit being, doing good and unable to attain it, the Anishnabeg learned.
>
> (Johnston 1976: 20)

As Sinclair states:

> Now, as before, stories reflect the experiences, thoughts, and knowledge important to Anishinaabeg, and collectively map the creative and critical relationships, and philosophies and histories of kin. Among other reasons,

stories create, define, and maintain our relations with each other and the world around us, and when shared cause us to reflect, to learn, to grow, as families, communities, and a People. Stories also indicate where we are in the universe, how we got here/there, and often indicate where we need to go … Anishinaabeg storytelling, therefore, is not a simple one-dimensional act but a complex historical, social, and political process embedded in the continuance of our collective presence, knowledge, and peoplehood.

(Sinclair 2010: 23)

Elder Brother stories conveyed Cowessess traditional law to its people. These stories functioned as a legal institution. Though this institution was unlike European institutions, it functioned in the same way. As Zion and Robert Yazzie explain, "When a legal institution articulates a norm or validates a custom, that is 'law'" (Zion and Yazzie 1997: 74). The Elder Brother stories explained the rules for expected normative behavior. These ideals were enshrined in the peoples' notion of themselves, with each retelling of Elder Brother stories and with each act that could be attributed to these stories.

A number of legal scholars have linked traditional narratives, whether stories, songs, or prayers, of Indigenous peoples to their traditional legal system (Auger 2001; Cruz 2001; Williams 1990; Yazzie 1994). For example, Williams points out that:

stories are told in tribal life to educate and direct young ones, to maintain the cohesiveness of the group, and to pass on traditional knowledge about the Creator, the seasons, the earth, plants, life, death, and every other subject that is important to the perpetuation of the tribe.

(Williams 1990: 84)

John Borrows states that the traditional tribal customary principles "are enunciated in the rich stories, ceremonies, and traditions within First Nations. Stories express the law in Aboriginal communities, since they represent the accumulated wisdom and experience of First Nations conflict resolution" (Borrows 2002: 14). Donald Auger asserts that "the knowledge gained by individuals from story-telling was that of relationships and the importance of maintaining balance and harmony" (Auger 2001: 124). Stories act to connect our "normative system to our social constructions of reality and to our vision of what the world might be" (Cover 1983: 10). Robert Cover explains the connection between narratives and law:

No set of legal institutions or prescriptions exists apart from the narratives that locate it and give it meaning. For every constitution there is an epic, for each Decalogue a scripture. Once understood in the context of the narratives that give it meaning, law becomes not merely a system of rules to be observed, but a world in which we live … in this normative world, law and narrative are inseparably related … every narrative is insistent in its demand for its prescriptive point, its moral.

(Cover 1983: 3–4)

The Elder Brother stories reflect the moral normative behavior that Cowessess people were expected to follow. Through these stories, as Johnston notes, "their sense of justice and fairness" were prompted (Johnston 2005: 103).

Elder Brother stories help to explain traditional kinship practices of the pre-reserve and early reserve periods, when Cowessess people easily incorporated others into their band, including the adoption of white children. However, the assimilation policies of the Canadian government sought to undermine the law of the people, including regulations guiding kinship practices. Though these attempts were in many respects successful, for many Cowessess people the notions of kinship as epitomized in Elder Brother's behavior continue to exist, demonstrating that the ideals of the traditional law of the people are still implicitly central principles guiding band members' social interactions. The extent to which current Cowessess band members tell Elder Brother stories or even know about them is not certain. However, what is apparent is that the values encoded in these stories have persisted to the present, and that the stories can be used to explain current kinship practices.

The *âtayôhkêwina* and *acimowina* stories not only give us insight on how Cree and Saulteaux societies operated, but can also provide a theoretical framework that can assist scholars. This is exactly what Neal McLeod advocates, as he states:

> the use of *âtayôhkêwina* – sacred stories or spiritual history, as one elder has described it – is one source of conceiving of a Cree critical theory; a narrative embodiment that creatively reflects on the situation and the world in which we find ourselves.
>
> (McLeod 2007: 97)

Applying traditional values and principles embedded in the ancient stories to assist in explaining contemporary peoples should be appealing to Indigenous Studies scholars.

Notes

1 *Wísahkécâhk*, variously spelled, is commonly referred to by his kinship term of Elder Brother. For some Cree people the term *Wísahkécâhk* was used only in the winter, the time when his stories were told, and the only term that could be used for him from spring to fall was Elder Brother. Though many Cree refer to him using the male designator of brother, others believe that this was a result of colonization and that traditionally *Wísahkécâhk* was neither male nor female. He falls in the category of trickster, though he is more like a cultural hero rather than a trickster.
2 For example, in the index of Smith's book it says: "Great Rabbit. *see* Nanabush" (1995: 228).

References

Ahenakew, Edward. 1929. "Cree trickster tales". *Journal of American Folk-Lore*, 42(1): 309–353.
Auger, Donald. 2001. "The Northern Ojibwe and their family law". Doctor of Jurisprudence, Osgoode Hall, York University.

Borrows, John. 2002. *Recovering Canada: The Resurgence of Indigenous Law*. Toronto: University of Toronto Press.

Brightman, Robert A. 1989. *Acaoohkiwina and Acimonwina: Traditional Narratives of the Rock Cree Indians*. Ottawa: Canadian Museum of Civilization.

Carlson, Nathan D. 2009. "Reviving Witiko (Wendigo): An ethnohistory of cannibal monsters in the Athabasca District of Northern Alberta, 1878–1910". *Ethnohistory*, 56(3): 359–394.

Cover, Robert. 1983. "Forward: Nomos and narratives". *Harvard Law Review*, 97(4): 4–68.

Cruz, Christina. 2001. "Tribal law as indigenous social reality and separate consciousness: [Re]incorporating customs and traditions into the law". *Tribal Law Journal*, 1: 1–27.

Cuthand, Stan. 1988. "On Nelson's text". In Jennifer S.H. Brown and Robert Brightman, eds. *"The Orders of the Dreamed": George Nelson on Cree and Northern Ojibwa Religion and Myth, 1823*. Winnipeg: University of Manitoba Press.

Doerfler, Jill, Heidi Kiiwetinepinesiik Stark, and Niigaanwewidam James Sinclair, eds. 2013. *Centering Anishinaabeg Studies: Understanding the World Through Stories*. Winnipeg: University of Manitoba Press.

Hallowell, A. Irving. 1975. "Ojibwa ontology, behavior and world view". In Dennis Tedlock and Barbara Tedlock, eds. *Teachings from the American Earth: Indian Religion and Philosophy*. New York: Liveright Publishing Corporation.

Johnston, Basil. 1976. *Ojibway Heritage*. Lincoln: University of Nebraska Press.

Johnston, Basil. 2005. "Is that all there is? Tribal literature". In Daniel David Moses and Terry Goldie, eds. *Anthology of Canadian Native Literature in English*. Toronto: University of Oxford Press.

Linklater, Eva Mary Mina. 1994. "The footprints of Wasahkacahk: The Churchill River Diversion Project and destruction of the Nelson House Cree historical landscape". MA Thesis, Simon Fraser University.

McLeod, Neal. 2007. *Cree Narrative Memory: From Treaties to Contemporary Times*. Saskatoon: Purich Publishing.

Martin, Keavy. 2012. *Stories in a New Skin Approaches to Inuit Literature*. Winnipeg: University of Manitoba Press.

Sinclair, James Niigaanwedom. 2010. "Trickster reflection: Part 1". In Deanna Reader and Linda M. Morra, eds. *Troubling Tricksters: Revisioning Critical Conversations*. Waterloo: Wilfrid Laurier University Press.

Smith, Theresa S. 1995. *The Island of the Anishnaabeg: Thunderers and Water Monster in the Traditional Ojibwe Life-World*. Moscow, ID: University of Idaho Press.

Wheeler, Winona. 2005. "Reflection on the social relations of Indigenous oral history". In Ute Lishcke and David T. McNab, eds. *Walking a Tightrope: Indigenous People and Their Representations*. Waterloo: Wilfrid Laurier University Press.

Williams, Robert A., Jr. 1990. *The American Indian in Western Legal Thought: The Discourses of Conquest*. New York: Oxford University Press.

Yazzie, Robert. 1994. "Life comes among the people: Torts and Indian courts". *New Mexico Law Review*, 24: 175–190.

Zion, James. 1984. "Harmony among the people: Torts and Indian courts". *Montana Law Review*, 45.

Zion, James and Robert Yazzie. 1997. "Indigenous law in North America in the wake of conquest". *Boston College International and Comparative Law Review*, 20(1): 55–84.

16 Histories with communities

Struggles, collaborations, transformations

Amy E. Den Ouden

Histories with communities may be an unsettling phrase for some in academia. It evokes engagement, collaboration, advocacy, even political activism. It is a phrase that asks us to consider the tensions and transformational possibilities that adhere in those contexts in which communities struggle (and sometimes engage with others, or "outsiders") to tell and record their collective history, convey that history to an audience that needs to know it, and perhaps also to disrupt and dismantle historical narratives or mythologies that have been imposed upon Indigenous peoples and used against them in ways that are distinctly political. Thus *histories with communities* is a phrase that refers to history-making, or historical production, as a political and social – as well as intellectual or academic – project. This is the understanding of the phrase that I wish to discuss here, from my perspective as a community-engaged, collaborative researcher, as well as an advocate and "outsider," who has worked with Native nations in southern New England for over two decades.[1] For these communities, as for other Indigenous peoples, history matters profoundly in everyday life, and to the preservation of rights to land, livelihood, governance, and community well-being – in essence, self-determination – in the present and in the future.

In this sense then, *histories with communities* embody and recount local histories of struggle, and draw our attention to history-making as a sometimes confrontational endeavor. Such confrontations can happen in the arena of discourse, when one seeks to write against the violence of colonial historiography's silencing mechanisms – the means by which Western notions of "legitimate" history have been and continue to be validated, and indeed used against communities. In the classic phrasing of Michel de Certeau, the established Western practice of producing history has been "expansionist": "it goes to the end of the world, toward those destined to receive it according to the objectives that it desires … With writing the Westerner has a sword in his hand" (1988: 216). More recently, in *History at the Limit of World-History*, Ranajit Guha has illuminated the colonial historiographical project as one not only of relegating the pasts of colonized peoples "into the wastelands of Prehistory," but one imposing upon, and strategically teaching "others," an exclusionary "World-history" in which

[w]hat is discarded is not only the pasts these so-called historyless people live by in their everyday existence but also the modes adopted by their languages to integrate these pasts in the prose of their respective worlds. In this way World-history has promoted the dominance of one particular genre of historical narrative over all the others.

(Guha 2002: 49)

"World-history," Guha explains, is the dominance of a historiography that is "powered by" the state, marginalizing and obscuring local, community-based historical prose, or "the narrative of being-with-others" (2002: 73).

Histories with communities does, and should, connote an intellectual and political practice that stands against the "World-history" Guha so cogently exposes, and that transforms conventional understandings of "other histories." Thus it is important to emphasize that histories with communities, as history-making projects, extend beyond the realm of historiography alone. They may directly engage the workings of law, policy, and governmental bureaucracies that amount to oppressive force. This has often been the case for Native peoples petitioning for federal acknowledgment in the late twentieth and early twenty-first century, who – in speaking their history to power – have been subjected to bureaucratic blockades and political manipulations bent on denying the legitimacy of community-based historical knowledge (see Den Ouden and O'Brien 2013). In the context of my own research, collaborations, and advocacy during my work for the federal acknowledgment petition of the Eastern Pequot Tribal Nation, I listened to, witnessed, and wrote about community history, as well as the individual and collective experience of enduring, and also defying, external disparagements of Indigenous community histories. Since this work also included extensive documentary research, along with careful analysis of the way particular interpretations, distortions, and obfuscations of documentary evidence can be used in attempts to turn history against communities, I learned something about what historical anthropologist Michel-Rolph Trouillot has referred to as "archival power": "the power to define what is and what is not a serious object of research and, therefore, of mention."[2] This is not simply discursive power. Those who are committed to histories with communities will likely come to understand the materiality of archival power as it has been employed against Indigenous peoples; but they will also be working in a local, community-based, partially textual archive, and thus may come to understand Indigenous archival power as well, and its importance to a critical analysis of the conventional archive.

Some of what I have said above presumes those engaged in histories with communities are "outsiders" or non-Natives. Of course this is not the case; nonetheless, I do write this as a non-Native, and as someone who teaches many students who are non-Natives and "outsiders," generally unfamiliar with the very notion of histories with communities. As such, I have now and always in my mind Vine Deloria Jr's trenchant critique of the "interested" outsider, which in my view remains an essential guideline for non-Natives who wish to engage in collaborations with Native communities, or who may seek to participate in histories with communities, as academics, advocates, or both. What motivates (or might transform the motivation of) such work? Culturally embedded assumptions and ideologies, along with popular and "authoritative" academic narratives "about Indians," perpetuate the notion that questions of power, politics, and rights should somehow be sifted out of outsiders' (especially academic outsiders') "interest" in Indigenous communities and histories. As Deloria put it in *We Talk, You Listen: New Tribes, New Turf* (1970), laying out a still-resonate critique of white liberalism during the Civil Rights era:

> Where whites "believe" in equality and are active in civil rights when they relate to the black community, they have been "interested" in Indians. It is rather like the way I am interested in collecting coins or someone else is interested in postage stamps.
>
> (Deloria 1970: 77)

In southern New England, where the histories and identities of Native communities have been subjected to distinctly racist "evaluation" for centuries, and where over the past several decades the local media and non-Native public have become so intensely "interested" in casinos owned and operated by tribal nations, it would be difficult to argue that non-Native public knowledge of tribal nations' sovereign rights – and of their centuries long struggles to defend those rights – has increased (Den Ouden 2005). Perhaps the fundamentally racist ideology that has propelled "interest in Indians" retains much of the meaning Deloria exposed in 1970. Whether or not that is the case, outsiders' collaborations with Native communities in recounting, writing, and publicly asserting history include profound responsibilities. Among them, as Dakota scholar Angela Cavender Wilson has explained, are those of a learner, which include first and foremost "placing oneself in a position of vulnerability" and acknowledging that one is not "an authority or expert on [the] history or culture" of the community, but rather "a student of theirs" (1997: 105).[3] As such, one will likely be a student of the community's shared experience of racial oppression, of the pain this has caused, and of the ways in which members of the community know their history in terms of history's impacts on relatives – siblings, cousins, parents, grandparents, aunts and uncles, and great grandparents – who have dealt with external threats to family and the continuity of community life over long periods of time. Without placing oneself in the position of vulnerability that Wilson describes, one cannot understand that to engage in histories with communities, to be a student of how community-based histories and knowledge are sustained over many decades and centuries, means that there will be many occasions when you must listen only: not write or record knowledge that has been shared with you, and not assume an entitlement (academic or any other kind) to convey it to a public audience because it has been shared with you.[4]

Here the distinction between the academic concept and the lived reality of community should be acknowledged. *Community* is a much problematized notion within some academic disciplines. It is a term sometimes still closely associated with, or used interchangeably with, an anthropological concept of "culture," and as such it has been described as having externally or "scientifically" identifiable "boundaries" or "features." It has also been theorized as essentially "imaginary" or "fictional." Yet, as we learn from Native historians engaged in histories with(in) communities, the local historical perspective teaches that the existence of community is (locally) self-evident but not necessarily accessible to external, "official" modes of identification – even though many Native people know well the experience of being targeted for collective destruction. With that in mind, I wish to offer two descriptions of community that defy the confines of academic debates. Ojibwe scholar Brenda J. Child's *Holding Our World Together: Ojibwe Women and the Survival of Community* (2012) conveys the power of collective historical experience, and helps us understand how such experience can be articulated in writing. In her Introduction, Child explains the centrality of Ojibwe women – such as her grandmother, Jeanette Jones Auginash – as "society builders," sustaining the bonds of kinship and community against the destructive impacts of US policies and institutions (among them, allotment, relocation, and residential schools), and "marshal[ling] much of the economy" (2012: xxvi). At the same time, Child explains why her own place and source of historical knowledge within the everyday life of her community at the Red Lake Reservation in Minnesota shapes her work as a historian:

> I come from an extraordinarily strong community with a powerful sense of place and a commitment to interpreting and remembering history. History is deeply rooted in our family stories and community life. We are descendants of earlier generations who were deeply affected by treaties and land and assimilation policies, and because of this we have a profound awareness of our survival as a people ... I grew up understanding that women figured prominently in Ojibwe families and communities and witnessing the tragedy of social problems and poverty. The elders were always a source of strength. We respected women who assumed demanding economic and cultural roles, and we deferred to a power and authority that seemed to grow even more concentrated with age and maturity. My work as a historian has always been inspired by the Auginash family and the people of Red Lake, as well as by my experiences working in archives and teaching history and American Indian studies in the university.
>
> (Child 2012: xxiv–xxv)

As Child helps us to understand, kinship-based power that is both tangible and intangible defines the contours of Ojibwe community *and* history; yet, as she goes on to explain, "the survival of that community has never been guaranteed" and "it came with a heavy price":

> Even today, our language and, with it, many aspects of our indigenous knowledge and culture continue to be endangered. It is therefore reassuring that many of our people still live close to the land and to history, allowing

Ojibwe historical knowledge to remain dynamic and survive in stories and places … My goal has been to remember the work and vision of generations of Ojibwe women who shaped life in their communities, a force greater than treaties that binds us to our homelands.

(Child 2012: xxviii)

Again, we are presented with the centrality of struggle in histories with communities. Having assigned *Holding Our World Together* to my own students for several years, I find myself reading that passage aloud in class each time, since the impact of Child's writing about her own experience of *history from within community* teaches us a great deal about responsibility to communities.

Child also beautifully conveys the power of land, of place, to the interweaving of community life and historical knowledge. So too does Lumbee historian Malinda Maynor Lowery eloquently teach us about this. In her essay "Racial Science and Federal Recognition: Lumbee Indians in the Jim Crow South," Lowery offers this remarkable description of the complexities and continuities of Lumbee community life in early twentieth-century Robeson County – a location of Lumbee resistance to the racial ideology and racist practices that sought to undermine that space of community life and Indian identity:

For Indians in Robeson County, their functioning social order revolved around identity markers of kinship and settlement and a decentralized, contested political structure. Indians in Robeson County had lived as Indians in that place for hundreds of years, but non-Indians surrounded them. Native Americans lived within a system of racial segregation that circumscribed their ability to express their identity as Indians. They scraped together a living in the midst of an economic depression that crippled much wealthier communities. These changes in the first part of the twentieth century had encouraged many nonwhites to leave the South in search of a better living. But Indians in Robeson County stayed in their homeland and maintained a sense of themselves as Indian people. To them, an Indian was not an isolated individual, standing on a platform, whose identity could be measured by scientific instruments. Instead, an Indian was part of a community of people, and Indians' identity expressed what their community thought was important. Hair, teeth, and skin color did nothing to help maintain their community in a society full of racial stereotypes; rather, the key to their identity was community residence, kin ties, and faithfulness to the tribe's social values and institutions.

(Lowery 2013: 72)

As Lowery explains, the "sense of belonging" that is at the core of Lumbee identity resides in the bonds among people as well as those between people and place, community and homeland. In the context of the real-world struggles for existence faced by Native communities, to be *surrounded*, as Lowery puts it, is to be engaged in everyday confrontations with and resistance to the material and ideological forces of racial hierarchy and racialized surveillance of Indianness. To be surrounded in this way is, then, to be subjected to a form of violence that permeates the social and geographic space of collective experience. The history of racial ideology as it has been employed in an effort to dissect Native identities and eradicate the Native body politic cannot be extracted from histories with communities.

During a summer of collaborative archival research sessions in the Connecticut State Library with Trudie Lamb Richmond and Ruth Garby Torres, both Schaghticoke educators and scholars, we spent a number of afternoons reading through and discussing the bureaucratic record of Connecticut's "Indian policy" in the late 1960s and early 1970s, wading through boxes and files that mark a sort of eruption of governmental "interest in Indians," a time when "oversight" of "Indian affairs" was being transferred from the state's Department of Welfare to the Department of Environmental Protection (DEP). As we divided up files and quietly shared our assessments of documents that offer up considerable insight into the racialized character of bureaucratic assessments of Indianness in that period, we kept in mind that among these boxes and files were documents that had become part of the official historical record for (and against) the federal acknowledgment petitions of the Eastern Pequot, Schaghticoke, and Golden Hill Paugussett tribal nations decades later. We also pondered – sometimes rather openly against the mandatory silences of the archival reading room – the more outrageous statements we came upon in those documents, which seemed in some instances to suggest that little understanding of the Civil Rights movement had reached the offices of some in the state bureaucracy by 1970, let alone knowledge of Native American rights and local Native histories. One of the documents I came upon in my stack of files stopped us cold for a while. In his December 1971 memo regarding the proposal from the Department of Welfare to shift "authority and responsibility for the management and maintenance of the property over the four Indian reservations in this State, including responsibility for the management and maintenance of the property," a DEP official commented:

> The Welfare Departments [*sic*] looks upon this as essentially a land management, rather than a people management, problem since there are not too many Indians in the State. (Of course, one may take the view, with General Custer, that even one Indian is too many Indians.)
>
> (Connecticut Archives, Record Group 079:018,
> Indian Affairs, 1836–1995. Series 6,
> Miscellaneous Docs., 1925–1977, Box 19)

Where to begin with such a statement? It reveals and connects to overlapping, persistent exertions of colonial power and racial ideology within and beyond the archive; to the rhetorical and real-world violence of "Indian policy" and policy-making as it seeks to position itself as legitimate historical documentation of Native peoples and their "disappearance." More importantly, it is a record, today, of how powerfully Native communities and their histories on the land have stood against the state-based narratives of conquest and historical denial. *Histories with communities* urge us, as students of Indigenous knowledge, to look back, and see ahead, to historical transformations.

Notes

1 I am immensely indebted to the historical knowledge of Native nations and community members in Connecticut, where I have worked on federal acknowledgment projects for the Eastern Pequot and Golden Hill Paugussett tribal nations beginning in 1991, and therefore I wish to note here that this chapter is dedicated to those mentors and friends. While I identify myself as an "outsider" here – as a way to denote the complex and sometimes fraught nature of collaborations in the context of communities' struggles to assert and defend their histories and their rights – warmth, openness, generosity, humor, and truthfulness have characterized the collaborative relationships I have been lucky enough to have with Native community members over the years. I would not have been able to understand the vitality and endurance of Eastern Pequot community life, kinship, and tribal sovereignty without the mentoring of Eastern Pequot Elder Darlene Hamlin, with whom I was so fortunate to have worked as an oral history interviewer over a decade ago, when we spent many hours visiting with Eastern Pequot Elders and other Eastern Pequot community members, recording oral histories about the importance of family, land, and the many essential contributions of Eastern Pequot women to past and present community life. From Darlene, and from many other Eastern Pequot women who shared time, history, wisdom, and, of course, laughter, with me over the years of work on the federal acknowledgment petition – including Katherine Sebastian, Mary Sebastian, Justine Perry, Brenda Geer, and Marsha Flowers – I learned that what the struggle for federal acknowledgment means to the Eastern Pequot Tribal Nation may not be intelligible to many outsiders. I am also ever thankful for (and overwhelmed by) all I have learned from Schaghticoke Elder, scholar, activist, and educator Trudie Lamb Richmond, who has been an ever patient and gracious mentor, friend, and colleague for twenty years now. We have co-taught, co-authored, and co-researched, and her vast knowledge of Native New England history and the wisdom that she has so generously shared with me have profoundly shaped my work as an educator. Likewise, Schaghticoke activist, scholar and educator Ruth Garby Torres has been a cherished friend, and over the past several years it has been a joy to research and discuss with her the unfolding implications of Connecticut's late twentieth- through early twenty-first-century "Indian policy." All of the teachings of these collaborations have been a gift.
2 As Trouillot explains, the historical "presences and absences" in the archives "are neither neutral or natural. They are created" (1995: 48). See also Stoler (2002) and Carter (2006).
3 Among other essential reading for students of Indigenous knowledge and community history is Smith (1999), Alfred (1999), Moreton-Robinson (2004), Barnhardt and Kawagley (2005), Alfred and Corntassel (2005), Wilson (2005) and McIsaac (2000).
4 Julie Cruikshank's discussion of her work as a product of collaboration, in her book *Life Lived Like a Story: Life Stories of Three Yukon Native Elders* (1992) offers crucial insights into how Cruikshank's research was transformed through years of collaboration and conversation with the Elders who shared their life stories with her, "Mrs. Sidney, Mrs. Smith, and Mrs. Ned": "Each of these women has taken an energetic role in determining both the direction of our work and the various forms in which it has already been published and distributed in her community. Under their tutelage my interests have shifted away from an oral history committed to documenting changes in social reality and toward an investigation of narrative forms for talking about, remembering, and interpreting everyday life" (1992: x; see also 12–20). Also important to

understanding the tensions and responsibilities of "outsiders" working in collaboration with Indigenous communities are the more recent discussions by Cruikshank (2007) and Chaat Smith (2007); see also Barber (2013).

References

Alfred, Taiaiake. 1999. *Peace, Power, Righteousness: An Indigenous Manifesto*. London: Oxford University Press.

Alfred, Taiaiake and Jeff Corntassel. 2005. "Being Indigenous: Resurgences against contemporary colonialism". *Government and Opposition*, 40(4): 597–614.

Barber, Katrine. 2013. "Shared authority in the context of tribal sovereignty: Building capacity for partnerships with Indigenous nations". *The Public Historian*, 35(4): 20–39.

Barnhardt, Ray and Angayuqaq Oscar Kawagley. 2005. "Indigenous knowledge systems and Alaska native ways of knowing". *Anthropology and Education Quarterly*, 36(1): 8–23.

Carter, Rodney G.S. 2006. "Of things said and unsaid: Power, archival silences, and power in silence". *Archivaria*, 61(61): 216–222.

Chaat Smith, Paul. 2007. "The terrible nearness of distant place: Making history at the National Museum of the American Indian". In Marisol de la Cadena and Orin Starn, eds. *Indigenous Experience Today*. Oxford and New York: Berg.

Child, Brenda. 2012. *Holding Our World Together: Ojibwe Women and the Survival of Community*. New York: Penguin.

Cruikshank, Julie. 1992. *Life Lived Like a Story: Life Stories of Three Yukon Native Elders*. Lincoln: University of Nebraska Press.

Cruikshank, Julie. 2007. "Melting glaciers and emerging histories in the Saint Elias Mountains". In Marisol de la Cadena and Orin Starn, eds. *Indigenous Experience Today*. Oxford and New York: Berg, 2007.

de Certeau, Michel. 1988. *The Writing of History*. New York: Columbia University Press.

Deloria, Jr, Vine. 1970. *We Talk, You Listen: New Tribes, New Turf*. Lincoln: University of Nebraska Press.

Den Ouden, Amy E. 2005. *Beyond Conquest: Native Peoples and the Struggle for History in New England*. Lincoln: University of Nebraska Press.

Den Ouden, Amy E. and Jean M. O'Brien, eds. 2013. *Recognition, Sovereignty Struggles, and Indigenous Rights in the United States*. Chapel Hill: University of North Carolina Press.

Guha, Ranajit. 2002. *History at the Limit of World-History*. New York: Columbia University Press.

Lowery, Malinda Maynor. 2013. "Racial science and federal recognition: Lumbee Indians in the Jim Crow South". In Amy E. Den Ouden and Jean M. O'Brien, eds. *Recognition, Sovereignty Struggles, and Indigenous Rights in the United States*. Chapel Hill: University of North Carolina Press.

McIsaac, Elizabeth. 2000. "Oral narratives as a site of resistance: Indigenous knowledge, colonialism, and western discourse". In George Sefa Dei, Dorothy Goldin Rosenberry, and Budd Hall, eds. *Indigenous Knowledges in Global Contexts: Multiple Readings of Our Worlds*. Toronto: University of Toronto Press.

Moreton-Robinson, Aileen. 2004. "Whiteness, epistemology and Indigenous representation". *Whitening Race: Essays in Social and Cultural Criticism*, 1: 75–88.

Smith, Linda Tuhiwai. 1999. *Decolonizing Methodologies: Research and Indigenous Peoples*. London and New York: Zed.

Stoler, Ann Laura. 2002. "Colonial archives and the arts of governance". *Archival Science*, 2(1–2): 87–109.

Trouillot, Michel-Rolph. 1995. *Silencing the Past: Power and the Production of History*. Boston: Beacon Press.

Wilson, Angela Cavender. 1997. "Power of the spoken word: Native oral traditions in American Indian history". In Donald L. Fixico, ed. *Rethinking American Indian History*. Albuquerque: University of New Mexico Press.

Wilson, Angela Cavender. 2005. "Reclaiming our humanity: Decolonization and the recovery of Indigenous knowledge". In Peter A. French and Jason A. Short, eds. *War and Border Crossings: Ethics When Cultures Clash*. New York: Rowman & Littlefield.

17 Places and peoples

Sámi feminist technoscience and supradisciplinary research methods

May-Britt Öhman

I am May-Britt Öhman Tuohea Rim, Forest and Lule Sámi of Sábme, the land of Sámi people, which stretches between three sea coasts and crosses the borders of four colonial settler states, Norway, Sweden, Finland and Russia. From my mother's paternal heritage, I belong to the Forest and Lule Sámi from Jokkmokk, of the Lule river – Julevädno. My father's paternal family is from Luleå in Swedish – Luleju in Lule Sámi – by the mouth of the Julevädno opening to the Bay of Bothnia. My maternal grandmother moved to Jokkmokk from another important river in Sábme, the Torne river, and my paternal grandmother moved to Luleju from north of Stockholm, a region named Roslagen.

I am a scholar, feminist and activist, engaging in the protection of lands of waters, future survival and decolonization of Sámi territories and Sámi bodies, analyzing and challenging the practices of destructive natural resource exploitation (mining, windpower, hydropower, forestry, militarization, railroads and roads, predator management policies) and their consequences for Sámi communities as well as all other humans and non-humans. I also engage in the work to propose alternative designs of technology and science.

Until its regulation by the Swedish state – finalized in the 1970s – Julevädno was a river rich in salmon, of which my family as most of all others in this river valley lived and prospered. It is also the river valley with the most reindeer on the Swedish side of Sábme, herded by Sámi herders, both nomadic mountain reindeer and the forest Sámi reindeer.

I left my hometown Luleju in 1990 for undergraduate studies at Uppsala University followed by a year at the Institute of Political Studies in Paris. I also studied Portuguese in Lisbon, Portugal, and spent six months in Bamako, Mali, 1996–1997, as a volunteer within international development assistance. I speak around seven languages, but only one of them, Swedish, is from my family's three languages: Sámi and Meänkieli were never transmitted to me.

I returned to Sweden in 1997 and became a PhD student of History of Science and Technology, at the Royal Institute of Technology in Stockholm, in late 1998. In 2007 I defended my PhD thesis focusing on hydropower exploitation funded by Swedish development assistance in Tanzania (Öhman 2007). I have never completely left my home region, returning for visits of family and friends several times per year. However, it was only after having finalized my PhD thesis that I also returned to do research.

Over the last few years, since 2008, using both personal means as well as research grants along with generous support from friends and family, I have been able to spend longer periods, in particular in Luleju and Jåkhåmåhkke/Jokkmokk. Over a year I am here around four or five times, spending from two to six weeks each time. Furthermore, I have organized several workshops and "roadshops" (workshops where we move between different places) along Julevädno and also other rivers, to learn together with local inhabitants and academic collaborators, about the different issues that are related to the particular land- and waterscapes.

Being a scholar at the Uppsala University, established in 1477 and in many ways the earlier and current heart of colonization of Sábme, I consider it to be of major importance to be active, living, in these places to experience first-hand perspectives and contexts as a researcher and to contrast them to the perspectives and contexts of the power centers of Uppsala and Stockholm. I reject the notion of performing "field studies" and instead consider it a normality to be an active part, citizen, of the territories and regions that I wish to research for and with.

In this chapter I reflect on the research theories and methodologies that I apply and work to develop.

The colonization of Sábme started with the establishment of the modern Swedish nation state in the sixteenth century. Until then, the Sámi were part of the power elite and Sámi fur trade was the basis for the wealth of the kings and lords. Archeological investigations have documented more than 2,000 years of Sámi history and culture and exchanges with Swedish culture. Eighteenth- and nineteenth-century colonial aggression had racism – eugenics – and industrial exploitation walking hand in hand (Larsson 2007; Zachrisson 1988; Össbo and Lantto 2011).

The first modern Sámi feminist and activist for decolonization, Elsa Laula (Renberg) (1877–1931), explains in her 1904 booklet directed at the Swedish parliament and at the Sámi ourselves the aspects and consequences of the colonization of Sábme (Laula 1904).

Laula urges all Sámi to take action, to organize, to educate ourselves to be able change the situation, to heal and develop the Sámi culture and advocate for Sámi rights to Sámi livelihood and identity, to demand human rights. Today, not much has changed since Laula's call and work for organizing Sámi resistance. In many ways, the situation is far worse. There is an increased aggressive colonial exploitation of Sámi territories in which traditional Sámi reindeer herding – a foundation of Sámi culture – is under immense pressure. In certain areas, reindeer herding is near collapse (Åhman et al. 2014), severely endangering not only an important part of Sámi traditional culture but also the region's food security as well. Also all other land-based economy and culture, including drinking water, are under serious threat from current industrial exploitations (Mikaelsson 2014; Persson and Öhman 2014).

Meanwhile, the majority of research projects on Sámi related issues was and still remains the purview of non-Sami. Simultaneously within the Swedish academic context academic scholars continue to find detrimental the open self-identification as Sámi (Öhman 2016b). Although many of non-Sámi scholars today studying Sábme and Sámi are raising their voices in support of the Sámi people's rights and many of these are also Sámi/Indigenous allies, still on the Swedish side of Sábme, the colonial situation prevails.

In 2008 I applied for and received a postdoctoral grant from the prestigious Swedish research council for the project named "Situated Perspectives on the Hydropower Exploitation in Sápmi: Swedish Technical Expansion in the 20th Century and its Impact on the Indigenous Population." It was my first attempt at working on my own region. I had – as a suggestion from a professor with origins in Sámi territories – stated in the application that "there's a void of studies which puts Sámi people as historical subjects instead of anthropological objects." At this point, I wasn't really sure what this sentence actually meant, nor what I thought I was going to do or how to do it.

There were – and still are – no demands of specific ethical protocols or background knowledge for studying Indigenous – Sámi – people's livelihoods and stories in Sweden. I was completely free to design my own "field studies," and in many aspects found myself falling into the pitfalls of colonial research practices.

Sending in the application, I was also still unaware that I myself was Sámi, that we had a Sámi history in our family. As my mother's origins were from Jokkmokk, which is a known Sámi area, I probably should have been able to guess. However my mother had fiercely denied any Sámi heritage ten years earlier and I had accepted this rejection. But as I set out to do this study, my uncle told me about our Sámi history. So from starting out to study Sámi people as the Others, thinking I was a non-Sámi outsider, I was sucked in and had to relate to the fact that I myself was among those that I wanted to study. It was an overwhelming experience which I have discussed partly in the chapter "Being May-Britt Öhman" (2010).

The revelation also remains a shock from which I am still recovering, seven years later as I approach fifty years of age. It was through being connected with Agneta Silversparf, Forest Sámi like me, and working with tracing Sámi families that I was introduced to the Sámi community and society, and also encouraged to become an active member. In 2011 I was elected to the board of the National Sámi Association, and in 2013 I was elected deputy of the Sámi parliament. Since 2011 I have been a member of the board of the Silbonah Sámesijdda, a Sámi association set up by Agneta Silversparf in 1997, and I have been a member of the Stockholm Sámi Association since 2009.

Over the years, through my research, being in the Julevädno region, interviewing, discussing and being part of everyday life, as well as by being active within the Sámi communities and associations, I have understood that my experiences are far from unique. The shaming of our Sámi heritage has been elementally powerful and paralleled Swedish nation building built on state-supported acts of Swedification. The objective was, and actually still is, to erase cultural markers of Sámi identity such as language, cultural traditions, norms as well as pointing out and shaming particular physiognomic traits found in many

Sámi persons, such as being short, having dark hair, high cheek bones, having a wide space between the eyes (see Sikku 2014).

It is a collective trauma, which plays out on our bodies and also takes its toll on us, including me personally. I have set out to challenge the status quo in Sweden, to fight it in different ways, to the point that this struggle – to reclaim, to remember – has become part of my research method. Furthermore, each year I understand better the aspects, the faces of colonization, and realize what it does to one's mind and understanding, as well as to colonized communities.

Along this process, my writing style has changed. I have passed via a writing style of explaining the stories of colonization of the Sámi toward a style where I switch perspectives. Ultimately I aim at developing a writing style from my own Sámi perspective. I say "*my* Sámi perspective," as there are several different Sámi perspectives, depending on personal experiences, geographical positions, cultural traditions in the areas, villages, cities, where we come from and live in, as with the different families and traditions we belong to.

Feminist technoscience – supradisciplinarity – Indigenous methodologies – Sámi methodologies

Already from the beginning as a PhD student I encountered scholars, theory and methodologies of the field of feminist technoscience. Read along with postcolonial authors (e.g., Said 1978; Mudimbé 1988), feminist technoscience is useful for understanding and analyzing and connecting places, peoples, human and non-human bodies, landscapes and waterscapes involved. In brief, scholars within feminist technoscience call for the recognition of non-existent boundaries between science and technology, for looking closer at the technical artifacts involved and also that we recognize a multitude of human and non-human actors involved in the making. Feminist technoscience calls for the use of feminist research and science critique to both explore and intervene in technoscientific practices, constantly reflecting over how to intervene and to consider the consequences of one's interventions. Although gender analysis is an integral part, scholars of the field also go beyond the relations of women and men and focus on epistemological and ontological issues (Haraway 1988; Hardinh 1986; Barad 1999). Furthermore, feminist technoscience scholars challenge the idea of a "gaze from nowhere" (Haraway 1988: 580), the idea that science is something performed by an all-seeing eye, an eye without a human body. Instead, feminist technoscience scholars emphasize that science, technology, its funders, its makers, its interpreters, all have human bodies, embedded in their contexts and experiences, and those that are recognized as scientists – scholars – are powerholders in society. This also includes the feminist technoscience scholar, who is challenged to discuss his/her own context and agenda in the research presentations, as well as his/her own experiences of the localities, the sites, involved.

As a PhD student, I was trained within the newly established cross-disciplinary academic field, history of science and technology, within which blending approaches from different academic disciplines is common and the analysis of nature, science and technical systems are basic parts. Within my doctoral dissertation I worked with interviews, site studies, conversations and archives. As I continued my work after my dissertation, made possible by three consecutive research grants, I have engaged in collaboration with co-researchers from other academic disciplines, including water resource management, political science, and archeology. Furthermore, I have continuously worked toward integrating knowledges and people outside of academia, consistent with feminist technoscience ideals.

In 2009, I was introduced to the concept "supradisciplinarity" by a feminist technoscience scholar, Marina Blagojevic, drawing on Donna Haraway's work (Blagojevic 2009). So far I have seen no written discussion about what this would be, but developing "supradisciplinarity" – in collaboration with others – I build on the ideals within feminist technoscience as described above.

Studying, interviewing regarding the hydropower exploitation and its consequences and risks, turned out to be somewhat an issue of the past. The struggles to protect the rivers were already lost or in some few cases won. I have therefore opted to focus on the one hand on the stories of the hydropower exploitation and all its consequences, but also on raising important aspects of "dam safeties" and human security, as part of feminist technoscience intervention and supradisciplinary methodologies (Öhman 2016a).

In 2012 I became involved in the anti-mining protests within Sámi territory, an ongoing struggle, which touches also on the already hydropower-exploited river valleys.

Attempting to apply "supradisciplinarity" makes it a necessity for me as a researcher, and as Sámi, to take a stance and not pretend to be "neutral" in the midst of colonial destructive natural resource exploitation of water- and landscapes. Being what is commonly seen as "neutral" would in reality be siding with the colonial aggression. I consider teaching, researching and acting as a scholar as activism, although it is commonly only those scholars such as myself that challenge norms that are pointed out as activists.

Since engaging with the work to protect Sámi land- and waterscapes against mining exploitations, I have become part of the protests and struggle. However, my work has been focusing on the areas that I have expertise in, such as "dam safety" and water resources, as well as analyzing colonialism and its impacts on local communities.

In feminist technoscience research intervention is considered normality. Most Indigenous scholars refer to "giving back" (Kuokkanen 2007) to the Indigenous communities as part of the method, while Kim TallBear speaks of "standing with" (TallBear 2014). I suppose that what I do is something like that, but I am also in front, pushing ahead. I challenge authorities, such as the Swedish government, counties and municipalities. I write complaints regarding decisions made and also continuously send emails and tweets to members of government and their staff. I also write debate articles and memos regarding risks of mining exploitations for water quality and the increased risks of dam failures. I organize and participate at manifestations, but also attend and ask questions at seminars organized within the dam, energy and mining sector.

Collaborating with other experts, both Sámi and non-Sámi, inside and outside academia, Sámi artists, activists, and also non-Sámi artists and activists, provides me with the possibilities to understand my own history, landscapes and waterscapes, as we perform research work and communication of our research together. I engage with reindeer herders both in my research work and in my activist work, by visiting and engaging on location, but also through following and interacting through social media.

As Indigenous studies – led by Indigenous scholars – as well as feminist technoscience, is very little represented within Swedish university education and research, I have worked toward a combination of teaching and research through supradisciplinary workshops, roadshops, symposiums and meetings. Among other activities, I have organized four symposiums to which Indigenous and Sámi activists and scholars were invited.

What is considered "real" academic work is commonly writing articles and papers, where the *informants* are filtered through the scholar. But, as in the anthology *Re:Mindings: Co-Constituting Indigenous/Academic/Artistic Knowledge* (Gärdebo et al. 2014), I explore how Sámi who are not academic scholars themselves can have a platform in their own right, to speak to the academic community, and other powerholders in the society. For instance, reindeer herders have lifelong training in their profession, culture and understanding landscapes and waterscapes although their own voices are rarely heard.

I came across Indigenous research methodologies, as described recently by, among others, Linda Tuhiwai Smith and Karen Martin. I am now attempting to figure out how my own work can be framed in this context (Smith 1999; Martin 2003). I also learn through exchange with Indigenous scholars whom I have gotten in touch with mainly through NAISA, the Native American and Indigenous Studies Association. Online discussions in social media are a huge aid for learning more and for exchanging ideas and understanding, as well as for me to understand that "I am not crazy," but that it is the colonial context that is abnormal and oppressive.

I now begin to realize that what I have referred to as a combination of feminist technoscience and postcolonial theory and method, supradisciplinarity, along with my attempts at trying to connect to realities of Sámi communities and territories, is indeed what can be considered as Indigenous theory and methodologies. I am – together with others – developing unique feminist technoscience and Sámi/Indigenous methodologies. My hope is that it will be possible to establish a permanent and stable platform for these perspectives within Swedish academia.

However, at the moment the prospects are not so good, so while waiting I do my best to promote the perspectives through websites, among other things. During 2015 I set up two websites. One is in my own name, www.maybrittohman.com, where I blog about the "supradisciplinary" work, explaining technical issues on dams, water, energy, technological design and impacts on Sámi culture as well as environmental issues. The other website is www.samelandsfriauniversitet.com and is a promotion of the "Sámiland Free University," a vision of how to challenge colonial academia, among other organizing supradisciplinary workshops and also contains a blog focusing on and experimenting with my Sámi perspectives.

All in all, to summarize, I have come to realize that what I do is to follow the summons by Elsa Laula to all Sámi; educate myself and work together to strengthen our society, support the weak, and struggle for the long-term survival as a people, including safeguarding the lands and waters for future generations. Is this action, activist, decolonial or just research methodology? I prefer to name it simply as "good research methodology."

References

Åhman, Birgitta, Kristin Svensson, and Lars Rönnegård. 2014. "High female mortality resulting in herd collapse in free-ranging domesticated reindeer (*Rangifer tarandus tarandus*) in Sweden". *PLoS ONE*, 9(10): e111509. doi:10.1371/journal.pone.0111509.

Barad, Karen. 1999. "Agential realism – feminist interventions in understanding scientific practices". In Mario Biagnoli, ed. *The Science Studies Reader*. New York: Routledge.

Blagojevic, Marina. 2009. "Scientific excellence beyond gender and locationality". Paper presented at the 3rd CG Ex Workshop, Centre for Gender Studies, Umeå, 26–27 March.

Gärdebo, Johan, May-Britt Öhman, and Hiroshi Maruyama, eds. 2014. *Re:Mindings: Co-Constituting Indigenous /Academic/Artistic Knowledges*. Uppsala: Hugo Valentin Centre.

Haraway, Donna J. 1988. "Situated knowledges: The science question in feminism and the privilege of partial perspective". *Feminist Studies*, 14(3): 575–599.

Harding, Sandra G. 1986. *The Science Question in Feminism*. Ithaca: Cornell University Press.

Kuokkanen, Rauna. 2007. *Reshaping the University: Responsibility, Indigenous Epistemes, and the Logic of the Gift*. Vancouver: UBC Press.

Larsson, Gunilla. 2007. "Ship and society: Maritime ideology in late Iron Age Sweden". PhD diss., Uppsala University.

Laula, Elsa. 1904. *Inför lif eller död? Sanningsord i de lappska förhållandena*. Stockholm: Wilhelmssons.

Martin, Karen. 2003. "Ways of knowing, ways of being and ways of doing". *Journal of Australian Studies*, 76: 203–214.

Mikaelsson, Stefan. 2014. "Winds of change: The role and potential of Sámi parliamentarians". In Johan Gärdebo, May-Britt Öhman, and Hiroshi Maruyama, eds. *Re:Mindings. Co-Constituting Indigenous /Academic/Artistic Knowledges*. Uppsala: Hugo Valentin Centre.

Mudimbé, Valentin Y. 1988. *The Invention of Africa*. Bloomington: Indiana University Press.

Öhman, May-Britt. 2007. "Taming exotic beauties". PhD diss., Royal Institute of Technology.

Öhman, May-Britt. 2010. "Being May-Britt Öhman: Or, reflections on my own colonized mind regarding hydropower constructions in Sápmi". In Pirjo Elovaara, Johanna Sefyrin, May-Britt Öhman, and Christina Björkman, eds. *Travelling Thoughtfulness: Feminist Technoscience Stories*. Umeå: Univ., Dept. of Informatics.

Öhman, May-Britt. 2016a. "Embodied vulnerability in large scale technical systems – vulnerable dam bodies, water bodies and human bodies". In Lisa Folkmarson Käll, ed. *Bodies, Boundaries and Vulnerabilities*. Rotterdam: Springer.

Öhman, May-Britt. 2016b. "TechnoVisions of a Sámi cyborg: Re-claiming Sámi body-, land- and waterscapes after a century of colonial exploitations in Sápmi". In Jacob Bull and Margaretha Fahlgren, eds. *Ill-Disciplined Gender: Engaging Questions of Nature/ Culture and Transgressive Encounters*. Rotterdam: Springer.

Össbo, Åsa and Patrik Lantto. 2011. "Colonial tutelage and industrial colonialism: Reindeer husbandry and early 20th-century hydroelectric development in Sweden". *Scandinavian Journal of History*, 36(3): 324–348.

Persson, Marie and May-Britt Öhman. 2014. "Visions for a future at the source of the Ume River, Sweden". In Johan Gärdebo, May-Britt Öhman, and Hiroshi Maruyama, eds. *Re:Mindings. Co-Constituting Indigenous/Academic/Artistic Knowledges*. Uppsala: Hugo Valentin Centre.

Said, Edward W. 1978. *Orientalism*. London: Routledge & Kegan Paul.

Sikku, Katarina Pirak. 2014. *Nammaláphán*, unpublished exhibition folder. Umeå: Bildmuséet.

Smith, Linda Tuhivai. 1999. *Decolonizing Methodologies*. London: Zed.

TallBear, Kim. 2014. "Standing with and speaking as faith: A feminist-indigenous approach to inquiry [research note]". *Journal of Research Practice*, 10(2): Article N17.

Zachrisson, Inger. 1988. "The so-called Scandinavian cultural boundary in northern Sweden in Viking times". *Acta Borealia*, 5(1–2): 70–97.

18 Oral history

William Bauer, Jr.

In January of 2002, I pulled my rental car into my grandmother Anita Rome's driveway, smashing the ice that had encrusted several potholes. I had scheduled an interview with Anita for my dissertation on Indigenous migrant workers from northern California's Round Valley Reservation. I knew from the outset of my dissertation research that I wanted to use oral history. Scholars had written too much of Round Valley's history without including Native voices and I hoped that oral histories would correct that oversight. Anita met me at the door of her mobile home dressed in her usual western-print long-sleeved shirt and blue jeans and curled black hair. We sat down at her dining table and I asked her to sign the mandatory Institutional Review Board (IRB) paperwork, which ensured consent to conduct, audiotape and use her interview in publications. Anita signed the papers, but balked at taping the interview. She explained that someone had previously recorded her without her permission (illustrating the importance of IRB's informed consent) and refused to allow anyone to tape her again. In our interview, she described growing up on the Round Valley Reservation, attending the Stewart Indian School in Carson City, Nevada, and migrant farm work in northern California. After a couple of hours, I left, and after lunch interviewed Anita's niece, Kathy Cook. Thankfully, this was not the only time I interviewed my grandmother. Whenever I returned to Round Valley on a research trip, I purposefully rented a truck so we could drive to the mountains, where she had grown up. On these trips, she discussed attending a grade school near the reservation and her father's many occupations.[1]

Oral histories, like those with my grandmother, are vital sources for understanding American Indian history. Oral histories are rooted in Indigenous ways of knowing the past, yet many non-Indian historians questioned their validity. In the 1950s, anthropologists and historians developed ethnohistory and the New Indian History and used oral histories to understand aspects of American Indian history that could not be found in traditional archives. Oral histories are useful, for instance, in understanding American Indian work and labor as well as the histories of Native women. Singularly, oral histories may appear mundane; taken together they stitch together an American Indian collective memory. Experiences, such as attending boarding schools, cut across tribal and national lines. Although Native people may not agree on boarding school experience, many remembered and told oral histories about those times. Finally, this chapter will assess how American Indians used oral histories to express sovereignty. American Indians employed oral histories to reclaim historical methods, understandings of the past and treaty rights.

American Indians stored and framed knowledge, especially about the past, using oral sources and methods. Choctaw Sarah Noah explained that her people were "great storytellers":

> Now and then, especially in the winter when all of the ... kitchen work, dining room, getting up wood and milking is finished, a big firewood is heaped up in the fire-place, all members of the family be seated around the fire when someone of the elder man or woman would begin to talk on some subject of the olden days.[2]

Noah revealed the position of oral histories and traditions within Choctaw ways of knowing. The telling of oral histories corresponded to specific moments: during the winter and after everyone completed their work. Additionally, oral histories operated within Choctaw kinship relationships. Noah observed that "all members of the family" were present as the elders told their oral histories and traditions. The elderly possessed the stories and established criteria for historical veracity. Age meant not a numerical age, but enough time on earth to learn oral histories and oral traditions and the wisdom to deploy them at the appropriate moment.

Despite oral history's importance to American Indian people and nations, many non-Indian scholars distrusted these sources. In 1917, anthropologist Robert Lowie wrote, "Indian tradition is historically worthless, because the occurrences, possibly real, which it retains are of no historical significance; and because it fails to record, or to record accurately, the most momentous happenings" (Lowie 1917: 165). Many historians similarly doubted Indigenous peoples' oral testimony, preferring the equally biased written sources. Historian Robert Utley, for instance, described Lakota sources about the Wounded Knee massacre as incoherent, "factually weak" and "interesting mainly for point of view" (Utley 1963: 298, 299, 300). Yet, he relied on military accounts and agent records that described the Ghost Dance as a "craze" (Utley 1963: 94).

Beginning in the 1950s, scholars began to utilize American Indian oral histories. After working on Indian Claims Commission cases, anthropologists, and later historians, developed the methodology of ethnohistory to study both sides of encounters between American Indians and Europeans and cultural change in American Indian communities. Practitioners of this method incorporated oral history and oral traditions into their intellectual toolkits, even though they may not have all agreed about how and when to use oral narratives.[3] The "New Indian History," born in the days of the American Indian civil rights movement, situated Indigenous people at the center of historical narratives. These intellectual projects welcomed the use of oral history.[4]

During the twentieth century, many people entered Indian Country to collect oral histories, providing evidence for ethnohistorians and New Indian histories. In

1930, Eleanor Hinman, a teacher and journalist from Lincoln, Nebraska, interviewed Lakotas on the Pine Ridge and Rosebud Reservations about the famous Oglala leader Crazy Horse. She hoped that "some Indians now living could throw light on an interesting personality and a debated episode in American history" (Riley 1998: 181–182).[5] In the 1930s, public works programs, such as the Works Progress Administration (WPA), canvassed American Indian communities to collect oral histories in order to understand the folk and multicultural underpinnings of American nationalism (Mangione 1972; Hirsch 2003). In 1936, the University of Oklahoma and the Oklahoma Historical Society secured a WPA grant to conduct oral history interviews. The subsequently named Indian Pioneer Papers contains interviews with nearly 80,000 Native and non-Native people in Oklahoma. Similar New Deal era projects existed in Minnesota and California.[6] Between 1967 and 1972, seven universities (Arizona, Florida, Illinois, New Mexico, Oklahoma, South Dakota and Utah) secured grants from the Doris Duke Foundation to create the American Indian History Project. The oral histories in these collections feature prominent American Indian leaders, such as Paiute Mel Thom and Diné Howard Gorman. Similar projects continued in the 1980s and 1990s. In Wyoming, the Warm Valley Historical Project interviewed Shoshones and Arapahoes on the Wind River Reservation.[7] The oral histories collected in all of these projects helped to revise American Indian history.

These collections and other oral history projects revealed aspects of American Indian history that could not be found in traditional archives. Oral histories exposed a rich history of American Indian work and labor. Choctaw Joseph Collins remembered, "Field work such as chopping cotton and thinning corn was done for one dollar per day, cotton picking was from sixty to seventy five cents per hundred pounds and other common labor pay was one dollar per day."[8] My grandmother added to this corpus of knowledge about work and labor in Indian country. "When I was ten," Anita remembered,

> I babysat Mildred Davis' children when she worked at the Hop Ranch [in Covelo, the reservation's bordertown]. We also went out of the valley and picked hops, grapes and prunes in Sonoma County. All five of us [Anita, Mildred and Mildred's three children] went. We stayed in camps for the workers. We stayed in cabins or houses that had running water and were fully stocked with stoves. I watched the children and cooked for them. Mildred made her dinner when she finished working.[9]

Oral histories of work and labor filled in the gaps one finds in the written, archival record. Government agents often noted that Indians worked, but rarely provided the intimate details and rich descriptions of work that one finds in oral histories.

Oral history aided historians in understanding American Indian women's histories. Historian Theda Perdue observes, "The complicating factor in writing the ethnohistory of native women is that European men, not women, wrote the vast majority of documents." European men often encountered Native men, not women, in "trade relations and military alliance" and simply lacked access to women's lives

(Perdue 1997: 73, 75–76). Oral histories center American Indian women in their respective nation's history. Diné scholar Jennifer Denetdale writes, "my work in oral history led me to recognize the ongoing centrality of concepts of matrilineality in Navajo society" (Denetdale 2014: 76). Shoshone Dorothy Peche recalled, "I used to go with my grandma … I think it was spring we went and we'd gather roots like the sago bulbs and bitter roots and all those kinds of things for our food."[10] Shoshone, Diné and other American women provided labor, participated in Indigenous politics, and stored knowledge that assisted in the survival of Indigenous people in the nineteenth, twentieth and twenty-first centuries.

In isolation, oral histories reveal everyday, perhaps mundane, activities. Considered together, oral histories create an American Indian collective memory. Beginning in the late nineteenth century and continuing into the 1960s, American Indian children attended boarding schools, often at locations far away from their families and homelands. Former students shared their oral histories of boarding school life with their family members. Ojibwe historian Brenda Child, whose grandmother Jeanette Jones Auginash, a second-generation boarding school student, attended a school in Flandreau, South Dakota, writes, "Like most Native Americans of my generation, I first learned about government boarding schools from a grandparent" (Child 2000: 1).

Former students remembered varied experiences at the boarding schools. Historian K. Tsianina Lomawaima used oral history interviews with her father and other former students to write a history of Oklahoma's Chilocco Indian School. Some students recalled Chilocco's positive attributes, such as learning work skills. Pauline, a Cherokee woman, remembered:

> I spent two years at Chilocco and they were the happiest two years of my life because I learned how to cook, I learned how to sew, I learned how to entertain, and I learned manners, and how to clean house, how to iron, how to wash, how to work in different things.
>
> (Lomawaima 1987: 245)

Arapaho Joe Creeping Bear attended the Seger Industrial School near Colony, Oklahoma. Creeping Bear said, "I wish that Mr. [John] Seger [the school's founder] was still living but he is gone. He gave me my schooling and all the rest of the Indians here wish for Mr. Seger." He continued, "Mr. Seger gave us lots of good things to eat while we attended school. Now I am old and can't work and just sit around and think of olden times." Creeping Bear likely looked back fondly on the school for, during the Depression, he was out of work because of a work-related injury.[11]

Other students disliked the boarding school experience. Anita shared stories of her time at the Stewart Indian School in Carson City, Nevada. "I went to school in Stewart, Nevada," she said.

> I lived in a dormitory. They had two matrons. One, Eleanor, was from Covelo and she was nice. However, one named Miss Winger, she was a dumpy

woman, with blondish hair she wore in a bun and walked like a sergeant. She was mean to the little children.[12]

Shoshone Dorothy Peche recalled similar teachers at her school:

[the school] had the meanest teacher down there that ever lived. She looked just like a witch. Skinny and … well just like a witch. She was mean. She was everlastingly popping the kids on the hand with a ruler.[13]

Oral histories revealed how the students resisted the worst aspects of boarding school life. Curtis, Lomawaima's father, recalled, "we used to deliberately do things … just to show [the school administrators] that we could do it and get away with it." The most common example of resistance was running away. Curtis said:

[I ran away] oh, I think I was about, I'm trying to remember, it must have been about 1934, '35, 1935 I guess it was … I just decided that the only way I was gonna get out of there was to just leave so, I just up and left. Hitchhiked to Oklahoma City, and caught a freight train and went to California.

(Lomawaima 1987: 248, 249)

Dorothy Peche recalled two examples of resistance: running away and liaisons between students of the opposite sex.

[The girls would] tie their sheets together and there'd be boys waiting outside to pick them up [to run away] … That's how [the boys] would get into the dormitories, crawled up the sheets … some of those girls would tie all their sheets together and bring [the boys] up to the dormitories. It would scare the rest of us half to death.[14]

Oral histories articulated a collective memory of attending boarding schools. Former students from different tribes related fond experiences at the school, hurtful teachers and the everyday forms of resistance that enabled students to persist at the school.

Oral histories articulated Indigenous sovereignty.[15] Rather than rely on academic historians, American Indians controlled the production of knowledge through oral histories. Anita, for instance, determined the manner in which we conducted the interview by refusing to have her words recorded on tape. Dakota Eli Taylor, with whom Waziyatawin worked, declared that he was going to discuss "Dakota history and culture" and the "difficult" history of Dakota–United States relations (Wilson 2001: 3). Anita and Eli claimed authority over the production of their respective histories.

American Indians understood how the standard historical practices, especially the reliance on written sources, silenced their voices and misinterpreted their history. Apache woman Eva Tulene Watt noted, "Lots is missing in those books because there's hardly no Indians in there. You can't see hardly nothing in there about how we used to live" (Jacoby 2008: 144). Lassik Lucy Young offered a similar reading on the silences of American history:

> If you could only know the truth of the Indian has been treated since the first white man came in into his part of the country, it would make an ordinary man shake and shudder. I would like to tell you the whole story from 1846 up to the present date. I am afraid it would not be allowed to be put in print.[16]

Watt and Young knew that United States history silenced or ignored American Indian people and histories. They also asserted that American Indians possessed their own ideas of historical veracity. Young witnessed certain historical events and orally transmitted them to anyone who might listen.

Oral histories reinterpreted and challenged conventional understandings of the past. Archaeologist Chip Colwell-Chanthaphonh argues Apaches used oral history to provide Apache understandings of the infamous Camp Grant Massacre of 1871, in which whites, vecinos and Tohono O'odhams attacked an Apache village in Arizona. "To write about the Camp Grant Massacre from the perspective of the Apache people empowers those voices that have previously been quieted and offers a much more intricate knowledge of the event because it spins another strand in the web of histories," Colwell-Chanthaphonh argues. Apache oral narratives agreed on the economic conditions at Camp Grant, mentioning the quantity and quality of rations and the necessity of working for extra rations and clothing (often cutting hay), which contributed to the massacre. Furthermore, Apaches noted that they had performed a ceremony the night before the massacre and fled into the mountains to escape their attackers, who assaulted the morning after the ceremony. Yet, Colwell-Chanthaphohn suggests, there was no one, authoritative Apache voice to interpret the Camp Grant Massacre; rather, "an array" of oral histories emerged, offering different understandings of, for example, the massacre's timing. Colwell concludes, "These [oral] stories from the Apache experience do not undermine previous writings so much as expand on them, compelling us to rethink the event from new angles" (Colwell-Chanthaphonh 2003: 640–641, 659).

Oral histories also defended Indigenous treaty rights. An example of the use of oral history to protect sovereignty occurred in 1973 and the famous case *United States* v. *Washington*. In the early 1970s, the United States, on behalf of the tribal nations in the Pacific Northwest, brought a lawsuit against the state of Washington for infringing on Indigenous peoples' fishing rights. Oral history provided testimony in support of treaty-reserved fishing rights. Lummi Forrest "Dutch" Kinley testified, "We gave up our land without any restrictions. But when it came to hunting and fishing, we wanted exclusive rights in certain areas. We felt that we were giving the citizens a right to fish in common with us." He continued by explaining the significance of American Indian oral histories in interpreting the treaty rights:

My father died at 103 years old, and I think it's been the tradition of our people – you have history books; our people, the duty of our old people was to inform us about our family and about our rights. I think that this is a tradition that has been as accurate as your history books.

(Kinley quoted in Wilkinson 2005: 2000)

As I wrote this chapter, Anita Rome passed away. Although I will not have another opportunity to drive up to her home, share a can of Mountain Dew and hear more about her life, I remain grateful for the way in which her oral histories taught me about how to research and write about American Indian history. Rooted in Indigenous ways of knowing that emphasize kinship, place and setting, oral histories and oral traditions have shaped the sources and methods used in the study of American Indian history. Anita, Dorothy Peche and Sarah Noah revealed aspects of American Indian women's experiences, often lost in non-Indian sources; added to the collective memory of American Indians who attended federal boarding schools; and claimed sovereignty over how people produce and interpret American Indian history as well as defend treaty rights. In the end, American Indians used oral histories to empower themselves and American Indian communities. They validate American Indian ways of knowing and understandings of Indian Country's past, present and future.

Notes

1 Anita Rome interview by author, January 21, 2003.
2 Sarah Noah interview by Pete W. Cole, Indian–Pioneer Collection, Western History Collections, University of Oklahoma, volume 67, interview 12367.
3 For surveys on the development of ethnohistory and the contested nature of oral history see Axtell (1979: 4 and 1978: 118).
4 For the origins of the New Indian History see Berkhofer (1971: 357–382). For a work in the vein of the New Indian History that used oral history interviews see Crum (1994).
5 Hinman never published a biography on Crazy Horse. Instead, she handed over her materials to Mari Sandoz, who wrote *Crazy Horse: The Strange Man of the Oglalas* (2004 [1942]).
6 Chantal Norgard's recent work on Ojibwe history has effectively used the WPA Ojibwe interviews (Norgard 2014).
7 On the proliferation of oral history collections and publications, see Fixico (2003: 31–32, 144).
8 Joseph Collins interview by Pete W. Cole, Indian-Pioneer Papers, Western History Collections, University of Oklahoma, volume 19, interview 6305.
9 Anita Rome interview by author, January 21, 2003.
10 Dorothy Peche, Warm Valley Historical Project, American Heritage Center, University of Wyoming.
11 Joe Creeping Bear interview by Ida B. Lankford, Indian-Pioneer Papers, Western History Collections, University of Oklahoma, volume 21, interview 8662. Creeping Bear explained, "I finished the ninth grade [at Seger's school] and could make a good living then and then I got hurt on a truck and now I am on relief. This accident happened in 1930 while I was unloading coal and a car backed on me."
12 Anita Rome interview by author, January 21, 2003.

13 Dorothy Peche, Warm Valley Historical Project, American Heritage Center, University of Wyoming.
14 Dorothy Peche, Warm Valley Historical Project, American Heritage Center, University of Wyoming.
15 Diné historian Jennifer Denetdale writes "[oral histories] revitalize and affirm the values and practices that undergird Native American belief systems and encompasses the spiritual, emotional, mental and physical aspects of Native Americans' lives" (2014: 69).
16 Lucy Young, Ethnological Documents of the Department and Museum of Anthropology, University of California, Berkeley, BANC FILM 2216, The Bancroft Library, University of California, Berkeley, reel 204(2), folder 204.23: 1757.

References

Axtell, James. 1978. "The ethnohistory of early America: A review essay". *William and Mary Quarterly*, 35: 110–144.
Axtell, James. 1979. "Ethnohistory: An historian's viewpoint". *Ethnohistory*, 26: 1–13.
Berkhofer, Jr., Robert. 1971. "The political context of a new Indian history". *Pacific Historical Review*, 40: 357–382.
Child, Brenda. 2000. *Boarding School Seasons: American Indian Families, 1900–1940*. Lincoln: University of Nebraska Press.
Colwell-Chanthaphonh, Chip. 2003. "Western Apache oral histories and traditions of the Camp Grant Massacre". *American Indian Quarterly*, 27: 639–666.
Crum, Steven. 1994. *The Road on Which We Came: A History of the Western Shoshone*. Salt Lake City: University of Utah Press.
Denetdale, Jennifer Nez. 2014. "The value of oral history on the path to Dine/Navajo sovereignty". In Lloyd L. Lee, ed. *Diné Perspectives: Revitalizing and Reclaiming Navajo Thought*. Tucson: University of Arizona Press.
Fixico, Donald. 2003. *The American Indian Mind in a Linear World: American Indian Studies & Traditional Knowledge*. New York: Routledge.
Hirsch, Jerrold. 2003. *Portrait of America: A Cultural History of the Federal Writers' Project*. Chapel Hill: University of North Carolina Press.
Jacoby, Karl. 2008. *Shadows at Dawn: An Apache Massacre and the Violence of History*. New York: Penguin Books.
Lomawaima, K. Tsianina. 1987. "Oral histories from Chilocco Indian Agricultural School, 1920–1940". *American Indian Quarterly*, 11: 241–254.
Lowie, Robert. 1917. "Oral tradition and history". *The Journal of American Folklore*, 30: 161–167.
Mangione, Jere. 1972. *The Dream and the Deal: The Federal Writer's Project, 1935–1943*. Boston: Little, Brown.
Norgard, Chantal. 2014. *Seasons of Change: Labor, Treaty Rights and Ojibwe Nationhood*. Chapel Hill: University of North Carolina Press.
Perdue, Theda. 1997. "Writing the ethnohistory of women". In Donald Fixico, ed. *Rethinking American Indian History*. Albuquerque: University of New Mexico Press.
Riley, Paul D. 1998. "Oglala sources on the life of Crazy Horse: Interviews given to Eleanor H. Hinman". In R. Eli Paul, ed. *The Nebraska Indian Wars Reader, 1865–1877*. Lincoln: University of Nebraska Press, 1998.
Sandoz, Mari. 2004 [1942]. *Crazy Horse: The Strange Man of the Oglalas*, with an introduction by Vine Deloria, Jr. Lincoln: University of Nebraska Press.

Utley, Robert. 1963. *The Last Days of the Sioux Nation*. New Haven: Yale University Press.

Wilkinson, Charles. 2005. *Blood Struggle: The Rise of Modern Indian Nations*. New York: W.W. Norton.

Wilson, Waziyatawin Angela. 2001. *Remember This! The Eli Taylor Narratives and Dakota Decolonization*. Lincoln: University of Nebraska Press.

III. Feminism, gender, and sexuality

19 Status, sustainability, and American Indian women in the twentieth century

Jacki Thompson Rand

Twenty years ago Nancy Shoemaker's introduction to the highly praised edited volume *Negotiators of Change: Historical Perspectives on Native American Women* assessed the previous twenty years of scholarship on post-contact North America (Shoemaker 1995). Heavily influenced by the work of feminist anthropologists Ruth Leacock and Michelle Rosaldo's *Women and Colonization*, Shoemaker explained, scholars had embraced the study of Native women's status as defined by gender equality based on the assumptions of constructed universal male dominance and female subordination, as rooted in colonization. Coming from a Marxist criticism of capitalism, Leacock and Rosaldo's approach to women's status through labor emphasized their economic contributions, which necessarily declined in the face of destructive impacts of colonialism and loss of tribal political strength (Shoemaker 1995: 4–5). Shoemaker's call for consideration of women's adaptive strategies in Native women's histories framed contributions to *Negotiators of Change* which examined the impact of colonialism on women's status and women's varied responses. Subsequently, studies of Native women in post-contact history continue to emphasize both women's status and decline at the expense of attention to women's adaptive strategies, despite this critical intervention (LeMaster 2014: 6).

Native women remained adaptable in the twentieth century, Shoemaker noted, as they entered wage labor economies while, paradoxically, experiencing increased political visibility, which my current research confirms (Shoemaker 1995: 10). Studies of twentieth-century Native women have thus far failed to take off in a sustained way, a curious lack given the obvious potential for scholarly inquiry in what one can only call a wide open field. One need only look to Wikipedia for lists of "prominent" Native women who have served as influential tribal chiefs and council members, as pioneers in journalism, the law, and academe, and as radical activists in domestic and international realms, not to mention the high representation of women in the arts, thus bearing out Shoemaker's observation about the rising visibility of twentieth-century Native women.[1] Such lists do not even exist for the legions of women from reservation and urban communities who devoted their energies to persistent social and health issues, politics, environmental concerns, and tribal code reforms. Absent, too, are women's initiatives in food sovereignty, language retention, and traditional manufactures and arts.[2]

Parenthetically, critiques of and projects related to violence against women, to alcohol, and to Native child adoption seem to garner most attention among legal scholars and social scientists.[3] These are not only women's initiatives, but men's as well, suggesting a rich field to mine on questions of gender, masculinity, divisions of labor, and political engagement.

Status, based on notions of gender equality and economic contribution, is far too limiting and should be, while not necessarily abandoned, rethought. Michelle LeMaster's "Pocahontas Doesn't Live Here Anymore: Women and Gender in the Native South before Removal" articulates a critique of scholars' persistent preoccupation with the question of status, which is potentially useful to scholars writing in all periods of post-contact history. LeMaster argues that the focus on women's power and status relative to men emphasizes questions that are of great concern to modern feminist scholars, but not necessarily to Native women in pre-modern societies, or, I would argue, in the twentieth and twenty-first centuries. The way status is framed is problematic in that it lacks attention to the experiences of Native women as perceived by them. It emphasizes a concept of power as understood in non-Native intellectual traditions without consideration for Native understandings of power. Simultaneously, it neglects the import of colonialism and how it structures power in the post-contact context. Status, as proposed and perpetuated by scholars, focuses primarily on economics while obscuring other important factors that influence women's position and leaves them frozen in a state of post-contact colonial domination of American Indian tribes (LeMaster 2014: 3–7). Patricia Albers's work on Devil's Lake Sioux Reservation refutes the assumptions of twentieth-century scholars that nineteenth-century women's status (arguably this applies to all eras) declined as tribal political power eroded (Albers 1983: 193). LeMaster would agree, "The loss of power of the people as a whole does not necessarily correlate to the loss of women's power relative to men" (LeMaster 2014: 7). Kimberle Crenshaw's work on intersectionality is relevant here with respect to her criticism of mainstream feminism's inattention to race and the invisibility it imposes on women of color (Crenshaw 1991).

I argue that status, as a scholarly preoccupation, is equally problematic to twentieth-century Native women. Based on my research in an American Indian tribe on the subject of violence against Native women in the twentieth century, American Indian women instead strongly identify with their tribes' experiences which remain marked by the impact of successive colonial regimes, including the United States, rather than with the politics of gender equality. Native Americans entered the twentieth century in the wake of a sea-change in power between the United States government and tribal governments, stripped of most sovereign powers as a result. A series of destabilizing policies, including the Indian Reorganization Act, Termination, and Relocation ensued, preventing Native communities from affectively recovering from their many problems. Native America reservation and urban life, lacking adequate schools, nutrition, housing, sanitation, health care, and legal protections while stuck in chronic unemployment, was one massive human rights violation. Structural poverty, marginalization, absence of resources, and settler and federal hostility to their existence contextualizes the history of twentieth-century Native women and their communities. These experiences shaped the direction and intentionality of their labors as concerned community members.

In "Political Theory in the Anthropocene: Sustainability and Human Rights," Leslie Paul Thiele examines the relationship between sustainability and human rights and the extent to which human rights might be grounded in and inspired by a concern for living in accordance with nature (Thiele 2014). Thiele further argues that "The integration and balancing of ecological, social, and economic welfare is a complex and dynamic challenge," one that can only be achieved "by means of creative cultures." Sustainability is "the effort to satisfy current needs without sacrificing future wealth through the balanced pursuit of ecological health, economic vitality, social empowerment, and cultural creativity, all of which correspond to the protection of human rights" (Thiele 2014: 1). The paradigm of sustainability, I propose, captures the "labor" of twentieth-century Native women whose politics and initiatives reflect a refusal of conquest-of-nature philosophy which has ushered the world into the Anthropocene, an era characterized by the consequences of the massive human impact on earth in which colonial projects have figured prominently (Thiele 2014: 3). Native American women's rejection of conquest of nature converges with the history of Western rights "talk" which, in its origins, posited that "with rights come duties."[4] Restoration of and ongoing defense of Native American human rights, routinely violated throughout successive waves of colonialism, is at the heart of Native American women's twentieth and twenty-first-century history.

But this is not to succumb to a romanticized history of Native America. The history of tribal government and of federal–tribal relations offers ample opportunity to explore tensions around and obstructions to women's sustainability work, such as child-rearing, social empowerment, community work, political activism, and family support. I have found in my research in the history of a southeastern tribe that the federal government's turn to tribal self-determination, which began to take root in the late 1950s, is a potentially productive point of inquiry. Formed in a federal discourse of "development," self-determination held out the promise of economic growth, jobs, wealth administration, and freedom from the heavy hand of the Bureau of Indian Affairs. Just as trade and politics drew eighteenth-century southeastern American Indians into an Atlantic commercial network that ultimately radically altered their economies to their detriment, self-determination initiatives, too, drew once-impoverished tribal communities into a modern global economy and particularly into investment networks that made possible manufacturing start-ups, but exposed them to risk. This scenario raises questions about the relationship between economic development, sustainability initiatives, and "rights with duties." Do they compete and, if so, what is the nature of that competition? What are the outcomes? Is this a gendered arena of competition? Self-determination led to, sometimes radical, tribal governmental and constitutional reforms. How did women's sustainability work fare under self-determination reforms? Such analyses not only shine a light on women's sustainability labor, as a complicating development in the creation of modern tribal economies and governments, but also forces the critical historicization of tribal self-determination.

My work on violence against women in the twentieth century has benefited from the work of Kimberle Crenshaw, who twenty-five years ago wrote about the consequences of the failure of anti-racist and feminist discourses to address intersections of race and gender. Theoretical silos, failing to intersect, "relegate the identity of women of color to a location that resists telling" (Crenshaw 1991: 1242), but race, gender, class, and sexuality do intersect in the lives of real people. During the second half of the twentieth century at least, prominent tribal leaders' fusion of anti-racist and self-determination discourses, and absence of attention to women as a class, were consistent with other liberation movements of the time. The War on Poverty subsumed tribal people and Native women as poor mothers and heads of household in particular under the rhetoric of dependency.[5] While attention to racial violence was heightened, violence against women, located at the intersection of race, gender, class, and anti-tribalism, remained invisible. It is incumbent upon scholars to interrogate Indigenous discourses and practices not only to identify the ways in which they abet disappearing Native women and eliding their concerns, but to contextualize their efforts to sustain family, community, and tribe as well, while simultaneously assuming diversity, as a function of historical experience, geography, culture, politics, and economy. While a foray into another substantial theoretical field is beyond the scope of this chapter, scholars might do well to consider the work of transnational feminist scholars such as Chandra Talpade Mohanty whose scholarship is informed by gender, race, and colonialism, simultaneously (Mohanty 2013).

Sources continue to be problematic for writing about Native women in the twentieth century and might explain the absence of sustained work in the period. The few scholars who work on the early twentieth century continue to rely on government documents, manuscript collections, organizational archives, and other conventional sources (Cahill 2013). Work in the second half of the twentieth century becomes more challenging, particularly as tribes begin to enter into the self-determination era and assume responsibility for preservation of their government documents. The National Archives and its various branches likely retain some documents during the transitional period, but the comparative dearth of records to earlier periods is obvious. In the face of an enormously challenging transition to self-determinative governance, tribes have given short shrift to document preservation and establishment of archives. The Cherokees in Oklahoma stand out as the exception, although the establishment of the Association of Tribal Archives, Libraries, and Museums in 2010 has been a source of support for other tribes who are committed to records preservation.

In the meantime, researchers were presented with another challenge with the creation of the American Indian Research Repository in Lenexa, Kansas as a result of the Cobell suit.[6] The Repository, although nominally under the administration of the National Archives, is not a public archive, nor are records maintained according to their protocols and standards, according to the staff of the National Archives. We cannot now know the scope and content of tribal records deposited at Lenexa. Procedures for gaining access to the records at the Lenexa facility are unclear as my own futile efforts at planning research at AIRR revealed.

Researchers might expect to receive advice about consulting with tribal research offices or filing Freedom of Information Act (FOIA) requests, but neither approach is a guarantee of success which is a source of discouragement to graduate students who feel the pressure of time to degree.

One area of research that has proven most fruitful to me is in the area of court records and legal documents, as inspired by Bethany Berger's fine article "After Pocahontas: Indian Women and the Law, 1830–1934" (1997). Berger uses court cases to discuss the status of American Indian women directly, the status of American Indian women as wives, and as mothers, relative to US courts and legislatures. By carefully mining these cases, contextualized in the history of federal Indian policy, Berger's fine-grained analysis persuasively historicizes women's personal experiences with land loss, imposition of cultural ideas such as the cult of true womanhood, social relationships, and loss of power. My research in the southeast has entailed combing through innumerable dockets of several county circuit courts which, while limited, can be as revealing for what they do not contain as for their actual contents, tracking down trial transcripts, and correlating events through large collections of local newspaper holdings. Oral histories have played an important role in my research, which necessarily entail advance work on Institutional Review Board (IRB) applications. Trial transcripts are particularly useful for fleshing out details of everyday life, perceptions and representations of Native women, locating women's voices in specific contexts, and local social, economic, and political environments. Every precaution should be taken when working with such materials, particularly in the twentieth century, to avoid causing harm to persons living and deceased who might be named in the materials. While such documents are public and accessible to researchers, one cannot be too diligent in considering the potential impact of using trial transcripts on a tribal community. The size of the tribal community might make it quite difficult to protect subjects' anonymity and it is the researcher's responsibility to proceed with due diligence to these and other issues related to working with "human subjects." Here it would be wise to take heed of the old saying that "The road to hell is paved with good intentions." Competence, understanding of American Indian history, sage guidance from an experienced researcher, and scrupulous self-awareness are critical.

Twentieth-century projects are frequently potential opportunities for public humanities projects, including building and adding on to tribal document collections, collaborating in museum exhibitions, and work in the digital humanities which opens up a new world of possibilities for collaboration, the core aim of the public humanities. Scholars and tribes now routinely use new digital tools in research and to visualize new knowledge. This takes the scholarly product far beyond the conventional book and article. Digital projects can visualize connections in comparative work. For example, you might create an interactive map and timeline about women's food sovereignty projects, about tribal code reforms regarding domestic violence or child adoption, about rates of violence against women, or any other topic based on research in multiple tribal communities which will allow readers to see those connections and changes over time.

Discoveries can be embedded in modest photographic essay projects. Collaborators can create mini-museum projects consisting of objects contextualized in various environments, with textual and visual references to pop culture, academic scholarship, community events, art, and anything the imagination can conjure.[7] Projects such as these are attractive to cross-generational, academic, and institutional partners.

Primary research and all the duties and responsibilities that come with it, however, remain at the heart of public humanities projects. The public humanities is predicated on the idea that research and production, usually the domain of isolated scholars and, less so, scholars working in collaboration, should extend the reach of knowledge dissemination and utility, which can be of paramount concern to American Indian tribes. Public humanities projects will influence the lamentable practice of ignoring Native women as historical actors and as modern shapers of tribal communities. This is particularly useful to tribal museums and cultural centers which typically organize cultural exhibits around a historical narrative. Unfortunately, some of the most ambitious and well-endowed tribal museum projects fail to integrate women into their exhibits and public programs. Public history and public humanities projects can be useful to reversing this unacceptable practice.

There is no doubt that the experiences of Native women in the twentieth century should be a priority for the field of American Indian Studies and for the discipline of history. Although greatly reduced in numbers and power when they entered the twentieth century, Native communities recovered in terms of population and withstood the assaults of federal Indian policies that threatened their existence. Native women, though still seemingly invisible, were critical agents in sustaining themselves as women, their families, and their communities through economic, political, social, and cultural contributions. In my experience, Native women are eager to share their experiences with well-prepared researchers who are willing to invest time in building relationships and are attuned to community priorities and protocols. As scholars we would be remiss to replicate the mistakes of the past which either captured what little we know about women in distorting frames of western assumptions and scholarly priorities or rendered them completely invisible. It is imperative that we pay more than lip service to Native women as historical actors for the good of the academic project and for future generations of Native Americans.

Notes

1   See http://en.wikipedia.org/wiki/Category:20th-century_Native_Americans.
2   A search of the Internet for "Native American food sovereignty" will yield numerous tribal sites and a site for a Food Sovereignty Alliance.
3   The literature is voluminous, but the interested reader might begin with the work of Sarah Deer, a Creek law professor, who has been instrumental in drawing attention to violence against Native women in the United States (Deer 2005: 455).
4   For a discussion on responsibilities and human rights, see Lauren (2003: 4–10).

5   See an excellent discussion on the discursive origins and politics of "dependency" talk in Fraser and Gordon (1994).
6   See this article in *Indian Country Today* for an overview: http://indiancountrytodaymedianetwork.com/2011/12/22/indian-records-repository-kansas-preserves-indian-records-69089.
7   Many thanks to Teresa Mangum, Director, Obermann Center for Advanced Study in the Humanities, University of Iowa, for her assistance and one-on-one tutorials on Public Humanities and Digital Humanities.

References

Albers, Patricia. 1983. "Sioux women in transition: A study of their changing status in a domestic and capitalist sector of production". In Patricia Albers and Beatrice Medicine. *The Hidden Half, Studies of Plains Indian Women*. Lanham: University Press of American, Inc.

Berger, Bethany Ruth. 1997. "After Pocahontas: Indian women and the law, 1830–1934". *American Indian Law Review*, 21(1): 1–62.

Cahill, Cathleen. 2013. *Federal Fathers and Mothers: A Social History of the United States Indian Service, 1869–1933*. New Directions in Southern Studies. Chapel Hill: University of North Carolina Press.

Crenshaw, Kimberle. 1991. "Mapping the margins: Intersectionality, identity politics, and violence against women of color". *Stanford Law Review*, 43(6): 1241–1299.

Deer, Sarah. 2005. "Sovereignty of the soul: Exploring the intersection of rape law reform and federal Indian law". *Suffolk University Law Review*, 38: 455–466.

Fraser, Nancy and Linda Gordon. 1994. "A genealogy of dependency: Tracing a keyword of the U.S. welfare state". *Signs*, 19(2): 309–336.

Lauren, Paul Gordon. 2003. *The Evolution of International Human Rights, Visions Seen*. 2nd edn. Philadelphia: University of Pennsylvania Press.

LeMaster, Michelle. 2014. "Pocahontas doesn't live here anymore: women and gender in the Native South before removal". *Native South*, 7: 1–32.

Mohanty, Chandra Talpade. 2013. "Transnational feminist crossings: On neoliberalism and radical critique". *Signs*, 38(4): 967–991.

Shoemaker, Nancy, ed. 1995. *Negotiators of Change: Historical Perspectives on Native American Women*. New York: Routledge.

Thiele, Leslie. 2014. "Political theory in the anthropocene: Sustainability and human rights (2014)". APSA 2014 Annual Meeting Paper. Available at SSRN: http://ssrn.com/abstract=2452696.

20 Representations of violence

(Re)telling Indigenous women's stories and the politics of knowledge production

Shannon Speed

For the last several years, I have worked with Indigenous – mostly Mayan – women migrants from Mexico and Central America to the United States. I set out to explore how women were continuing to pursue their rights on the complicated terrain of neoliberal multicriminalism,[1] and I found that what stood out in women's stories was a staggering level of violence. Their stories are invariably compelling; they reflect both devastating intersectional vulnerability to violence and astounding agency and courage. They are hard stories to hear and harder stories to retell, particularly when that retelling takes place in the context of academic research. While the stories offer the opportunity to critically analyze a variety of violent state landscapes as the women move through them, as well as the possibility of speaking to a broad and (often hostile) public about the human experience of Indigenous migration, they also pose significant ethical dilemmas. As an Indigenous feminist anthropologist, with all of the tensions that that particular set of identifications entails,[2] I confronted a series of questions: Can the stories be told, and analysis be generated, without rendering Indigenous women's lives "raw material"[3] or "verifiable data"? Can the stories be told, in all of their pain and devastation, without falling into near-pornographic voyeurism into the suffering of others? Can the stories be told in a way that highlights how Indigenous women's race, gender, and class render them vulnerable to violence in a myriad of ways, without casting them as victims? And the question overarching all of the above, which is can the stories be told, and analysis wrested from them, without doing the fundamental anthropological work of re-colonizing them? In this chapter, I will consider these questions in relation to my work with the Hutto Visitation Project (HVP) and the Indigenous Women Migrants Oral History Project in Austin, Texas. I will argue that while the dilemmas and contradictions of anthropological representation are significant and never fully resolvable, engagement with those dilemmas and contradictions through critically engaged feminist research can produce knowledge that moves us toward greater social justice and a more decolonized discipline.

> Virgilia departed her home in southern Mexico, fleeing a domestic partner who had been beating her for years, breaking her clavicle twice and leaving permanent scars on her face and back. A Tzotzil speaker from the highlands

of Chiapas, she had been living in the city of San Cristobal since she was 14, when she left her community to become a live-in domestic servant in the home of a Ladino family. One of her main motivations in leaving her community was to escape her father, who drank heavily and abused her, as well as her mother and siblings. She had two children with her partner, ages four and seven when she fled, whom she left in the care of her sister. The decision to leave her children "broke her heart," but she was certain that it was only a matter of time before her partner, who had become involved in illegal smuggling activity and regularly carried weapons, would kill her. She paid a coyote $3000 to bring her north, most of it borrowed from her sister and the family she worked for. The journey was perilous. Although she lived in the town of San Cristobal, 25-year-old Virgilia was not worldly. The life of indigenous women in domestic servitude in San Cristobal is highly proscribed, and their activities are largely socially restricted to home, place of work, and market. Her Spanish remained limited. She was terrified. There was good reason to fear. She and others were stranded for days – eventually without food and water – when the train they were riding on broke down in a remote area. A man who offered her and two others shelter in his house threatened to rape her in the middle of the night. She was held for ransom by drug cartels in Reynosa. Freed after a brother living in Oklahoma City paid the ransom, she spent days in the desert after crossing the border and was abandoned by her coyote when Border Patrol approached and she could not run fast enough to keep up. He shouted, "Córrele pinche india! Apúrate!" ("Run, damned Indian! Hurry up!") as he ran off. Virgilia was apprehended by the Border Patrol. Agents attempted to coerce her into accepting voluntary departure to Mexico, but Virgilia refused, insisting that she was afraid to return. She was placed in political asylum proceedings and sent into the vast immigration detention system. I met her some time later in the T. Don Hutto immigration detention facility in Taylor, Texas. Shortly thereafter, an asylum officer who interviewed her by video conference and in Spanish deemed her not to have a "credible fear." Virgilia was deported.

Virgilia's story is emblematic of the devastating experiences of migration for Indigenous women from Latin America. It quickly became clear to me when I began visiting women in Hutto that women want – indeed need – to tell their stories. For the women, it is cathartic to relate their experiences, gratifying to know that others care, and comforting to learn that they are not alone in what they have experienced. The Oral History Project also offered the opportunity to discuss the larger structures of power that shape women's lives and that mark them for such violence.

And yet, the task of retelling such stories is thornier than one might imagine. To begin with, I do so from the bowels of the most colonized and colonizing of disciplines. Anthropology was birthed from the colonial project; the undertaking of anthropological representation itself constituting the quintessential violence of transforming sovereign human beings into the colonizable Others of "civilization."

At least since Vine Deloria, Jr. declared that "Indians have been cursed above all other people in history. Indians have anthropologists" (1969: 78) and signaled anthropologists' tendency to be "intolerably certain that they represent ultimate truth" (1969: 100), the coloniality of anthropology[4] for Native peoples has been blisteringly clear. In the intervening years – not because of Indian critiques, but rather because of theoretical interventions emanating from European intellectuals regarding the nature of "truth" in modernity and post-modernity – anthropologists have engaged in considerable hand-wringing regarding our representations. Anthropologists have focused overly on the subjective nature of observation and analysis (which should be a given), and the proffered solutions have been to "situate ourselves" (acknowledging our subjective location) and a recourse to the textual (there is no Truth, so all writing is fiction), rather than a much-needed critical engagement with the politics of knowledge production (the understanding that all knowledge produced has political effects on its subjects). In other words, anthropologists (with some notable exceptions) largely continue to side-step the simple question Deloria posed regarding anthropological research nearly 50 years ago: "The question for Indian people, and the ultimate question for Americans, is: What effect will it have over the lives of people?" (1969: 99).

In past work, I have argued for the value of a *critically engaged feminist/ activist research* that combines critical feminist analysis and collaboration that is directed toward some form of shared social justice goal (Speed 2006, 2008). This engagement means taking Indigenous peoples' interpretation of their experiences seriously, putting those in dialogue with the researcher's own critical analysis, and directing them consciously toward some type of shared end that is of use in peoples' lives.[5] I have also explored the problematics of such work, and this project offered much new fodder for reflection.

My work with Indigenous women migrants fit reasonably well within this framework. It was born of an activist collaboration with the Hutto Visitation Project (HVP), a social justice organization that provides accompaniment to detainees, and emerged out of the needs and interests of the women migrants themselves. Further, it offered the opportunity to reflect on settler colonial and neoliberal conditions, and the attendant race, class, and gender ideologies that structure the field of experience within which the women's lives take place. It gave the women the ability to retake control of their own stories (something they are deprived of in the course of unfolding events so entirely out of their control), and at the same time offered me the opportunity to analyze from these stories about Indigenous women's oppression. It allowed us to bring our different knowledges to the work, to create something we all hoped would give other women strength and help build social change.

However, a plethora of issues cropped up for me as soon as I undertook the project. Perhaps most immediate were questions regarding representation and truth.[6] In my academic writing, as can be seen in the example of Virgilia's story, I am not doing strict oral history, i.e. recording and reproducing verbatim what Virgilia said. There are ample debates in the field of oral history and *testimonio* regarding the merits of verbatim transcription, editing, contextualizing and, above all, analyzing. Institutional Review Boards in the United States, for example, take oral history to be such a restricted field (recording people's memories and preserving them) that it does not constitute "research," and thus is not subject to human subjects review. This is problematic because, as Blackwell argues, "*Testimonio* and oral history are often received … as the supposedly pure Other or subaltern through a supposedly unmediated narrative" (2011: 42). There has been a fair amount of deliberation about how oral history/testimony works as unmediated "data" and particularly whether peoples' oral recountings can or should be taken as truth given the vicissitudes of memory.

Those debating oral histories' worth as data rarely address the ethical question of regarding people's lives as something comparable to documents or other data sources, and tend to focus instead on their verifiability (or not). I am asked on an alarmingly regular basis, by academics and other generally progressive people, whether I should consider the possibility that the women are fabricating their stories in order to gain political asylum. My short answer is, "No." The longer answer is that I am astounded at the mental lengths people are willing to go to in order not to confront the appalling levels of violence that Indigenous women are subject to. If details of women's stories shift, or chronology is off, rather than deception, it is likely due to one or more of the following: 1) trauma (well-known to cause memory elisions and blocks), 2) cultural difference (particularly notable in relation to narrative and chronology), and 3) fear and anxiety (Are people understanding my poor Spanish? How can I tell this story so that people will understand that my life is at stake?). All of these constitute part of the women's experience, and are as "true" as an aspect of their narration.

Indigenous feminists have tended to be less concerned with such questions, for several reasons: we tend to be more comfortable (without falling into facile stereotypes) with storytelling as a mode of knowledge transferal (Cavender Wilson 1996, Archibald 2008); we tend not to be invested in hierarchically positioned Western positivist notions of truth (Smith 1996, Yellowbird 1995), and, relatedly; we tend to hold Indigenous women's experience and its telling as a valid form of theorization (Archuleta 2006). Thus, my interest in this project is not to provide a history that is testable and verifiably "true" in some abstract sense. Nor am I particularly interested in deconstructing women's testimony in order to show how one or another thing has led them to remember or recount in "incorrect" ways. The women's memory of their experience is itself the *embodied experience* of what has happened to them, and in that sense is the "real" story I am interested in, and which presents a source of knowledge not bound by hegemonic ideological frames.

While I do not analyze their embodied stories in the deconstructive sense, I am interested in what they tell us regarding how race, class, and gender are working in the current context. These ideologies shape what experiences the women have, making them vulnerable for violence at every step. But they also shape how women experience events in their lives, and how they remember those experiences. It is thus crucial that we ask how gender, race and class, as structural and ideological relations, shape the construction of historical memory, not to make claims *about* their stories (as true/false) but rather to make claims *from* their stories. For example, Virgilia recounts how a man who offered her and other immigrants shelter for the night threatened to rape her. I asked Virgilia how he had threatened her. She replied, "I don't remember. Maybe he didn't say anything. I just knew that he would." That Virgilia both experienced it as a rape threat and remembers it as one, in the absence of verbal or physical evidence of a threat, is a product of her positionality as an Indigenous woman, vulnerable to such violence due to her race and gender. What I take from this is not that her story is faulty, but that race and gender fundamentally structure the way Indigenous women experience the world. Oral histories present one way of grasping this knowledge. Stephen argues that "oral testimony as an embodied speech act permits people to represent personal histories within fused/inseparable identity categories of gender, race, ethnicity, class, sexuality and more" (2015: 9). The women's stories often in this way bypass the categorizations so prevalent in Western academic theorizing: of "race" as analytically separable from "gender," etc., which inevitably invisibilize Indigenous women, and instead, departing from their complex self-representations, offer new ways to think about the fields in which they are multiple constituted as social actors.

The fact that the women's stories are so deeply imbued with violence presents another layer of complexity. I have grappled with the question of how to write the stories so that they conveyed the full weight of the women's experience – with all of the pain and fear and anguish that attend such violent experiences – yet not engage in what might be termed "pornographics of violence," rendering their stories titillating entertainment for the privileged who will never experience it. Matthews and Goodman (2013) have critically analyzed the ways in which violence is framed, mediated, and regulated through representations. As a Native feminist, I am highly cognizant of the increased dangers when representing Indigenous women and gender violence because of the dual potential for anthropological representations to "delve into two central western fantasies – the eroticization of domination and the eroticization of 'the (dominated) Other'" (Harvey and Gow 2013: 2). Yet, the ways the women were marked for violence in multiple forms and in many contexts was precisely what I found compelling about their stories.

My approach to this has been to look to the women's stories for guidance. How do they understand and talk about the violence to which they have been subject? This exercise led me to the insight that the women themselves did the opposite of sensationalizing: that violence is so much a naturalized part of their lives that they do not find any of these events particularly exceptional. Not pleasant, not desirable, but simply the norm of their interaction with the world. We can see one example in Virgilia's story: she experiences multiple forms of violence since her earliest formative years and expects it to characterize her interactions – even, for example, with the person who was ostensibly offering her shelter. In other words, seeking a path to appropriate representation of their stories led me to new knowledge that they conveyed through their narration, perhaps not explicitly, but multiple registers (Blackwell 2011).

The aspiration to a *critically engaged feminist research* carries with it all manner of tensions and contradictions, only a few of which I have considered here. However, by taking Indigenous women's stories seriously as organic theorizations, which we put into dialogue with our critical analysis, we can move toward a shared knowledge production that has some common ends. This does not resolve the power imbalances that inhere – in the end I still have the final control over these representations – but by presenting them in ways that allow women not just to tell the stories but to give validity to the knowledge they generate, we might do something akin to what Emberley has called an *analytics of (dis)memberment*, in which "representational strategies that seek to tell the truth of the body's pain, suffering, joy and pleasure, must both re-member knowledge of the body and dis-member officially sanctioned truths as to what constitutes this knowledge" (2010: 223). As Blackwell has framed the issue, "through [subaltern women's oral histories] a different way of knowing or new epistemologies are introduced into the (warped) historical record" (2011: 39). While such knowledge production will not, of course, end violence in women's lives or the conditions of oppression in which they live, it gives sustained attention to not affecting further violence through the representational process, and to "re-membering" the violence Indigenous women suffer in ways that challenge the hierarchies of knowledge and truth that enjoy hegemonic power in the colonized world. We can hope that the shared authority ultimately generates knowledge that might be of help to other women in their search for understanding and healing, and ultimately contributes to a better comprehension of the working of power in the current moment, in order to better contest and resist it.

Notes

1 "Neoliberal multicriminalism" is a term I use to refer to states such as Mexico, which are characterized by all the devastation of unrestrained neoliberal economies, without the benefit of the democratic politics, rights regimes, and rule of law that neoliberal reform was supposed to bring with it. This has resulted in mass-scale illegal economies, and states simultaneously engaging in authoritarian governance and militarization to combat illegality, while blatantly participating in it to reap some of the profits. See Speed (2016).
2 The problematics of anthropology and Indigenous peoples is dealt with later in the text. Both the nature and the merits of "Native/Indigenous feminisms" have been long discussed. It is outside the scope of this text to cover these debates, but I will say briefly that while I acknowledge the argument that feminism is a foreign concept (in the United States/Canada usually understood as pertaining to white women, in Latin America as a product of urban/academic/hegemonic thinking), Indigenous women from throughout the continent have increasingly appropriated the term to describe and contest the interrelated forms of oppression that are mutually constitutive in our lives.
3 Lourdes Tiban, Kichua activist/attorney/scholar, in a 2005 workshop of the Ford Foundation-funded project "Governing in Diversity," regarding the role of Indigenous researchers: "No soy material prima" (I am not raw material [of this research]).
4 With "coloniality of power" Quijano theorized the legacy of colonialism in contemporary (Latin American) societies, particularly the racialized hierarchical social orders imposed by European colonialism that systematically attribute value to certain peoples and justify the subordination of others (Quijano 2000). I use "coloniality of anthropology" to signal anthropology's key function in regard to that system. For a critique of Quijano's work from an Indigenous standpoint, see Rivera Cusicanqui (2012). For a gender critique, see Lugones (2007).

184   *S. Speed*

5   I would note (lest Vine Deloria, Jr. haunt me) that this is a very different undertaking
    from APPLIED anthropology, designed by anthropologists to "help" Indian people.

References

Archibald, Jo-ann. 2008. *Indigenous Storywork: Educating the Heart, Mind, Body, and Spirit*. Vancouver: UBC Press.

Archuleta, Elizabeth. 2006. "'I give you back': Indigenous women writing to survive". *Studies in American Indian Literatures*, 18(4): 88–114.

Blackwell, Maylie. 2011. *Chicana Power! Contested Histories of Feminism in the Chicana Movement*. Austin: University of Texas Press.

Cavender Wilson, Angela. 1996. "Grandmother to granddaughter: Generations of oral history in a Dakota family". *American Indian Quarterly*, 20(1): 7–13.

Deloria, Jr.,Vine. 1969. *Custer Died for Your Sins*. New York: Macmillan.

Emberley, Julia. 2010. "To spirit walk the letter and the law: Gender, race, and representational violence in Rudy Wiebe and Yvonne Johnson's 'Stolen Life: The Journey of a Cree Woman'". In Cheryl Suzack, Shari M. Hundorf, Jeanne Perreault, and Jean Bartman, eds. *Indigenous Women and Feminism: Politics, Activism, Culture*. Ontario: University of British Columbia Press, pp. 218–238.

Harvey, Penelope and Peter Gow, eds. 2013. *Sex and Violence: Issues in Representation and Experience*. New York: Routledge.

Lugones, María. 2007. "Heterosexualism and the colonial / modern gender system". *Hypatia*, 22(1): 186–209.

Matthews, Graham and Sam Goodman, eds. 2013. *Violence and the Limits of Representation*. London: Palgrave Macmillan.

Quijano, Anibal. 2000. "Coloniality of power, Eurocentrism, and Latin Amercica". *Nepantla: Views From the South*, 1(3): 533–580.

Rivera Cusicanqui, Silvia 2012. "*Ch'ixinakax utxiwa*: A reflection on the practices and discourses of decolonization". *South Atlantic Quarterly*, 111(1): 95–109.

Smith, Linda Tuhiwai. 1996. *Decolonizing Methodologies: Research and Indigenous Peoples*. London: Zed Books.

Speed, Shannon. 2006. "At the crossroads of human rights and anthropology: Toward a critically-engaged activist research". *American Anthropologist* 108(1): 66–77.

Speed, Shannon. 2008. "Forged in dialogue: Towards a critically engaged activist research". In Charles R. Hale, ed. Engaging *Contradictions: Activist Scholarship in Interdisciplinary Perspective*. Berkeley: University of California Press, pp. 213–236.

Speed, Shannon. 2016. "States of violence: indigenous women migrants in the era of neoliberal multicriminalism." *Critique of Anthropology* 36:3

Stephen, Lynn. 2015. "Bearing witness: Truths, audiences, strategies, and outcomes". *LASA Forum*, XLVI(3): 4–14.

Yellowbird, Michael. 1995. "Tribal critical thinking centers". In *For Indigenous Eyes Only*. Santa Fe: School of American Research, pp. 9–30.

21 Indigenous interventions and feminist methods

Mishuana Goeman

It is a common misperception that feminism reflects a man-hating, idealistic, naive, and frivolous set of goals and that angry white women set this agenda. Feminists thus are also depicted as promoting agendas that are not important to a majority of Indigenous communities. This is especially true of Indigenous communities who are fighting for self-determination and sovereignty, a fight which differs from a rights paradigm that demands inclusion into the nation-state. The notion that feminism has only three waves and that it originated solely with Euro-Americans at the time of suffrage movements (early 1900s) has hindered the development of feminist conversations that have much to add to many disciplinary fields. Developments of Native and Indigenous feminist methodologies demonstrate the importance of revisiting these assumptions. Gendered analysis needs to move beyond early framings of "loss" of culture leading to "loss" of status and present a much more complex, intersectional assessment of pivotal issues in Indigenous communities. Indigenous feminist methods intervene and provide the distinction of alternative gender norms and relationships to governance at multiple scales: from roles in one's community to larger peoplehood (Anderson 2000; Allen 1986; Medicine et al. 2001), from Indigenous nation to nation (Allen 2012; Huhndorf 2009; Stark 2012), from Indigenous nation to settler nation-state, to larger global communities.

Currently, feminist traction is needed to address the policies and structures that can be the difference between life and death for Indigenous women and children around the globe. Claims of feminism conceived of in mainstream temporal and racialized ways has a material impact on Indigenous communities. That is, it is not just a matter of erasure from the historical record or the need to add Native women's voices, rather it frames the conversations around politics, economics, and the issues that need to be addressed external and internal to communities, such as domestic violence, sexual assault, poverty, the prison system, and other commonplace issues. What is missing in these particular and commonplace feminist scenarios is the long-standing struggles and work of Indigenous women both historically and in the contemporary moment. Early Native feminist Luana Ross ends her essay on the conception of feminism as the "F word" in Indian country by questioning the role of a feminist methodology: "Must women of color renounce feminism in order for racism to be dealt with effectively by white women? This question reminds us of the fragility of feminist sisterhood and the pervasiveness of racism in the United States" (Ross 2009: 49). We must ask, as Lisa Hall in the context of Native Hawaiian feminism does, "Who benefits by the repeated assertions of a Euro-centric trajectory and timeline to describe feminist theory and activism in the US?" (Hall 2009: 26). Indeed, Native feminist scholars go a step further to ask who benefits on a transnational scale and in global economies and politics by such a Euro-centric spatial, temporal, geographical, and racialized definition of feminism.

The development of feminism is situated in the event, the Seneca Falls Convention, that would lead to women (racialized as white) voting across many Westphalian nation-states in the 1920s. This so-called first wave occludes much of black women's work toward abolition as well as the influence that Native cultures surrounding them had on the movement. Disrupting common discourses about whitestream feminism, while not the primary goal of Native feminist methodology, began early in the field of Indigenous studies. Paula Gunn Allen and Rayna Green call upon scholars to address weak constructions of feminism made from either excluding Native women from the narrative, such as in Allen's "Red Roots of White Feminism," or appropriating and playing Indian in their earlier machinations, such as explicated in Green's very early intervention "Pocahontas Perplex" (Green 1975). Dominant genealogies and etymologies of feminism are a colonial entrapment that helps to sustain mainstream feminist ideologies, feminist colonial practices, white supremacy, and colonial patriarchy.

Acclaimed feminist scholar, Estelle Freedman, notes in *No Turning Back: The History of Feminism and the Future of Woman*, that from the start the "term was always controversial" and proceeds to argue that the rise of capitalism in state economies displaced early forms of familial reliance. Accompanying this was a reconfiguration of statehood focused on the rights of the individual (Freedman 2003). However, in this premise does Freedman speak to the displacement, dispossession, and destruction of Indigenous land and lifeways that made possible these transitions. Scholars must examine colonial dispossession in the trajectory of feminism in order to understand better the nexus of power that continues to undergird a unilaterally patriarchal settler power. For instance, acknowledgement that early suffragists gained the first US Senate stage to discuss the suffrage of white women in 1887 was in large part because of westward expansion and the violent dispossession of Native lands and bodies resituates our understanding of complex gender and nation-building roles (Sneider 2008: 58). Settler states, ones of liberal democracy, are built on individual property accumulation. Suffragists were often quick to write against the obtainment of citizenship for Indians in these new "representational governments," the very same institutions that Freedman speaks to as a burgeoning transition points of feminist movements. These early feminists fought to obtain property and be included in its inheritance. White women used the Indian Citizenship Act to garner traction for the vote, promoting the fear of supposedly savage Indian men having authority over white women who would then in turn treat them as beasts of burden. This constructed and well-circulated gender iconography of male/female relationships in Indigenous communities enabled suffragists to gain the political mobility needed to advocate for their own full citizenship rights.

Margaret Jacobs in *Mother to a Dark Race* explores the relationship between white women in Australia, the United States' involvement in maternalist movements, and those feminists involved in the removal and gender disciplining of Indigenous bodies and tribal communities (Jacobs 2009). This sustained archival study documents early whitestream feminist complicity in settler patriarchy. Suffragists' adamant claims to white superiority and Indigenous savagery laid the groundwork for *their individual advancement as white women* into settler regimes of power. This power would later continue to follow these settler common-sense notions and expand to many continents outside the commonwealth states, moving into the Pacific Islands and other continents. Concepts of Indian savagery continue today in development of laws and policies that undermine Indigenous sovereignty.

It is the simultaneous control over the definition of feminism and the lack of addressing this history that has had such long-lasting, memorable and documented effects for tribal communities, making it a difficult path to claim feminism as a movement or as a methodology for those seeking healthy Indigenous communities, self-determination, continuity, and sovereignty. Native feminisms, however, as a methodology often engage in politics of refusal; that is, as Audra Simpson (2014) states, refusal to let settlers define subjectivity, communities, politics, history, or stories. She positions the colonial context as a coercive way that the settler state demands the colonized to govern, identify, act, or resist in order to receive minor advancements. Simpson prompts a refusal of a politics of inclusion that encompass certain forms of political belonging and citizenship, stating: "The primary way in which the state's power is made real and personal, affective in its capacity, is through the granting of citizenship and, in this, the structural and legal preconditions for intimacy, forms of sociability, belongings, and affections" (2014: 106). This refusal to allow a whitestreaming of Indigenous women's politics and organizing enables Indigenous feminists to not only define intellectual engagements from the site of their communities, but in doing so it creates a practice that pays attention to the particularities of community needs on the ground. Refusal thus enables a generative questioning of directions in research.

For instance, many Indigenous women refused forced citizenship into the United States or Canada and still do. Rather than accept forms of belonging, solutions that feminists at the time were scrambling for, these early women knew that adherence meant a step toward eradication of their nation, treaties, laws as well as their sovereign space in the world. Not everyone agreed with this refusal, as Native people – women and men – debated about the best path forward in the context of colonialism. As ethnologist Alice C. Fletcher makes clear in an 1888 *Report of the International Council of Women*, Indian women "have met with but one response. They have said: As an Indian woman I was free. I owned my home, my person, the work of my own hands, and my children should never forget me. I was better as an Indian woman than under white law." The imposition of the 1924

Indian Citizenship Act took place against the will of many Indigenous nations, particularly Haudenosaunee on whose lands the first feminist convention occurred. This is not a geographic coincidence, but rather the *Seneca Falls Convention* took place in a territory where land is entrusted to Haudenosaunee women and where that land is not inanimate property, but rather the center of political, social, cultural, and economic life (Goeman 2015). Indigenous women often still view their primary citizenship relationship to that of their Indigenous nation.

However, this nation-to-nation relationship analysis by Native peoples differed significantly in how white suffragists viewed settler law and the bodies managed under its auspices. For some community members the vision of white suffragists fighting against the subjugation and extraction of labor of vulnerable subjects was evidence that the settler citizens did not hold the moral high ground. Their contemporary political activist, Laura Cornelius Kellogg, who played an influential role in Oneida tribal politics, as well as tribal politics on a national stage, at the time was active in defining Indigenous politics from housing to labor to reservation economics. Rather than working through the narrow limits of equal rights, she strove to work through what she determined were "new conditions" brought on by colonization and often had scathing critiques of the very ranks white suffragists were trying to join. In one such instance, she definitively stated in regards to child labor, "No, I cannot see that everything the white man does is to be copied" (SAI 1912: 46–48). Kellogg, like many other Indigenous women working to ensure the physical and cultural survival of their communities at the time, disrupts the wave genealogies of feminisms: "It is a cause of astonishment to us that you white women are only now, in this twentieth century, claiming what has been the Indian women's privilege as far back as history traces" (Ackley and Stanciu 2015: 30). Freedman's widely accepted analysis of suffrage debates largely positions disagreements about the organization of rights around distribution of property. Mainly white women were concerned about universal rights, including that of property (bodily property, children, and material), and the right to suffrage that would ensure property protection. This differed from those concerned with the right to motherhood and still others were concerned with the concentration of rights defined by the middle class. While white suffragists in some camps fought for the right to their children, many of these camps were the ones that denied Indigenous women's rights to raise children without threats of death or removal. In fact, in later years policy would dictate a gendered process of domesticating Indian bodies that went hand in hand with the domestication of Indian land.

In particular, Matilda Josyln Gage would "demand citizenship denied" to American Indians on the basis of "political degradation" of "She, educated, enlightened, Christian" who "in vain begs for the crumbs cast contemptuously aside by savages" (SAI 1912: 58). Margaret Jacobs makes clear not only the complicity of feminists in enacting gendered forms of violence on Indigenous communities, but also how it actively drove forward their own objectives:

> Changing indigenous gender roles, transforming indigenous homes through promoting domesticity, and monitoring girl's bodies and containing their

sexuality figured prominently in white women's agenda. To achieve these aims, the women resorted to measures of surveillance and control that differed little from the state's approach.

(Jacobs 2009: 282)

Indigenous feminist methods raise awareness of these histories and in doing so upset the teleology of gender equity development and obscuring of the outright racist attitude of early suffragists that relied on the dichotomy of either the dying noble savage or the savage that must be eliminated by brute force. For Indigenous women, the heteropatriarchial state *is* the violent actor, not the protector of rights. The early moments of feminism spoken about above orbited around making the boundaries of the early nation-state manageable and by necessity, this meant controlling gender and sexuality (Rifkin 2014), while articulating US belonging. The borders and creation of property was done so through gendered violence, a main theme that runs throughout the field of Native and Indigenous feminisms (Goeman 2013; Robinson 2015). Mainstream forms of feminism, or whitestreaming forms of feminisms that may also include people of color who hold those ideals (Grande 2004: 9, 181), still rest in these "affections" rooted in white supremacy. Historians and mainstream feminists often distil a complicated story of race-making and violent territorial expansion into a singular narrative of heroic white women fighting for suffrage and full citizenship, and Indigenous feminist studies complicate this teleology. The method of categorizing and containing these movements into the waves of feminism is part of the project of elimination, a technique meant to uphold settler-governing structures (Wolfe 2006).

Turning to the coining of the word "feminism", for instance, exposes an important distinction in Indigenous feminist methods of situating gender analysis within tribal contexts. This method creates an intervention into rigid categorizations. Freedman outlines the etymology from a largely European and North American context (one in which she tangentially includes Indiegnous presence). The word "feminism" was first used in English in 1892 to designate a movement of women, though there were earlier iterations pertaining to the perceived "nature" of women traced to the word *femme* and the suffix *ism* that denotes a movement took place. At the convention in Paris, *féminique* was foundational to the discourse; it was a title derived from the biological determinate caricatures of feminine qualities thus defining what it meant to be a woman (Haslanger et al. 2014). In these conversations, the disciplining of binary gender constructions produced a widely accepted normative binary of man/ woman that precluded other formations. However, this constructing of a normative biological idea of womanhood coincided with decades of mass physical and cultural genocide of Indigenous peoples that had numerous genders, multiple constructions of womanhood and relationships to the non-human. These gendered philosophies stemmed from non-dualistic ways of being which often did not privilege the human (Calhoun et al. 2007). In her foundational book, *The Sacred Hoop: Recovering the Feminine in American Indian Traditions*, Allen disrupts western notions of gender and sexuality by putting forth various tribal perspectives. Allen's important work reminds us that Indigenous feminist methods should not be nostalgic:

> Modern American Indian women ... are deeply engaged in the struggle to redefine themselves. In their struggle they must reconcile traditional tribal definitions of women with industrial and postindustrial non-Indian definitions ... Indian women must somehow harmonize and integrate both in their own lives.
>
> (Allen 1986: 43)

Anthropologists who examined differing gender and sexuality constructions in Indigenous and Native communities also buttressed the work of gender construction in Indigenous communities.[1]

Relationships in Indigenous communities did not solely orientate between men and women but rather promoted the well-being of the communities through various roles. An Indigenous feminist analytic compels us to push beyond constructions of assimilation that only deals with the nexus of race and demands we account for gender and sexuality. Gender and heteronormative violence enacted in colonial policy and military operations had at its core a compulsion to a dominant understanding of gender and sexuality as it enforced marriages, stymied reproduction as well as choice, prevented the continuation of gender roles, and, as Mark Rifkin writes, entailed "an effort to make them [Indians] straight" (Rifkin 2011: 8). As early feminist Beth Brant writing in the 1980s and later Qwo-li Driskell and Scott Morgensen remind us, Native peoples who presented as "queer" or living outside of a heteronormative lifestyle became targets of violence (Morgensen 2011; Driskill et al. 2011).

Native and Indigenous feminist studies' methodology, however, is less concerned with the description of these alternative knowledges that can then be engaged with by individual members or appropriated into LGBTTQ movements. Instead, it constellates its engagement with these alternative ways of being by questioning how its repression is necessary to the structuring of colonial power and how legibility of these issues must be addressed on the ground in communities and within our theorizing and organizing. Addressing gender and sexuality in our moves to decolonize is not optional. Mark Rifkin, in *When Did Indians Become Straight*, addresses the eradication of Indigenous forms of gender and sexual orientations as beyond that of just mere oppression, in fact he astutely observes that modern forms of sexuality *were formed in the colonial moment* and against the gendered practices of Native and Indigenous nations:

> If "every civilization" has acknowledged the "unique bond" of heteroconjugality, what about those parts of history, and peoples, that have not been characterized as having "civilization," that have provided the savage counterpoint against which to define the civilized and that have been made the object of a mission to bring to them the saving grace of enlightenment?
>
> (Rifkin 2011: 4)

Rifkin proposes that Native nations in the United States must become legible through implementation of these newly introduced forms of gender and sexuality.

Native feminist studies have clearly laid out what the implications of addressing Native women and queer subjectivity and politics would mean, and as Deborah Miranda fiercely states:

> The crimes against humanity committed in the name of colonization become visible alongside these women, while the U.S. constitution and the Bill of Rights, as well as every treaty ever written and every protest against genocide in "other countries," suddenly become testimony that strangles American mythology and Identity. In other words, we cannot be allowed to *see* indigenous women in all their erotic glory without also *seeing* and acknowledging all that has been done to make those women – their bodies and culture – extinct.
>
> (Miranda 2002: 145)

Distrust and contention with feminism stems from the dominant mainstream narrative that center European Americans and their settler systems. What often is not dismissed in Indigenous communities is the strength of women and their necessity for ongoing growth of communities. Sandy Grande self-describes as "Indigena," asserting: "I theorize and act in public life from a standpoint that presumes *decolonization* (not feminism) as the central political project" (Grande 2004: 329). That is not to say that the mainstream or "whitestream" feminist targets of sexism, homophobia, or injustice does not occur in communities (which I widely define as not just reservation but urban and rural based as well), or forms of patriarchal control do not exist. Joanne Barker in writing about *The Indian Act* in Canada reminds us that even after correcting years of sexist legislation that withdrew Indian women's status based on nineteenth-century racial and gender logics, the consequent reiterations "did not create gender-based inequalities or sexism within Indian communities" but rather "represented and perpetuated a much longer process" that "contributed to the normalization and legitimization of Indian male privilege within band governments" (Barker 2008: 262–263). The tentacles of patriarchy are deep and must be reckoned with if we are to move toward creating even healthier communities.

In Native and Indigenous feminist studies, scholars bravely critique the following: the rhetoric of a nostalgic past that evades the real work and responsibilities it took and takes to maintain healthy communities; the rhetoric of tradition that is used to exclude or discipline bodies; the construction of culture as stagnant and not accounting for continued growth since time immemorial; the belief of state permanence, legitimacy and ongoing sustainability of capitalism in its current forms; and the rhetoric of sovereignty that puts aside rights of some of its citizens and expects compliance even against one's own (and extended families) interest. Indigenous feminisms asserts a relationship between the naming and the doing – that is that many of the concepts above are unstable and being reformulated on individual, clan, and nation levels to ensure survivance. The plurality of Native feminisms reflects the doing on the ground and the necessity of communities to determine the direction of these practices.

Many fields of inquiry have yet to engage with, much less exhaust, the rich contributions of Indigenous feminisms. Utilizing Indigenous feminist methodologies in a multitude of rigorous conversations is an important step to unsettling ongoing state violence. It promotes a consideration for how gendered colonialisms continue to form many of the issues Indigenous communities face. By moving beyond an additive or lip-service model of Indigenous feminist inclusion into multiple fields, new questions and methods arise that restructure questions around the political, cultural, and social. As Deborah Miranda reminds us, "If Native women, who bear the scars from five hundred years of erotic murder in this country, suddenly become visible, there is hell to pay" (Miranda 2002: 145). The various methods employed by Indigenous feminist studies asks us all to rethink the structures that make possible great injustices that often have an intersectional gendered undergirding, and they ask us to consider moves toward justice that do not reaffirm the power of the state. An Indigenous feminist methodology restructures settler colonial hierarchies that rely on normative gender, sex, and racial hierarchies. By asserting the importance of Indigenous values and histories, Indigenous women have redefined commonly held notions of feminism. They have fashioned it into an important instrument for those working for social justice to utilize in their development of anti-colonial tactics, to push decolonization beyond the metaphor (Arvin et al. 2013: 25), and assert a self-determination that works for all.

Note

1   Here I am referring to work by Beatrice Medicine, one of the first women anthropologist who would pay particular attention to the importance of gender roles in communities. This was followed by those looking for alternative sexualities that at time would present unfortunate and controversial terminology such as the Berdache, see Gilley (2006), Lang (1998) and Roscoe (1998).

References

Ackley, Kristina and Christina Stanciu, eds. 2015. *Laura Cornelius Kellogg: Our Democracy and the American Indian and Other Works*. Syracuse: Syracuse University Press.

Allen, Chadwick. 2012. *Trans-Indigenous: Methodologies for Global Native Literary Studies*. Minneapolis: University of Minnesota Press.

Allen, Paula Gunn. 1986. *The Sacred Hoop: Recovering the Feminine in American Indian Traditions*. Boston: Beacon Press.

Anderson, Kim. 2000. *A Recognition of Being: Reconstructing Native Womanhood*. Toronto: Sumach Press.

Arvin, Maile, Eve Tuck, and Angie Morrill. 2013. "Decolonizing feminism: Challenging connections between settler colonialism and heteropatriarchy". *Feminist Formations*, 25(1): 8–34.

Barker, Joanne. 2008. "Gender, sovereignty, rights: Native women's activism against social inequality and violence in Canada". *American Quarterly*, 60(2): 259–266.

Calhoun, Anne, Mishuana Goeman, and Monica Tsetblikai. 2007. "Achieving gender equity for Native Americans". In Susan S. Klein, ed. *Handbook for Achieving Gender Equity Through Education*. 2nd edn. New York and London: Routledge, pp. 525–552.

Driskill, Qwo-Li, Chris Finley, Brian Joseph Gilley, and Scott Lauria Morgensen, eds. 2011. *Queer Indigenous Studies: Critical Interventions in Theory, Politics, and Literature*. Tucson: University of Arizona Press.

Freedman, Estelle B. 2003. *No Turning Back: The History of Feminism and the Future of Women*. New York: Ballantine Books.

Gilley, Brian J. 2006. *Becoming Two-Spirit: Gay Identity and Social Acceptance in Indian Country*. Lincoln: University of Nebraska Press.

Goeman, Mishuana. 2013. *Mark My Words: Native Women Mapping Our Nations*. Minneapolis: University of Minnesota Press.

Goeman, Mishuana. 2015. "Land as life: Unsettling the logics of containment". In Stephanie Nohelani Teves, Andrea Smith, and Michelle H. Raheja, eds. *Native Studies Keywords*. Tucson: University of Arizona Press, pp. 71–89.

Grande, Sandy. 2004. *Red Pedagogy: Native American Social and Political Thought*. Lanham: Rowman & Littlefield.

Green, Rayna. 1975. "Pocahontas perplex: The image of Indian women in American culture". *The Massachusetts Review*, 16(4): 698–714.

Hall, Lisa Kahaleole. 2009. "Navigating our own 'sea of islands': Remapping a theoretical space for Hawaiian women and Indigenous feminism". *Wicazo Sa Review*, 24(2): 15–38.

Haslanger, Sally, Nancy Tuana, and Peg O'Connor. 2015. "Topics in feminism". In Edward N. Zalta, ed. *The Stanford Encyclopedia of Philosophy*. http://plato.stanford.edu/archives/spr2014/entries/feminism-topics.

Huhndorf, Shari M. 2009. *Mapping the Americas: The Transnational Politics of Contemporary Native Culture*. Ithaca: Cornell University Press.

Jacobs, Margaret. 2009. *White Mother to a Dark Race*. Lincoln and London: University of Nebraska Press.

Lang, Sabine. 1998. *Men as Women, Women as Men: Changing Gender in Native American Cultures*. Austin: University of Texas Press.

Medicine, Beatrice, and Margaret Jacobs. 2001. *Learning to be an Anthropologist and Remaining "Native": Selected Writings*. Urbana: University of Illinois Press.

Miranda, Deborah A. 2002. "Dildos, hummingbirds, and driving her crazy: Searching for American Indian women's love poetry and erotics". *Frontiers: A Journal of Women's Studies*, 23: 135–149.

Morgensen, Scott L. 2011. *Spaces Between Us: Queer Settler Colonialism and Indigenous Decolonization*. Minneapolis: University of Minnesota Press.

Report of the International Council of Women Assembled by the National Woman Suffrage Association, Washington, D.C., U.S. of America, March 25 to April 1, 1888. 1888. Washington, DC: Rufus H. Darby.

Rifkin, Mark. 2011. *When Did Indians Become Straight? Kinship, the History of Sexuality, and Native Sovereignty*. New York: Oxford University Press.

Rifkin, Mark. 2014. "Making peoples into populations: The racial limits of tribal sovereignty". In Audra Simpson and Andrea Smith, eds. *Theorizing Native Studies*. Durham, NC: Duke University Press, pp. 149–187.

Robinson, Aileen. 2015. *The White Possessive: Property, Power, and Indigenous Sovereignty*. Minneapolis: University of Minnesota Press.

Roscoe, Will. 1998. *Changing Ones: Third and Fourth Genders in Native North America.* New York: St. Martin's Press.

Ross, Luana. 2009. "From the 'F' word to Indigenous/feminisms". *Wicazo Sa Review*, 24(2): 39–52.

Simpson, Audra. 2014. *Mohawk Interruptus: Political Life across the Borders of Settler States.* Durham, NC: Duke University Press.

Society of American Indians (SAI). 1912. *Report of the Executive Council on the Proceedings of the First Annual Conference of the Society of American Indians Held at the University of Ohio, Columbus, Ohio, October 12–17*, 1911. Washington, DC: SAI.

Sneider, Allison L. 2008. *Suffragists in an Imperial Age: U.S. Expansion and the Woman Question, 1870–1929.* Oxford and New York: Oxford University Press.

Stark, Heidi Kiiwetinepinesiik. 2012. "Marked by fire: Anishinaabe articulations of nationhood in treaty-making with the United States and Canada". *American Indian Quarterly*, 36(2): 119–149.

Wolfe, Patrick. 2006. "Settler colonialism and the elimination of the native". *Journal of Genocide Research*, 8(4): 387–409.

22 History and masculinity[1]

Brendan Hokowhitu

There are two points that should be made clear from the outset. First, Masculinity Studies has until very recently been consumed with the analysis of masculine forms of whiteness. Second, the majority of post-Enlightenment history, including colonial/postcolonial history, has not only been tacitly infused with a masculine worldview, but also ostensibly about white masculinity itself. The fact that colonization, for example, was/is a gendered project remained unspoken until very recently. Part of this silence included an assumption that the settler heterosexual male embodied the power of human reason and, thus, represented the interests and will of humanity. Reason, as conceived of as dispassionate and disembodied, was/is in fact settler masculine reason and, consequently, the liberal humanist appeal to the individual is, more succinctly, an appeal to an idealized universal European masculinity, where European bourgeois heterosexual masculinity came to represent humanity itself: "this Man, rational, self-determined and, since Descartes at least, the center of his universe, serves as the privileged unmarked term against which all humans are measured" (Drichel 2008: 594). I begin with these related points because they in part answer why Masculinity Studies in general is juvenile (i.e., because the bounds of reason and thus alterity were defined by men) and signify a will to occlude the omnipresence of masculinity within scholarship more broadly. In history, for instance, John Beynon argues, "Historians have largely taken masculinity for granted and, therefore, it has passed largely unquestioned" (Beynon 2002: 58).

In many ways, the long absence of masculinity as a field of study reflects what Bob (now Raewyn) Connell referred to as 'Patriarchal Dividend' in that the surplus associated with simply being a man, in Western cultures at least, speaks to the tacit ways that power works through gender. Indeed, it wasn't until Connell's ground-breaking book *Masculinities*, first published in 1995, that Masculinity Studies began to germinate proper. Central to Connell's ideas was the elucidation of the masculine/feminine binary in that, "masculinity does not exist except in contrast with femininity … [m]asculinity is in effect defined as not-femininity" (Connell 2005 [1995]: 68–70). More crucial to this discussion was the development of concepts such as 'Patriarchal Dividend' and 'Hegemonic Masculinity':

> Hegemonic masculinity can be defined as the configuration of gender practice which embodies the currently accepted answer to the problem of the legitimacy of patriarchy, which guarantees (or is taken to guarantee) the dominant position of men and the subordination of women ... it is the successful claim to authority, more than direct violence, that is the mark of hegemony.
>
> (Connell 2005 [1995]: 77)

Following on from the seminal work of feminists in the 1970s, such as Ann Oakley who wrote *Sex, Gender and Society* (1972) and Sandra Bem (1974), Connell's work was underpinned by an anti-essentialist foundation. That is, while the biological category of 'men' remained there was not an essential ontological core to being a man. Thus, masculine domination was seen as a discursive propagation, produced, internalized and effected through male bodies, but was not male domination per se. Put more positively, there was nothing biologically determined nor culturally essentialist about masculine oppression, yet the men produced through ideologically dominant forms of masculinity were/are very real and had/have very real consequences for women, children and other men.

Prior to Connell, the majority of scholarly work published about 'men' was uncritical and derived from the imbecilic 'men's movement' popular in many quarters of US society in particular from the 1970s to the 1990s and, yet, remains today discursively through various forms of masculine culture and pop-culture (e.g., *Fight Club*). As Connell remembers, "[t]he main direction taken by [white privileged] masculinity therapy in the 1980s was this attempt to restore a masculinity thought to have been lost or damaged in recent social change" (Connell 2005 [1995]: 207). The core notion of 'loss' underpinned what came to be referred to as 'masculinity in crisis' (Clare 2000); the postmodern fracturing of traditional performances of men in work, education, family, sexuality and health.

Unsurprisingly, the white men's movement or scholarship forming around the movement did not seek to work with feminism to uncover the structural inequalities faced by women. Rather, it sought to reassert masculine physicality (as the historical core to masculine dominance), while trying to reestablish masculine power by usurping the increasingly vaunted qualities of women. In an edited collection entitled *The Male Body* (a response to an edited collection on the female body), for instance, Laurence Goldstein outlines, "[i]f recent writings, including those in this collection, are any indication, the task of men's studies is to recover from history, and from empirically observed behaviors in the present day, that sense of choice and variety in self-definition that so many women have embraced as a means of personal and social liberation" (cited in Edwards 2006: 159).

While analyses of the so-called 'crisis' typically focused on the debilitation of US and British white, middle- to upper-class, and straight masculinities (Edwards 2006), the fracturing of modernity's traditional masculine roles was probably primarily felt by those men most disenfranchised by neoliberalism, that is, working-class men of color. Yet, much of the research focused on masculine formations of non-whiteness simply ignored structural critiques of neo-capitalism and neo-colonialism and, in so doing, served to pathologize men of color. In 1986, renowned masculinity theorist James Messerschmidt, for example, argued: "[t]he marginalized male expresses himself through a collective toughness, a masculine performance observed and cheered by his buddies. Members of the macho street culture have to maintain a strong sense of honor" (cited in Beynon 2002: 82). This ilk of scholarship served to frame 'violence' as a natural performance of masculine alterity, yet, failed to acknowledge the structural, symbolic and physical violence that subordinated forms of masculinity suffered at the hands of white privilege on a daily basis. Ironically enough, the broader discourses surrounding the white men's movement sought to pathologize what they had lost (e.g., physical violence) through accounts of the masculine Other, while providing 'back-to-nature' spaces such as men's camps to facilitate 'physical bravado' as an inherent right of access to 'the deep masculine.' Often such masculine self-improvement camps involved some form of romanticization surrounding the nobility of Indigenous men (read 'savage').

The few critical analysts within Masculinity Studies, in contrast, concluded that the men's movement had very little to do with the reclamation of lost or damaged forms of masculinity but rather was an attempt to reassert various forms of disaffected hegemonic masculinities. A handful of scholars took this moment of 'postmodern fracturing' to attack traditional Western masculine ontologies as figments of discourse, for instance. As John MacInnes in his influential book *The End of Masculinity*, argues:

> [w]hat were once claimed to be manly virtues (heroism, independence, courage, strength, rationality, will, backbone, virility) have become masculine vices (abuse, destructive aggression, coldness, emotional inarticulacy, detachment, isolation, an inability to be flexible, to communicate, to empathize, to be soft, supportive of life-affirming).
>
> (MacInnes 1998: 47)[2]

The contextualization to Masculinity Studies (read White Middle-Class Masculinity Studies) I provide here is by no means exhaustive as there is a plethora of research on masculinities seen through various lenses. Yet, there are three ideas that should be taken methodologically out of this introduction. First, Masculinity Studies has been largely auto-ethnographic. It was forged on the coattails of white feminism, fashioned out of discourses of white privilege and coincided with the so-called postmodern turn.[3] Hence, the focus on melancholic visions and consumption of nostalgia related to past masculinities, which in turn helped demonstrate the blankness and depthlessness of white masculinity. Moreover, when 'masculinity' was referred to (and without reference to a qualifier like 'African American') there was a tacit assumption that the research focused on white masculinity. Even in Connell's work, for instance, there was an assumption that 'hegemonic masculinity' be read as dominant forms of white masculinity, whereas little thought was given to hegemony beyond the confines of whiteness.

Second, when Masculinity Studies did focus on masculine alterity it typically pathologized and displaced the structural violence of capitalism and colonialism onto the ontologies of Other men, not as a symptom of structural violence but as an inherent cultural artifact. Lastly, the recentness of Masculinity Studies as a discipline and invisibility of the patriarchal dividend historically, means that methodologically the scholarly focus on masculinity has been grounded in cultural studies, which in turn has largely meant an ahistorical treatment of masculinity. For instance, Beynon lists six methodologies for looking at masculinity, including, representations in literature, in media, in 'spectacles' (e.g., sport), in autobiographies and documentary, how men experience masculinity in their lives, and the constructed and contextual nature of masculinity (Beynon 2002: 146–147). That is, masculinity was researched in terms of being a product of contemporary culture, with very little thought to a genealogical method.

Indigenous Masculinity Studies

Indigenous scholarship focused or ostensibly related to masculinity and settler colonialism has tended to concentrate on Pacific masculinities, including the seminal book *Native Men Remade: Gender and Nation in Contemporary Hawai'i* (Tengan 2008) and other works by Ty Kāwika Tengan, the work on Pacific masculinity, sport, and seafaring by Vicente Diaz (2002, 2007, 2011), the scholarship focused on masculinity and militarism in the Pacific by Keith Camacho including his book, *Cultures of Commemoration: The Politics of War, Memory, and History in the Mariana Islands* (2011), Isaiah Walker's analysis of underground Hawaiian masculine surf culture culminating in his book, *Waves of Resistance: Surfing and History in Twentieth-Century Hawai'i* (2011), Lisa Uperesa's work on Sāmoan football, April Henderson's scholarship on diasporic Sāmoan masculine culture in hip hop and football, and my own work focused on Māori masculinity, physicality, sport and media. Only recently has Indigenous masculinities scholarship coming out of the continental United States and Canada surfaced more cogently with the publication of Lloyd Lee's book *Diné Masculinities: Conceptualizations and Reflections* (2014), the 2014 publication of *Masculinidians: Conversations about Indigenous Manhood* by Sam McKegney, and the edited collection by Rob Innes and Kim Anderson entitled *Indigenous Men and Masculinities: Identities, Legacies, Regeneration* (2015).

From this brief and incomplete overview of the burgeoning field, it is clear that a concentration on sport, physical activity and militarism defines the research area thus far. Indeed, a new wave of scholarship stemming from earlier work has emerged focused on Indigenous masculinity and what might erroneously be referred to as 'hyper-masculine' pursuits. The recent 2014 special issue of *The Contemporary Pacific* edited by Lisa Uperesa and Tom Mountjoy, for instance, is populated by authors who are either new professors or recently completed PhDs signifying that sport and Indigenous masculinity, in the Pacific at least, has become a recognized area of research. Although named "Global Sport in the Pacific" the special issue is more accurately concerned with sport and masculinity in the Pacific, given that almost the entire issue focuses on the production of Indigenous masculinity through sports such as football, rugby union, soccer and rugby league.

The concentration on sport, militarism and physical activity within Indigenous Masculinity Studies is consistent with Masculinity Studies in general in that a cultural studies focus relies upon analysis of contemporary identity production. However, unlike the typical ahistorical treatment of masculinity within the general field, Indigenous masculinity scholarship is linked to the tenets of Indigenous Studies more broadly. As a consequence, the method is characteristically genealogical in that most scholars have tended to locate the production of contemporary Indigenous masculinities within the broader frames of settler colonialism and colonial history. This contrast speaks to the criticism I outline above in relation to how the general field has dealt with alterity. That is, typically anthropological or criminological studies of masculine alterity have sought and located violence or dysfunction and, subsequently, described such traits as simply reflective of a patriarchal hyper-masculine culture that is in turn symptomatic of an un-evolved society. The approach, unlike Indigenous masculinity scholarship, ignores the structural violence of colonialism and/or capitalism as precursors to dysfunction.

In contrast, Indigenous male dysfunction within Indigenous Studies has typically been treated as a symptom of colonization. For instance, a growing yet hesitant voice has begun to narrate the mimicry of invader masculinity by Indigenous men, and the subsequent creation and traditionalization of the feminine/masculine binary (i.e., the ontological exclusion of the feminine). According to such scholarship, the foundation of post-contact Indigenous masculinity mimicked Victorian masculinity's divestment of the feminine because of its perceived weakness and frailty. In turn, this has led to ritual displays of physical manliness and hyper-masculinity, along with the traditionalization of heterosexuality, homophobia and patriarchy.[4]

The prevalent Indigenous Masculinity Studies methodology, therefore, does not simply unveil contemporary identity, rather it reveals how, for instance, general masculine traits of 'assertiveness' or 'muscularity' are re-appropriated through colonial discourses to manifest as aggressive, violent bodies over-reliant on physicality; or rather the animation of colonialism through the dysfunction of Indigenous men.[5] The integration of colonial history within Indigenous Studies in general then, lays the groundwork for Indigenous masculinity scholars to work with Indigenous feminist scholars to lay waste the constructions of masculinity that serve to oppress Indigenous communities. This disciplinary convention serves to unite and marks a clear methodological fissure with Masculinity Studies in general that, as described above, has tended to focus 'on men' as opposed to focusing on the discursive and historical structures of settler/colonial power that have enabled and continue to enable male privilege.

In many ways, therefore, the treatment of masculinity within Indigenous Studies has followed the methodology of its discipline. That is, it has sought to disprove the dysfunction of today by revealing the infection of colonialism and, accordingly, the purity of the pre-colonial past. For example, Māori scholar Annie Mikaere argues: "evidence abounds which refutes the notion that traditional [read pre-colonial] Māori society attached greater significance to male than to female roles" (Mikaere 1994: 1). While genealogical analyses of Indigenous identity construction reveals a temporal depth of analysis in relation to the diaphanous nature of Masculinity Studies in general, the romanticization of the pre-colonial in Indigenous Studies tends to divorce agency from agents, and authentic conceptions of indigeneity from the *immediacy* of Indigenous realities. Accordingly, although the general field of Masculinity Studies (as a sub-field of cultural studies) might be criticized for being ahistorical, its focus on the 'everyday' can inform the development of research on the *immediacy* of the Indigenous condition.

Beyond binaries

The relatively recent genesis of Indigenous masculinity as a site of study not only reflects the emerging nature of the broader field described above, but possibly also an unwillingness of Indigenous Studies scholars to imagine the discursive nature of power through another binary other than the colonizer/colonized. This unwillingness can also be understood as an aversion to impose a gender binary onto Indigenous conceptions of the world. In relation to the latter point Connell argues that "masculinity does not exist except in contrast with femininity" (Connell 2005 [1995]: 68); this is true and exactly why some Indigenous people and Indigenous Studies scholars reject the very premise of gender, for the gender binary confines Indigenous understandings of 'being' to the discursive power of Western gender constructions.

As alluded to in the previous section, *ressentiment* fueled by the colonizer/ colonized binary lies at the heart of the Indigenous Studies discipline, currently at least. As also aforementioned, a significant branch of the general field of Masculinity Studies has reacted to the postmodern diffusion of power by pitiably laying claim to an inherent male right to power in various guises such as 'the deep masculine.' Habitually, masculinity theorists have failed to comprehend masculinity beyond the frames of 'men's rights' (as a mirror image of feminism). For instance, Beynon outlines:

> whereas feminists framed their struggle as a battle against men, men have no clearly defined enemy who they can point to with certainty as oppressing them. Thus, the male model of confrontation, appropriated so successfully by women is, ironically, now unsuitable for men.
>
> (Beynon 2002: 142)

Again, the tacit implication of what Beynon outlines is a focus on privileged white men and a singular binary construction of power, given that 'Other' masculinities do have distinct frameworks that can be pointed to in relation to oppression, whether that be race, class and/or colonialism.

These two underpinnings of the two disciplines that inform Indigenous Masculinity Studies point to crucial methodological variances in analyzing masculinity in general versus Indigenous masculinity in particular. In Indigenous Studies it would be disingenuous to conceive of Indigenous masculine power vertically, where all Indigenous men hold symbolic power. Simply constructing Indigenous men, for instance, as the subordinators of Indigenous women fails to comprehend the construction of indigeneity itself that (as is so evident with Indigenous masculinity) should be conceived of as both repressive and productive. Of significance here is how the study of Indigenous masculinities can aid in the theoretical analysis of power. Indigenous masculinities and associated cultural performances in particular can and should be treated as a largely untapped rubric for examining the propagation of power in the colonial context. Indigenous masculinity, in serving two essentialized binary masters (i.e., colonized/colonizer and man/woman), creates a model for looking at power within the colonial context where the two essentialized notions associated with the dominance of colonized man over the Indigenous man, and man over woman, create the ambivalent figure of the Indigenous heterosexual patriarch. The dialectics between hetero-patriarchal masculinity and feminism, and colonized/colonizer become complicated, as Indigenous masculinities are both imbibed with privilege and denied; both performing colonial hetero-patriarchy and resistant to it. Simply put, Indigenous masculinity allows us to clearly form an understanding of power as post-hegemonic, as productive; as both oppressor and oppressed.

One of the most significant methodological departures that Indigenous Masculinity Studies enables, therefore, is the movement beyond binaries that tend to anchor Western thought. For instance, as described above, Connell formulated the idea of 'hegemonic masculinity' referring to a form of masculinity that subordinated others. Hegemonic masculinity is possibly useful in thinking about postcolonial formations of Indigenous masculinity where, in certain 'traditional' ceremonies for instance, simply being a man enables authority and subordinates women and/or excludes women from the so-called traditional activities. Perhaps due to the diligence and care that is required when working within one's own communities, simplistic binaries fade, as people are 'aunty' or 'uncle' as opposed to some amorphous group of 'hegemonic men.' Such attention to complexity and community can be seen in the work of Tengan who refuses to lay simplistic binaries upon his community:

> Indigenous men in the Pacific engage in both hegemonic and marginalized gender practices and have historically occupied differently gendered positions of power and disempowerment depending upon the context … Hegemonic masculinities and subaltern masculinities should not be seen as two homogenous and discreet productions that are separated by distinct boundaries. To do so would be to replicate the debilitating dichotomies upon which colonial hegemonies and authority rests, as well as to miss the complexities of what actually takes place "on the ground".
>
> (Tengan 2002: 239–241)

The will to unpack postcolonial formations of masculinity also reveals another problematic for Indigenous Studies scholars that most masculinity scholars do not face; tradition. Although 'the end of masculinity' is proclaimed by white masculinity theorists, who are conterminously unaware of their own privilege in being able to pronounce such a position, Indigenous theorists in contrast have to grapple with, on the one hand, the untenable notion that gender roles are rigidly fixed by tradition and, on the other, the fact that corporeal manifestations of masculine traditions hold (or held) strategic value to communities, not to mention the fact that traditions (false or otherwise) are embodied by very real community members. The inanimate academic jargon of 'hegemonic masculinity' or 'patriarchal dividend' bandied about in general masculinity research not only elides the complexity of Indigenous communities, it is potentially damaging. That is, there is very real fear of destabilizing "the very identities, narratives and analytical tools that had charged a long history of popular anti-colonial struggles" (Featherstone 2005: 18).

Here Indigenous Studies scholars tread carefully, unpacking those ontologies that remain to suppress, while strategically reinforcing those ontologies that strengthen communities. Although the constructed nature of ontology is commonly understood within poststructural frameworks, at least, the tendency of cultural studies academics to ridicule essentialist notions typically occurs in a vacuum where scholars can speak in abstract terms. Seldom do such privileged scholars have to look into the faces of their subjects of ridicule. The method of Indigenous scholars is not to disavow the genuineness of ontology rather it is to, in a careful way, comprehend how Indigenous men, for instance, came to be seen as 'the holders of traditional knowledge.' As Gayatri Spivak outlines, "[d]econstruction does not say there is no subject, there is no truth, there is no history. It simply questions the privileging of identity so that someone is believed to have the truth" (Spivak 1988: 28).

Conclusion

I want to take the reader back to the initial premise of gender itself, which could be defined as an overarching Western taxonomy that precipitated the conditions of the subordination of women and, later, hastened the need for Western feminists to create anti-sexist methodologies that, ironically, came to nurture popular discourses surrounding masculinity and femininity. Indigenous masculinity scholars have demonstrated that Indigenous men were not immune to a Victorian patriarchal dividend. In turn, the subjugation of Indigenous women through processes of exclusion masked as 'tradition' have compelled Indigenous women to enter into the discourses of third-wave feminism, which, similarly, reinforces an imposed gender taxonomy. Of significance, then, is the centrality of alterity to Indigenous Studies, which allows scholars to imagine ontologies that live beyond the masculinity/femininity framework. The first method then is to strategically unpack those 'traditions' that strengthen communities, and/or simultaneously perform a form of necropolitics. The second method is to imagine beyond the taxonomy of gender; to think about ontology beyond the limits of a Western epistemology.

Notes

1　When referring to 'masculinity' I am not referring to a stable singular concept, rather as an area of study, with the inherent understanding that there are multiple masculinities.
2　What MacInnes highlights here is captured uniquely within the film *Fight Club*, where recourses to middle-class male violence are enabled via the devolution of masculine roles as caused by the domestication of the workplace ('the office'). The main character's split personality disorder symptomatic of postmodern fracturing and what white middle-class masculinity has become and what it has lost; the right to senseless physical violence on others.
3　According to Jameson, the consumption of nostalgic images by the subject of postmodernity has led to a cultural 'depthlessness' and 'blankness.' For example, in the television program *The Sopranos*, lead character Tony Soprano consumes American heroic white masculinity through his viewing of old movies featuring Gary Cooper, Clarke Gable and the like. The consumption of nostalgia demonstrates the blankness and depthlessness of Tony's masculinity as he imbibes male self-confidence from a bygone era. A subjectivity based on image construction (as opposed to the belief in a stable core identity) is inherently destabilized or, in the case of Tony Soprano, stricken by 'panic attacks.' Jameson views the decentering of the subject as tied to a loss of confidence with which 'truth' was conveyed under the conditions of modernism.
4　Here patriarchy is defined as including crude acts of aggression, but more importantly as "men's control of women's bodies and minds ... deeply entrenched in rituals, routines and social practices" (Beynon 2002: 85).
5　This methodology, although inherently truthful, is of course not unproblematic for it can also divest Indigenous men of culpability in their complicity with false traditions.

References

Bem, Sandra. 1974. "The measurement of psychological androgyny". *Journal of Consulting and Clinical Psychology*, 42: 155–162.

Beynon, John. 2002. *Masculinities and Culture*. Buckingham and London: Open University Press.

Camacho, Keith. 2011. *Cultures of Commemoration: The Politics of War, Memory, and History in the Mariana Islands*. Honolulu: University of Hawai'i Press.

Clare, Anthony. 2000. *On Men: Masculinity in Crisis*. London: Chatto & Windus.

Connell, Robert. 2005 [1995]. *Masculinities*. 2nd edn. Berkeley: University of California Press.

Drichel, Simone. 2008. "The time of hybridity". *Philosophy and Social Criticism*, 34: 594–615.

Edwards, Tim. 2006. *Cultures of Masculinity*. New York: Routledge.

Featherstone, Simon. 2005. *Postcolonial Cultures*. Edinburgh: Edinburgh University Press.

Innes, Rob and Kim Anderson, eds. 2015. *Indigenous Men and Masculinities: Identities, Legacies, Regeneration*. Winnipeg: University of Manitoba Press.

Lee, Lloyd. 2014. *Diné Masculinities: Conceptualizations and Reflections*. CreateSpace Independent Publishing Platform.

MacInnes, John. 1998. *The End of Masculinity*. Buckingham: Open University Press.

McKegney, Sam. 2014. *Masculinidians: Conversations about Indigenous Manhood*. Winnipeg: University of Manitoba Press.

Mikaere, Annie. 1994. "Maori women: Caught in the contradictions of a colonised reality". *Waikato Law Review*, 2. www.waikato.ac.nz/law/wlr/1994/article6-mikaere.html.

Oakley, Ann. 1972. *Sex, Gender and Society*. London: Temple Smith.

Spivak, Gayatri. 1988. "Subaltern studies: Deconstructing historiography". In Ranajit Guha and Gayatri Spivak, eds. *Selected Subaltern Studies*. New York: Oxford University Press, pp. 3–32.

Tengan, Ty. 2002. "(En)gendering colonialism: Masculinities in Hawai'i and Aotearoa". *Cultural Values*, 6(3): 239–256.

Tengan, Ty. 2008. *Native Men Remade: Gender and Nation in Contemporary Hawai'i*. Durham, NC: Duke University Press.

Uperesa, Lisa and Tom Mountjoy, eds. 2014. "Special issue: Global sport in the Pacific". *The Contemporary Pacific*, 26(2).

Walker, Isaiah. 2011. *Waves of Resistance: Surfing and History in Twentieth-Century Hawai'i*. Honolulu: University of Hawai'i Press.

23 Indigenous is to queer as …

Queer questions for Indigenous Studies

Mark Rifkin

The United Nations Declaration on the Rights of Indigenous Peoples, approved by the UN General Assembly in 2007, nowhere defines the word Indigenous.[1] The term/concept signifies shared histories of invasion and occupation in which people(s) from elsewhere come and create governments that seek to extend jurisdiction over the bodies, polities, and lands of those peoples who preceded them in what becomes the "domestic" space of those new nations (settler-states). The concept of indigeneity provides a means of challenging settler political and social norms, but it also can allow certain formulations of indigeneity to become the norm through which the concept implicitly is defined. The term Indigenous gestures toward particular modes of inhabitance, governance, and social life that distinguish such peoples from the legalities, institutions, and imperatives of the settler-state, and certain kinds of, in the Declaration's terms, "social structures" and "traditions" can come to be seen as more truly expressive of indigeneity than others.[2] A similar tension operates within the term *queer*, and attending to the work performed by that term, and the ways queer studies has sought to unpack and trace the implicit normalizations enacted through its use, can aid Indigenous studies in thinking about what's at stake in the ways the concept of Indigenous/indigeneity circulates. To be clear, I am not suggesting that Indigenous peoples are queer, that non-native queers are like Indigenous peoples, or that Indigenous and queer politics and struggles are in any way synonymous (or even necessarily consonant). Rather, I want to suggest a resonance between the kinds of conceptual and political work performed by *queerness* and *indigeneity* in order to highlight the possibilities for hierarchies of authenticity and/or relevance within Indigenous movements.

Queer gains its meaning and force from marking something other than the normal, particularly forms of sexual and gender deviance.[3] In this vein, one could define the work of queer studies as developing strategies for tracing how processes of (hetero)normalization produce modes of queerness along various axes and in a range of interdependent areas of social life. Doing so focuses less on the experiences of those deemed perverse than on the dynamics through which the perverse/deviant/aberrant is continually (re)constituted as such, the mechanisms through which that process occurs, and the interests served through such differentiation/denigration.[4] Furthermore, an investment in queerness entails recuperating practices, relationships, communities, representations in their deviance from dominant ideals and institutional standards instead of seeking to cast them as ultimately compatible with such norms.

While the scholarly and political reclaiming of queer works to challenge ideas of the normal, certain kinds of persons and groups included within that category can come to serve as the privileged referent for it in ways that limit its possible range and oppositional force. In "Punks, Bulldaggers, and Welfare Queens," Cathy J. Cohen observes, "In queer theorizing, the sexual subject is understood to be constructed and contained by multiple practices of categorization and regulation that systematically marginalize and oppress those subjects thereby defined as deviant" (1997: 439), but she also notes that "queer politics has often been built around a simple dichotomy between those deemed queer and those deemed heterosexual" (1997: 440). Setting "queer" and "heterosexual" in a binary relationship effaces the ways that the "'nonnormative' procreation patterns and family structures of people who are labeled heterosexual have also been used to regulate and exclude *them*" (1997: 447). Cohen points specifically to how people of color are deemed perverse by virtue of a supposed failure to fulfill social norms of home and family associated with whiteness.[5] Thus, while queer seemed to enable a broad-based coalition and analytical framework capable of addressing a range of kinds of oppression linked through their reliance on charges of deviance, one form of deviance – homosexuality defined in terms of object-choice (the sex of the person with whom one wants to have sex) – comes to provide the model such that other ways of defining sexual normality (such as whiteness) vanish from view, while also speaking as if all non-heterosexuals were oppressed equally and in the same ways. Furthermore, Mel Y. Chen notes how the shift from adjective (deviation from the normal) to noun (a kind of personal identity) leads to a less dynamic understanding of the meaning of queer: "the very condition for its definition, that it be defined *in relation to the norm*, is easily made opaque by a renormalization of the category *queer* itself, which is that it too must have a center and a periphery" (Chen 2012: 78). In other words, the fact that queer was mobilized as a way of challenging varied, interwoven ideas of normality fades from view as it comes to designate a particular group, one whose "center" is object-choice such that other personal and political dynamics (like gender, race, class, ability) and issues of perceived aberrance (kinds of household and family formation, forms of gender expression, sites and sorts of intimacy or eroticism) appear secondary or peripheral. The shift from queer as a critique of heteronormativity broadly conceived to a kind of identity not only limits the scope of queer analysis/activism but treats the "queer" identity (defined as against "heterosexual") as if it were inherently free from the broader set of power dynamics queer initially was invoked to oppose.

As with queerness, the momentum of the term/concept Indigenous lies in opposing the obviousness of extant norms, in this case the self-evidence and inherent legitimacy of settler governance and jurisdiction, and identifying with/as Indigenous also moves away from a politics of inclusion toward one of self-determination. However, are there also forms of normalization at play in the ways Indigenous gets used, implicitly delimiting the possibilities for what the concept of Indigenous might mean or do? In the US context, blood quantum, federal recognition, connections to Indianness,[6] and faithfulness to "tradition" all serve as ways of assessing the relative authenticity and legitimacy of claims to indigeneity. The example of queerness provides a methodological caution to a perhaps over-hasty optimism in the capacity of notions of indigeneity to fully escape the orbit of the dynamics of settler colonialism in which the concept Indigenous arose and which serve, in Chen's terms, as "the very condition for its definition." The notion of indigeneity gains meaning through its opposition to settlement, collating together varied peoples in their shared subjection and resistance to colonial domination through "domestic"-ation by the nation-states that claim them and their lands. However, in being articulated as an identity, Indigenous can shift away from that critique by *renormalizing* aspects of settler governance and popular sentiments as taken-for-granted facets of Indigenous identity, as the de facto center against which other people(s) or forms of (collective) self-expression appear as aberrant or inauthentic.

Work by queer Native intellectuals points toward such difficulties, highlighting how certain formulations of Native identity come to be privileged as more truly expressive of indigeneity in ways that not only can enact harm toward other Native people(s) but implicitly can take heteronormative ideals as their basis.[7] In *Writing as Witness*, Beth Brant (Mohawk) explores how homoeroticism comes to be understood as not properly Native:

> Our sexuality has been colonized, sterilized, whitewashed ... When we fight amongst ourselves as to who is a better Indian, who is a more traditional Indian, we are linking arms with the ones who would just as soon see us dead. Homophobia has *no* justification within our Nations.
>
> (Brant 1994: 59–60)[8]

Brant further observes, "I have been hurt and ostracized by some Natives, men and women, who have made it clear that being a lesbian, or *saying* it out loud is not good for our community," and she responds, "I believe what they are really saying is – you embarrass me with your sexuality, therefore you embarrass our people, and *white* people will have even more ammunition to use against us," further suggesting that such people may be "frightened by what can be taken away. And why shouldn't they be? Everything else has been stolen" (1994: 76–77). Brant's presence as a lesbian strains against a de facto model of indigeneity in which straightness helps provide the center, in which tradition has itself been "colonized, sterilized, whitewashed" in ways that normalize white "values." Brant addresses how the colonial dynamics of settlement pit Native people against each other. Non-straight desire becomes another form of "ammunition," and as such, it can be disavowed and disowned as destructive to continued Native survival, cast as something not truly Indigenous.[9] However, in marking and refusing such efforts (whether explicit or implicit) to compromise with dominant, non-native notions of normality, she offers an analysis of how settler colonialism enacts, in Cohen's words, "multiple [and intersecting] practices of categorization and regulation."

The distancing of indigeneity from non-normative sexuality, then, winnows down the diversities and complexities of Indigenous peoples' histories, cultures, and sovereignties in ways that respond to settler pressures and stereotypes.

Daniel Heath Justice (Cherokee) explores the ways that ideas about proper (racial) genealogy limit the potential for forms of alliance among Indigenous peoples and for more robust critique of the processes through which the United States normalizes its claims to Native lands (Justice 2008). Challenging the claim that Native people(s) in Connecticut "are not Indians" because "The blood is gone," he observes that such an argument

> follows the line of logic used by many anti-Native forces, namely, that blood quantum and phenotypically "Indian" features are the fullest measure of cultural authenticity and that those who are lacking in these qualities are, by definition, no longer Indian—if they ever were.
>
> (2008: 156)

While not seeming to be about sexuality, this line of thought concerns the ways that Indianness, or indigeneity more broadly, comes to be understood as a function of racial substance passed down lineally: certain kinds of reproductive couplings can transmit it and others cannot (or do so only in a severely diminished fashion). A vision of procreatively transmitted racial identity becomes centered as the norm through which to assess Indigenous being. Such narratives cast what it means to be Indigenous in terms of the possession of certain physical "qualities" or amounts of "Indian blood" rather than as active participation within peoplehood, which Justice characterizes as "the tribal web of kinship rights and responsibilities that link the People, the land, and the cosmos together" (2008: 151). In contrast to the (hetero)normalization of Indigenous identity around blood, Justice suggests that kinship offers a more flexible sense of indigeneity as a multifaceted matrix of ongoing relations. The idea of fulfilling of one's "responsibilities" to one's people and to others, thinking of kinship as a verb (2008: 150), moves away from the more static sense of belonging to a specific kind of racialized family structure defined around reproductive union (in ways that parallel the nuclear family model). Justice highlights the potential for other configurations of intimacy, eroticism, care, and enduring connection than those at play in the heteroreproductive calculus of inherited "Indian" blood substance. He observes:

> among most eastern indigenous nations—indeed, among most tribal nations in this hemisphere—intermarriage was an honored method of developing kinship bonds with other peoples ... an act both intimately familial and overtly political—and many of us reflect that tradition in our skin and features.
>
> (2008: 158)

In addition, he suggests that the idea of bloodedness as the measure of indigeneity largely arises out of histories of settler imposition and settler interests (including the notion that generationally diminishing bloodedness eventually will mean the absence of "Indians" who can make collective claims to land and governance).[10] "Kinship" offers a means of moving away from a singular means of defining Indigenous identity – like object-choice for queerness – to addressing a wider range of (kinds of) relations/affiliations/alliances, thereby better registering the multiplicity of forms of survival, sovereignty, and self-determination within ongoing processes of settler domination, regulation, and attempted erasure.

Queerness, as a concept or movement, does not inherently turn toward an engagement with Indigenous peoples. As Brant observes, "we have learned that a hegemonic gay and lesbian movement cannot encompass our complicated history ... Nor can a hegemonic gay and lesbian movement give us tools to heal our broken Nations" (1994: 45), and one might add that such cautions also apply to those intellectual and political projects organized under or around the rubric of "queer."[11] However, I have sought to suggest that the efforts within queer studies to grapple with the dynamics of "queer" – as both a means of opposing multiple forms of normalization and a vehicle through which existing forms of privilege can end up being renormalized – might be instructive for Indigenous studies in considering the conceptual and political work performed by "Indigenous" and "indigeneity." From this perspective, queer Native intellectuals, such as Brant and Justice, become particularly important in their attention to the tendency for concepts like "tradition" or "blood" to convey the coherence of Indigenous identity by flattening the diversities and intricacies of Native social life and histories, especially by marginalizing those deemed deviant in sexual/reproductive terms.

Notes

1   On that process of nondefinition, the politics circulating around it, and the various nonofficial definitions that precede and surround the document, see Montes and Cisneros (2009). On the taking up of the term Indigenous by those peoples so designated, see Allen (2002: 195–220) and Engle (2010).

2   The Declaration states, "Indigenous peoples have the right to self-determination. By virtue of that right they freely determine their political status and freely pursue their economic, social and cultural development" (2007: 4). For efforts to elaborate the meaning of "self-determination" for Indigenous peoples under international law and custom, see Anaya (1996); Charters and Stavenhagen (2009); Engle (2010); Lâm (2000).

3   On the reappropriation of the term "queer," see Butler (1993: 223–242); Chen (2012: 57–88); Jakobsen (1998); Warner (1993: vii–xxxi).

4   The emphasis within queer analysis on the critique of processes of normalization instead of the defining and defending of a particular identity or subject position has been characterized as "subjectless critique." See Eng et al. (2005: 3). As I will suggest, this idea has come under fire for the ways it can implicitly install a white gay male perspective as the de facto norm for queer theorizing while speaking as if identity had been displaced as a basis for intellectual work. For such discussion, in addition to the scholars I address in greater detail, see Driskill (2010); Holland (2012); Perez (2005); Puar (2007).

5   As Roderick Ferguson suggests, "African American familial forms and gender relations were regarded as perversions of the American family ideal ... heterosexual but never *heteronormative*" (2004: 86–87), meaning that the line for defining the normal versus

the perverse was not solely gay/straight but also black/white, and David Eng observes that in the contemporary United States "intimacy might be regarded as a type of racialized property right that remains unequally and unevenly distributed among gay and lesbian populations today" (2010: 45), given the ways that populations of color are subjected to much more extensive and intensive forms of state surveillance and are presumed deviant in ways that make intimacy less a form of privacy than a perceived threat to the welfare of the nation.

6 By this phrase, I mean both being understood as Indian rather than belonging to another non-white racial group (particularly not being of African descent) and being compared to Indians as the prism through which to be recognized as Indigenous. On the repudiation of non-white racial identity (especially blackness) in relation to Indian identity, by both Natives and non-natives, see Den Ouden (2005); Lowery (2010); Mandell (2008); Saunt (2005); and Sturm (2002). On the ways federal and state policy is seeking to model relations with Native Hawaiians on federal Indian policy, thereby limiting the potential for Hawaiian self-determination, see Kauanui (2013: 311–336). On the process of "making Indian" populations that the US government targets for imperial violence, see Byrd (2011).

7 I should note that Native feminist work has offered expansive analysis of the ways Native authenticity gets organized around heteropatriarchal presumptions institutionalized by the settler-state. For examples, see Barker (2011); Denetdale (2006); Goeman (2013); Lawrence (2004); Million (2013); and Simpson (2014).

8 While limitations of space lead me to focus on only two writers, Beth Brant and Daniel Heath Justice, I also could have turned to the work of a number of other queer Native intellectuals, such as Chrystos, Qwo-Li Driskill, Janice Gould, Deborah Miranda, Greg Sarris, James Thomas Stevens, and Craig Womack.

9 Elsewhere, I describe this dynamic as "the bribe of straightness." See Rifkin (2011).

10 For discussion of the problems of defining indigeneity in terms of quanta of "Indian blood," see also Barker (2011); Lowery (2010); Rifkin (2011); and Sturm (2002).

11 In fact, many of those queer studies scholars most attentive to the relations between racialization and sexuality themselves invest in the notion of diaspora as a way of conceptualizing the aims and horizon of queer critique – or at least challenge the idea of place-based political collectivity – in ways that leave little conceptual room for engaging with Indigenous peoples' self-determination as landed polities. For examples, see Eng (2010); Ferguson (2004); Gopinath (2005); Puar (2007); Reddy (2011). For discussion of this dynamic within queer studies and the problems it poses for Indigenous studies, see Driskill (2010).

References

Allen, Chadwick. 2002. *Blood Narrative: Indigenous Identity in American Indian and Maori Literary and Activist Texts*. Durham, NC: Duke University Press.

Anaya, S. James. 1996. *Indigenous Peoples in International Law*. New York: Oxford University Press.

Barker, Joanne. 2011. *Native Acts: Law, Recognition, and Cultural Authenticity*. Durham, NC: Duke University Press.

Brant, Beth. 1994. *Writing as Witness: Essay and Talk*. Toronto: Women's Press.

Butler, Judith. 1993. *Bodies That Matter: On the Discursive Limits of "Sex"*. New York: Routledge.

Byrd, Jodie. 2011. *The Transit of Empire: Indigenous Critiques of Colonialism*. Minneapolis: University of Minnesota Press.

Charters, Claire and Rodolfo Stavenhagen, eds. 2009. *Making the Declaration Work: The United Nations Declaration on the Rights of Indigenous Peoples*. Copenhagen: IWGIA.

Chen, Mel. 2012. *Animacies: Biopolitics, Racial Mattering, and Queer Affect*. Durham, NC: Duke University Press.

Cohen, Cathy J. 1997. "Punks, bulldaggers, and welfare queens: The radical potential of queer politics?" *GLQ*, 3(4): 437–465.

Den Ouden, Amy E. 2005. *Beyond Conquest: Native Peoples and the Struggle for History in New England*. Lincoln: University of Nebraska Press.

Denetdale, Jennifer Nez. 2006. "Chairmen, presidents, and princesses: The Navajo Nation, gender, and the politics of tradition". *Wicazo Sa Review*, 21(1): 9–28.

Driskill, Qwo-Li. 2010. "Doubleweaving two-spirit critiques: Building alliances between native and queer studies". *GLQ*, 16(1–2): 69–92.

Eng, David. 2010. *The Feeling of Kinship: Queer Liberalism and the Racialization of Intimacy*. Durham, NC: Duke University Press.

Eng, David, Judith Halberstam, and José Esteban Muñoz. 2005. "What's queer about queer studies now?" *Social Text*, 23(3–4): 1–17.

Engle, Karen. 2010. *The Elusive Promise of Indigenous Development: Rights, Culture, Strategy*. Durham, NC: Duke University Press.

Ferguson, Roderick. 2004. *Aberrations in Black: Toward a Queer of Color Critique*. Minneapolis: University of Minnesota Press.

Goeman, Mishuana. 2013. *Mark My Words: Native Women Mapping Our Nations*. Minneapolis: University of Minnesota Press.

Gopinath, Gayatri. 2005. *Impossible Desires: Queer Diasporas and South Asian Public Cultures*. Durham, NC: Duke University Press.

Holland, Sharon. 2012. *The Erotic Life of Racism*. Durham, NC: Duke University Press.

Jakobsen, Janet R. 1998. "Queer is? Queer does? Normativity and the problem of resistance". *GLQ*, 4(4): 511–536.

Justice, Daniel Heath. 2008. "'Go away, water!': Kinship criticism and the decolonization imperative". In Native Critics Collective, eds. *Reasoning Together*. Norman: University of Oklahoma Press, pp. 147–168.

Kauanui, J. Kēhaulani. 2013. "Precarious positions: Native Hawaiians and U.S. federal recognition". In Amy E. Den Ouden and Jean M. O'Brien, eds. *Recognition, Sovereignty Struggles, and Indigenous Rights in the United States: A Sourcebook*. Chapel Hill: University of North Carolina Press, pp. 311–336.

Lâm, Maivân Clech. 2000. *At the Edge of the State: Indigenous Peoples and Self-Determination*. Ardsley: Transnational Publishers, Inc.

Lawrence, Bonita. 2004. *"Real" Indians and Others: Mixed-Blood Urban Native Peoples and Indigenous Nationhood*. Lincoln: University of Nebraska Press.

Lowery, Malinda Maynor. 2010. *Lumbees in the Jim Crow South: Race, Identity, and the Making of a Nation*. Chapel Hill: University of North Carolina Press.

Mandell, Daniel R. 2008. *Tribe, Race, History: Native Americans in Southern New England, 1780–1880*. Baltimore: Johns Hopkins University Press.

Million, Dian. 2013. *Therapeutic Nations: Healing in an Age of Indigenous Human Rights*. Tucson: University of Arizona Press.

Montes, Adelfo Regino and Gustavo Torres Cisneros. 2009. "The United Nations Declaration on the Rights of Indigenous Peoples: The foundations of a new relationship between Indigenous peoples, states and societies". In Claire Charters and Rodolfo Stavenhagen, eds. *Making the Declaration Work: The United Nations Declaration on the Rights of Indigenous Peoples*. Copenhagen: IWGIA, pp. 138–168.

Perez, Hiram. 2005. "You can have my brown body and eat it, too!" *Social Text*, 23(3–4): 171–192.

Puar, Jasbir K. 2007. *Terrorist Assemblages: Homonationalism in Queer Times*. Durham, NC: Duke University Press.

Reddy, Chandan. 2011. *Freedom with Violence: Race, Sexuality, and the US State*. Durham, NC: Duke University Press.

Rifkin, Mark. 2011. *When Did Indians Become Straight? Kinship, the History of Sexuality, and Native Sovereignty*. New York: Oxford University Press.

Saunt, Claudio. 2005. *Black, White, and Indian: Race and the Unmaking of an American Family*. New York: Oxford University Press.

Simpson, Audra. 2014. *Mohawk Interruptus: Political Life Across the Borders of Settler States*. Durham, NC: Duke University Press.

Sturm, Circe. 2002. *Blood Politics: Race, Culture, and Identity in the Cherokee Nation of Oklahoma*. Berkeley: University of California Press.

United Nations Declaration on the Rights of Indigenous Peoples. 2007. New York: United Nations.

Warner, Michael, ed. 1993. *Fear of a Queer Planet: Queer Politics and Social Theory*. Minneapolis: University of Minnesota Press.

IV. Indigenous literature and expressive culture

24 State violence, history, and Maya literature in Guatemala

Emilio del Valle Escalante

In this chapter, I explore how Maya authors have engaged with the violent legacies of the Guatemalan military dictatorships while elaborating a new poetics that dignifies their distinct cultural and linguistic identities, propose intercultural ways of coexistence, and register Maya voices and experiences in the hegemonic literary and cultural history of Guatemala. I will critically examine Maya Q'anjob'al poet Sabino Esteban Francisco's poetry book, *Gemido de huellas* [The Moan of the Footprints], a poetic autobiographical account that registers the experience of Maya peoples who were displaced during the armed conflict in Guatemala (1960–1996), and consequently joined the Comunidades de Población en Resistencia, or Communities of Population in Resistance (CPR) in the early 1980s. By narrating experiences of violence, pain and chaos, I argue, Francisco not only discloses the operations of settler colonialism (Wolfe 1999), but also aims to "re-member" the Maya social body by confronting the past. In doing so, he rewrites or re-*rights* history (Smith 2012: 29) in order to inscribe into the hegemonic Guatemalan narrative the memory of the Maya peoples who joined the CPR.

In 1982, in the region of Ixcán in Guatemala – composed of populations coming from the regions of Huehuetenango, Quiché, Totonicapán, Quetzaltenango, and San Marcos – under the most precarious and inhumane conditions, thousands of Indigenous families started a long exodus, leaving behind their lands of birth, their crops, their belongings, searching for a place where they could safely survive the Guatemalan army's military incursions in the region. The forced displacement that Maya families in Ixcan experienced can be thought of as a contemporary Indigenous Maya "trail of tears"[1] impregnated by pain, chaos, and uncertainty. In their long walks, thousands of Maya peasants went to Mexico, hoping that as soon as they crossed the border, they would find immunity from the political persecution. Among those thousands of people who walked this journey was the Maya Q'anjob'al family Esteban Francisco, who carried in their arms Sabino, a little boy of one year. Subsequently, this family and others found refuge in the compounds of the CPR which emerged during this time.

Making reference to this particular context, an unnamed war survivor tells us that those who went into exile in the region of Ixcán followed three different paths. Some, like the Esteban Francisco family, found refuge in Mexico, others enrolled in the "model communities" compounds established by the Guatemalan army and the Self-Defense Civil Patrols (PAC), and others, the CPR, remained in the Ixcán jungles, surviving and resisting the counterinsurgency campaigns. Victoria Sanford tells us that for the CPR life in the mountains became

> even more precarious, the realities of staying alive day to day were so harsh as to deny both humanity and dignity to massacre survivors. Civilians in the mountains suffered extreme hardship with no shelter, no clothing, no medicines, and no stable food or water sources.
>
> (2003: 131)

Indeed, according to a witness, members of the CPR "hid in the forests, in the folds of the ravines, on the high peaks, or wherever they could remain outside the military's reach. That was how a total of nearly twenty thousand people formed the Communities of Population in Resistance" (Moller and Falla 2004: 57) in Quiché and in the rain forest of the Petén region, in the north of Guatemala. Amidst military pressure, the CPR began to survive on basic crops of beans, corn, and greens. As Ricardo Falla indicates, they

> organized astonishing internal systems of production, defense, education, hygiene, health, pastoral care and even sports ... they no longer believed that they would be in the jungle for the short term; they now saw that they would be there for an undefined period that could last ten or fifteen years.
>
> (cited in Moller and Falla 2004: 58)

In 1983, as an act of cooperation with the Guatemalan army, the Mexican government removed its support to thousands of Guatemalan refugees on Mexican soil, obliging them either to migrate to the United States or to return to Guatemala. Among those who decided to return, were the Esteban Francisco family, who in 1984 incorporated to "Los limones" (the limes), one of the compounds of the CPR in Ixcán. From these surroundings, from those long walks which were infused with fear, anguish, and uncertainty, but also with hope and the landscapes of the Ixcán jungles, Sabino Esteban Francisco obtained his first life lessons. There, in the jungle, he grew up, composing his first verses, writing them "in a little table/ with remnants of carbon" (2007: 63). There, he survived on the very basic, quenching the silences of his throat (67) with corn grains, *pixtones* (101), *quiletes*, papaya roots, and zapote seeds (79), and struggling not only against the repressive forces that sought to eliminate the CPR, but also against misery and curable diseases provoked by the precarious conditions under which he and his family lived. These are the elements and the habitual contexts described in *Gemido de huellas*, Esteban Francisco's first poetry book, which articulates a poetics of survival with an extraordinary expressive force.

In this book, the poetic voice registers the experiences of persecution, survival, and tenacity of the CPR in the jungles of Ixcán. It does not describe an experience of victimization or abandonment, but rather acts of courage and survival that feed the dignity, hope, and tenacity of Maya peoples. Intense and devastating images that highlight institutional violence against Indigenous peoples, are contrasted with songs that celebrate the environment and human courage to transcend the highest obstacles. The "moan of the footprints" in this sense symbolizes a song to life that serves to disarticulate the failed attempt of those who have sought to silence Indigenous peoples. These moans or poems, characterized by their apparent simplicity, have the capacity to awaken the most profound sentiments and move the reader with their intense communicative capacity. The poems simultaneously inscribe a traumatic experience and underscore the dignity and pride of the CPR. Additionally, they serve as songs to the jungle that sheltered members of the CPR and that witnessed these members' harassment and ultimate survival.

The poetry book constitutes what Brian Swann calls "a poetry of the historical witness" (1988: xvii); that is, it is not just in the voice and from the perspective of someone who observes history, but also someone who embodies it. The book is written in Q'anjob'al Maya and Spanish in order to make it accessible to broader audiences. Given my limits in Q'anjob'al, the following critical analysis is based on my interpretations from the poems translated into Spanish by the author. In turn, I provide my own free English translations of the poems in Spanish.

Gemido de huellas particularly underscores the necessity to "remember" and to speak out about the traumatic experiences inherited from the armed conflict in Guatemala. Francisco's objective is to inscribe and authorize the "small voices of history" (Guha 1996) in the hegemonic historical records. Out of the poetry book emerge five prominent themes. First, testimonial poems like "*Ceiba* Tree base camp" (2007: 123), "Among the Trees" (115), and "Stage" (23) highlight the moments of uncertainty that the CPR experienced in the jungles of Ixcán. Second, poems like "Mending" (*remiendo*) (117), "Rebirth" (137), and "Resistance" (173) underscore the tenacity and perseverance of the CPR. Third, poems like "Long Walk" (109), "Xalbal" (111), "Wings and Roots" (121) seek to re-vindicate Maya cultural identity; specifically, they employ the image of "footprints" in order to evoke re-signified millenarian images to organically tie the past and the present of the Maya peoples of the CPR. Fourth, in poems like "Guatemala," "Diversity," and "Rainbow", the poetic voice re-imagines the nation-state as intercultural, recognizing its multilingual and multiethnic character. Finally, there are several poems dedicated to nature. As we will see later, these poems are organically related to the other themes in the sense that remembering the history of genocide and re-vindicating Maya cultural history, identity, and the nation-state also entails the re-vindication of the environment.

Although some poems contained within the collection play with form, the majority of them are written in free verse. Significantly, they draw on a conversational language reminiscent of the poetics of the Committed Generation,[2] or the poetic style of other Maya poets like the Francisco Morales Santos (Kaqchikel) and Humberto Ak'abal (K'iche'). Francisco employs various literary resources that, among others, include alliteration, onomatopoeia (e.g., "Laugh river", "Weaves," and "Morning song"), calligram ("Echo"), and *jitanjáfora*. These literary elements evoke the context of the Ixcán jungle and often use personification, the literary recourse most employed by the Q'anjob'al poet.

Personification serves to give life to the natural surroundings represented within the poems. Indeed, Francisco endorses the Law of Ecology: "Everything is connected to everything else" (Rueckert 1996: 108), developing a context where he argues that all things that inhabit the earth – people, animals, and plants – are organically connected. This idea is represented through a Maya *traje/hupil* or "traditional dress" whose harmony is displayed with each of its strings and diverse colors: "The seas / the animals / the people / and everything that exists / we are strings and conjugated colors" (2007: 17), the poetic voice indicates. This is why all the plots evoked in the poems occur within natural contexts; that is, animals, plants, and people all move within the jungles of the Ixcán, the main literary trope in *Gemido de huellas*.

Environmental elements like rivers, trees, and animals (for the most part aquatic and those with wings) are the most evoked, usually as allegorical representations of the subjects and experiences described in Ixcán. In addition, these natural elements often serve as metaphorical bridges that lead us through diverse temporal and spatial contexts that include the civil war, the post-war period, or settings where the poetic voice simply takes the time to appreciate and contemplate his surroundings in Ixcán. In these poems, Francisco shows a patient poetic gaze that evokes nature's elements in a mood of playful exaltation. In "Last night," for instance, we find that the old trees catch a cold, "All of them [awake] / with a piece of mist / tied in their heads" (2007: 81). In "Dried tree," a woodpecker is sad to see a tree dying. He decides to open a hole in the tree's chest to build a nest. The tree comes back to life and ever since then, the poem concludes, "Every morning from the tree / his heart goes out flying" (2007: 61). At times, these environmental elements acquire mythological dimensions. This is the case with the poem, "A day," which objectively explains the origins of the night. The poetic voice tells the story of a day who dares to touch the sun. In doing so, he burns himself to the point that he is blackened (*tiznado*). For his "daring," the sky gives him the moon as a present, and "in memory / of the event / nowadays this day still repeats itself as the night" (2007: 97).

Instead of representing contradictions between the natural elements of daily life, what emerges from Francisco's poems is a vision of environmental bonding and reciprocity in which natural elements complement one another within a persistent cycle of revitalization. Natural elements bond to give life to one another, like the tree that comes back to life with the woodpecker and in turn the tree that serves as a home where the woodpecker lives. "Dried tree," in this sense, endorses a biocentric perspective that aims to erase the opposition between humans and nature in order to suggest instead that they are equal and depend from one another to exist. In addition, the poem could be interpreted allegorically: It is the story of the CPR, whose presence in the jungle gives life to it and in turn receives sustenance from it, thus maintaining a mutually productive relationship. It represents, at the same time, an imagined world and environmentalist political project that underscores the relationship between Mother Earth and the Indigenous peoples constituted in reciprocal harmonic exchanges.

The environmental perspective endorsed by Francisco, as we can see, acquires an almost pastoral dimension that is characterized, significantly, by what it does not mention. These are scenes where Nature and the people of the CPR operate in a harmonious ways, outside the influences of modernity, untouched by its tentacles. Nowhere in the poems do we find the presence of technological objects like radios or TVs. Nature acquires an authority that overdetermines the experience of the CPR. It is only when pastoral peace and harmony give way to poems that evoke memories of catastrophe that the reader is exposed to chilling snapshots the CPR confronted in the mountains. It is here where images of persecution, the struggle for survival, and death are evoked.

In the poem "Pleading," the people's pleas not to be killed are met with gunshots. The voices of the innocent "acquired the burned stench of human flesh / in a clandestine / cemetery" (2007: 183). The people saw them die, the poetic voice tells us, listing an inventory of terrorist tactics carried out against them by the Guatemalan army: "drowned, / hanged, / stroked with machetes, / bombed, / burned alive" (2007: 43). The eyes of the witnesses, the poem concludes, are today, "clandestine cemeteries / and their tears / the most transparent exhumation." In this context, as a witness and mediator for his community, Francisco discloses the operations of settler colonialism by highlighting the efforts of the nation-state to "eliminate the native." The poem "Pleading" can be associated with the "storm" that Aime Cesaire describes in his seminal text, "Discourse of Colonialism"; that is, the counterinsurgency campaigns depicted by Francisco resemble colonialist strategies that rest upon entire "societies drained of their essence, cultures trampled underfoot, institutions undermined, lands confiscated, religions smashed, magnificent artistic creations destroyed, extraordinary *possibilities* wiped out" (Cesaire 1994: 178). This is indeed, what the civil war represented for the CPR, an experienced marked by memories of terror, fear, and political persecution.

Yet, in poems like "Caves" and "Among the trees," Francisco describes how survivors escape, hide in the jungle, and manage to survive. Their stories of persecution and survival are consequently narrated and recorded as a way to underscore the courage of a people who in the most extreme conditions found ways to maintain their existence, continuance, and hope. Memories of pain activate memories of resistance that aim to sustain and dignify the history of the CPR, and in turn, that of Indigenous peoples who have survived colonialism.

In the poem "Caves," Francisco describes how Indigenous families hide from the Guatemalan army in caves in the jungles of Ixcán. The poet brushes a morbid painting that features irony and sarcasm within a context marked by extremity. The poem describes a game of hide and seek played between adults and children inside a cave in order to entertain the children, and thus to distract them from the violent noises of planes, gunshots, and bombs heard outside the cave. This is the "chorus of the earth," the poetic voice tells us, where people experience the night "inside" while there is a party of lights and fireworks "outside." Through its dichotomous structure, the poem marks the difference between inside and outside, life and death. The survival of people takes place amidst a disturbing context of destruction and fear.

Similarly, the poem "Among the trees" draws some of the strategies the CPR used to survive in the jungle. The poem reads:

> In Emergency Plans
> of the armed conflict
> of hunger screamed
> the children of the CPR:
> a rag
> in their mouth was placed
> to silence their scream
> before the *pintos* [soldiers].
> Instead of tortilla
> they swallowed their scream.
> Today the scream of many
> still has an echo of hunger.
>   (Francisco 2007: 115)

The "silence" and the "screams" evoked in the poem are powerful. The effort to silence the screams of the children so the soldiers don't find the hiding places of the CPR acquires a significance associated with not only survival against premeditated death, but also the misery inherited by many in the aftermath of the civil war. The verse "Today the scream of many" evokes the Peace Accords that were signed in 1996 to end the armed conflict. It suggests that while there was a formal, diplomatic solution to formally end the civil war, it did not stop poverty and the hunger of those who have survived modernity or globalization in conditions of subalternity. In turn, the poem depicts the silencing of screams as an act of narration and the performance of memory to address a traumatic experience. By evoking the "silencing of the children" and "screams" (to suggest hunger), the poem establishes the authority of the CPR. Remembering experiences like this one not only means confronting the past, highlighting and denouncing the activities of the nation-state and its efforts to eliminate Maya peoples, but also re-*membering* the Maya social body. They significantly invoke resistance against the "storm" that Cesaire talks about above, as well as the resilience of the CPR to survive the army's military operations.

Gemido de huellas in this sense marks the limits of colonialism, its failure to entirely destroy a people. In addressing the experiences of the peoples of the CPR in the jungles of Ixcán, Francisco's poems tell us something about the nature of modernity itself. That is, its project has been constitutive of what it has violently aims to suppress and destroy. However, for Francisco and the CPR, it is now time to re-member the Maya social body and the beginning of "national culture" as understood by Franz Fanon. That is, *Gemido de huellas* delves into the traumatic past "in order to find coherent elements which will counteract colonialism's attempts to falsify and harm" (Fanon 1994: 44): it describes the "whole body of efforts made by a people in the sphere of thought to describe, justify and praise the action through which that people has created itself and keeps itself in existence"

(Fanon 1994: 44). Indeed, Francisco's poetry book demonstrates how Maya peoples self-represent their own experiences and persistence despite more than 500 years of systematic attempts of genocide and assimilation. By inviting his readers to consider the experiences of those who perished and survived the atrocities of one of the most shameful chapters in Guatemalan history, Francisco's poetry represents an example of "witness literature." It is a "poetry that puts us in touch with raw facts of existence rather than effects produced by rhetorical technique" (Vogler 2003: 174), and in doing so, he not only challenges the hegemonic versions of history endorsed by the Guatemalan state, but also registers a courageous testimony that aims to restore our spirits and dignity as Indigenous peoples.

Notes

1   The Trail of Tears is a name given to the forced relocation of Native American nations from southeastern parts of the United States following the Indian Removal Act of 1830. The removal included peoples from the Cherokee, Muscogee, Seminole, Chickasaw, and Choctaw nations. For this particular historical event, see Jahoda (1995 [1975]).
2   The Committed Generation refers to a generation of poets that emerged in the 1960s in Central America. Many of the writers felt that writing poetry was not enough to change the world. Consequently many of them joined revolutionary movements in their struggles for freedom. Several of these writers, like Guatemalan Otto Rene Castillo and Salvadorian Roque Dalton, were assassinated for their efforts.

References

Cesaire, Aime. 1994. "Discourse on colonialism". In Patrick Williams and Laura Chrisman, eds. *Colonial and Post-Colonial Discourse*. New York: Columbia University Press, pp. 172–180.
Fanon, Franz. 1994. "On national culture". In Patrick Williams and Laura Chrisman, eds. *Colonial and Post-Colonial Discourse*. New York: Columbia University Press, pp. 36–52.
Francisco, Sabino Esteban. 2007. *Sa'aqaw yechel aqanej / Gemido de huellas*. Guatemala: Editorial Cultura. Extracts reproduced with permission.
Guha, Ranajit. 1996. "The small voice of history". In Shahid Amin and Dipesh Chakrabarty, eds. *Subaltern Studies: Writings on South Asian History. V IX*. Delhi: Oxford University Press, pp. 1–12.
Jahoda, Gloria. 1995 [1975]. *Trail of Tears: The Story of the American Indian Removal 1813–1855*. New York: Random House.
Moller, Johathan and Ricardo Falla, eds. 2004. *Our Culture is Our Resistance: Repression, Refuge and Healing in Guatemala*. New York: Power House Books.
Rueckert, William. 1996. "Literature and ecology: An experiment in ecocriticism". In Cheryll Glotfelty and Harold Fromm, eds. *The Ecocriticism Reader: Landmarks in Literary Ecology*. Athens and London: University of Georgia Press, pp. 105–123.
Sanford, Victoria. 2003. *Buried Secrets: Truth and Human Rights in Guatemala*. New York: Palgrave Macmillan.
Smith, Linda Tuhiwai. 2012. *Decolonizing Methodologies: Research and Indigenous Peoples*. London and New York: Zed Books.

Swann, Brian. 1988. "Introduction: Only the beginning." In Duane Niatum, ed. *Harper's Anthology of Twentieth Century Native American Poetry*. New York: Harper, pp. ix–xxxii.

Vogler, Thomas. 2003. "Poetry witness: Writing the real". In Ana Douglass and Thomas Vogler, eds. *Witness and Memory: The Discourse of Trauma*. New York: Routledge, pp. 173–206.

Wolfe, Patrick. 1999. *Settler Colonialism and the Transformation of Anthropology*. London and New York: Cassell.

25 Pieces left along the trail

Material culture histories and Indigenous Studies

Sherry Farrell Racette in conversation with Alan Corbiere and Crystal Migwans

> I asked him if they had any swords associated with Indians and he said, "Just this one that belonged to a 'Little Knife'." I saw it, held it, and knew it was Mookomaanish's and I was really excited to find it. After I left that storage facility and was heading back to the hotel I just started running, and jumping, I was so damn excited! I had a really strong reaction to finding the sword. I was ecstatic. I couldn't sit still, nor just walk, I had to run.[1]

Alan Ojiig Corbiere, former director of the Ojibwe Cultural Foundation on Manitoulin Island, shared this story of joyous discovery in response to questions I posed while preparing this chapter.[2] Having written a reflective essay, I questioned the limits of a single perspective on material histories. I also wanted to consider a broader question – are Indigenous historians simply using conventional material culture and museum collections research strategies or is there something inherently or uniquely Indigenous about how we approach collections and *do* material culture research both inside and outside the frame of museums? Are there Indigenous material culture research methodologies?

Most scholarly writing about museums and "source communities" focuses on the important work museums around the world are doing with elders, knowledge keepers and community groups (see Clifford 1997; Fienup-Riordan 2003). This critical work has been under way for several decades and is integrated into most museum studies programs. There is significant scholarship describing the problematic history of collections and the shift (however tentative) toward collaboration and community-driven projects.[3] In the United States, the Native American Graves Protection and Repatriation Act (1990) was a change stimulus, while in Canada *Turning the Page: Forging New Partnerships Between Museums and First Peoples* (1992) was the catalyst.[4] Subsequent projects tended to facilitate community access to museum collections, sought the deep cultural knowledge of elders, or initiated the process of repatriation. As a historian and artist, I don't fit neatly into these categories of engagement, nor do the relatively small number of Indigenous scholars who incorporate material culture into our broader research lives, or the growing number of Indigenous museum professionals.

To explore larger questions of Indigenous material culture research, I initiated a conversation. Discussions moved from social media, to email correspondence, and finally animated conversations, with our heads crowded together, peering at images on computers and smart phones at the 2015 Native American Indigenous Studies Conference in Washington, DC. A common core of experiences, practices and epistemological approaches has begun to emerge.

Into the museum

In 2001 when Alan Corbiere began research for an exhibition commemorating the 1862 Manitoulin Island Treaty, he came across a description of a sword gifted to a chief who fought alongside the British during the War of 1812. Later, while doing archival research in Ottawa, he made a cold call to the Canadian War Museum, hoping to borrow a few circa War of 1812 era items. It was there he discovered the sword. Where Alan ran jumping with joy down the streets of Ottawa, I jumped up and down, fist-pumping in the air, after opening a trunk of items collected by the Earl of Southesk from the Canadian plains in 1859–1860. I was in the Kinnaird Castle library on the east coast of Scotland, supervised by a (momentarily forgotten) man. I froze when I saw his astonished face, but asked, "Do you play bingo here?" When he nodded, I returned to my dance, shouting "Bingo!" I did a similar dance in the Montana Historical Society where I found a saddle belonging to Gabriel Dumont.[5] This is the pure joy felt when a lost object is found, when an object described in a historic text appears before you, when a story moves from orality to the material presence of an object-witness.

Like Alan, I went to museums looking for something that was lost, dropped along the trail. I experience strong emotions when I'm inside a museum: joy, anger, sorrow, awe. Now, after many years in museum collections, I also have collegial relations and friendships with several curators, and returning to a collection is often like visiting old friends. Other times it is not. A few years ago, while viewing an exhibition, I came upon a disconsolate young Indigenous women weeping before a dress. She kept saying, "It shouldn't be here. It shouldn't be here." She had no previous knowledge of the dress; her distress was spontaneous. Later, the curator told me the dress had a disturbing story, and shouldn't have entered the museum collection. Somehow the dress communicated its pain. A heightened sensitivity to objects and stories is entangled within Indigenous methods; whether it is love stitched into beadwork, bravery honored or a wrenching story of trauma and loss.

Perhaps the work of Indigenous artists best illustrates our troubled relationships with museums – the spaces we negotiate to see and touch the objects of our material heritage – and the authoritative voices who have defined, analyzed and categorized the objects within them.[6] Artists gave visual form to the late-twentieth-century challenge that questioned that authority. James Luna (Luiseño, USA) and Rebecca Belmore (Anishinaabe, Canada) became living artifacts, replacing museum objects with their own bodies (Blocker 2009; Cooper 2007: 24). In *The Artifact Piece* (1987–1990), Luna disrupted museological order by lying quietly in a glass case surrounded by objects and labels. In *Artifact 671B* (1988), Belmore, similarly caged and labeled, sat (in sub-zero weather) protesting *The Spirit Sings* exhibition at the Calgary Winter Olympics. These works, and the issues they addressed, have been integrated into the discourse of museum studies, but more recent works suggest resolution remains elusive. In 2006 Wayne Youle addressed the "alive-ness" of objects in a series of interventions created from museum storage boxes. Desperate knocking emanated from *Jack (Haki) in the Box*, and from another the sounds of someone/thing struggling for air (Raymond and Salmond 2008). Tlingit artist Nicholas Galanin addressed seizure and dispersal in his dizzying *Who We Are* (2006), a visual reunification of 25,000 Tlingit objects dispersed among many museums.[7] These works give visual form to thoughts and emotions that dog any Indigenous historian working with museum collections. I usually surrender to the joy of discovery, but one never forgets. Drawers with objects draped with white cloth haunt me; and I am often overwhelmed by the loss of knowledge collections represent. It is why I am there. Similarly, Alan Corbiere reflected, "I am looking for pieces of our past, our identity, pieces of our foundation so we can build it up again."

Negotiating museum systems

From the beginning, my forays into collections required negotiating an array of surprisingly resilient museum conventions. The dominant mode of categorization in ethnographic museum storage and display is the ubiquitous culture area. A surprising number of people are unaware of the role museum-based anthropologists played in the development of the culture area concept, and its principle function as a means to exhibit and order collections.[8] The culture area construct has difficulty accommodating the notion of movement and seeks to confine entire nations within distinct environmental regions. While many museums have changed their curatorial approach in gallery spaces, old paradigms generally rule behind the scenes. "Ethnographic" collections are often organized by culture area, subdivided by object type and are generally managed separately from other collections. If one's research focus falls neatly within ethnographic paradigms, these systems will work for you. If not, one must learn to negotiate them. My primary focus, Métis material culture, immediately puts me at odds with the authority of the museum. Métis material culture has either eluded categorization or been ignored and subsumed within generic regional identifies. Occasionally catalogued outside ethnography, Métis objects can also be found in "pioneer" or "settlement" collections. My research invariably straddles and transgresses categories, requiring me to work with several curators and departments, negotiating storage and catalogue systems.

Each museum, unless it is very tiny, will have at least one functioning catalogue system to facilitate collections management. Cataloguing systems have changed over time and tend to be idiosyncratic, unique to particular museums and information trends.[9] Researchers are generally directed toward the most current catalogue, and it may take some negotiation to gain entry to the deeper archive of collections documentation.[10]

Newcomers to collections research might be astonished at the sparseness of many museum files. Items are often bereft of provenance or any record of community origin or maker. A file is sometimes a mere lineage of speculation gradually accepted as an object's truth – with each researcher and curator adding her or his "best guess" to the accumulated body of knowledge. One might reconstruct an object's circuitous post-collection movement, but information on where and when an item was first acquired is rare. Objects have lost home – or perhaps home has forgotten them – and the path has grown over. The knowledge we bring into museums is critical, whether family and community names, stylistic markers, designs, or half-remembered stories. This knowledge grounds us. Museum systems are useful road maps, but we must never accept their authority without question or be limited by their impositions. We must pose our own questions, and be prepared to open every drawer, peek in every shelf, and challenge structural categories.

Learning to see, drawing as conversation

Material culture is visual culture; in order to study it one must learn to see. My methodological approach, both as teacher and practitioner, begins with developing a maker's eye. It is grounded in the notion of objects as master teachers, as animate storytellers. You must train your eyes to *see* stories. I ask an object, "Where did she start?" Her process reveals itself – the first bead, the sequence of stitches. This is my methodological foundation. One object tells a story, sometimes several stories. Multiple objects reveal interconnected stories, but as they communicate visually, one sees stories rather than hears them.

Initially my principal tools for studying objects were a pencil and a sketchbook, but with the advent of digital technology I went through a period when the camera briefly replaced the pencil. Invariably, however, when compiling visual data, my drawings and sketchbook notes – no matter how rough – are more reliable aides-memoire. Drawing helps one listen to an object. It compels you to sit quietly and make friends. One draws, looks at the object, notices incongruities between what you "saw," what you drew, and the object before you. It forces you to look many times, and teaches you to distrust what you think you see.

Drawing is an old museological tool. Early museum catalogues and registry books often include drawings. I was unaware of that history when I first brought my sketchbook into a museum. It is the way I learn. I look, draw, measure and count. I rough out the construction. How many pieces to make it? How is it sewn together? How many colours? I look for patterns, not only in the actual designs, but the overall rhythm of the object. It's extraordinary how many there are.

As I considered drawing-as-research, I contacted Crystal Migwans, an artist–scholar who also employs drawing in collections research.[11] We discussed drawing as the opposite of photography – to use Crystal's phrase, the antithesis of the "authoritative shot."[12] Drawing is a record of our own looking, she reflected, tracing "the eye's path over the object." Drawing is a conversation or rather the act of drawing with the object before us is the conversation, while the drawing itself serves as the memory of that conversation. Drawings substantially enhance photographs, although photography ostensibly reproduces objects with greater reality. Drawings hold more memory.

Since Crystal and myself are concerned with reclaiming and revitalizing artistic practices, we considered drawing as "the step before making." Drawings were links to the invisible artist. At one point in the conversation, we realized we were addressing objects as "she" – seeing objects as manifestations of the artist. We "were trying to see her hands." Drawing traces the moving hands of an unknown artist.

Visiting and bringing it home

"Listening" and "visiting" were recurring words and ideas that were expanded throughout our conversations. The notion that objects are alive and infused with spirit is articulated throughout the Indigenous world. Alan Corbiere observed:

> As you know, pipes, drums, scrolls, and pouches have a spirit and some people can feel that, others can communicate with it, and this is why we address these items as *N'mishoomis*, "My grandfather." I am not able to receive messages the way some people do, but it is the reflexive process afterward wherein that spirit may inspire you … I have burned tobacco at various museums, if there is a facility to do so, and if not, I will place some outside by a tree.

In these instances, we listen and speak to objects through word, prayer or gesture. At other times, communication is silent. Listening to objects is multi-layered. We listen to the object itself, reading storied texts of stitches and marks. We may learn stories left by makers and stories of use and function. Visiting quietly with an object in reflective contemplation is often at odds with the assembly-line mode adopted when researchers have limited time in a museum. We might call such deep looking and listening, "slow" research. It extends time in collections and requires accommodation by researchers and hosting museums. All relationships, even with objects, take time to nurture.

The stories objects reveal are amplified by rigorous searching to reconstruct an object's history, linking it with archival documents, community stories and other objects. Alan Corbiere's interdisciplinary approach does not always begin with objects:

> It is a great puzzle with many pieces scattered and I feel like I am going around trying to make the picture whole again, not just with collections research but with oral tradition research, with cultural practices, and I always try to include our language. So I collect elders' stories, read old ethnographies, and now material culture research has added another dimension to the research I do. I love looking at these woven bags, looking at the symbols, symbols that also appear on bark, hide, drums, pipe stems, pipes, and try to

relate the images to episodes in our stories and teachings, but also do the inverse, use the images to tell the stories.[13]

At NAISA, Crystal Migwans had a work-in-progress wrapped around her wrist. It was a narrow piece of fingerweaving, applying the knowledge she had drawn (literally) from museum collections. From time to time, she would pause and make a few quick stitches. This, perhaps, is the key element of Indigeneity in material culture research. We search collections, not to replicate the past, but rather to learn from it and reclaim it in the present. As Alan Corbiere reflected, "it comes back to this 'finding items left alongside the road' and picking those up again; trying to understand their purpose and re-incorporate them into our lives again." We seek to bring them home.

Notes

1 Alan Ojiig Corbiere, bne doodem (Ruffed Grouse clan), was Executive Director of the Ojibwe Cultural Foundation for five years. He is now Anishinaabemowin Revitalization Program Co-ordinator for M'Chigeeng First Nation, Manitoulin Island (Mnidoo Mnising), unceded territory, Ontario. Alan Corbiere, personal communication, May 15, 2015.
2 Alan Corbiere and Crystal Migwans, personal communication March 25 and May 14, 2015.
3 Scott Manning Steven's "Cultural Mediations: Or How to Listen to Lewis and Clark's Indian Artifacts" (2007) was a plea to acknowledge knowledge and authority residing in communities. See also Knowles (2011) and Krmpotich and Peers (2011).
4 See Phillips (2011) for a discussion of *The Spirit Sings* and the Task Force on Museums and First Peoples, 48–70; also the Great Lakes Research Alliance for the Study of Aboriginal Arts and Culture, est. by Philips in 2004, 277–297. For a discussion of NAGPRA and shifts in museum practice see Lonetree (2013).
5 Gabriel Dumont (Métis, 1837–1906) was military leader of the 1885 Saskatchewan Resistance.
6 A significant percentage of "Canadian" First Nations items in museum collections were acquired under Section 114 (later Section 149) of the Indian Act, which outlawed traditional forms of government, ceremonies and associated cultural practices. See Pettipas (1994) and Brown (2014).
7 Nicholas Galanin lecture at Evergreen State College, 13 October 2010, Olympia, Washington, posted on Nicholas Galanin, http://galan.in/post/1541687004/evergreen.
8 The culture area map was first used by Otis Mason in 1907 and by Clark Wissler at the American Museum in 1912 (Lyman et al. 1997: 123–129).
9 See Parks Canada (1992) for a modified Chenhall system and SHIC Working Party (1993). Both systems undergo frequent revisions and cataloguer discretion determines an object's assignation.
10 The importance of preserving the catalogue archive was emphasized by Jonathan King's "Fragile Paradigms" presented at the Museum Ethnographers Group conference, Manchester Museum, Manchester UK, May 2005. King demonstrated valuable details lost with each systemic shift.
11 Crystal Migwans (Anishinaabe, Wikwemikong Unceded First Nation) worked at the Ojibwe Cultural Foundation, and as a research assistant for the GRASAC project. She is currently a PhD student in Art History at Columbia University, New York.

12 Crystal Migwans, personal communication at the Native American Indigenous Studies Association Conference, Washington DC, June 5, 2015. Quotation marks indicate notes from our conversations, most are Crystal's thoughts.
13 Alan Corbiere, personal communication, May 15, 2015.

References

Blocker, Jane. 2009. "Peoples of memory: James Luna and the production of history". In *Seeing Witness: the Visuality and Ethics of Testimony*. Minneapolis: University of Minnesota Press, pp. 13–28.

Brown, Alison. 2014. *First Nations, Museums, Narrations: Stories of the 1929 Franklin Motor Expedition to the Canadian Prairies*. Vancouver: UBC Press.

Clifford, James. 1997. "Museums as contact zones". In *Routes: Travel and Translation in the Late Twentieth Century*. Cambridge, MA: Harvard University Press, pp. 188–219.

Cooper, Karen Coody. 2007. *Spirited Encounters: American Indians Protest Museum Policies and Practices*. Lanham: AltaMira Press.

Fienup-Riordan, Anne. 2003. "Yupik elders in the museum: Fieldwork turned on its head". In Laura Peers and Alison Brown, eds. *Museums and Source Communities: A Routledge Reader*. London: Routledge, pp. 28–41.

King, Jonathan. 2005. "Fragile paradigms: Ethnographic displays in London c.1740–1940". Museum Ethnographers Conference, Manchester Museum, Manchester, UK, 9 May.

Knowles, Chantal. 2011. "'Objects as ambassadors': Representing nation through museum exhibitions". In Sarah Byrne, Anne Clarke, Rodney Harrison and Robin Torrence, eds. *Unpacking the Collection: Networks of Material and Social Agency in the Museum*. New York: Springer, pp. 231–248.

Krmpotich, Cara and Laura Peers. 2011. "The scholar-practitioner expanded: An Indigenous museum research museums collaborative network". *Museum Management and Curatorship*, 26(5): 421–440.

Lonetree, Amy. 2013. *Decolonizing Museums: Representing Native America in National and Tribal Museums*. Chapel Hill: The University of North Carolina Press.

Lyman, R. Lee, Michael O'Brian, and Robert C. Dunnell. 1997. *Americanist Culture History: Fundamentals of Time, Space and Form*. New York: Springer Science + Business Media.

Parks Canada. 1992. *Classification System for Historical Collections*. Ottawa: Canada Communications Group.

Pettipas, Katherine. 1994. *Severing the Ties That Bind: Government Repression of Indigenous Religious Ceremonies on the Plains*. Winnipeg: University of Manitoba Press.

Phillips, Ruth B. 2011. *Museum Pieces: Toward the Indigenization of Canadian Museums*. Montreal and   Kingston: McGill-Queen's University Press.

Raymond, Rosanna and Amiria Salmond, eds. 2008. *Pasifika Styles: Artists inside the Museum*. Cambridge: Museum of Archaeology and Anthropology, Cambridge University.

SHIC Working Party. 1993. *Social History and Industrial Classification (SHIC): A Subject Classification for Museum Collections*. London: Museum Documentation Association [Collections Trust].

Stevens, Scott Manning. 2007. "Cultural mediations: Or how to listen to Lewis and Clark's Indian artifacts". *American Indian Culture and Research Journal*, 31(3–4): 181–202.

26 Authoring Indigenous Studies in three dimensions

An approach to museum curation

Gabrielle Tayac

Like my colleagues who have contributed to this volume, I was rigorously trained as an academic scholar – more specifically as a political and historical sociologist. The written word was to be my primary form of knowledge transmission and professional currency. Text production was to be frequently enhanced with teaching and in my own practice, both local and international Indigenous activism for sovereignty rights.

Several months before my dissertation defense, I received a phone call. It was Dr. Charlotte Heth, the noted Cherokee ethnomusicologist who had been my mentor when I was an undergraduate at Cornell and had been checking in on my progress (or lack thereof) in graduate school. She told me that she had taken on a position at the National Museum of the American Indian (NMAI), not yet built, and that she wanted me on board with her to create educational programs. NMAI was in my Piscataway tribal homeland, after all, she encouraged, and their Native consultants wanted to make sure that the museum honored place and ancestry.

Charlotte's offer, by any standards, would be a dream job. But I hesitated – this is a museum, I countered, what about human remains? Deaccessioned, working on returning everything, she said. What about all of the stolen sacred objects? Caring for them with tribal awareness and working on repatriation, she added. Besides, I didn't know anything about museums at all, I recklessly said to her. That, Charlotte answered finally, was exactly why she wanted me there. NMAI called itself "The Museum Different" and it would be about the living, in honor of the ancestors, for the future generations.

I went in to see Charlotte the next morning. That was in 1999, five years before NMAI became a physical place. At the time of this writing, I have been working at NMAI for over fifteen years. I specialize in curating exhibits that take on an interdisciplinary, collaborative approach with the direct purpose of creating social change leading to wide public support for Indigenous human rights.

I am still interrogating how museums can be indigenized space, an intersection for reconciliation and civic engagement. I remain ever aware of the massive hemispheric accountability in such a visible venue as well as the weight of stewardship for collections that were at times acquired unethically during dark times for Native peoples.

I took up word count to begin with personal narrative, because I understand that many of us in Indigenous Studies wrestle with the colonialist legacies ongoing in our venues. Museums have a peculiar weight in that relationship, although it is shifting radically over the past several decades especially since the passage of the Native American Graves Protection and Repatriation Act of 1990. Here I am presenting a concept for museology, specifically curatorial practice that goes toward a more profound inscription for the place of museums and exhibits as sites of three-dimensional authorship. Three-dimensional authorship, as I will describe it here, is beautifully suited as a methodology for the delivery of Indigenous Studies research. Museum-based sources, including collections, archives, images, and live presentation can be even further reclaimed in their indigeneity. My agenda here is to entice, enlighten, and encourage Indigenous Studies students and scholars to exercise three-dimensional authorship as a complement to publication. More selfishly, perhaps on behalf of my museum colleagues, I would also like to elevate museum-based scholarship and curation to parity with published products across fields beyond where it is now recognized in fine arts disciplines. To explain the process, I will refer to the National Museum of the American Indian and share a current example of work that utilizes three-dimensional authorship.

Three-dimensional authorship

Curation is a practice that produces knowledge and transmits understanding mostly through museum-based, or spatially located, sensory experience. Curators select objects, images, words, sound, and media to compose a point of view assembled in surrounding, designed space. The resulting composition is known as an exhibit, and although static in nature, it can be enlivened through dynamic interaction presented in accompanying programs. Visitors actively engage with, participate in, and move through that space we call an exhibit. In this context, curators are authors working in three dimensions and visitors are not only readers but also physically present participants moving through the assembled experience.

Exhibits lend themselves to a constructivist approach, which is essentially sensuous, kinesthetic, multi-dimensional, and experiential (Hein 1998; McLean 1993; Simon 2010). Visitors have some freedom of choice in learning sequence, selecting focus of attention although design can encourage directions. Exhibits are often a social experience, encountered in conversation and with others. Exhibits might measure success through didactic intellectual learning, but at their best elicit emotional attachment. Exhibits are not books on walls – ideally they reach visitors through largely non-verbal communication although text and speech are additional explanatory means. Text is a component in curatorial interpretation, most usually presented in label copy, but it is enhancement. Exhibits are fully complementary to books, articles, and other media – and are contained and formed through authorship.

One-and-a-half million visitors come to the Smithsonian's National Museum of the American Indian per year. A University of Indiana study shows that the public trusts museums as the most reliable sources of historic information, demonstrating that the impact that an exhibit can have in knowledge transfer is profound (American Alliance of Museums 2014). If that knowledge and means of transfer anchors in Indigenous constructions, then a more mindful encounter with Native perspectives can be achieved. Form meets content when an exhibit incorporates directions expressed knowledge in sensory, intellectual, and material forms as well as ideas embedded in the written word.

In Indigenous contexts, knowledge – ancestrally integrated throughout societal institutions – often transmits in orality, expressive practices, experiential embodiment transformations, social and ceremonial interaction, and material culture (Barnes and Talamantez 2006; Berlo and Phillips 1998; Heth 1998; Ong 2002; Penney and Horse Capture 2004). Describing, analyzing, and recording Indigenous knowledge merely through writing is inadequate, I argue, to fully disseminate Native concepts not only to scholars and academic students but also to other sectors of the public who may benefit from varying, appropriate degrees of understanding Indigenous perspectives.

Peter Jemison, Seneca educator, artist, and culture bearer commented, "knowledge is earned" (personal communication, August 2012). In a public arena, the task is to communicate unearned knowledge in the sense that highly esoteric information reserved for tribal people who achieve access through their own process is not on display – but that still leaves a great deal of content for mass relation. An essential means for such dissemination can be developed through an indigenized museology.

Museums becoming Native space: the NMAI example

Museums classically come with many negative connotations for Indigenous communities. Museums were founded originally as cabinets of curiosity, trophy cases full of wonders or treasure houses tantalizing elites with the reach of imperial Europe. Early museums such as Tradescant's Ark (now in the Ashmolean Museum at Oxford) entertained viewers with the exotic, strange world of the other (MacGregor 1983). In many ways, these seventeenth- and eighteenth-century versions of museums assumed that Native peoples would be in situ, odd, bizarre, even monstrous, yet self-determined nonetheless.

Social sciences in the nineteenth century focused on misguided notions of evolution involving the erroneous scale of savagery to civilization. The concept of cultural hierarchy and racial ranking interacted with policies meant to dismantle tribal societies. Museums, then, embarked on the intensive project to capture as many objects, images, and even bodies belonging to peoples who were believed to not possibly withstand the might of civilization (Lonetree 2012; Sleeper-Smith 2009). Most certainly, US action and policy intended that Native peoples would vanish entirely by the mid-twentieth century as distinct cultural, sovereign entities. In the most terrible cases, physical genocide continued during that era (see Chapter 32 in this volume).

The National Museum of the American Indian now stewards a collection originated by the passion of a single wealthy man, George Gustav Heye. Heye collected with that early twentieth-century fervor to record those certain to disappear. Alone, he amassed a collection encompassing 10,000 years of Native American expression, representing nearly 700 unique Indigenous communities ranging over the entire Western Hemisphere. In about fifty years, Heye assembled nearly one million objects. Some were displayed in his Museum of the American Indian (MAI), located on 155th Street in Manhattan – at the time a luxurious neighborhood called Audubon Terrace. The remainder of the materials was warehoused in a collections facility in the Bronx. A 40,000-volume library, extensive photographic and paper archives, and a publication series rounded out the collection.

Native peoples actively resisted the plan of cultural extinction. Rather, powerful late twentieth-century movements pushed massive reforms. A policy era for self-determination and sovereignty opened – at least in regulation and intent. In this context, as the old MAI fell into disrepair and loneliness in Dominican Harlem, then generally perceived by many potential museum-goers as a remote neighborhood, Native activists and allies sought a reclamation of Indigenous voice through the reclamation of the magnificent Heye collection. Knowing that so many of these materials were ripped out of the lives of peoples, there would be a chance to regenerate knowledge, connect with relatives, restore Indigenous authority through the collection's objects.

With great heart and political force, following pathways of such groundbreaking scholars as Hartman Lomawaima and Vine Deloria, Jr. who insisted on re-asserting the Native voice, the Smithsonian's National Museum of the American Indian came into being through a 1989 Congressional act. The Act also provided for a repatriation program across the Smithsonian, mandating collections inventory leading to a process for return of culturally affiliated human remains and objects of cultural patrimony. NMAI opened in 2004, elevating Native voice to primary validation in permanent exhibits. NMAI's mission stated:

> The National Museum of the American Indian (NMAI) is committed to advancing knowledge and understanding of the Native cultures of the Western Hemisphere—past, present, and future—through partnership with Native people and others. The museum works to support the continuance of culture, traditional values, and transitions in contemporary Native life.

The inaugural exhibitions were community curated, meaning that NMAI staff invited culture bearers and community-based scholars to select the materials and storylines in the galleries. Situating itself as a massive tribal museum moving away from objectifying living peoples, presenting objects was less important than showcasing Native oral account. Exhibit, landscape, and architectural design mirrored Native cosmologies and philosophies. Even the elevators had stunning ancestral bird motifs signifying flight. Expressive culture through live programs gained equal stature to exhibitions. Intensive community interactions were seeded as keystone responsibilities and reciprocities. For all the successes in flipping the script to prioritize Native perspective (although always including extensive academic scholarship, contrary to some perceptions), we still had much work to do in order to merge the dynamism of lived culture and relevance of history with the static nature of museums. Most importantly, we had to make the experience accessible to visitors and learners while also supporting the needs of our Native constituents. Both extensive community support and substantial critique emerged with NMAI's opening on the National Mall (see Cobb and Lonetree 2008). Taking those matters to heart, the undeniable statement, "we are still here," would become irrevocable in its placement next to the US Capitol.

After ten years, NMAI is coming of age. It is at this juncture that a more confident stance in curation, partnered with community and academically based scholars, that a deeper melding of Indigenous concepts and practices with museology can emerge. There are vast resources at NMAI and museums around the world, much of them artifacts of earlier museum practices. Three-dimensional authorship, implemented through material, sensorial, and intellectual expression effectively transmits Indigenous knowledge.

Sky Dome: a proposed section for Native New York

I would now like to take some time to explicate my current curatorial practice in three-dimensional authorship and describe a work in progress that will illuminate process. It may be that, as an unfinished project, all sorts of events might unfold that will lead to a different path for research and exhibition. Nonetheless, the following example shows how indigenized curatorial methodology and museum sources can begin to shape scholarly work that will lead to the planned exhibit, "Native New York: Where Nations Rise." The exhibit will serve multiple audiences with special attention to the educational needs of thousands of New York City public school students.

Our team began with forays into NMAI collections, archives, media, educational material, and photographic resources based on directions that we developed from a core consultant group of Indigenous scholars that met for two days in August 2012 (Lori Quigley, Rick Hill, Jr., Peter Jemison, Lisa Brooks, and Cedric Woods). The initial consultation established the exhibit's central theme, nation-building, and supporting variables for further research shaped by further community based field consultations and educational guidance. Along with NMAI curatorial resident, Korah English (Concow Maidu), I made twenty-five consultative visits to Haudenosaunee and Algonquian communities to meet with cultural experts and scholars as well as to museum and public history sites dealing with relevant Native subjects to sharpen focus on exhibit content. A series of object research visits by Seneca, Lenape, and Mohegan experts to the NMAI collection also informed the work.

By 2014, Haudenosaunee (Peter Jemison, Kay Olan, Tom Porter, Louise McDonald, Randi Rourke Barreiro, Kahente Horn-Miller, and Beverly Cook), Abenaki (Lisa Brooks, Judy Dow, and Joe Bruchac), and Mohegan consultants (Stephanie Fielding, Melissa Tantaquidgeon Zobel, and Rachel Sayet) were particularly focusing on the ongoing presence of sacred creation narrative manifested in the Sky Dome, which is the realm from which creation springs (Mohawk 2005; personal communication with Tom Porter, July 2013; personal communication with Beverly Cook and Louise MacDonald, July 2013; personal communication with Peter Jemison, July 2013). In Haudenosaunee and some Algonquian representations, Sky Dome appears as a repeating half circle with parallel curved lines emerging from the top. Among peoples in Southern New England including the Long Island Sound, Sky Dome takes the shape of a symmetric flower with four petals, with the celestial tree design ascending from the cross spaces (personal communications with Melissa Tantaquidgeon Zobel, July 2013 and August 2014; White 2015; Logan 2015). Sky Dome may also be analogous to the Four Wigwams, which can appear as a cluster of four circles.

To be utterly brief in summarizing an extensive, complex origin narrative held by Haudenosaunee (there are many variants), Sky Dome is Sky World, the place from which Sky Woman fell through a hole created by the uprooted Celestial Tree. Falling through space and pregnant, Sky Woman was buoyed by a flock of geese or swans. The world below was all water, and a great turtle emerged. Yet, the shell was hard, and a series of animals dove beneath the surface to bring up earth. The muskrat was ultimately successful. Please take this description as you would a similar reduction of any sacred narrative such as the Torah, the Vedas, or the Sutras.

Sky Woman landed on Turtle's back, and danced to sprout the seeds falling from her fingers to create a living earth, known as Turtle Island (personal communication with Marissa Corwin, March 2014; personal communication with Jamie Jacobs, June 2014). This dance, known as Women's Dance, is the continuous enactment of that eternal moment. Women massage the earth to bring the plant world into being (personal communication, Kay Olan, July 2016). Women traditionally are the agriculturalists, interplanting corn, beans, and squash (the Three Sisters) to best maintain soil nitrogen cycles and fertility. Haudenosaunee government, an ancient continuous democracy, institutes male chiefs via clanmothers. The Bean Dance also respects the Three Sisters, moving in a vine-like motion.

In exhibition, Women's Dance might easily and commonly be shown on a media piece. Additionally, however, the Bean Dance motions that intertwine the dancers could also be laid out as a pathway on the floor. Visitors could experience the points about the three sisters not only by object, label, image, and kinesthetic body movement but also by putting together the concepts of interdependence into the very design of that gallery section. The practice of auditory anthropology brings in a soundscape not merely as background music but also as the "sound of indigeneity" (Schoer and Lewy 2014). Individual visitors see installations such as these in different angles, and richness in display invites return visits with new insights to offer at each turn.

Sky Dome does not only represent an external universe or singular creation moment. Rather, Sky Dome is also found inside the body as the uterus, according to Akwesasne Mohawk Council Chief and nurse, Beverly Cook (personal communication, July 2013). She also connects the fall of Sky Woman to ovulation, describing that creation is carried and repeated by human generations constantly connecting external to the internal environments, the body to the galaxies. This concept is used in healing from substance abuse, addressing domestic violence, and women's health initiatives. Sky Woman, as Kahnawake Mohawk scholar, Kahente Horn-Miller (2014), notes, manifests in the lives of present-day, ordinary Haudenosaunee women. Working with the ideology that all carry Sky Woman within their own experiences – in the here and now – Horn-Miller clarifies the interconnecting strands between esoteric deep time and current daily relevance.

Sky Dome and Celestial Tree can be found on most historic and contemporary Haudenosaunee traditional clothing. Contemporary art also frequently brings in Sky Dome and Sky Woman as central themes. An installation of these materials, with time progression, enhanced by audiovisual media, and interactives incorporating movement and design elements could offer the visitor an experience to understand facets of Sky Dome, Sky Woman's journey, and why it resonates in contemporary life. As a curator, I am proposing that designers consider not only an aesthetic that would incorporate the sensibility of Sky Dome, but also create ways to have visitors move through that exhibit area in ways consistent with lived practice reflecting Sky Woman and Sky Dome. Ultimately, it may not be feasible, and the lines between cultural appropriation and ethical display might well not work, but this is the process in consultation that I am working with to further Indigenous museology for a wide audience.

Among the Mohegan, Pequot, Shinnecock, Abenaki, Mahican – and further research may reveal relevance in others – Sky Dome appears as a symmetric flower, the four wigwams (traditional homes), or as a multi-directional set of domes. The motif can be seen on the Mohegan and Shinnecock flags, printed on baskets, painted on bark boxes, and sewn into traditional clothing and accessories. It is carpeted throughout Mohegan Sun Casino.

I am proposing that the gallery section that encompasses integral ancestral practices be constructed to reflect the four domes. Materials demonstrating nation-building themes could be arranged under four domes, immersing the visitor in philosophic space while they learn about what may be considered more secular areas although the sacred always pervades societal institutions up through the present day.

Sky Dome, pervasive among many of the peoples Indigenous to lands now known as New York, is danced, sung, embroidered, painted, printed, embodied over time and space. With Sky Woman as the Haudenosaunee emissary to current creation, falling and dancing between dimensions, Indigenous teachings can also be transmitted in sensuous space – in a physically encountered exhibit. Evoking the wigwam shape, also Sky Dome, reintroduces Native space within building walls. Sky Dome's societal manifestations are distinct, yet linked among peoples in the region. Research conversations leading to new questions have triggered different ways of understanding meanings and practices relating to Sky Dome. In a public museum setting, knowledge that goes out on the floor does not have to be earned. In the museum context, Sky Dome strives to be widely seen and sensed and experienced – even at the most basic comprehension – again in New York City.

Museums as Indigenous form and content

Native objects and archives in museum collections are primary sources, the direct expressions of Indigenous peoples. Certain classes of objects are more prevalent than others depending on the collector's interests. Building collections from an Indigenous Studies perspective we might develop pieces to steward for further research or to compose into spatially experienced exhibits that are reconnected to Indigenous knowledge.

Because Native societies contain knowledge in forms that are not always written, and transmit that knowledge in ways that are not always written, then exhibit curation offers another methodology to consider for Indigenous Studies scholarship. While we have thought of museums as institutions developing out of colonial enterprises, we now can claim that space as a venue for inscribing scholarly three-dimensional authorship of Indigenous experience.

References

American Alliance of Museums. "Museum facts". Accessed 1 October 2014, www.aam-us. org/about-museums/museum-facts.

Barnes, Linda L. and Ines M. Talamantez. 2006. *Teaching Religion and Healing*. New York: Oxford University Press.

Berlo, Janet Catherine and Ruth B. Phillips. 1998. *Native North American Art*. New York: Oxford University Press.

Cobb, Amanda and Amy J. Lonetree. 2008. *The National Museum of the American Indian: Critical Conversations*. Lincoln: University of Nebraska Press.

Hein, George E. 1998. *Learning in the Museum*. New York: Routledge.

Heth, Charlotte. 1998. *Native American Dance: Ceremonies and Social Traditions*. Washington, DC: National Museum of the American Indian.

Horn-Miller, Kahente. 2014. "We walk with her: Sky Woman's journey as meta-narrative toward healing and discovery". Native American and Indigenous Studies Association Annual Meeting, Austin, TX, 31 May.

Logan, Linley. 2015. "Bringing it home: Artists reconnecting cultural heritage with community". National Museum of the American Indian Artists Leadership Program, Washington, DC, 9 December.

Lonetree, Amy. 2012. *Decolonizing Museums: Representing Native Americans in National and Tribal Museums*. Chapel Hill: University of North Carolina Press.

MacGregor, Arthur. 1983. *Tradescant's Rarities: Essays on the Foundations of the Ashmolean Museum, 1683*. Oxford: Clarendon Press.

McLean, Kathleen. 1993. *Planning for People in Museum Exhibitions*. Washington, DC: Association of Science-Technology Centers.

Mohawk, John. 2005. *Iroquois Creation Story: John Arthur Gibson and J. n. B. Hewitt Hewitt's Myth of the Earth Grasper*. Buffalo: Mohawk Publications.

Ong, Walter J. 2002. *Orality and Literacy*. New York: New Accents.

Penney, David W. and George Horse Capture. 2004. *North American Indian Art*. New York: Thames & Hudson.

Schoer, Hein and Matthias Lewy. 2014. "Toward an Auditory Anthropology". *Soundscape Journal*, 3. Accessed 1 January 2015, www.soundingmuseum.com.

Simon, Nina. 2010. *The Participatory Museum*. Museum 2.0.

Sleeper-Smith, Susan. 2009. *Contesting Knowledge: Museums and Indigenous Perspectives*. Lincoln: University of Nebraska Press.

White, Kevin J. 2015. "Examining the evolution of the twin's names in Hewitt's cosmological narratives of the Haudenosaunee". Native American and Indigenous Studies Association Annual Meeting, Washington, DC, 6 June.

27 Future tense

Indigenous film, pedagogy, promise

Michelle Raheja

Framing the future

John Ford's first Technicolor film, *Drums Along the Mohawk* (1939), released during the height of Hollywood's "golden age," exemplifies the complicated ways Native Americans have been represented in cinema. Seneca actor Isaac Johnny John (aka Chief John Big Tree) plays Blue Back, a Christian convert who is sympathetic to the settlement of the Mohawk Valley in New York by American colonists in the late eighteenth century.[1] He befriends Gilbert Martin (Henry Fonda) and in a scene that encapsulates representations of Native Americans in film history, Blue Back frightens Martin's newlywed, Magdalena (Claudette Colbert), when he enters their cabin unannounced. While lighting strikes intermittently, a Lon Chaney-like, somnambulant Blue Back enters the Martin's cabin, encased in a robe, cradling his rifle against his shoulder. He walks slowly and silently to the fireplace to get warm and dry off while the camera pans to his impassive face.

Magdalena is horrified by Blue Back's presence and begins screaming, only to be silenced when Gilbert slaps her. In a predictable filmic turn, Gilbert establishes himself as the patriarchal, colonial site of power in this scene, subduing both the "hysteric" domestic space of his cabin and the female unruliness within, as well as the potentially violent, incommensurable, and frightening "savage" space beyond the cabin's door.

Eve Tuck and Rubén A. Gaztambide-Fernández argue that settler colonial texts such as this engage in a "project of *replacement*, which aims to vanish Indigenous peoples and replace them with settlers, who see themselves as rightful claimants to land, and indeed, as indigenous" (Tuck and Gaztambide-Fernández 2013: 73, emphasis in original). Additionally, as Patrick Wolfe has contended, settler colonialism is predicated on a "logic of elimination" that nearly always compels the settler colonial state to commit genocide in order to have unimpeded access to territory (Wolfe 2006: 409). Hollywood film representation, drawing from earlier colonial visual and literary histories, engages both the project of replacement and the logic of elimination through its rehearsal of stereotype and the fantasy of the first contact narrative. At the very advent of motion picture technology, silent film directors were deeply invested in creating films with Indian themes, both as a strategy of salvage anthropology to capture Native people on film before their putative disappearance (replacement) and to solidify the amnestic desire to figure European settlers as domestic and Indigenous and Indians as external, violent threats to the nation (elimination).[2] As the growing body of scholarship on Native Americans in film demonstrates, Indigenous people, when they are represented at all, are nearly always fixed in the past with no viable future.

Yet Blue Back's presence in Ford's film is not predicated solely on replacement and elimination. At the end of the film, he stands at a church pulpit, smiling and wearing the eye patch of his British enemy in a symbolic form of counting coup. Native people have always contested the idea that the future is an over-determined, foreclosed one, even within the powerful representational institutions of the dominant culture. Not only is Blue Back portrayed as the smiling victor at the end of the film, even as he is immersed in the trappings of assimilation, but the actor Isaac Johnny John made a career for himself playing Native roles, many of which were complicated and demonstrated his investment in the technological and representational futures of film.[3] While Indian representations in Hollywood films have been deployed to signify absence and justify settler colonial presence, I have previously argued that these images, alongside the off-screen work of Native American actors, directors, and spectators, enable Indigenous futurity on the virtual reservation of cinema, as well as in the lived experiences of Native people in land-based, real time territories since the silent era (Raheja 2011). The work of Luther Standing Bear, Lillian St. Cyr (Red Wing), Edwin Carewe, and Jay Silverheels, to name a few, critiqued these representations and is credited by Joanna Hearne with "reframing the Western imaginary" through their insistence on "exert[ing] control over both film scenarios and the politics of representation" (Hearne 2013: 90). In the 1970s and 1980s, with the rise of many more Native American directors in the United States and Canada, Alanis Obomsawin, Sandra Osawa, Larry Littlebird, and many more continued to forward powerful critiques of Hollywood representations. Since the 1990s, there has been a resurgence in global Indigenous film production, as the success of Chris Eyre's *Smoke Signals* (1998) and Igloolik Isuma's *Atanarjuat (The Fast Runner)* (2001) attest. The sheer number of Indigenous filmmakers working in animation, documentary, experimental, and fiction films is too lengthy to list in this chapter, but in the United States and Canada include Jeff Barnaby, Dustinn Craig, Thirza Cuthand, Tracey Deer, Yves Sioui Durand, Helen Haig-Brown, Sterlin Harjo, Zoe Hopkins, Tasha Hubbard, Lisa Jackson, Blackhorse Lowe, Billy Luther, Andrew Okpeaha MacLean, Shelley Niro, N. Bird Runningwater, and Reaghan Tarbell.[4]

Native people involved in film production from the silent era to the present were and are much more sophisticated than they are given credit for and are especially invested in how film representations work toward an Indigenous future This investment in the future has been particularly present in recent film, video games, literature, music videos, and performance work by Native American artists. Some of the most compelling work on Indigenous futurity has been produced by Upper One Games, a project of the Cook Inlet Tribal Council, the first Native-owned videogame developer. Their puzzle-platform video game, *Never Alone* (Kisima Inŋitchuŋa), tracks the efforts of a young Iñupiat girl, Nuna, and her Arctic fox partner as they interact with spirit beings to search for the source of the "eternal blizzard" that threatens their communities. The game features contemporary Iñupiat storytellers as the game progresses, features a strong female point of entry protagonist, and, although it is based on a traditional story, the historical period in which it is set could be the past, present, or future.

Articulations of Indigenous futurity have been particularly present in recent science fiction texts and scholarship by Native American cultural producers, including Hokulani Aikau, Grace Dillon, Brian Hudson, Stephen Graham Jones, Elizabeth La Pensée, Karen Recollet, and others. For the remainder of this chapter, I will engage with what I call the "filmic future tense" to consider how "first contact" historical and science fiction narratives are taken up by Aboriginal filmmakers to imagine what kind of impact contemporary work by Indigenous filmmakers will have on the "future." I will consider Helen Haig-Brown's film, *?E?ANX: The Cave* (2009), to think about what kinds of political and pedagogical projects by Native filmmakers accomplish.

Contemporary Indigenous filmmakers, especially those working in the science fiction and experimental genres, engage in projects that teach us how to productively imagine an alternative future to the one offered up by dominant culture narratives. As Hearne notes, "the ways Native films foreground imaginative visions of Indigenous futures … facilitates an overt acknowledgement of the world-making qualities of visual media and articulates the political stakes of public culture images of Indians" (Hearne 2013: 19). Film provides a particularly productive way of imagining the future because, according to Vivian Sobchak, "the *moving picture* is a visible representation not of activity finished or past but of activating coming-into-being" (Sobchak 2004: 146, emphasis in original). By screening the filmic future tense, Native filmmakers offer powerful and critical interventions that imagine a future marked by complexity, humor, and creativity in spaces where Aboriginal experience is aligned with a vanishing, romanticized past. Rather than providing a lens that corrects inaccurate, outdated images of Native people, these film projects dispense with discourses of authenticity, offering up a hermeneutics of Indigenous experiences of time and space instead.

First contact

One of the most enduring literary and visual culture forms of the US and Canadian settler states has been narratives of so-called first contact. In visual culture, these narratives provide a powerful and damaging colonial genealogy from the earliest representations of Aboriginal people in the early sixteenth century to contemporary science fiction films. First-contact narratives are perhaps the most ubiquitous of all stories about Native people and with very few exceptions inflict historical and discursive euthanasia on Aboriginal people shortly after the imagined moment of contact. And they continue to be popular narratives, as the reprisals of Westerns such as *The Lone Ranger* (2013) and *Apocalypto* (2006), as well as science fiction films like *Avatar* (2009) and *John Carter* (2012) attest. Narratives of first contact are arguably the most prevalent theme of the science fiction genre.

Conventional first-contact narratives transform settler colonial space into what is perceived as domestic and white homelands through the use of non-Native characters as the primary points of entry for the reader/spectator, while Aboriginal people are metaphorized as terrify, primitive, alien, and non-individuated others that require either subjugation or annihilation (thus justifying violence and genocide). Ridley Scott's *Alien* (1979) is a classic example of this process whereby "exploration" becomes a euphemism for the invasion of Indigenous territories. The protagonists, who in another context would be read as rapacious invaders, are represented as human and heroic, whereas the nameless aliens are rendered violent, villainous, and cannibalistic, in a narrative that mirrors that of Christopher Columbus' representations of Indigenous people as radically "Other" in what is now known as the Caribbean 500 years previously.

First-contact narratives, either in the form of historical primary sources or subsequent filmic versions, neither permit an Indigenous past nor a future. The past is rendered unavailable because Indigenous history prior to the fetishized moment of contact is insignificant. What matters instead in these narratives is the arrival of the European or humanized figure. Indigenous access to a future is also foreclosed as violence and genocide become "natural" outcomes of both scientific curiosity and resource extraction and the future belongs solely to those in power.

When we think of the future as it is expressed in science fiction films, there are generally two possible outcomes: the future is utopic and technology brings improvement to our lives or the future is dystopic and apocalyptic, portending the destruction of Earth and humankind.[5] We will either be cyborgs living in a sterile, disease-free, homogenized future or we will have survived the apocalypse by the skin of our teeth (or the skin of our neighbor's skin). In either case, the future is one in which Indigenous people are not present.[6]

Yet people have created and continue to create speculative narratives in ways that are radically different from the contact narratives so popular in mainstream science fiction.[7] Narratives like the Haudenosaunee history of origin (nearly all Aboriginal origin narratives, actually) and figures like Sasquatch, Nanabozho, Yellow Woman, and the Windigo engage in speculative narratives about the past, present, and future. Gerald Vizenor, who has written about Anishinabe creation stories and supernatural figures, argues that Native people have always engaged in the future.[8] In the first book on Indigenous science fiction, Grace Dillon writes, "Indigenous sf is not so new, just overlooked" (Dillon 2012: 2). She coins the term "Native slipstream" to think about "a species of speculative fiction within the science fiction realm, infuses stories with time travel, alternate realities and multiverses, and alternative histories" (Dillon 2012: 3). Native slipstream, according to Dillon, reflects "models of cultural experience of reality" that have been "around for millennia, anticipated recent cutting-edge physics, ironically suggesting that Natives have had things right all along" by engaging with the "multiverse … which posits that reality consists of a number of simultaneously existing alternate worlds and/or parallel worlds" (Dillon 2012: 4).

Helen Haig-Brown, *The Cave* (2009)

Tsilqot'in filmmaker Helen Haig-Brown's *The Cave* represents a Native slipstream in that it allows the filmmaker "to recover the Native space of the past, to bring it to the attention of contemporary readers, and to build better futures" (Dillon 2012: 4). Simultaneously, it rewrites the first-contact narrative, radically unhinging it from its colonial trajectories. *The Cave* was filmed on location on the Stone Reserve in British Columbia and engages in Native filmmaking practices similar to those advocated by Standing Bear and others in the early twentieth century: Haig-Brown employed as many Tsilqot'in crew as possible and the film is based on a narrative told by Haig-Brown's great-uncle and recorded by her mother about a Tsilqot'in bear hunter who accidentally stumbles across a cave that leads to a multiverse. According to Haig-Brown, *The Cave* conforms to Tsilqot'in representational protocols. She uses her great-uncle's voice recording at the beginning of the film, employs cultural advisors, and credits everyone who participated in the project, including first aid providers, camp helpers, and catering services. Dillon claims that it is "the first sf film to be shot entirely in an Indigenous language" (Dillon 2012: 5). It was commissioned by the imagineNATIVE Film Festival and "was named one of Canada's Top Ten Short Films of 2009" (Dowell 2013).[9]

The Cave undermines almost every convention of the first-contact narrative. Rather than a group of white explorers, the spectator's point of entry is an unnamed Tsilqot'in bear hunter from 1961 (played by Tsilqot'in actor Edmond Lulua) who stumbles across a time traveling portal accidentally. Rather than traveling to another planet, the "Spirit Beings" he encounters are in Gwetsilh (a place in historical Tsilqot'in territory) and speak Tsilqot'in rather than an unintelligible language.[10] He experiences a feeling similar to Freud's concept of the uncanny when he recognizes the alternate universe he stumbles upon that is visually similar to the place where he was bear hunting, but also unfamiliar in that he experiences a kind of sensorial assault when he emerges from the cave – his nose starts to bleed, he is blinded by the harsh light, and the people he encounters seem to move and breathe differently than those from the world from which he comes.

Rather than facing conventionally high-tech aliens, the bear hunter finds a group of people who are what many would consider naked and engaged in so-called primitive tasks like fishing and starting fires with sticks. And rather than either acquiring the superior technology of the seeming aliens or wow-ing them with his own technological sophistication, he is telepathically told by a young woman, "This is not the place for you. You're not ready yet. Wherever you have crawled from, crawl back." She and her small community express no curiosity or interest in him and any interest that he might have taken in them is refused. The protagonist is addressed as though he were an infant or an animal when he is entreated to "crawl back" to the place from which he comes. This punctures the conventional first-contact narrative in two ways. Instead of being hailed by a patriarchal, male counterpart, it is a young woman who addresses him. In fact, his embarrassment about seeing women's breasts when he enters this alternative world points to the effects of colonization on Aboriginal communities on whom

Christian principles of post-lapsarian, gendered shame have been inflicted. Also, the film is not invested in equating technology with Western markers of teleological sophistication (machines, computers, weaponry). The advanced technology of the Spirit Beings is their ability to repulse the hunter with sound and manipulation of physics, as well as communicate with him telepathically. And while they're familiar with the world from which the hunter comes (evidenced by a burnt stick inside the cave), they have chosen an existence that radically upsets dominant culture notions of civilization and teleology by living sustainably outside of a capitalist system.

Evoking the Rip van Winkle story, when he returns to the cave and when he emerges on the other side, the hunter finds that so much time has passed that his horse has died and is now a pile of bleached bones. In an interview with Krisin L. Dowell, Haig-Brown states:

> in Tsilqot'in cosmology, the Spirit World is a world of deceased ancestral figures existing in the same plane and at the same time as the present world, although there is a temporal difference between the two ... What feels like only a few hours or minutes in the Spirit World is many years in this world.
>
> (Dowell 2013: 167)

The evocative way Haig-Brown creates this multiverse in her film imagines the future in ways that puncture Western teleological notions of time (here the Spirit Beings simultaneously exist in the past, present, and future) and forwards a project of visual sovereignty aimed at providing intellectually engaged, therapeutic spaces for Aboriginal spectators to imagine the future in ways that are disarticulated from first-contact representations in film that foreclose Indigenous futurity. The pedagogy of this kind of filmic representation of Indigenous concepts of time and space creatively structures a visual history and critical reassessment for Indigenous peoples that embeds Native people in the present and future, rather than the sealed past that films like John Ford's *Drums Along the Mohawk* and other film genres with Native representation offer.

Notes

1 Throughout this chapter, I use the terms "Native American," "Indigenous," and "Aboriginal" interchangeably, recognizing the complicated contexts and histories of all three terms. Likewise, I employ the term "Indian" to refer to stereotypical images of Native Americans by the dominant culture, primarily in Hollywood films.

2 Joanna Hearne provides close analyses of many of these silent films in *Native Recognition* (2013). While most silent film and early "talkies" figured Native Americans as anachronistic and vanishing, there were notable exceptions, as both Hearne and Angela Aleiss have contended. Aleiss has argued that the silent film era is also "surprising" in terms of its representations of contemporary Native people's struggles with boarding schools, assimilation, land dispossession, and military participation (see Aleiss 1995, 2005).

3 Isaac Johnny John attended Carlisle Indian Industrial School and had a nearly forty-year film career. He starred in over fifty films, including *Red Fork Range* (Alan James,

1931), *The Golden West* (David Howard, 1932), and his last film, *She Wore a Yellow Ribbon* (John Ford, 1949).

4   These lists of Indigenous filmmakers are in no way meant to be exclusive. Festivals and organizations that have helped support Native filmmakers in the United States and Canada include the imagineNative Film + Media Arts Festival in Toronto; the Native American Film + Video Festival at the National Museum of the American Indian; the Native Lab Fellowship at the Sundance Institute; Présence Autochtone/Montreal First Peoples Festival; the American Indian Film Festival in San Francisco; the National Film Board of Canada; Wapikoni Mobile; the Los Angeles Skins Fest; and the American Indian Film Institute. In addition, Indigenous film is produced in Sápmi (the Sami homelands of the Arctic Circle), the Pacific Islands, Australia, New Zealand, and Latin America.

5   Both of these categories – utopia and dystopia – are particularly Western projections of the future and are both, to some extent, invested in forms of violence. Frederic Jameson calls utopias the "by-products of Western modernity" and are marked by "a simple, a single-shot solution to all our ills." Because utopias are grounded in "the alleviation and elimination of the sources of exploitation and suffering," they advocate a totalitarian system that may be as oppressive as the chaos of the post-apocalyptic future (Jameson 2005: 11–12).

6   Exceptions include Afrofuturist texts and films, as well as work by Indigenous science fiction writers.

7   Although Mark Bould and Sherryl Vint claim that there can be no single definition of science fiction, George Mann defines it as "a form of fantastic literature that attempts to portray, in rational and realistic terms, future times and environments that are different from our own" (see Bould and Vint 2011; Mann 2001).

8   Almost all of Vizenor's work offers up narrative play about the future and its relationship to what we call the past and present. Of particular interest is his neologism "survivance," a term that marks the survival of Native people in the past under various settler regimes, as well as the aesthetic, representational, and creative Native people have engaged in to ensure a present and future (see Vizenor 2000, 2008).

9   In honor of imagineNATIVE's tenth anniversary, Haig-Brown and six other Indigenous filmmakers from Canada, the United States, New Zealand, and Australia were commissioned by the Embargo Collective to create films that pushed them outside of their comfort zones in terms of filmmaking style and subject. The filmmakers imposed restrictions on each other and worked collaboratively to create their films over the course of two years. The one universal guideline was that their films had to be in an Indigenous language.

10 Haig-Brown names her characters "Spirit Beings" in the film's credits.

References

Aleiss, Angela. 1995. "Native Americans: The surprising silents". *Cineaste*, 3: 34–36.

Aleiss, Angela. 2005. *Making the White Man's Indian: Native Americans and Hollywood Movies*. Westport: Praeger.

Bould, Mark and Sherryl Vint. 2011. *The Routledge Concise History of Science Fiction*. London: Routledge.

Dillon, Grace. 2012. *Walking the Clouds: An Anthology of Indigenous Science Fiction*. Tucson: University of Arizona Press.

Dowell, Kristen. 2013. *Sovereign Screens: Aboriginal Media on the Canadian West Coast*. Lincoln: University of Nebraska Press.

Hearne, Joanna. 2013. *Native Recognition: Indigenous Cinema and the Western*. Albany: State University of New York Press.

Jameson, Frederic. 2005. *Archaeologies of the Future: The Desire Called Utopia and Other Science Fictions*. New York: Verso.

Mann, George. 2001. *The Mammoth Encyclopedia of Science Fiction*. New York: Running Press.

Raheja, Michelle H. 2011. *Reservation Reelism: Redfacing, Visual Sovereignty and Representations of Native Americans in Film*. Lincoln: University of Nebraska Press.

Sobchak, Vivian. 2004. *Carnal Thoughts: Embodiment and Moving Image Culture*. Berkeley: University of California Press.

Tuck, Eve and Rubén A. Gaztambide-Fernández. 2013. "Curriculum, replacement, and settler futurity". *Journal of Curriculum Theorizing*, 29(1): 72–89.

Vizenor, Gerald. 2000. *Fugitive Poses: Native American Indian Scenes of Absence and Presence*. Lincoln: University of Nebraska Press.

Vizenor, Gerald. 2008. *Survivance: Narratives of Native Presence*. Lincoln: University of Nebraska Press.

Wolfe, Patrick. 2006. "Settler colonialism and the elimination of the native". *Journal of Genocide Research*, 8(4): 387–409.

V. Indigenous peoples in and beyond the state

28 Stories as law

A method to live by

Heidi Kiiwetinepinesiik Stark

Treaty with the Hoof Nation

In *The Gift is in the Making*, Anishinaabe theorist and storyteller Leanne Simpson retells the story of the Treaty with the Hoof Nation. As she reminds us, the Anishinaabe had taken their relationships with the Hoof Nation for granted. They had neglected their responsibilities and obligations to these relatives. They had failed to act respectfully. After some time, the Hoof Nation decided to leave the territory. As one season transitioned into another, the Anishinaabe began to realize they had not seen their Hoofed relatives for nearly a year. They began to worry and with the passing of some time, decided they should send out their fastest and strongest runners to find the cause for this absence. They soon learned that the Hoof Nation had left their territory because the Anishinaabe had been disrespectful. They felt the Anishinaabe no longer honored their relationship with the Hoof Nation. Determined to restore this relationship, the Anishinaabe petitioned the Hoof Nation to meet in council. Simpson notes:

> After some negotiation, the people learned that the Hoof Clan had left their territory because the Nishnaabeg were no longer honoring them. They had been wasting their meat and not treating their bodies with the proper reverence. The Hoof Clan had withdrawn from the territory and their relationship with the Nishnaabeg. They had stopped participating.
>
> (Simpson 2013: 11)

The Anishinaabe listened. They listened to these grievances. They listened to the stories and teaching that the Hoof Clan shared. They spent many long days listening. They acknowledged their errors and mistakes; they discussed remedies, and negotiated the best approaches to restoring their relationship. They each thought about what they could do to restore their relationship.

The Anishinaabe agreed to honor and respect the lives of their Hoofed relatives, taking their bodies only when needed and using the flesh wisely. They promised to protect their relatives and the homelands that sustained them. They committed to sharing the meat the Hoofed Ones gave to the Anishinaabe, ensuring nobody went without and would rely on other food sources when times were tough for their Hoofed relatives. And they promised they would demonstrate their respect and reverence, offering tobacco and holding ceremonies to honor the Hoof Nation. In exchange, the Hoof Nation agreed to return to the territory of the Anishinaabe, committing to give up their lives when the Anishinaabe were in need (Simpson 2013: 9–12).

This opening story of the Anishinaabe treaty with the Hoof Nation provides critical insights into Indigenous law and diplomacy. Like many Indigenous stories, we learn that Anishinaabe life was precarious. The people failed to honor their relationships with their Hoofed relatives. They were no longer upholding their obligations and responsibilities. Their failure to honor these relationships, to carry out their obligations in good faith, had a detrimental impact on their relatives, causing the Hoofed Ones to leave. This produced grave results for the Anishinaabe who struggled to survive the harsh winters that characterized life on the prairies and around the Great Lakes without the sustenance provided by their hoofed relatives. Recognizing the errors of their ways, the Anishinaabe sat in council with leaders of the Hoof Nation. They listened carefully. They acknowledged their wrongdoings and they worked diligently to rectify these wrongs and ensure they would not persist. Perhaps one of the oldest recorded stories of reconciliation, the Treaty with the Hoof Nation illustrates the importance of listening and hearing, admitting and acknowledging wrongdoings, and restoring respectful relationships to ensure the end of harm and the reinstatement of reciprocity.

Stories are law. Once relegated to the field of folklore or mythology, little attention was paid to these rich sources. Recently, critical approaches to the study of Indigenous law have elucidated this point, noting stories lay out the central principles for how people order their world (Borrows 2010; Napolean 2010; Stark 2013). Indigenous nations have largely been cast as lawless peoples in dominant narratives, while European law has generally been revered as a robust body of legal reasoning comprised by rational, civilized, enlightened thinkers (Williams 1990, 2005). This chapter seeks to demonstrate that understanding story as law not only unearths a rich body of thought containing alternate pathways for Indigenous–state relations, it also dispels the inviolability of law, demonstrating that law is, likewise, a set of stories. When we closely examine these legal narratives we can see how Western law took form and how these stories function to legitimate the settler state through the dispossession of Indigenous nations of their lands and rights. Subsequently, Western law was born out of a will for empire and thus continuously reproduces and is always conditioned by settler colonialism. The study of Indigenous law, in presenting alternative frameworks for the restoration of Indigenous–state relations, contains the potential to not only produce new methodological approaches but may also unearth alternate methods for living together differently.

Instruments of empire: law, colonialism and the rise of the settler nation-state

The rise of the settler state was made possible through European laws that enabled these nations to assert legitimacy in the international arena. As Lumbee scholar

Robert Williams Jr. has argued, "Law, which Europeans have long revered as their instrument of civilization, became the West's perfect instrument of empire in the heart of darkness that was America" (Williams 1990: 93). This law operated within a settler colonial logic that centered on, what scholar Patrick Wolfe has coined as, "the elimination of the native." Recognizing colonialism as a structure, not an event, Wolfe argues, "Settler colonialism destroys to replace" (Wolfe 2006). This was not achieved exclusively through the physical elimination of Indigenous peoples but through a figurative recasting of Indigenous nations that persists as an organizing principal of settler society. Indeed, we can see this in settler law. Indigenous peoples (and specifically their treaty relationships or lack thereof) continue to structure settler society, and thus cannot be eliminated, as the settler state's own legitimacy and authority is contingent on the recognition of Indigenous sovereign authority. This recognition is nonetheless entangled in settler discomfort and fears that reconfigure Indigenous sovereignty as a threat to the stability of the state. Thus, Western law became the instrument through which the settler state sought to perfect their claims to Indigenous lands (Ford 2010). As Chickasaw scholar Jodi Byrd notes, "settler sovereignty requires the indigenous as sovereign at the same time that it seeks to conquer it, appropriate it, and render it contained, if not nullified once and for all" (Byrd 2014).

Scholarship interrogating the relationship between empire, law and settler colonialism (Wilkins and Lomawaima 2001; Wilkins 1997; Deloria and Wilkins 1999; Bruyneel 2007; Rifkin 2009), that seeks to expose the colonial logics enabling courts to render devastating blows to Indigenous rights and tribal sovereignty on the one hand, while simultaneously recognizing Indigenous nations' unique relationships to the state on the other hand, has further elucidated what seminal Lakota scholar Vine Deloria famously noted in the US context, that settler law is a

> mythical creature because it is composed of badly written, vaguely phrased and ill-considered federal statutes, hundreds of self-serving Solicitor's Opinions and regulations; and state, federal, and Supreme Court decisions which bear little relationship to rational thought and contain a fictional view of American history that would shame some of our country's best novelists.
>
> (Deloria 1989: 203)

Methods and approaches to the study of Western legal thought that expose how the logics of settler colonialism continues to structure Indigenous–state relations through settler law dispel the sanctity of law, demonstrating that law is a set of stories. I contend we can understand settler law as the creation stories of the settler state, as it is through seminal decisions that these states narrate themselves into existence and maintain their fictive authority (Stark 2013). As scholar Bain Attwood notes:

> In the case of settler societies, colonizers have found it necessary to persuade others as well as themselves that the land they have appropriated as their basis

is rightfully theirs. This is done in large part through the formulation of legal stories of one kind or another, since the law plays a crucial role in creating boundaries between what is deemed to be legitimate and what is not.

(Attwood 2011: 190)

More troubling, perhaps, than the narratives crafted to legitimate state authority is the power settler law has in determining the bounds of their relationships with Indigenous nations. Indeed, much of the litigation that makes up federal Indian law in the United States and Aboriginal law in Canada is the result of competing interpretations of not just how Indigenous peoples came into relationships with these states (treaties), but more importantly, revolve around the contours of these relationships (treaty interpretation). Indigenous nations not only contest the interpretation of the historical documents produced through these relationships that codified their responsibilities and obligations to one another. Crucially, Indigenous nations dispute the very framing of these relationships through a language of rights, which has too often obscured and buried central questions around responsibilities and obligations. As Anishinaabe scholar John Borrows notes, "If everyone acts as if they only have rights and do not affirm their obligations, society is in danger of coming apart at its seams" (Borrows 2007: 211). Legal research thus must both ask how we understand the past as well as how we bring these interpretations into the present in shaping our contemporary relationships and responsibilities. This point is starkly present in the 2014 Canadian Supreme Court opinion in *Grassy Narrows First Nation* v. *Ontario*.[1]

Grassy Narrows First Nation v. *Ontario*: a Canadian approach to reconciliation

On July 11, 2014, two weeks after the Supreme Court of Canada handed down a landmark decision granting a declaration of Aboriginal title in *Tsilhqot'in Nation* v. *British Columbia*, it issued its opinion in *Grassy Narrows First Nation* v. *Ontario (Natural Resources)*.[2] While both cases considered provincial governmental authority to develop resources in First Nations' territories, they turned on different questions: application of provincial law over Aboriginal title lands in *Tsilhqot'in* versus Treaty lands in *Grassy Narrows*. In *Grassy Narrows,* the court found the province was unrestrained by federal authority in "taking up" Treaty 3 lands.[3] Despite being exceedingly prominent at trial, where the Grassy Narrows First Nation was victorious, Anishinaabe perspective is silent in this decision. The *Grassy Narrows* decision illuminates an approach to reconciliation, one that differs dramatically from the approach outlined in the story of the Treaty with the Hoof Nation.

The Grassy Narrows Ojibwe (Anishinaabe) have persistently protested industrial logging of their traditional lands, expressing concern about the environmental impacts and increased mercury poisoning that has wreaked havoc on their community, lands and relationships with creation since the 1960s when a Dryden Ontario paper mill dumped mercury in the English-Wabigoon River.[4] In addition to maintaining the longest running blockade to industrial activities, the Grassy Narrows First Nation took legal action in 2005, seeking resolution of its conflict with Canada, which sanctioned these logging activities. A decade later, the highest court in Canada took a narrow approach to this relationship. While recognizing Crown obligations persist whether First Nations are contending with the federal or provincial level of government, the court failed to address Ojibwe concerns about the scope and application of crown obligations, as Grassy Narrows First Nation was seeking federal oversight of provincial activities that have often worked against the interests of Indigenous nations. The court was able to achieve this reconfiguration of Ojibwe concerns by reframing and narrowing the question in front of the court until the possible answers were absent any potential for meaningful change. Instead of considering whether Ojibwe signatories to Treaty 3 understood the Crown would act honorably in their relationship and be held accountable for breaches, the court instead found "nothing in the text of the history of the negotiation of Treaty 3 suggests that a two-step process requiring federal supervision or approval was intended."[5] Through this narrow framing of the question, the court was able to avoid consideration of what it meant to act honorably, what the provincial and federal obligations and responsibilities are to the Grassy Narrows Ojibwe.

The court cautioned nonetheless that provincial power was not unbridled. It noted:

> Ontario's power to take up lands under Treaty 3 is not unconditional. When a government—be it the federal or provincial government—exercises Crown power, the exercise of that power is burdened by Crown obligations toward the Aboriginal peoples in question. Here, Ontario must exercise its powers in conformity with the honour of the Crown, and the exercise of these powers is subject to the fiduciary duties that lie in the Crown in dealing with Aboriginal interests.

Specifically, the court argued, "For Treaty 3 land to be taken up, the harvesting rights of the Ojibway over the land must be respected." While this seems promising, a closer reading of this case raises concern regarding the parameters of this respect. The court contended, "If the taking up leaves the Ojibway with no meaningful right to hunt, fish, or trap in relation to the territories over which they traditionally hunted, fished, and trapped, a potential action for treaty infringement will arise."[6] Consequently, this produces trepidation about the degree to which the province can impair treaty rights, so long as they are not completely absent (read: eliminated). Is it only after all their relatives, hoofed and otherwise, leave their territory that Ojibwe have cause for action? How are the Ojibwe to honor their treaty with the Hoof Nation if state action impairs them from being able to do so? While the courts will not expressly eliminate the "rights" that flow from Indigenous treaties (at least without remedy) to keep the settler state legitimacy intact (which is dependent on these agreements), they are too often willing to take a narrow interpretation of these relationships so they are void of the original spirit and intent that animated them.

With the *Grassy Narrows* decision, we can see how settler colonial logics close off any potential for meaningful reconciliation. "While courts can offer a forum to find remedies when a treaty has been breached," Anishinaabe scholar Aimie Craft notes, "they are not a holistic truth-finding mechanism. They are entrusted with resolving discrete legal questions rather than uncovering the complete understanding of treaties. Given that treaties are living, breathing documents built on the foundations of indigenous laws, courts may not be the ultimate forum for treaty interpretation" (Craft 2014: 4). Indeed, Borrows reminds us: "One of the main functions of legal systems is to authoritatively provide enforceable remedies for breaches (anticipated or otherwise) of the rights and obligations they confer." He cautions:

> Aboriginal peoples are increasingly appealing to the law's principles to adjudicate the bounds of propriety in their interactions with the Crown. While justiciability in this sense can be beneficial for Aboriginal peoples, remedial access comes with a cost. The more Aboriginal peoples use the law, the more tightly they are drawn into a relationship with the Crown.
>
> (Borrows 2007: 214)

A relationship that continues to reproduce the very colonial logics that Indigenous nations approach the court to find relief from. But what if we considered a different approach for reconciling grievances? What if we took Indigenous law seriously and considered the alternative methods for living together presented by this body of law?

An Anishinaabe framework for grievances

The Anishinaabe have long been seeking remedial approaches for our all too human faults. It is in these messy moments of life, often contained in stories, that we can unearth the approaches and principles that enabled the development or restoration of proper relationships with others. As the opening story illustrates, a core principle of proper relationships is recognition of these relationships' ongoing nature. As many stories and diplomatic speeches of Anishinaabe leaders will attest, Anishinaabe relationships were and remain contingent on respect, recognition of responsibilities to one another, and a continuous renewal of these relationships through the enactment of one's responsibilities in a respectful manner (Stark 2010).

Indigenous law not only persists and adapts but also underpins and gives shape and meaning to Indigenous engagement with other nations, namely the settler states they find themselves contained within today. The advent of newcomers to Indigenous territories necessitated the development of new relationships, often carried out through treaties. With the rise of the settler state, made possible by destructive colonial policies and practices and failure to implement treaties in accord with their original spirit and intent, Indigenous peoples have found their pre-existing relationships and obligations to creation to be significantly impaired. If we analyze the story of the Treaty with the Hoof Nation in order to draw out principles for reconciling grievances between nations we find a meaningful restoration of an impaired relationship requires the offending party to: 1) listen and hear the grieved; 2) recognize (take account for) and rectify the wrongdoing; and 3) develop mechanisms to ensure harms won't persist. Indigenous nations, such as the Grassy Narrows Ojibwe, continue to look for approaches to hold the settler state accountable for their responsibilities and obligations, not just to the Indigenous parties to these treaty relationships, but to all of creation as she prefigures and conditions Indigenous and settler nations alike.

An analysis of stories as law may not just posit alternative methodological approaches for the study of law but aspires to also illuminate alternative pathways for restoring relationships. The Anishinaabe, like other Indigenous nations, do not have the luxury of walking away from their relationships with the settler state (unlike our Hoofed relatives). Our pre-existing obligations to creation, which also conditioned Anishinaabe relationships with the settler state, necessitate that we do our part to honor our treaties, both with creation and with the settler state. We must speak for our relatives; we must uphold our commitments to the land, water, animals, flora and fauna. We have an obligation to protect creation. We are accountable for the damages being wreaked upon the land and water. Our survival necessitates we find ways to hold the settler state to the original spirit and intent of our treaties, which were and remain conditioned by our legal obligations to creation. Methods are not just a tool for the study of the past and present. They illuminate pathways forward. When understood through Indigenous stories, methods are also ontological; they are about a way of being, a method for living.

Notes

1 *Grassy Narrows First Nation* v. *Ontario (Natural Resources)*, 2014 S.C.C. 48.
2 *Tsilhqot'in Nation* v. *British Columbia*, 2014 S.C.C. 44; *Grassy Narrows First Nation* v. *Ontario (Natural Resources)*, 2014 S.C.C. 48.
3 The court was tasked with interpreting the "taking up" clause of Treaty 3. The written text of the treaty states: "Her Majesty further agrees with Her said Indians that they, the said Indians, shall have right to pursue their avocations of hunting and fishing throughout the tract surrendered as hereinbefore described, subject to such regulations as may from time to time be made by Her Government of Her Dominion of Canada, and saving and excepting such tracts as may, from time to time, be required or taken up for settlement, mining, lumbering or other purposes by Her said Government of the Dominion of Canada, or by any of the subjects thereof duly authorized therefor by the said Government."
4 For a detailed study of blockade efforts by the Grassy Narrows Ojibwe, see Willow (2012).
5 *Grassy Narrows First Nation* v. *Ontario (Natural Resources)*, 2014 S.C.C. 48.
6 Ibid.

References

Attwood, Bain. 2011. "The Batman legend: Remembering and forgetting the history of possession and dispossession". In Hester Lessard, Rebecca Johnson, and Jeremy Webber, eds. *Storied Communities: Narratives of Contact and Arrival in Constituting Political Community*. Vancouver: UBC Press, pp. 189–210.

Borrows, John. 2007. "Let obligations be done". In Heather Raven Hamar Foster and Jeremy Webber, eds. *Let Right Be Done: Aboriginal Title, the Calder Case, and the Future of Indigenous Rights*. Vancouver: UBC Press, pp. 201–215.

Borrows, John. 2010. *Canada's Indigenous Constitution*. Toronto: University of Toronto Press.

Bruyneel, Kevin. 2007. *The Third Space of Sovereignty: The Postcolonial Politics of U.S.-Indigenous Relations*. Minneapolis: University of Minnesota Press.

Byrd, Jodi. 2014. "Follow the typical signs: Settler sovereignty and its discontents". *Settler Colonial Studies*, 4(2): 151–154.

Byrd, Jodi A. 2011. *The Transit of Empire: Indigenous Critiques of Colonialism*. Minneapolis: University of Minnesota Press.

Craft, Aimee. 2014. "Living treaties, breathing research". *Canadian Journal of Women and Law*, 26(1): 1–22.

Deloria, Vine, Jr. 1989. "Laws founded in justice and humanity: Reflections on the content and character of federal Indian law". *Arizona Law Review*, 31(2): 202–223.

Deloria, Vine, Jr., and David E. Wilkins. 1999. *Tribes, Treaties, and Constitutional Tribulations*. 1st edn. Austin: University of Texas Press.

Ford, Lisa. 2010. *Settler Sovereignty: Jurisdiction and Indigenous Peoples in America and Australia 1788–1836*. Cambridge, MA: Havard University Press.

Napolean, Val. 2010. "Living together: Gitksan legal reasoning as a foundation for consent". In Jeremy Webber and Colin M. Macleod, eds. *Between Consenting Peoples: Political Community and the Meaning of Consent*. Vancouver: University of British Columbia Press, pp. 45–76.

Rifkin, Mark. 2009. *Manifesting America: The Imperial Construction of U.S. National Space*. Oxford and New York: Oxford University Press.

Simpson, Leanne. 2013. *The Gift Is in the Making: Anishinaabeg Stories*. Winnipeg: Highwater Press.

Stark, Heidi Kiiwetinepinesiik. 2010. "Respect, responsibility, and renewal: The foundations of Anishinaabe treaty making with the United States and Canada". *American Indian Culture and Research Journal*, 34(2): 145–164.

Stark, Heidi Kiiwetinepinesiik. 2013. "Transforming the trickster: Federal Indian law encounters Anishinaabe diplomacy". In Jill Doerfler, Niigaanwewidam James Sinclair, and Heidi Kiiwetinepinesiik Stark, eds. *Centering Anishinaabeg Studies: Understanding the World through Stories*. East Lansing: Michigan State University Press, pp. 259–278.

Wilkins, David E. 1997. *American Indian Sovereignty and the U.S. Supreme Court: The Masking of Justice*. Austin: University of Texas Press.

Wilkins, David E. and K. Tsianina Lomawaima. 2001. *Uneven Ground: American Indian Sovereignty and Federal Law*. Norman: University of Oklahoma Press.

Williams, Robert A. 2005. *Like a Loaded Weapon: The Rehnquist Court, Indian Rights, and the Legal History of Racism in America*. Minneapolis: University of Minnesota Press.

Williams, Robert A., Jr. 1990. *The American Indian in Western Legal Thought: The Discourses of Conquest*. New York: Oxford University Press.

Willow, Anna J. 2012. *Strong Hearts, Native Lands : The Cultural and Political Landscape of Anishinaabe Anti-Clearcutting Activism*. Albany: State University of New York Press.

Wolfe, Patrick. 2006. "Settler colonialism and the elimination of the native". *Journal of Genocide Research*, 8(4): 387–409.

29 Métis in the borderlands of the northern Plains in the nineteenth century

Brenda Macdougall and Nicole St-Onge

John Francis (Johnny) Grant, born at Fort Edmonton in 1833 on the banks of the North Saskatchewan River, lived much of his life across the 49th parallel. In 1891, traveling along old prairie trails that had once been open to Plains peoples, Johnny observed that now "many places [along] the old road was [*sic*] fenced" (Ens 2008: 315). He further noted that in Saskatchewan a portion of the old trail to Edmonton was now a private road on a settlers' homestead causing them to travel eight miles out of their way to access the trail again (Ens 2008: 316). This division of homeland, places the Métis had crossed through as they hunted buffalo, must have been particularly troubling to Grant whose life was embedded in the history of a large, extended family that lived throughout the northern Plains – a region bounded today by three western Canadian provinces (Manitoba, Saskatchewan, and Alberta) and three states in the western United States (North Dakota, Montana, and Idaho).

The son of a Métis woman, Marie Anne Breland, and Hudson's Bay Company (HBC) servant, Richard Grant, Johnny's maternal family originated in the amiskwâciwaskahikan (Beaver Hills House) between the north branch of the Saskatchewan and the Battle River (Goyette and Roemmich 2004: 20). Marie Anne was born in amiskwâciwaskahikan around 1800 to voyageur Pierre Breland and Louise Umphreville, daughter of Edward Umfreville, a North West Company trader, and an unnamed Gros Ventre or Cree woman.[1] By the age of 16, Grant was living with his father at Fort Hall, an HBC post in the Idaho Territory. Deciding against being a fur trader, Johnny instead built a financial empire trading cattle along the Oregon Trail while maintaining a ranch in Montana's Deer Lodge Valley. He operated here until the late 1860s when the discovery of gold fostered an increasingly racist atmosphere as prospectors and settlers moved into the region. Furthermore, according to Grant, their presence led to the establishment of Montana as an American territory which brought with it government, laws, and bureaucracy; Grant said:

> After a time the Territory was established, then counties, and then officers were elected. Then came Assessors and the Collectors annoying me with their lists and tax collections and laws for this, that and the other, and I concluded to leave for Manitoba.
>
> (Ens 2008: xiii)

In making this decision, Grant wrote to his maternal relatives at Red River, asking whether it would be appropriate to relocate his family north. Johnny's uncle, the Honourable James McKay, husband of Johnny's aunt, Margaret Rowand, invited this branch of the family – which by now included Grant's eighth wife, Clothilde Bruneau, and 14 of his children, along with 105 additional Métis families for whom he was responsible – to join them (Ens 2008). By the late 1880s Johnny and his family moved westward to Alberta where he eventually died in 1907 not far from where he was born – he had come full circle (Ens 2008: xxxvi).

Embedded in Grant's life is a theme that is repeated in other Métis families – the ability of this extended and highly mobile family to maintain relationships despite the passage of time and extreme distance. Grant had likely not seen his maternal family since he left Fort Edmonton, and it was unlikely he had ever met McKay, yet there was no social distance; somehow this family maintained a shared knowledge of one another, and felt confident enough to call upon their common bond in times of need. Furthermore, what is relevant is how this style of life represented the borderland. Across national, territorial, and eventually state and provincial boundaries, this family, and others like it, thrived economically and socially until the beginning of the twentieth century because of the liminality and ambiguity of that space. For those who lived in the northern Plains, the political, economic, and social space created because of, as well as in spite of, the once porous 49th parallel changed with the imposition of new national identities by the end of the century. It was then that this mobile society was trapped by a foreign intellectualization of space and place.

Borders demarcating separations necessarily exist. Establishing boundaries – physical, social, economic, cultural, racial, sexual, intellectual, religious, or biological – is how human societies create safe zones separating the *us* from *them*. Kyle Conway and Timothy Pasch noted that borders do not just interrupt spaces, they interrupt time: "to cross the border is to leave one temporal frame of reference and national timeline, replete with its own history and sense of order, and arrive in another [entering] into a new relationship with the past, and consequently with the present and the future" (Conway and Pasch 2013: 3). Canada and the United States have very different interpretations of history along their shared border, but conversely its very existence sutures their historical narratives together because they necessarily overlap and inform one another (Conway and Pasch 2013: 3). The creation of the 49th parallel destabilized the control Aboriginal people had over their territories, including the economic processes that necessitated following animals on annual migratory routes, and socio-cultural understandings of their histories, families, and inter-tribal relations. There are scholarly accounts analyzing how First Nations/American Indian communities along the international border were divided and segmented as Canada and the United States asserted economic and political dominance (Bellfy 2013; McCrady 2006; Rensink 2011; Samek 2011; Simpson 2014). Similarly, there are studies demonstrating how Indigenous peoples transgressed that border by asserting themselves as the original peoples as they were confined by colonial policies. Regardless, the effect of the border on Aboriginal societies was that, like their lands, they were divided, segmented, and incorporated into the intellectualization of space and place of nation-states. What these societies became, how the people were labeled or categorized depended on where they stood when the border was surveyed. The Métis experience was no different. The first study of Métis along the border was Joseph Kinsey Howard's transnational interpretation of Métis history, describing the 49th parallel as an artificial boundary that obstructed their ability to move through their homeland (Howard 1952: 49). More recently, Nicholas Vrooman characterized the Métis as a people whose history is best understood in a continental context, while Michel Hogue argued that the Métis are a people of the northern Plains, not simply a western Canadian phenomena (Vrooman 2012; Hogue 2009: 3).

The imprint of the Plains Métis within this transnational context is revealed through 15 petitions sent to the Canadian and/or American government between 1847 and 1883, asserting a clear political ideology and determination to be recognized as rights-based communities.[2] Within the text of these petitions Métis signatories presented themselves as possessing inherent rights to land and economy as the original people, "old settlers," natives, or half-breeds of the northern Plains. Several petitions requested reserves, noting that the signatories were willing, in time, to assume private ownership of those reserve lands and pay the necessary taxes. Importantly, these petitions expressed a sense of togetherness and shared enterprise among the signatories. The 31 signatories of the Qu'Appelle Lakes petition dated September 11, 1874 referred to their "*brethren* [emphasis added] scattered across the prairies" while the 30 signatories of the 1874 Fort Walsh petition stated that they were speaking for their *brothers* spread out across the four districts of Assiniboia, not just themselves.[3]

These petitions spoke to the changing circumstances of the late nineteenth century on the Plains and a determination by the Métis to locate a path forward under often challenging circumstances. They pointed to the hard times the Plains Métis were experiencing because of the collapse of the buffalo herds. The 1878 Cypress Hills petition, for instance, noted that government policy prevented Métis from hunting buffalo as early as November, yet permitted Indians to hunt until February. They noted that this policy was not simply unfair, it had created an atmosphere of shame among men who were unable to provide for their families.[4] Similarly, the 1874 Qu'Appelle Lakes petition requested that Métis hunting and fishing rights be respected and protected in a manner consistent with their way of life.[5] In return for their rights being protected within a nation-state, the Métis consistently stated that they were willing to function inside its (Canadian or American) legal systems in return for protections of their rights. Without detracting from the rights of Indians, the Métis repeatedly stated that they simply wished that their rights were protected as well. The Métis, like other Indigenous nations, were dealing with the influx of settlers and nation-state policies that prevented them from freely crossing the border. Within this new environment, it is understandable that they were concerned about what the future held. But they are not without hope; the petitions represent a plan for dealing with the impending changes.

Historian Tony Ballantyne argued that although there have been calls for the creations of transnational histories, "historians need to produce critical work that thinks under as well as across the nation" to consider how histories were made and remade by networks, connections, and webs of exchange (Ballantyne 2012: 246). Analysis of nineteenth-century Métis involvement in petition writing speaks to this approach. To see the Métis as historical actors, we need to erase the border and understand the contexts of treaty making, economic colonialism, and the military occupation of the northern Plains by emergent nation-states. But it also requires us to look at how the system of family networks, combined with their hyper-mobile economy, was a strength (and not a weakness) in the history of this society (Ballantyne 2012: 288, 295). Johnny Grant's story certainly demonstrated that mobility did not undermine his family's social construction or cohesion, and other Métis families had similar experiences along the borderland.

Similarly, at Turtle Mountain (North Dakota), St. Vital (Manitoba), Pembina (North Dakota), and in the Judith Basin (Montana), the Wilkie family forged a community built on alliances with the Azures clan. Jean Baptiste Wilkie, son of Alexander Wilkie, a Scottish born NWC voyageur, and Josephte Mijakammikijikok, an Ojibwe/Chippewa woman, was a buffalo hunter who became one of the leading political figures at Pembina by 1849. Married to Amable Elise Azure, daughter of Pierre Azure, another buffalo hunter, and Marguerite Assiniboine, Jean Baptiste appears in a number of documents that, when read together, point to a life that straddled the 49th parallel. The Wilkies appear in seven Red River censuses between 1830 and 1843, by which time the family, comprised of Jean Baptiste and Amable and their seven children, had ten acres under cultivation in the parish of St. Vital, owned six carts, four horses, and two oxen.[6] Between 1843 and 1847, the Wilkies left St. Vital and moved south to the Pembina district. According to geographer W.F. Rannie, Red River was marked by extremes in temperature and annual flooding, The winter of 1847–1848 was the most severe ever recorded, with many horses and cattle starved to death (Rannie 2010). Pembina just south of St. Vital had slightly better climatic conditions and was a place from where buffalo hunting expeditions had been launched since the early nineteenth century.

By the middle of the summer of 1848, Jean Baptiste Wilkie, along with other Métis buffalo hunters, fought the Dakota at O'Brien's Coulee (near Olga, ND). Wilkie was one of the leaders at this battle, along with the Chippewa chiefs Old Red Bear and Little Shell II. The Métis at Pembina generally, and the Wilkies specifically, were described as "Chippewa" Métis. Furthermore, Wilkie and the other Métis at Pembina were closely related to and aligned with both the Turtle Mountain Band of Chippewa and the Little Shell Band.[7] While Jean Baptiste's mother was Chippewa, Amable Azure Wilkie was descended from the Assiniboine, and other family members were connected to the Cree and Sioux. Yet, perhaps the most significant identity at this time was economic – they were buffalo hunters/ traders/provisioners, or they were not.

In 1849, Jean Baptiste and four of his sons, as "the principal hunters, who … returned in advance of the main body" signed the Pembina Petition.[8] Sent to Governor Alexander Ramsey of the Minnesota Territory, the 1849 petition put forward a number of requests, including that the Americans stop the HBC from crossing the border to arrest Métis free traders. By this time, there was across the Red River Valley an active free trading movement where Métis hunters refused to sell their goods to the HBC in favour of the American Fur Company or others who offered better prices. From the HBC's perspective, these Métis free traders were trading in violation of the Company's economic monopoly. Wilkie and his hunting brigade were asking the American government to protect them in the borderlands. A year later, the entire Wilkie family appeared in the 1850 Minnesota Territorial census as hunters alongside their extended family.[9] Within the context of the United States in this era, there was no option to being Métis – the choice was to be Indian and sign treaties, or be white, which would confer citizenship. And so it was within this narrowly prescribed system of categories that some of the Wilkie children entered treaty, appearing on the annuity rolls for the Turtle Mountain and Pembina Chippewa bands. In 1867–1868 Jean Baptiste, Jr. appeared on the annuity list of the Pembina, and by 1893 several more children and grandchildren appeared on the Turtle Mountain Indian census.[10]

By looking at the lives of Plains Métis families, it seems clear that one of the most significant borderlands created by the 49th parallel was the legal and racial construction of the space between the categories of Indian and Métis. For a time, fur companies and foreign nation-states valued the Plains Métis' physical and intellectual mobility, but, by the end of the century, that outlook was re-evaluated. Because commercial hunters moved regularly and purposefully to both hunt and trade, their way of life was centered on creating and maintaining extensive familial relationships spread across multiple geographic spaces. However, nation-states wanted to define and categorize people by discrete communities based on racial myths and to discourage "roaming" in favor of settlement.

Part of the effort, then, is to understand mobility within a culturally grounded set of principles, where space was as central as place to understanding who people were. Pembina and Red River parishes were places where people recorded their lives in censuses, petitions, and other official record-keeping activities. In this reckoning, Red River and Pembina were central nodes where some Métis rooted themselves by planting crops, erecting permanent dwellings and churches, and participating in western-styled governmental processes. Focus on these places obscures that they were simply one place within a series of nodes or periodic habitation sites where Plains Métis lived their lives. For a people who moved frequently in pursuit of buffalo and then to trade the products of their hunts, it is the lines between the nodes that we need to focus on to understand how mobility impacted the construction and function of Métis nationalism. Place is not a point on a map, but a specific set of constellations that are themselves the product of social relations that cut across particular locations in a multiplicity of ways. The Métis must be regarded as a set of relational constellations – kinscapes – where families such as the Wilkies or Grants connected to others, building extensive economic networks based on inter-generational extended family networks across the northern Plains (Lakomäki 2014).

Recent Canadian provincial court decisions in Saskatchewan (*R* v. *Belhuemeur*, 2007), Manitoba (*R* v. *Goodon*, 2009), and Alberta (*R* v. *Hirsekorn*, 2010), and an American adjudication by the federal Department of the Interior on the nature of tribes in Montana (*In Re Federal Acknowledgement of the Little Shell Tribe of Chippewa Indians of Montana*, 2013) made inquiries into how the Métis existed, functioned, and thrived along the border and in the borderlands between nation-states particularly relevant. The Canadian Prairie provinces have attempted to place impermeable boundaries around the scope of Métis Aboriginal rights by solidifying what features constituted historical communities – settlements and not mobile kinscapes. The focus on settlements, with fixed and bounded physical structures of parishes, villages, towns, posts, is the imposition of an intellectual border as much as it is geographic one. Furthermore, the courts relied on an antiquated agro-centric, settlement-oriented model as the defining feature of an historic community (Ray 2012: 106–108). The history of Johnny Grant and his extended family established the broadest form of physical movement and fluidity of place. Although not a buffalo hunter, he lived the life of a mobile trader of commodities, and each move reflected an attempt to adapt to the changing circumstances in which he lived as his opportunities constricted within the borderlands.

The US Interior Board of Indian Appeals did much the same to the Little Shell tribe, an Indigenous people who define themselves as "descendants of mixed-blood bands of primarily French-Chippewa buffalo hunters." The Wilkie family whose descendants today are in the Little Shell and Turtle Mountain tribes as well as in the Métis Nation demonstrated the mobility and fluidity of cultural and social processes. However, whether they were on the American or Canadian side determined whether they were Indian and Métis depending on the nation-state's administrative categories. Within the American system of Indian recognition, the Little Shell people, despite this history, cannot claim a Métis history because there were/are no Métis from the United States – they are aliens who crossed the border from Canada in the latter decades of the nineteenth centuries. To claim to be Métis is to nullify any claim to Indigeneity within the American context, and so the Little Shell people, by necessity, must assert a tribal, an Indian, identity, history, existence. This is not just an issue of linguistic hair-splitting. The implications of this is that the American colonization of Métis history is completed at the same time that Canada's is validated. The imposition of Canadian and American nationalities and tribal identities on Indigenous peoples is the most insidious form of colonization. In this case, the borderland is a liminal space where this people existed based on the acceptance of the nation-states, not actual historical events that happened in that region. Within this framework, it is understandable that the Appeal Board ruled there was no evidence the Little Shell people were/are a distinct community because of their mixed-blood heritage. The "mixed" nature of the people was, in short, regarded as evidence of their borderlessness. Families like the Wilkies, then, must be Indian according to this logic because there is no alternative state of Indigenity in a contemporary American context for it has been eradicated from American consciousness. Yet within Canadian historiography, the Wilkies were Métis, not Indians and not white.

Duane Champagne, a member of the Turtle Mountain Band of Chippewa, suggested that the Canadian Métis are not a society (or even Indigenous), but rather simply representative of a new ethnicity composed of mixed-blood individuals with varying degrees of Aboriginal ancestry. This misconception promotes the notion that the Métis are both Indigenous to Canada and not the United States (where mixed-bloods are perceived to undermine tribal authenticity) and simply a lesser, inauthentic form of being Indian (Champagne 2013). Any claim to a collective identity as Métis in the United States today, Champagne argued, was a "separatist" posture claimed by mixed-bloods that invalidates what it meant to be Indian and not a true representation of their historical reality (Champagne 2013). Within this interpretation, there is no possibility that there were ever Métis in the United States, let alone in his own tribe, contrary to all historical evidence. That members of the Wilkie clan became enrolled members of the tribe was not necessarily an positive affirmation of a Chippewa identity, but rather an historically logical choice as the world Plains people created shrank around them, confining them to identities not of their making.

Champagne's dismissal of the Métis as a distinct people reinforces the profound lack of understanding of the history of the origins and connectivity between Métis in Canada and the United States and reinforces Canadian and American colonial historiographies and political logics. Chris Andersen pointed to this type of rationalization of space and people by Indigenous people themselves as *seductive integration*, a process that confers "status, rights, and privileges in a context whereby 'minorities *want* [emphasis in original] to integrate into the dominant norm'" because this will improve their chances politically, economically, and socially (Andersen 2014: 23). The intellectual legacy of seductive integration discounts the boundaries that the Métis created to set themselves apart as a distinct people within the economic geo-political world of the Great Plains on either side of the 49th parallel. It validates Canadian and American ideologies that categorize and define who is and who is not authentically Aboriginal. Studying the Métis through the lens of empires and nation-states can reveal how they defined their own geo-political world, while examining their sense of community, tribalism, or nationhood contributes to a new understanding of the Métis nation. It is the study of borders, frontiers, and hinterlands that reflects how Métis society evolved and how this people saw themselves as they responded to larger colonial pressures. Documenting the history of this Métis society – these so-called separatists – is something that has been undertaken by a number of scholars in both countries over the years, but thus far little has been done to connect the history of these Métis societies to a transborder narrative of the northern Plains within a framework of borderlands theory and methodology. The records exist to do this work, we just need to read them differently.

Notes

1　"Edward Umfreville," Dictionary of Canadian Biography Online. www.biographi.ca/en/bio/umfreville_edward_4E.html, accessed August 18, 2014.
2　The Métis Family and Community Research lab at the University of Ottawa began collecting the petitions a couple of years ago and in 2014–2015 research assistant

Michael Walton transcribed and documented each petition, creating the "Petitions Database."

3 "Métis Petition to Join Treaty Four"; "Petition from Augustin Brabant and Others, 11 September 1874," 291–292. *Epitome of Parliamentary Documents in Connection with the North West Rebellion, 1885* (Canada, Dept of the Secretary of State: McLean, Roger, & Co.), 291–292.

4 "Petition from Half-Breeds Living in the Vicinity of Cypress Hills Received Through the North-West Council, not dated, Covering Letter from the Lieutenant Governor of the North-West Territories dated 30 Sept 1878," *Canada Sessional Papers*, no. 45, 1886: 10–12.

5 "Petition from Augustin Brabant and Others, Dates Lake Qu'Appelle, 11 September 1874," *Epitome of Parliamentary Documents in Connection with the North West Rebellion, 1885* (Canada, Dept of the Secretary of State: McLean, Roger, & Co.), 291–292.

6 Hudson's Bay Company Archives, E.5/1, Red River Settlement Census Returns, 1843, p. 24.

7 Vrooman's *"The Whole Country was ... 'One Robe'"* (2012) was based on the report written on behalf of the Little Shell Tribe as they pursued federal recognition of their Indian status within Montana.

8 "Memorial from the Half-Breeds of Pembina," *Journal of the Council During the First Session of the Legislative Assembly of the Territory of Minnesota* (St. Paul: McLean & Owens, Territorial Printers, 1850), 197–199.

9 Minnesota Territorial Census, Pembina County, August–September 1850.

10 US Office of Indian Affairs, M360, Chippewa Annuity Rolls, 1841–1907, "Pembina Band, 1867–1876, vol. 1" and "Pembina Band, 1877–1897, vol. 5." The reality is that they appear on almost every tribal census and annuity list in the latter half of the nineteenth century.

References

Andersen, Chris. 2014. *Métis: Race, Recognition, and the Struggle for Indigenous Peoplehood.* Vancouver: University of British Columbia Press.

Ballantyne, Tony. 2012. *Webs of Empire: Locating New Zealand's Colonial Past.* Wellington: Bridget Williams Books.

Bellfy, Phil. 2013. "The Anishnaabeg of Bawating: Indigenous people look at the Canada-U.S. border". In Kyle Conway and Timothy Pasch, eds. *Beyond the Border: Tensions Across the Forty-Ninth Parallel in the Great Plains and Prairies*. Montreal: McGill Queen's University Press, pp. 199–222.

Champagne, Duane. 2013. "The challenge of mixed-blood nations". *Indian Country*, 25 April. Accessed 1 May 2013, http://indiancountrytodaymedianetwork.com/2013/04/25/challenge-mixed-blood-nations-148961.

Conway, Kyle and Timothy Pasch. 2013. *Beyond the Border: Tensions Across the Forty-Ninth Parallel in the Great Plains and Prairies*. Montreal: McGill Queen's University Press.

Ens, Gerhard J., ed. 2008. *A Son of the Fur Trade: The Memoirs of Johnny Grant.* Edmonton: University of Alberta Press.

Goyette, Linda and Carolina Jakeway Roemmich. 2004. *Edmonton in Our Own Words.* Edmonton: University of Alberta Press.

Hogue, Michel. 2009. "Between Race and Nation: The Plains Métis and the Canada-United States Border". University of Wisconsin, dissertation.

Howard, Joseph Kinsey. 1952. *Strange Empire: A Narrative of the Northwest*. New York: William Morrow & Co.

Lakomäki, Sami. 2014. *Gathering Together: The Shawnee People Through Diaspora and Nationhood, 1600–1870*. New Haven: Yale University Press.

McCrady, David G. 2006. *Living with Strangers: The Nineteenth-Century Sioux and the Canadian-American Borderlands*. Lincoln: University of Nebraska Press.

Rannie, W.F. 2010. "'One damned thing after another': The environmental challenges of the Red River Settlement". In *Papers of the Rupert's Land Colloquium 2010*, Centre for Rupert's Land Studies. Winnipeg: University of Winnipeg, pp. 353–374.

Ray, Arthur J. 2012. *Telling it to the Judge: Taking Native History to Court*. Montreal: McGill-Queen's University Press.

Rensink, Brenden W. 2011. "Cree contraband or contraband Crees? Early Montanan experiences with transnational natives and the formation of lasting prejudice, 1880–1885". In Elaine Carey and Andrae M. Marak, eds. *Smugglers, Brothels, and Twine: Historical Perspectives on Contraband and Vice in North America's Borderlands*. Tucson: The University of Arizona Press, pp. 24–43.

Samek, Hana. 2011. *The Blackfoot Confederacy, 1880–1920: A Comparative Study of Canadian and US Indian Policy*. Santa Fe: University of New Mexico Press.

Simpson, Audra. 2014. *Mohawk Interruptus: Political Life Across the Borders of Settler States*. Durham, NC: Duke University Press.

Vrooman, Nicholas C.P. 2012. *"The Whole Country was ... 'One Robe'": The Little Shell Tribe's America*. Helena: Drumlummon Institute.

30 Plotting colonization and recentering Indigenous actors

Approaches to and sources for studying the history of Indigenous education

Margaret D. Jacobs

Indigenous peoples do not fit neatly into national narratives about education. Histories of education in the United States tend toward progressive plots. Plantation masters notoriously denied their slaves literacy and an education. With emancipation, freed people clamored for education, only to be increasingly isolated in substandard segregated schools. Latino/as, too, have been denied educational opportunities and subjected to segregation. Jews experienced educational discrimination, and women had to fight for the right to higher education. Denial of education erupted as a major issue during the civil rights movement of the late twentieth century. For Indigenous people in the United States and Canada, however, the extension of education by the government – primarily through boarding or residential schools – functioned less as a tool of liberation and more as a weapon of colonization. Yet Indigenous people seized upon education as their own weapon of resistance and resilience.

The sources and methodologies that researchers have used to uncover the unique nature of education in Indigenous histories have influenced their interpretations. Scholars who have used government archives and the papers of non-Indigenous reform organizations and individuals, have tended to dwell on the oppressive nature of schooling for Indigenous children. Other scholars who have drawn more upon family correspondence, first-hand narratives, and oral accounts often capture greater ambivalence about the role that governmental and Christian education played in Indigenous communities. Some scholars have taken a panoramic approach by comparing Indigenous education in disparate colonial contexts, while others have produced focused studies of particular schools or the role of education in the lives of one community.

Though studies of boarding and residential schools have garnered the greatest attention, other researchers have looked to earlier and later periods to gain greater understanding of the contested space of education in Indigenous histories. Scholars working in the colonial North American period are often limited to sources produced by non-Indigenous people. In contrast scholars working in the twentieth century have used Indigenous archival and oral sources to show that Indigenous self-determination movements made control of education a key demand.

Boarding and residential school education

Much of the literature on Indigenous education in North America has focused on federal boarding schools in the United States or Indian residential schools in Canada that the government contracted with religious groups to operate. Many scholars have utilized traditional archival sources to gain an understanding of what motivated each government to enact this type of schooling. The autobiography and papers of Richard Henry Pratt, the primary instigator behind the US boarding schools, and of reform organizations such as the Women's National Indian Association and the Indian Rights Association show, on their surface, humanitarian intentions in establishing the US boarding schools (Pratt 1964; Women's National Indian Association 1994; *Proceedings of the Annual Meetings of the Lake Mohonk Conference of the Friends of the Indian* 1883–1929). Church and missionary records, too, particularly in Canada, offer a rich source for understanding non-Indigenous justifications for and perspectives on Indigenous education.[1] Government archives help scholars trace institutional histories and compile studies of policy.[2]

A reliance on reformer papers, church records, and government archives, however, often gives a skewed view. The "official written record—reports of commissioners, superintendents, inspectors, agents, teachers," as Jacqueline Fear-Segal writes, "inevitably exerts a strong centripetal pull on interpretation and encourages us to take at face value the stated intentions of white educators and overlook the muted voices of Indians" (Fear-Segal 2007: xvii). Scholars such as David Wallace Adams, J.R. Miller, and John S. Milloy have read these archival sources with a critical eye and uncovered the harsh treatment that boarding and residential school authorities meted out to their "inmates," as they called the students (Adams 1995; Miller 1996; Milloy 1999).

Comparative work on boarding schools and other educational institutions in several different national contexts has further revealed the oppressive nature of government-sponsored Indigenous education. A recent edited collection on Indigenous education in both North and South America enables readers to contemplate how various colonial and national regimes often used education to undermine Indigenous people's aspirations (Child and Klopotek 2014). Michael Coleman compares the US boarding schools to English schools for Irish children, my work analyzes the forcible removal of Indigenous children to schools and other institutions in both the United States and Australia, and Andrew Woolford brings boarding schools in the United States in comparison with residential schools in Canada (Coleman 2007; Jacobs 2009; Woolford 2015). These comparative studies underscore how numerous colonial regimes have used education to discipline and punish Indigenous communities and to accomplish colonial aims of land dispossession, modernization, and the creation of an unskilled labor force.

The study of Indigenous education in other colonial contexts has played out differently. In Hawaii and New Zealand, early missionaries and later government officials promoted boarding-school education for Indigenous elites. The system did not involve the forcible removal of children or their abuse within institutions, as it did on the North American mainland and in Australia. Nevertheless, it produced complicated colonial identities among the trained elites.[3]

While some scholars have taken a broad panoramic view of Indigenous education across several colonial contexts, others have studied particular schools as a way to comprehend the meaning of education for its students. Such scholarship tends to focus on the gap between policy and practice in the implementation of the schools. It often yields critical insight into the spaces of resistance that opened up in institutions, and how Indigenous children and their families made use of such spaces to survive and turn the schools to their own purposes (Gilbert 2010; Ellis 1996; Riney 1999; Hyer 1990; Trennert 1988).

Still other interpretations of boarding and residential schools center on Indigenous-produced narratives and elicit other perspectives. Michael Coleman's *American Indian Children at School* relied on dozens of first-person written accounts by American Indians. His book revealed the great ambivalence with which American Indian children experienced the schools (Coleman 1993). Classic autobiographies by Indigenous authors such as Francis La Flesche (1978), Zitkala-Sa (Gertrude Bonnin) (2003), Basil Johnston (1990), and Margaret Tucker (1977) provide invaluable perspectives on early institutional experiences. Indigenous authors continue to produce these vital sources, including Adam Fortunate Eagle's *Pipestone* (2010), Bev Sellars's *They Called Me Number One* (2013), and Doris Pilkington's *Rabbit-Proof Fence* (2013).

A generation of scholars, many of them of Indigenous backgrounds, turned to oral history sources, often within their own families, to provide student-centered narratives of the schools (Child 1998; Lomawaima 1994). Tsianina Lomawaima conducted interviews with 61 people who had attended Chilocco Indian School or been employed there for her classic pathbreaking book, *They Called It Prairie Light*. Lomawaima's methodology enabled her to move beyond an account dominated by government policy statements and teacher reports. Although boarding schools "were often harsh and repressive institutions," she found "boarding-school students had the resilience of children." Some despised their school upbringing, but some "count their years away at school among the happiest and most carefree of their lives." Lomawaima's recovery of Indian voices "instruct us in adaptation, accommodation, resistance, and revolt" (Lomawaima 1994: xiv, xv).

Other Indigenous historians sought Indigenous voices and evidence of their actions in the archives as well as in their family histories. For *Boarding Schools Seasons*, Brenda Child sifted through hundreds of letters in the government archives for Flandreau and Haskell Indian Schools to uncover the stories of Ojibwe children and their families from her community at the Red Lake Reservation in Minnesota. Her quotation from letters written by members of her own family lends a particular poignancy to her book. These seemingly "inconsequential" unpublished letters from everyday Indian people reveal insights into the boarding school experience that are unavailable in the official record (Child 1998).

Scholars who want to understand more about the schools from the perspective of the Indian students have also looked to extracurricular activities in the schools, especially sports and music, as a means to grasp the complexity of the experience. John Bloom's *To Show What an Indian Can Do* uses familiar archival sources in concert with interviews to argue that sports "posed specific possibilities for Native American students to creatively reimagine their cultural memories, traditions, and identities" (Bloom 2000). Similarly, John Troutman finds that boarding school students expressed their political views and critiques of federal assimilation policy through musical performance (Troutman 2009).

The historiography on Indian boarding schools in the United States has become rich and led to some tension between narratives centered on oppression and others centered on resilience. Several scholars have raised concerns with the creation of a single narrative on the trauma of boarding school experience that might stifle competing viewpoints. Brenda Child has spoken of this danger in her perceptive article, "Boarding School as Metaphor" (2014). Ronald Niezen has critiqued Canada's Truth and Reconciliation Commission as well for creating one common narrative of abuse and tyranny that makes it difficult for former students to tell alternative stories (Niezen 2013). Similarly, Bain Attwood has argued that the accretion of Stolen Generation testimonies in Australia has led to a formulaic story that does not capture the full and complex history of Indigenous experience or government practice (2001). Alternatively, narratives emphasizing the trauma of boarding and residential schools and other institutions have served as important correctives to popular conceptions of the benevolence and humanitarianism of such endeavors.

Some new scholarship approaches the schools using theories and methodologies from multiple disciplines. Jacqueline Fear-Segal deftly analyzes the "white managed built environment of schools … using techniques and concepts borrowed from landscape historians and human geographers," the anthropologist James Scott, and the historical theorist Michel Foucault. With her spatial analysis, Fear-Segal thus broadens the scope of sources to include archival photographs, maps and charts, school buildings, structures, and roads, paths, fences, entrances, and exits (Fear-Segal 2007).

K. Tsianina Lomawaima and Teresa McCarty offer another insightful interpretation of boarding school education through innovating a new theoretical framework they call the "safety zone" to explain why government authorities seemingly tolerated Indigenous cultures and languages in particular historical eras. They argue that each generation developed "an area where dangerously different cultural expressions might be safely domesticated and thus neutralized." Lomawaima and McCarty's framework integrates three perspectives: federal policy, institutional practice, and Native and non-Native individual experiences. This approach enables them to tack back and forth between official efforts and Native actions, showing an ongoing dialectical encounter and power struggle in the spaces created for Indigenous education (Lomawaima and McCarty 2006: xxii).

Several scholars have applied the insights of labor history to the boarding schools. Cathleen Cahill crafted a labor history of the teachers who worked in the schools, noting that a significant percentage of the teachers were of Indigenous descent. Such a finding complicates further any simple notion that the policy of assimilation through education easily translated into its reality (Cahill 2011). Victoria Haskins studied the many young American Indian women students whom boarding schools trained and then "outed" to work as domestic servants in white Tucson homes (Haskins 2012).

The bulk of scholarship on Indigenous education, at least in the United States, has focused on boarding schools, but many scholars have studied other aspects of Indigenous education. Margaret Connell Szasz hunted through personal papers, church archives, and the papers of the New England Company in the eastern United States to reconstruct American Indian education in the British American colonies (Szasz 2007a). In a later book she connected the efforts of the Society in Scotland for the Propagation of Christian Knowledge (SSPCK) to colonize the supposedly savage Scottish Highlanders with their endeavors to proselytize Iroquois and Algonquin people in the American colonies (2007b).

Scholars have been keen to analyze how Indigenous people themselves have sought to control and direct the education of their own members. Some researchers have looked to earlier periods when Indigenous people seized control of their own educational system. Devon Mihesuah's groundbreaking book, *Cultivating the Rosebuds*, examined how the Western Cherokee Nation established the Cherokee Female Seminary in 1851 in order to help young Cherokee women adapt to the changing world around them. Mihesuah's use of Cherokee National Records and personal papers enabled her to tell the story of this unique school (Mihesuah 1993; Reyhner and Eder 2004: 251–330; Davis 2013).

More commonly this scholarship has concerned the link between self-determination movements and education in the late twentieth century. Margaret Connell Szasz penned one of the earliest such studies in the midst of American Indian self-determination efforts to gain control of Indigenous education in the United States. She supplemented governmental records with dozens of interviews with Indian leaders, such as those at the Navajo (Diné) Rough Rock Demonstration School, who were engaged in developing new models of education to better serve their people (Szasz 1999 [1977]). More recently, Julie Davis reconstructed the history of the survival schools of the American Indian Movement in the Twin Cities through oral history interviews with school founders, parents, administrators, teachers, and students. She revealed how important the control of education proved to be to those who sought greater sovereignty and self-determination for Indigenous peoples and linked the survival schools to global Indigenous decolonization movements since the 1960s (Davis 2013). Other recent studies emphasize the necessity of bilingual and bicultural education under the control of Indigenous communities to both the self-determination of Indigenous communities and the realization of true democracy (Lomawaima and McCarty 2006: 114–149; Goodyear-Ka'opua 2013; see also Reyhner and Eder 2004: 251–330).

The *Journal of American Indian Education* has been an important voice for new research on all aspects of Indigenous education since its inception in 1961. Although it is rooted in issues related to the education of American Indian/Alaska Natives, the *Journal* has included scholarship on educational issues pertaining to Indigenous people worldwide. The journal aims "to improve Native Education through knowledge generation and transmission to classrooms and other educational settings. It encourages dialogue between researchers and teachers through research-based scholar and practitioner articles elucidating current innovations in the classroom."[4]

New sources on Indigenous education are arising in some surprising places: as a byproduct of efforts by some modern settler colonial nations to reckon with the complicated past of Indigenous schools. The government of Canada established the Truth and Reconciliation Commission in 2009 as a requirement of the Indian Residential Schools Agreement of 2006. The Commission has held seven national events at which it has gathered testimony from hundreds of Indian residential school survivors. Their testimonies will become part of an archive and research center at the University of Manitoba in Winnipeg. In Australia, the Stolen Generations Inquiry into the Separation of Aboriginal and Torres Strait Islander children from their families resulted in the formation of the Bringing Them Home Oral History Project, housed at the National Library of Australia. Like its Canadian counterpart, it has created new sources for current and future generations of historians.

The study of Indigenous education is a rich and vibrant field. Its documentation challenges the progressive narratives of American history and adds new dimensions to studies of colonialism worldwide. The sources that scholars use to examine Indigenous education have influenced their approaches and interpretations. Those using government records and the papers of missionary and reform groups have leaned more toward emphasizing the oppressive nature of Indigenous education while those prioritizing the use of Indigenous-authored sources have given more weight to the ambivalent experiences of Indigenous survivors and how Indigenous communities have sought to gain control of education as a key means of asserting sovereignty. Taken together these competing approaches and interpretations provide a complex view of the role of education in Indigenous histories.

Notes

1   See for example the General Synod Archives of the Church of England and the United Church of Canada Archives in Toronto.
2   The National Archives and Records Administration, Records of the Bureau of Indian Affairs, Record Group 75, based in Washington, DC, holds records for government officials responsible for the US boarding schools. Many of the records for particular schools are held at the regional branches of the National Archives throughout the United States. Records of the Department of Indian Affairs (Record Group 10) are held in the National Archives of Canada in Ottawa, but many official records are available in provincial archives and the papers of religious organizations. In Australia, national and state archives provide insight into official justifications for the institutionalization of children as well as the development of policy.
3   There has been much less writing about these boarding schools and other Indigenous education in New Zealand and Hawaii. For some recent work, see Barrington (2008) and Goodyear-Ka'opua (2014).

4   Website of the *Journal of American Indian Education*, published by the Center for Indian Education of the School of Social Transformation at Arizona State University, http://jaie.asu.edu/about.html, accessed August 6, 2014.

References

Adams, David Wallace. 1995. *Education for Extinction: American Indians and the Boarding School Experience, 1875–1928*. Lawrence: University Press of Kansas.

Attwood, Bain. 2001. "'Learning about the truth': The Stolen Generations narrative". In Bain Attwood and Fiona Magowan, eds. *Telling Stories: Indigenous History and Memory in Australia and New Zealand*. Sydney: Allen & Unwin/Bridget Williams Books, pp. 183–212.

Barrington, John. 2008. *Separate But Equal? Maori Schools and the Crown, 1867–1969*. Wellington, New Zealand: Victoria University Press.

Bloom, John. 2000. *To Show What an Indian Can Do: Sports at Native American Boarding Schools*. Minneapolis: University of Minnesota Press.

Cahill, Cathleen D. 2011. *Federal Fathers and Mothers: A Social History of the United States Indian Service, 1869–1933*. Chapel Hill: University of North Carolina Press.

Child, Brenda. 1998. *Boarding School Seasons: American Indian Families, 1900–1940*. Lincoln: University of Nebraska Press.

Child, Brenda J. 2014. "The Boarding School as Metaphor". In Brenda Child and Brian Klopotek, eds. *Indian Subjects: Hemispheric Perspectives on the History of Indigenous Education*. Santa Fe: School of Advanced Research Press, pp. 267–284.

Child, Brenda and Brian Klopotek, eds. 2014. *Indian Subjects: Hemispheric Perspectives on the History of Indigenous Education*. Santa Fe: School of Advanced Research Press.

Coleman, Michael. 1993. *American Indian Children at School, 1850–1930*. Jackson: University Press of Mississippi.

Coleman, Michael C. 2007. *American Indians, the Irish, and Government Schooling: A Comparative Study*. Lincoln: University of Nebraska Press.

Davis, Julie. 2013. *Survival Schools: The American Indian Movement and Community Education in the Twin Cities*. Minneapolis: University of Minnesota Press.

Eagle, Adam Fortunate. 2010. *Pipestone: My Life in an Indian Boarding School*. Norman: University of Oklahoma Press.

Ellis, Clyde. 1996. *To Change Them Forever: Indian Education at the Rainy Mountain Boarding School, 1893–1920*. Norman: University of Oklahoma Press.

Fear-Segal, Jacqueline. 2007. *White Man's Club: Schools, Race, and the Struggle of Indian Acculturation*. Lincoln: University of Nebraska Press.

Gilbert, Matthew Saskietewa. 2010. *Education Beyond the Mesas: Hopi Students at Sherman Institute, 1902–1929*. Lincoln: University of Nebraska Press.

Goodyear-Ka'opua, Noelani. 2013. *The Seeds We Planted: Portraits of Native Hawaiian Charter School*. Minneapolis: University of Minnesota Press.

Goodyear-Ka'opua, Noelani. 2014. "Domesticating Hawaiians: Kamehameha schools and the 'tender violence' of marriage". In Brenda Child and Brian Klopotek, eds. *Indian Subjects: Hemispheric Perspectives on the History of Indigenous Education*. Santa Fe: School of Advanced Research Press, 2014.

Haskins, Victoria K. 2012. *Matrons and Maids: Regulating Indian Domestic Service in Tucson, 1914–1934*. Tucson: University of Arizona Press.

Hyer, Sally. 1990. *One House, One Voice, One Heart: Native American Education at the Santa Fe Indian School*. Santa Fe: Museum of New Mexico Press.

Jacobs, Margaret. 2009. *White Mother to a Dark Race: Settler Colonialism, Maternalism, and the Removal of Indigenous Children in the American West and Australia, 1880–1940*. Lincoln: University of Nebraska Press.

Johnston, Basil H. 1990. *Indian School Days*. Norman: University of Oklahoma Press.

La Flesche, Francis. 1978 [1900]. *The Middle Five: Indian Schoolboys of the Omaha Tribe*. Lincoln: University of Nebraska Press.

Lomawaima, K. Tsianina. 1994. *They Called It Prairie Light: The Story of Chilocco Indian School*. Lincoln: University of Nebraska Press.

Lomawaima, K. Tsianina and Teresa L. McCarty. 2006. *To Remain and Indian: Lessons in Democracy from a Century of Native American Education*. New York: Teachers College Press.

Mihesuah, Devon. 1993. *Cultivating the Rosebuds: The Education of Women at the Cherokee Female Seminary, 1851–1909*. Urbana: University of Illinois Press.

Miller, J.R. 1996. *Shingwauk's Vision: A History of Native Residential Schools*. Toronto: University of Toronto Press.

Milloy, John S. 1999. *A National Crime: The Canadian Government and the Residential School System, 1879–1986*. Winnipeg: University of Manitoba Press.

Niezen, Ronald. 2013. *Truth and Indignation: Canada's Truth and Reconciliation Commission on Indian Residential Schools*. Toronto: University of Toronto Press.

Pilkington, Doris. 2013. *Follow the Rabbit-Proof Fence*. St. Lucia, Australia: University of Queensland Press.

Pratt, Richard Henry. 1964. *Battlefield and Classroom: Four Decades with the American Indian, 1867–1904*, ed. Robert Utley. New Haven: Yale University Press.

Proceedings of the Annual Meetings of the Lake Mohonk Conference of the Friends of the Indian. Lake Mohonk, NY: Lake Mohonk conference, 1883–1929.

Reyhner, Jon and Jeanne Eder. 2004. *American Indian Education: A History*. Norman: University of Oklahoma Press.

Riney, Scott. 1999. *The Rapid City Indian School, 1898–1933*. Norman: University of Oklahoma Press.

Sellars, Bev. 2013. *They Called Me Number One: Secrets and Survival at an Indian Residential School*. Vancouver: Talonbooks.

Szasz, Margaret Connell. 1999 [1977]. *Education and the American Indian: The Road to Self Determination Since 1928*. Albuquerque: University of New Mexico Press.

Szasz, Margaret Connell. 2007a. *Indian Education in the American Colonies, 1607–1783*, with a new introduction by the author. Lincoln: University of Nebraska Press.

Szasz, Margaret Connell. 2007b. *Scottish Highlanders and Native Americans: Indigenous Education in the Eighteenth-Century Atlantic*. Norman: University of Oklahoma Press.

Trennert, Robert. 1988. *The Phoenix Indian School: Forced Assimilation in Arizona, 1891–1935*. Norman: University of Oklahoma Press.

Troutman, John. 2009. *Indian Blues: American Indians the Politics of Music, 1879–1934*. Norman: University of Oklahoma Press.

Tucker, Margaret. 1977. *If Everyone Cared*. Melbourne: Grosvenor Books.

Women's National Indian Association. 1994. Records, 1880–1951, microfilm. Bronx: Hunting Free Library.

Woolford, Andrew. 2015. *This Benevolent Experiment: Indigenous Boarding Schools, Genocide, and Redress in Canada and the United States*. University of Nebraska Press.

Zitkala-Sa (Gertrude Bonnin). 2003. *American Indian Stories*, with an introduction by Susan Rose Dominguez. Lincoln: Bison Books.

31 Laws, codes, and informal practices

Building ethical procedures for historical research with Indigenous medical records

Mary Jane Logan McCallum

Introduction

This chapter discusses some of the procedures historians undergo when researching modern institutional records pertaining to Indigenous people, in particular, restricted medical records. After describing my early encounters with the Sanatorium Board of Manitoba (SBM) records, I discuss the complicated nexus of codes of ethics and the Researcher Agreement that regulate my research.[1] Last, I reflect on some of the methodological difficulties, impacts, and responsibilities of researching archives of institutions like the SBM that collected private and personal information about Indigenous people while operating without their consent or involvement.

Historian meets the Sanatorium Board of Manitoba history and historical records

Manitoba is home to Ojibwe, Cree, Oji-Cree, Dene, Dakota, and Métis people, as well as other Indigenous people and settlers from all over the world. Colonial relations from the fur trade through settlement have shaped all aspects of its modern institutions, and this is no less evident when examining the province's twentieth-century history of tuberculosis (TB). From the late-nineteenth century to the first half of the twentieth century tuberculosis became a major public health concern, and in Canada many more First Nations, Inuit, and Métis people than non-Aboriginal people proceeded from being infected to having active, serious, and deadly cases of the disease.[2] This led to the widespread assumption that people of Indigenous ancestry were racially or biologically susceptible to the disease. Rather, dislocation, poverty, malnutrition, and inadequate housing contributed to its high incidence – conditions fueled by the processes of colonization (see, for example, Kelm 1998; Lux 2001; Daschuk 2013; Burnett 2010; Hackett 2005; Hackett et al. 2006; Grygier 1994; Stevenson 2014). Until the 1940s, governments committed very few resources to addressing tuberculosis among Indigenous people (Lux 2010: 420). But in the 1930s, Manitoba medical professionals increasingly warned of the "menace" First Nations people with tuberculosis posed to public health in the province (Hackett 2008: 118). The

Sanatorium Board of Manitoba, a voluntary organization charged with conducting a preventive campaign against tuberculosis, committed to a relationship with the federal government to manage on its behalf a segregated TB program of surveying, hospitalizing, and rehabilitating First Nations in Manitoba and some parts of north-western Ontario, some Inuit from the central Arctic, and some Métis. This era of health service has had an enormous impact on Manitoba's medical history and its health care delivery models as well as present relations within our systems of care.

The SBM records constitute a "colonial archive" (Stoler 2002; Burton 2006; Perry 2016). The Board collected qualitative and quantitative information about Indigenous people for the purposes of administering a diverse and changing racially segregated TB service funded by the state, municipalities, patients, the province, and private donations. The records are generated in the context of "public health" and they were also used to discipline Indigenous people (and "protect" white people). The records are evidence of both colonial governance of Indigenous health and the justification of the *need* to govern Indigenous health and all that this entails, including bodies, communities, and relations. Scientific and distant at some times and yet downright sociable at others, the SBM archives record the activities of a wide range of people including doctors and nurses; patients and visitors; orderlies and nurses' aides; hospital administrators and government officials; teachers, social workers, rehabilitation specialists and volunteers; church ministers and missionaries; cleaning staff, accountants, and engineers. While the purpose of the collection and preservation of these records was primarily to document the SBM as an institution, the archive speaks to other histories as well.

Modern institutions such as the SBM produce some common forms of records that are readily available to researchers. For example, my initial research was based on the SBM's *Annual Reports*. This type of record is a public document that provides summarized details about the activities of the administrative branches of an institution (such as finances, operations, and personnel) and will often include some photographs and graphs. Having read the *Annual Reports* and wanting more details about the organization, I began the process of finding and accessing the SBM's institutional records. Although the SBM ran three Indian hospitals with First Nations health funds, it operated as a private, non-government institution – and was not required to make its records public. Instead, the SBM records were only accessible with special permission of the Board itself. When I applied for access, the organization initially gave me permission to view its *News Bulletin*, a regular periodical for patients and the public that was useful in learning more about the SBM's social history.

Both the *Annual Reports* and the *News Bulletins*, like many institutionally created records, tend to unwaveringly support the organization; indeed, their purpose was to promote the SBM among medical professionals, politicians, and citizens. Nonetheless, drawing from these two sources, I began to formulate a number of research questions about the Indigenous history of TB in Manitoba relating to admissions, discharges, and deaths at TB hospitals, hospital physical plant, policies and architecture, food, education, and social and medical treatment.

As I began to pose these questions to health professionals and others in the province, I found that the enthusiastic support for the SBM contained within its *Annual Reports* and *News Bulletins* was widespread. To many Manitobans, the SBM was an important, positive, and benevolent force in medical history. More problematically, however, I was told on more than one occasion that I could find any information I needed for my project in books already published on the topic (for example, Stewart 1999; Wherrett 1977) even while for more than ten years, First Nations have repeatedly prioritized an examination of First Nations history of hospitalization and health care in Manitoba (McKinley 1998: 44).[3] The Indigenous history of TB in Manitoba is in fact not well known and the SBM archives provide some important quantitative and qualitative information that can supplement and complement local and oral history.

I was also confronted by a concern that my approach not be "too critical" of the Board. Since institutional records were used in the successful legal claims of Indian Residential School survivors against the Canadian government and churches, historians often encounter defensiveness about institutions that collected information pertaining to Indigenous people.[4] A desire to engage with this information can put historical researchers wanting to access restricted records in an especially difficult position and researchers have undertaken various strategies to navigate this defensiveness, at times either consciously or unconsciously crafting how they describe their project – knowing that this could influence the quantity and quality of records they see.

When I first encountered the records, the SBM was in the process of donating them to the Archives of Manitoba. This took many years in part because of the lengthy process of constructing a Finding Aid. The massive fonds of the SBM, covering 1900–1987, is organized into 15 series and contains administrative and operational files and patient records.[5] The highly structured nature of the collection reveals one of the great benefits of working with modern institutional records as opposed to private or older records. Another benefit is that they are often typed and therefore easier to read. All the same, as I describe in the next section, twentieth-century records can have other mitigating circumstances that can make them as difficult to access as any others.

Codes, applications, agreements, and competing priorities: Indigenous historical researchers' responsibilities to multiple jurisdictions

Once the SBM records were transferred to the Archives of Manitoba, they became subject to provincial regulations regarding access to personal and personal health information.[6] In Manitoba, the Health Information and Privacy Committee (HIPC) oversees the application of the Personal Health Information Act (PHIA),[7] which regulates the storage, use, and disclosure of information about individuals that is collected by governments and public and private organizations. In Canada, such laws date to the 1960s, when citizens became concerned that expanding governments functioned without laws permitting access to or restricting the amount, nature, and use of information they collected. Privacy standards in Manitoba cover all health information that has been collected at any time and do not expire after the death of an individual or at any other point.[8]

HIPC's application for access to documents containing personal health information is ten pages long and comprehensive. It requires a general description of the research project, including its purpose and proposed methodology; a list of specific research questions and the objectives or hypotheses to be tested; a description of exactly what data will be accessed; a rationalization of the level of intrusion associated with the research project; and an explanation of where the data will reside, how confidentiality will be protected, how the data will be accessed, and any plans for publication. Applications must show institutional (in my case, a university) Research Ethics Committee approval and proof of research funding, both of which require that projects are informed by the codes of ethical conduct in research developed by Canada's three main federal granting agencies, or the "Tri-Council".[9] My research project specifically needed to be informed by Chapter 9 of the *Tri-Council Policy Statement: Ethical Conduct for Research Involving Humans* (TCPS), "Ethics of Health Research Involving First Nations, Inuit and Métis People," and the Canadian Institute of Health Research's "Guidelines for Health Research Involving Aboriginal People." Finally, in Manitoba, researchers applying for access to personal health information relating to First Nations people need to show proof of the support of the Assembly of Manitoba Chiefs' Health Information Research and Governance Committee (HIRGC), which requires a separate application to the HIRGC describing the research and how it addresses HIRGC principles of ethical research.[10]

These codes require researchers to commit to a range of responsibilities – and many times these responsibilities will in fact conflict with one another. Moreover, most research ethics codes are framed for scientific, psychological, and medical research, and can be an awkward fit for historical methods. There were three main points of conflict arising in this process. First, in order to undertake the research, I needed to access a large amount of personal health information (health data linked with identifiers such as names, addresses, and health numbers). Since the nature and relevance of documents are only clear once they were read, I needed full access to sift through a significant number of them. In its interpretation of the PHIA, the HIPC saw this as contradicting the ethical principle of limiting access to restricted records, especially as the Committee normally only dealt with requests for information that had been de-identified (information where personal details had already been redacted). While de-identifying records may be consistent with medical and scientific research principles of objectivity and anonymity, it is at odds with Indigenous methodologies, which prioritize acknowledgement – of the past, people, and place (Kulchyski 2000). In response to my application, the HIRGC explained:

> First Nations … wish to understand their family histories and wish to have the First Nations communities named, so that the research will provide the overall policy and health environment for people to understand the history of that time, and its impact on the health of First Nations from then on.[11]

Researching and writing in ways that protect individual privacy while respecting and acknowledging Indigenous history is actually difficult to legislate and regulate and in the end I agreed to remove only individual names and other identifiers, such as band numbers. This method of de-identifying case files fit well with historical methodologies – which are often shaped to develop general (as opposed to individual) narratives about this past – while allowing for the parallel analysis of community-specific experiences.

Following this, the second point of contention was defining the research project's "level of intrusion." The HIPC considered the project to be at the highest level of intrusion, "highly sensitive," first because the information included people's names and second because the information was about a "dependent" population. The Committee suggested that I first gain the consent of all individuals whose information I accessed. However, as the information was collected many years ago, implicates tens of thousands of people, and many, if not most, have passed on, this would be impossible. Procedurally, I would also need to see the documents before I could ascertain whose consent was required. Framing the research as highly intrusive based on the notion that First Nations people are "dependent," or, in other ethics procedures, "vulnerable," was just as problematic. The term "intrusion" also suggested that I was being careless and nosy and studying a history that was an individual and private matter. Labelling my research as "intrusive" conflicts with the general commitment of historians to free and open inquiry[12] and risks protecting instead an organization that was in fact highly intrusive to First Nations, Inuit, and Métis people. After all, the SBM had operated without the consent of or accountability to Indigenous people while accepting public funds to do so. Inevitably, I spent a lot of time describing what a professional historian does and how our education prepares us to work with medical records. I maintain that in general, the professionalization of history has not served Indigenous researchers or Indigenous history well, but there is no place for ambivalence in research laws, codes, and ethics.

Finally, the HIPC was concerned that the amount of identifiable information and the level of "intrusion" was not justified by the "benefits" of the research. In health research, benefits often include advances in medical science, health administration, or medical training and it is difficult to justify institutional historical research with the same credence. My original justification – that First Nations, Inuit, and Métis communities deserve to know what happened to them and that a critical examination of this past can equip Manitobans to better understand ongoing issues in health care – was considered too "vague." In the end, I argued that the project's significance outweighed its "intrusion" because the treatment of Indigenous people and their experiences of hospitalization are matters of public concern and public policy.

Because my request was "complex," the Committee asked me to revise and resubmit the application; after the second submission, they sought legal advice for several months before granting approval. At that point, the application was forwarded to the Archives of Manitoba, which began to work with the provincial government's Civil Legal Services to develop a Researcher Agreement to support my access to and the protection of the personal health information found in these records. Researcher Agreements are binding contracts signed by institutions and researchers that outline how information will be protected and the consequences for not complying. The Researcher Agreement that Civil Legal Services developed for access to the Sanatorium Board of Manitoba records was 54 pages long and it seemed obstructionist.[13] With the help of another researcher working with the documents, as well as an archivist and the Assembly of Manitoba Chiefs, the Researcher Agreement was simplified to 13 pages. It is still long and punitive[14] but much less so than before.

Archives and Indigenous historical research ethics

The conditions under which I research the SBM records have been somewhat negotiated, but they are ultimately subject to Manitoba's Health Information Privacy Act, the ethics codes of my university and the Tri-Council, the HIRGC principles of the Assembly of Manitoba Chiefs, and the Researcher Agreement between the Archives of Manitoba and myself. In practice, these conditions include: all restricted documents are consulted in a separate and private room at the Archives of Manitoba; all personal information and personal health information is kept in strict confidence and never used in such a way that an individual could be identified; I may only produce notes about original documents and these are saved in encrypted files on a password-protected computer until they are transferred to a password-protected external hard drive that is kept in a locked drawer in my office; and any and all material made public is subject to prior review by the Health Information Management Branch of Manitoba Health.[15] But what procedures are taken by historians who consult archives that are not restricted and which are not governed this way? Do historians have special ethical responsibilities toward the archives they consult? How do we describe and practice these responsibilities?

Indigenous research ethics is interested predominantly in what is called "research involving humans" and the use of "Indigenous knowledge," both of which are defined fairly narrowly as knowledge that is transmitted orally and experientially. The structures guiding ethical research therefore tend to pre-empt Indigenous literacy and exclude information about and by Indigenous people that is stored in public or private archives, libraries, or other institutions. Such records, however, can and do observe and record Indigenous activities and people.[16] In light of this, I wanted to see what the Canadian Historical Association (CHA) had to say about ethics and Indigenous historical research. The CHA's guidelines assumed a readership of "outsider" or non-Aboriginal researchers:

> Doing history inevitably involves researching and writing about individuals and groups distanced from ourselves by time and social circumstances … Part of our ethical role is to continually question if, and how, our historical research and writing might have a contemporary impact on these individuals and communities.

After an obligatory reference to the Tri-Council Policy Statement and a summary of that document's references to "suggested good practices for research on Aboriginal peoples," the CHA then referred readers to the Department of Indian Affairs and Northern Development (DIAND) website for more information on ethical research! Needless to say, deferring to DIAND on matters of ethics is highly problematic.[17]

Importantly, Indigenous history writing and research ethics have a place in a long history of a lack of privacy protection for Indigenous people. The Indian Act allowed the federal government to track people's movements, to enter homes at will, to correspond about marriages, families, and living arrangements, to determine the health and diet of individuals and communities, and to discuss people's income and how they spent their money. At the same time that the government had all four corners of people's lives flayed open for inspection, judgment, discipline, and documentation, the record of this knowledge was removed from the people most affected by it and kept by "private" institutions or the state. What ethical responsibilities do scholars have when they read material produced in these circumstances? (Larocque 2010: 14, 62).[18] The more extreme response from some scholars is to not review or use the material at all; some even suggest that its use innately "colonizes" a research project. This response sometimes comes from not knowing what is in the archives in the first place, likely because the information was collected a long time ago and without any follow up. To be sure, institutional records are often distressing and even repulsive to read, but this response avoids altogether the fact of colonization.[19] Another approach, historian Lynette Russell suggests, is to enable Indigenous people "the right of reply" and for archives to develop opportunities for interactive and performative interventions (Russell 2005: 165). In part Indigenous historical research itself can be a practice of reply.

In my work with Manitoba TB history, I read archival documents to learn about the experiences of Indigenous people; this is sometimes called reading "against the grain" because most of the documents were written by and for non-Indigenous people. For example, we can retrieve glimpses of Indigenous experience in the ways doctors and nurses wrote, or did not write, about Indigenous people. Especially in the context of institutions imposing uniformity and anonymity, even brief encounters such as letters or photographs take on great significance. When I do encounter knowledge in archives that is personal and private, I use pseudonyms and sometimes also change details to prevent disclosure, even when the document is not by law restricted. I am thus constantly evaluating what "risk" is and how to ensure that in efforts to do no harm I'm not also obscuring or concealing the work of the institutions themselves. Describing the nature and functions of institutions themselves is also my concern. This is sometimes called "reading with the grain," or reading for patterns of treatment and policy with respect to Indigenous people.

Committing to reading Indigenous health history in SBM institutional records has, over time, impacted my research procedures and my writing as well. The records are, for the most part, about violence in a variety of different forms. They are informed by racist thought, they justify life-threatening inequality and they are infuriatingly fragmentary. Exceptional circumstances aside, I limit contact with them to four hours at a time. In reading materials that are distressing and at the same time not being able to directly confront anyone about them, certain statements inevitably stand out and stick, sometimes to the point of defining an institution or one of its employees. Institutional records tend to reflect institutional administration, and their structures can be inadvertently reproduced in my writing. Also, when describing especially problematic or detailed historical developments, I will overload my writing with evidence, a habit that has been criticized as "too academic." At the same time, researchers working on institutions that operated without consultation with Indigenous people and that withheld their information are obliged to be as thorough, clear, thoughtful, and transparent as possible; our evidence is knitted to complicated histories that have long been silenced or misunderstood. Last, especially in well-known or widespread public institutions, many people feel personally or professionally invested in the research. In practice, this will often mean generously consulting with individuals who want to know more about their family's history and experiences in institutions and those who want to learn about how to consult the records themselves.

Conclusion

As privacy legislation and ethics codes are commonly applied in our research projects, it is important to think about how they impact our methodologies. Indigenous historical research is often responsible to multiple jurisdictions and requires patience and flexibility from the researcher as well as an ability to defend and explain work to a range of audiences, many of whom are unfamiliar with not only the historical context and the materials we examine, but also the kinds of work that historians do. All researchers need to be prepared for the often hidden, complicated, and time-consuming procedures that can restrict and even pre-empt historical research on institutions. And yet institutional records remain a crucial resource, and their access and responsible use by historians is imperative to gaining a fuller understanding of our past.

Notes

1   For the purposes of this chapter, I'm using a definition of ethics by Marlene Brant Castellano: "Ethics refers to rules of conduct that express and reinforce important social and cultural values of a society. These rules may be formal and written, spoken or simply understood by groups who subscribe to them" (2004: 98).
2   We are currently at a critical juncture where TB rates and multi-drug resistance and co-morbidity with HIV are on the rise and threatening so-called "at risk" populations while entrenched policies and procedures for TB health care continue to lack engagement with the very people who are at risk. A 2010 report from the Public Health Agency of Canada documented continuing high infection rates of TB among First Nations populations (31 times higher than non-Aboriginal people in Canada) and that rates in Manitoba are worse; in some communities, rates of 600 cases of TB per 100,000

were reported, whereas the national average is five (Curry 2010; Skerrit 2010; see also Jen Skerrit's series on tuberculosis in the *Winnipeg Free Press* in 2009).

3 In 2008 and 2010 the Assembly of Manitoba Chiefs (AMC) and the Manitoba Keewatinowi Okimakanak (MKO) respectively made resolutions to support the identification and commemoration of gravesites of ancestors who were in tuberculosis sanatoria in the province. For more, see MKO and AMC websites: www.mkonorth. com and www.assemblyofmanitobachiefs.com.

4 Most publicly and recently, for example, in 2012, the Truth and Reconciliation Commission (TRC) made news in its efforts to access historical documents. Under the agreement that established the TRC, the government of Canada and the churches were obliged to provide "all relevant documents in their possession or control" to the Commission. However, the federal government prevaricated, blaming the time and costs associated with finding and reproducing the estimated 2–5 million documents. In late December 2012, the TRC took legal action to compel the federal government to produce the documents it was still withholding. After the court ruling in late January 2013 in favor of the TRC, the federal government continued to waffle on what it considered to be "relevant documents" and the Commissioners feared that records may not be able to be reviewed anyway due to the limited time available for the Commission to do its work. This case prompted one of the few public discussions of archival research related to Indigenous history in Canada and illuminates some of the challenges faced by researchers. The TRC's access to these documents was supposed to be guaranteed as part of a class action legal settlement resulting between Residential School Survivors and the federal government and churches. One might ask where this leaves smaller projects without such substantial support and backing.

5 The fonds consists of 22 metres of textual records, including 1,325 photographs, 60 volumes of textual records, 24 film reels (4hr, 59 min), and 72 architectural and presentation drawings. Contents include Correspondence and Administration Files, Minutes, Payroll and Financial Records, Patient Records, reports of mobile TB clinics, and historical files.

6 While the Freedom of Information of Protection of Privacy Act (FIPPA) deals with information collected by the government (including most Indian hospital records), PHIA deals with personal health information collected by both public and private institutions.

7 The Province defines "Personal Health Information" as "information about an individual's health or health care history, provision of health care to the individual or payment for health care provided to the individual which, alone or in combination with other information, could potentially identify an individual and … includes Personal Information." It defines Personal Information as "information about an identifiable individual and any other information about an individual which, alone or in combination with other information could identify that individual." The Personal Health Information Act can be found at the Province of Manitoba website: www.gov.mb.ca/health/phia/.

8 This is far more restrictive than the American Health Insurance Portability and Accountability Act (HIPPA), for example, which protects an individual's health information for 50 years after death. See the Federal Register Website at: www. federalregister.gov/articles/2013/01/25/2013-01073/modifications-to-the-hipaa-privacy-security-enforcement-and-breach-notification-rules-under-the.

9 The Tri-Council is made up of Canada's three federal funding agencies for university-based research: SSHRC (Social Science and Humanities Research Council of Canada), NSERC (Natural Sciences and Engineering Research Council), and CIHR (Canadian Institutes of Health Research).

10 The HIRGC was founded in the mid-1990s to oversee the Regional Health Survey (the only First Nations-governed health survey in Canada, which amassed health information on reserve and northern First Nations communities from the late 1990s to the early 2000s). Its role is to review academic proposals for research concerning First Nations;

to promote First Nations benefits through research, including partnerships; and to ensure that research is based on free, prior, and informed consent, First Nations OCAP Principles (Ownership, Control, Access, and Possession), and First Nations Ethical Standards. The HIRGC developed a program, called "Enigok" which means "Work Hard" in Ojibwe, to gather information about Indigenous concepts of ethical research and to make it available to research communities in Manitoba. The HIRGC is part of a larger movement within Aboriginal health research to codify ethical research conduct. Such efforts have been driven in part by a history of poor research relationships that have involved theft of bodily material, failure to share the results, concerns about experimentation and unethical conduct, and the decontextualization of research results, resulting in misunderstandings of Aboriginal cultures and pathologization. First Nations research codes tend to be shaped by two main issues: self-determination – the need for First Nations people to determine what research needs to be done, how it will be done, how it will be shared and developed – and worldview – the need for both research informed by Indigenous understandings of the relationships between individuals and the world around them, responsibilities, and respect.

11 Correspondence, Kathi Avery Kinew, Assembly of Manitoba Chiefs to Members of the Manitoba Health, Health Information Privacy Committee, August 26, 2011.
12 See the Canadian Historical Association Website: www.cha-shc.ca/english/about-the-cha/statement-on-research-ethics.html#sthash.RQgTRP1N.dpbs.
13 Researcher agreements and other issues confronting historians working with freedom of information legislation in Canada are explored in Clément (2015).
14 The consequences of not following these procedures include the termination of the research and the Agreement and any suspicion of wrongful activities can be reported to the HIPC, my university, and professional associations with jurisdiction to sanction, discipline, and regulate me professionally.
15 In addition, all members of the research team underwent training from the province in the handling of Personal Health Information.
16 This information, Australian historian Lynette Russell argues, "is not immediately or obviously Indigenous knowledge as it is knowledge not by but rather about indigenous people … material housed in archives and libraries in general is [not] indigenous knowledge per se, [however] such material can become Indigenous through reclamation processes which can be facilitated by libraries and archives" (2005: 170).
17 I wrote to the CHA and this has since been changed. See the Statement on Research Ethics at the Canadian Historical Association's Website: www.cha-shc.ca/?lid=WVJBJ-WNEB5-USA7E#sthash.hnUCOn8U.dpbs.
18 Larocque remarked on the "overwhelming presence of Eurocentric and hate material in our archives" that "remains protected and continues as currency for the colonizers' archives." She calls these "colonial texts" "Hate Literature."
19 Dale Turner and Audra Simpson write: "[c]olonialism is an unavoidable dimension of our reality; yet, making sense of it and, more importantly, making our understandings of colonialism ultimately do work for us in ways that empower us as Indigenous peoples is quite another matter. Part of Indigenous leadership must think about the global world and act in it *because* we are part of it, and therefore we ought to have a say in how humanity should evolve. We cannot do so unless we come to grips with what colonialism means and how it is put to use in the world" (2008: 5).

References

Burnett, Kristin. 2010. *Taking Medicine: Women's Healing Work and Colonial Contact in Southern Alberta, 1880–1930*. Vancouver: University of British Columbia Press.
Burton, Antoinette, ed. 2006. *Archive Stories: Facts, Fictions, and the Writing of History*. Durham, NC: Duke University Press.

Castellano, Marlene Brant. 2004. "Ethics of Aboriginal research". *Journal of Aboriginal Health Research*: 98–114.

Clément, Dominique. 2015. "'Freedom' of information in Canada: Implications for historical research". *Labour/Le Travail*, 75: 101–131.

Curry, Bill. 2010. "Aboriginals in Canada face 'Third World' level risk of tuberculosis". *Globe and Mail*, 10 March.

Daschuk, James. 2013. *Clearing the Plains: Disease, Politics of Starvation, and the Loss of Aboriginal Life*. Regina: University of Regina Press.

Grygier, Pat. 1994. *A Long Way From Home: The Tuberculosis Epidemic among the Inuit*. Montreal and Kingston: McGill-Queen's University Press.

Hackett, Paul. 2005. "From past to present: Understanding First Nations health patterns in a historical context". In "Aboriginal Health Research and Policy: First Nations-University Collaboration in Manitoba", supplement to the *Canadian Journal of Public Health*, 96(Supplement 1): S17–21.

Hackett, Paul. 2008. "Tuberculosis mortality among the students of St. Joseph's residential school in 1942–43: Historical and geographical context". In J. Littleton, J. Park, A. Herring, and T. Farmer, eds. *Multiplying and Dividing: Tuberculosis in Canada and Aotearoa New Zealand, Research in Anthropology and Linguistics*, 3: 113–133.

Hackett, Paul, J. Daschuk, and S.D. MacNeil. 2006. "Treaties and tuberculosis: First Nations people in late 19th century Western Canada, a political and economic transformation". *The Canadian Bulletin of Medical History*, 23(2): 307–330.

Kelm, Mary-Ellen. 1998. *Colonizing Bodies: Aboriginal Health and Healing in British Columbia, 1990–1950*. Vancouver: University of British Columbia Press.

Kulchyski, Peter. 2000. "What is Native Studies". In Ron F. Laliberte, Priscilla Settee, James B. Waldram, Rob Innes, Brenda Macdougall, Lesley McBain, and F. Laurie Barron, eds. *Expressions in Native Studies*. Saskatoon: University of Saskatchewan Press, pp. 13–26.

Larocque, Emma. 2010. *When the Other is Me: Native Resistance Discourse, 1850–1990*. Winnipeg: University of Manitoba Press.

Lux, Maureen. 2001. *Medicine That Walks: Disease, Medicine and Canadian Plains Native People, 1880–1940*. Toronto: University of Toronto Press.

Lux, Maureen. 2010. "Care for the 'racially careless': Indian hospitals in the Canadian West, 1920s–1950s". *Canadian Historical Review*, 91(3): 407–434.

McKinley, Rob. 1998. "Rumours of abuse, cover-up at clinics". *Windspeaker*, 18 September.

Perry, Adele. 2016. *Aqueduct: Colonialism, Resources, and the Histories We Remember*. Winnipeg: ARP Books.

Russell, Lynette. 2005. "Indigenous knowledge and archives: Accessing hidden history and understandings". *Australian Academic and Research Libraries*, 36(2): 161–171.

Skerrit, Jen. 2010. "TB cases on rise in Manitoba". *Winnipeg Free Press*, 10 March.

Stevenson, Lisa. 2014. *Life Beside Itself: Imagining Care in the Canadian Arctic*. Oakland: University of California Press.

Stewart, D.B. 1999. *Holy Ground: The Story of the Manitoba Sanatorium at Ninette*. Killarney: J.A. Victor David Museum.

Stoler, Ann Laura. 2002. "Colonial archives and the arts of governance". *Archival Science*, 2: 87–109.

Turner, Dale and Audra Simpson. 2008. "Indigenous leadership in a flat world". Research paper for the National Centre for First Nations Governance, May, 5. See National

Centre for First Nations Governance Website: http://fngovernance.org/ncfng_research/turner_and_simpson.pdf.

Wherrett, George Jasper. 1977. *The Miracle of the Empty Beds: A History of Tuberculosis in Canada*. Toronto: University of Toronto Press.

32 Toward a post-Quincentennial approach to the study of genocide

Jeffrey Ostler

Introduction

Although Raphael Lemkin coined the word genocide in 1944, it was not until almost fifty years later – at the time of Columbus Quincentennial – that the term became widely used to characterize the European conquest and colonization of the western hemisphere. In the run up to Columbus Day 1992, American Indian Movement protesters in Denver carried signs reading, "No parades for genocide," and on the day itself as many as 50,000 Indigenous people in La Paz, Bolivia, marched against "500 years of genocide and mourning" (Lemkin 1944: 79; Kubal 2008: 163, 94). During the Quincentennial writers indicted Columbus and the invasion he initiated as genocidal in essays, newspapers, and books. Two works became particularly influential: David Stannard's *American Holocaust: The Conquest of the New World* and Ward Churchill's *A Little Matter of Genocide: Holocaust and Denial in the Americas, 1492 to the Present* (Stannard 1992; Churchill 1997).[1]

As their titles announced, Stannard and Churchill made their case by arguing for a moral and analytical equivalence with the Holocaust. Their narrative strategy was to relate horrific event after horrific event (massacres, enslavements, epidemics), indict Europeans for their greed, racism, and bloodlust, and link these to statistics underscoring the drastic decline of Indigenous populations in the Americas, thus creating an impression of an unrelenting, intentioned, and unambiguously evil process that resembled and indeed exceeded the Nazis' systematic annihilation of the Jews.

Although the argument for the pervasiveness of genocide in the Americas has the status of fact in some areas of Indigenous Studies and genocide studies, it has had remarkably little impact on the writing of American Indian history.[2] In part, this is because of a generally conservative disposition among many academic specialists in colonial American and US history, though the way Stannard and Churchill made the case has made it easier for skeptics to brush it aside. In part, too, one of Native American history's most important commitments over the past several decades – to replace narratives of Indians as victims with Indians as agents – has seemed to logically repel or at least discourage attention to genocide.

If the Quincentennial moment has now passed and the debates it engendered ossified, new approaches that account for the distinctive conditions of settler colonialism suggest a basis for reorienting the study of genocide in the Americas (Smithers 2010). The concept of settler colonialism as a specific type of colonialism was initially theorized primarily by scholars of Australia in the late 1990s and early 2000s, a period of intense academic and public debate about the Stolen Generations and the larger issue of Australia's genocide of Aboriginal peoples. Those arguing for the occurrence of genocide in Australia (and similar cases, the United States and Canada included) contended that settler colonialism inherently carried what Patrick Wolfe termed a "logic of elimination." Settler colonists, in other words, wanted to get rid of Native people so that they could possess their lands, but the means of elimination were manifold and could include assimilation, concentration, removal, as well as mass killing. The task then became to specify the conditions under which genocide in the strong sense of the term as physical annihilation became the chosen means of elimination. A. Dirk Moses provided a useful generalization in specifying the "intensity of Indigenous resistance" as the "mechanism of policy radicalization." Thus, "the colonization of Australia" was "a dynamic process with genocidal potential that could be released in circumstances of crisis" (Wolfe 2006; Moses 2004: 33).[3] Applying this approach to the Americas avoids forcing a 500-year history to conform to the Holocaust and other commonly recognized twentieth-century genocides, events of relatively brief duration and sustained, total intensity. Instead it opens space for an analysis of genocidal or potentially genocidal processes as they unfolded over long periods of time with varying degrees of intensity and with an uneven impact on a large number of distinct peoples, while at the same time allowing Indigenous agency to emerge as a crucial variable. This chapter identifies several areas where new approaches might be developed. My focus is mainly on the areas of North America that eventually became part of the United States through the nineteenth century, although there are a wealth of possibilities in other geographies and time periods.

The problem of definition

Before considering approaches for the post-Quincentennial study of genocide in North America, it is necessary to address a problem that has plagued genocide studies: the problem of defining the field's central term. The authoritative legal definition is the 1948 United Nations Convention on the Prevention and Punishment of the Crime of Genocide, which defines genocide as:

> any of the following acts committed with intent to destroy, in whole or in part, a national, ethnical, racial or religious group, as such:
> (a) Killing members of the group;
> (b) Causing serious bodily or mental harm to members of the group;
> (c) Deliberately inflicting on the group conditions of life calculated to bring about its physical destruction in whole or in part;
> (d) Imposing measures intended to prevent births within the group;
> (e) Forcibly transferring children of the group to another group.

Despite its legal standing, however, scholars have proposed several alternative definitions. Some have argued that other groups (e.g., political groups) should be included; others have insisted on physical extermination as the central if not the only means of destruction; others have required clear demonstration of national government planning to establish intent; others have advocated that intent be judged less by formal government policy than by the effects (including indirect effects) of societal and national projects.[4] To move beyond the apparent intractability of the debate about definitions, the best approach, at least for the moment, may be to resist the tendency to "prove" that genocide occurred or did not occur under a particular definition and instead develop careful analyses of intersecting forces of destruction operating against American Indians (and the contexts for these forces) and the ways in which Native communities comprehended and chose to deal with these forces.

Disease

A logical place to begin is with disease, since there is a consensus among scholars, regardless of their position on genocide, that in the western hemisphere post-1492 more Indigenous people perished from disease than any factor. Debate has centered on the issue of intentionality. Those arguing that disease was genocidal have sometimes made the case by linking the spread of disease to other more clearly intentional colonial actions (e.g., enslavement, forced removals, destruction of resources, war) and at other times by citing examples of Europeans intending to spread disease by distributing blankets or other items infected with smallpox or other diseases. Those arguing that disease was not genocidal maintain that linking disease to other colonial actions is insufficient to establish intentionality and are skeptical about most cases of alleged biological warfare.

Either way, protagonists in this debate have taken an "arithmetic" approach with those arguing for genocide citing figures for a very high pre-Columbian population and highlighting rapid population declines following initial contact (80 percent or more), thus establishing a demographic catastrophe far in excess of the Holocaust.[5] Ironically, however, this line of argument allows opponents to respond that the vast majority of deaths were inadvertent. It can be argued, however, that the extent of initial depopulation is less crucial to assessments of genocide than the impact of disease in conjunction with other forces of destruction in relation to specific colonial projects developed after the moment of initial invasion. Thus, although Paul Kelton's opening argument in *Epidemics and Enslavement* that Spanish exploration of what became the southeastern United States in the sixteenth century did not introduce major epidemics or cause major destruction runs counter to the Quincentennial narrative of genocide, his subsequent contention that when smallpox did appear in the late 1690s it was linked to the emerging British slave trade in Indian captives challenges inadvertency. This does not resolve the debate about genocide (Kelton himself does not address the issue), but it shows how disease interacted with an overtly destructive colonial project (Kelton 2007).

Other studies also suggest useful new approaches. In examining the background to the horrific smallpox epidemic that broke out on the upper Missouri River in 1837, J. Diane Pearson does not attempt to argue, *á la* Churchill, that Army officials or traders intentionally created the epidemic by distributing smallpox infected items. Instead, she offers a critical reading of the 1832 Indian Vaccination Act, contending that it functioned to establish colonial authority and could be used as a weapon. In the event, she contends, government officials labeled Indians on the upper Missouri "aggressor nations" and so withheld vaccination from them, thus explaining their vulnerability to the spread of smallpox. Whether this qualifies as an act of genocide or not would depend on what definition is used, though Pearson's analysis establishes a link between government policy and disease that goes beyond inadvertency or negligence (Pearson 2003).

Beyond attention to well-known epidemics, there is much about disease that remains to be investigated. Take, for example, disease and the well-studied removal of southeastern Indians. Although the work of Russell Thornton and other scholars has established some of the basic demographic facts (Thornton 1987: 113–118), the "trail of tears" metaphor has deflected attention away from what happened in the months after southeastern nations had completed their forced journeys west. Although some scholars such as Donna L. Akers have begun to document post-removal conditions, more work remains to be done (Akers 2004: 112–113).[6] The relationship between disease and the policy of removal itself also merits further interrogation. Scholars have appropriately begun labeling removal as ethnic cleansing (see, for example, Perdue and Green 2007: 42; Kiernan 2007: 330; Anderson 2014: 151–172), though this term is sufficiently elastic to encompass actions requiring a range of assessments. In other words, it would be one thing if the United States had moved eastern Indians all at once without fully realizing that many would die, but the fact that the United States continued to force Indians west year after year *knowing* of mounting death tolls requires a categorically different evaluation.

There is also a need for work on poor health and mortality, and their connections to malnutrition, poverty, starvation, and social stress in lesser known situations involving, for example, nations forced to remove multiple times (e.g., Delawares forced from Ohio to Missouri to Kansas to Oklahoma) or Indians confined to reservations in the late nineteenth and early twentieth centuries. A case study of tuberculosis on Lakota reservations in David S. Jones's *Rationalizing Epidemics* provides a useful model. From a different direction, Jacki Thompson Rand's *Kiowa Humanity and the Invasion of the State* provides an analysis of the insufficiency of rations, resulting from congressional parsimony and neglect but also because government officials used rations as a weapon, that establishes a crucial context for disease, declining life expectancy, and infant mortality (Jones 2004: 145–168; Rand 2008: 90–91). Finally, little attention has been given to Native agency in connection to foreign disease. We have ethnographic studies of "traditional" medical practices and know something of the disruptive impact of epidemics on Indigenous medical knowledge, but too often accounts of disease focus on providing examples of Indians responding to disease in a way that made things worse, as for example, by sweating (see, for example, Ewers 1997). We know less about how Native practitioners sought to understand European diseases and developed ways to deal with them over time.[7]

War and massacre

European warfare against Indians is often considered separately from disease, yet in many instances war's most destructive consequence was the creation of conditions that encouraged the spread of disease. The emphasis on military campaigns, battles, and massacres in much of the literature has tended to obscure this. A good example is the Continental Army's 1779 invasion of Iroquoia. Facing a huge military force, Haudenosaunees decided that rather than risk losing hundreds or more non-combatants (i.e., suffering genocide) they would abandon their towns. As a result, when American troops burned their towns and food supplies, Haudenosaunees were destitute. Many more Haudenosaunees died from starvation and disease after the US invasion than were directly killed by soldiers. Though the United States did not intend this precise outcome, it would be narrowly legalistic to dismiss it as inadvertent. The government's intention was to inflict as much destruction on the Haudenosaunees as possible (Calloway 1995: 139).

Because so much has been written on events of European violence against Indians, it may seem that there is little room for new work, but for scholars interested in new approaches to genocide, there are many possibilities. In addition to studying the intersection between warfare and other forces of destruction (disease, starvation, dispossession), there is considerable room for contextualizing particular events and phases. One avenue, suggested by Karl Jacoby's exploration of exterminatory rhetoric prior to the 1871 Camp Grant massacre, is to provide thick local contexts for massacres by piecing together material in sources like newspapers, settler diaries, and pioneer histories. Another, following Benjamin Madley's analysis of how California state officials and the federal government itself provided material support to local militias that pursued sustained Indian killing during the California Gold Rush, would be to probe for similar connections in other instances, using, for example, government records documenting appropriations for local militias. From a different angle, following the work of Lisa Brooks, who has shown how Indians in the northeast indicted the English for destroying resources, rejecting an ethic of reciprocity reflected in the metaphor of the "common pot" and turning the world upside down, scholars might develop a more robust history of Indigenous critiques of colonialism, including frequent allegations that colonists intended not only to take their lands but to kill them all to do it (Jacoby 2008; Madley 2008; Brooks 2008: 60–61).[8]

Beyond new focuses on specific cases, much could be clarified by systematic identification of patterns. John Grenier's *The First Way of War* reveals a consistent American approach to Indian warfare involving the regular killing of non-combatants and systematic destruction of material resources, and goes a considerable distance toward countering the still-common characterization of specific massacres as somehow anomalous (Grenier 2005). Other than attributing

America's violent propensities to ideological dispositions (Slotkin 1973; Drinnon 1980) or the cultural imperatives of nation building (Silver 2008; Smith-Rosenberg 2010), however, we lack careful consideration of patterns of violence. To move beyond narratives that rely on a strategy of serially relating horrific acts of violence (critical work, but ultimately insufficient), a post-Quincentennial approach to the question of genocide would recognize that as a general rule European imperial and settler governments did not generally pursue policies that called for outright extermination in the first instance and that there were many periods of relatively non-violent interaction between Indians and non-Indians. Even in situations when colonizers pursued war against Indians they were often not successful, partly because of their own incapacities and incompetence, but also because of Native agency, including skills of warfare and intelligence gathering, an ability to evacuate non-combatants when necessary, and so on. What is needed, then, is an analysis of the variables that explain patterns of violence. There are many questions that might be asked: When were massacres likely to occur and under what conditions? What explains why massacres occurred in some situations but not in others? Under what circumstances did imperial and settler governments authorize exterminatory violence? To the extent that military forces exercised restraint, what factors, material (e.g., the utility of captives) and ideological (e.g., the imperative to disguise genocidal impulses), explain this? What tactics did Indian communities employ to preempt or avoid massacre?

Policy

Though scholars who have theorized genocide under conditions of settler colonialism have usefully argued for replacing an "intentionalist" with a "structuralist" approach, thus emphasizing "society-led" instead of "state-led" genocides (Moses 2004: 23–28; Barta 1987), it would be a mistake for these orientations to foreclose new analyses of the place of violence and warfare in the thinking of government officials and the policies they devised.

With some exceptions, historians of US federal Indian policy have limited their focus to policymakers' statements of first preference, that is, what policymakers ideally hoped (or fantasized) would happen. In general – and consistent with the priorities of settler colonialism – policymakers envisioned scenarios, legally enacted, in which Indians would willingly give up their lands through treaties in exchange for protection from settler abuse and assistance toward becoming "civilized" with assimilation as the mechanism by which Indians as distinct peoples would vanish. Some tribal leaders agreed to treaties ceding land, though almost always under pressure, including open or veiled threats of exterminatory war. In many instances, however, tribal leaders refused to cede their lands and asserted the right of self-defense against settler invasion. When Indians resisted the US "gift" of civilization for land, policymakers sanctioned exterminatory war. Though historians have often characterized war as some unforeseen or unfortunate breakdown of policy, in fact policy was structured as a series of options, which ultimately sanctioned wars of extermination when the United States deemed

Indians to be illegitimately resisting its demands for land cessions. From this perspective, President Thomas Jefferson's 1807 statement to resisting Indians near Detroit that "if ever we are constrained to lift the hatchet against any tribe, we will never lay it down till that tribe is exterminated, or driven beyond the Mississippi,"[9] was not simply rhetoric, as scholars commonly treat such utterances. It articulated official policy. Approaches linking ideologies and discourses to a broader conception of policy and then tracing them to on-the-ground actions and outcomes would usefully integrate levels that have often been treated in isolation from one another.

Demography

As scholars come to a better understanding of the manifold and intersecting forces of destruction under settler colonialism, it is important to develop new demographic histories. Given current evidence and methodologies, it is doubtful that much progress can be made resolving debates about the pre-Columbian population of the Americas. Clearly it was substantially higher than scholars thought prior to Henry Dobyns's important intervention in the 1960s, but exactly how high may be unknowable (Thornton 2002: 68–70). What can be done, however, is to attempt to reconstruct population histories for particular nations or regions over key periods of post-1492 history. For example, as US settler colonialism operated against Indians between the Appalachians and the Mississippi River from the 1770s to the eve of removal in 1830, what was its impact on the Indian population of the region? Perhaps surprisingly, although secondary and primary sources supply abundant data (Tanner 1987; Morse 1822), the scholarly literature contains no aggregate figures for Indian populations over time for this or other regions. Relatedly, genocide studies' tendency to give narrative and analytical priority to demographic collapse, a tendency that risks replicating settler colonialism's ideological preoccupation with Indian disappearance,[10] has deflected attention from histories involving population stability, recovery, and growth even in the face of oppression and destruction. My own preliminary inquiry into Creek demography, for example, indicates that although the Creek population likely declined by 3,000 or more during 1813–1814 (a time in which an internal Creek civil war overlapped with a US invasion), the Creeks rapidly rebuilt their population in its aftermath; by 1830, the Creek population was almost certainly higher than it had been prior to the catastrophe of 1813–1814. Comparative studies of demographic trends among several tribes would help clarify the conditions under which Indians were able to maintain and rebuild their populations. The retention of a land base even in the face of some dispossession seems crucial, while repeated removals, near-total dispossession, and initial reservation confinement appear strongly correlated with population declines even in the absence of direct violence. This and similar hypotheses, however, remain to be systematically explored.

Survival

Finally, a post-Quincentennial approach to the question of genocide must attend to concerns that accounts of genocide and destruction risk depicting Indians, in William Bauer's words, as "a vanishing and culturally degraded people." Bauer's work, which focuses on wage labor as a crucial component of the economic strategies of California's Round Valley Indians, emphasizes "stories of Indian survival," though without ignoring the history of violence, enslavement, and dispossession that made survival necessary. Similarly, Brenda J. Child's study of Ojibwe women over several centuries and Alyssa Mt. Pleasant's of the rebuilding of a Haudenosaunee community after the devastation of the Revolutionary War provide rich accounts of the networks and cultural resources that undergirded what Gerald Vizenor calls *survivance*, a "moving beyond our basic survival in the face of overwhelming cultural genocide to create spaces of synthesis and renewal" (Bauer 2009; Child 2012; Mt. Pleasant 2007; Vizenor 1994: 53).[11]

Although narratives of survival have sometimes been seen as logically incompatible with those of genocide, there is no inherent reason why both cannot be combined (White 1998: 234; Anderson 2014: 11). After all, all genocides have survivors. For scholars with a commitment to document the forces of destruction operating against American Indian communities and expose the operations of settler colonialism, whether writing within a framework of genocide or not, there is a challenge to avoid the trap of reinscribing Indians solely as victims. It is essential, then, to analyze not only the devastation that threatened and afflicted Indian communities but also the concern for community survival at the heart of Indians' decision-making during moments of crisis; to document not only the brutal facts of destruction but the specifics of community rebuilding in its aftermath; to reveal not only the inhumane logic of empire but also the ways in which Indian people have recognized that inhumanity and practiced humane alternatives.

Notes

1 Activists and writers used the term *genocide* in the 1970s, but it did not gain traction until later. For early uses, see First International Indian Treaty Council at Standing Rock Indian Country (1979: 44) and Norton (1979).
2 As an indication of the absence of genocide in the writing of American Indian history, note that the authoritative *Blackwell Companion to American Indian History* (Deloria and Salisbury 2002) contains barely a mention of the subject.
3 On the emergence of settler colonialism, see Veracini (2013); see also Veracini (2010).
4 For an overview of definitions, see Straus (2001); the UN Convention is widely available online.
5 See, for example, Todorov (1984: 133), who after providing figures indicating a demographic collapse of 90 percent (70 million) for the Americas, concludes that "If the word genocide has ever been applied to a situation with some accuracy, this is here the case."
6 See also the estimate of a government official that 3,500 Creeks died from "bilious fevers" shortly after their arrival in Oklahoma as reported by Foreman (1930: 120).

7 For a recent work that demonstrates how this deficiency can be overcome, see Kelton (2015).
8 For evidence of Indians charging colonizers with an intent to kill them all, see Ostler (2015).
9 William Hull to Henry Dearborn, Nov. 1807, in *American State Papers: Indian Affairs*, 2 vols. (Washington, DC: Gales and Seaton, 1832), 1:745.
10 For an analysis of the construction of vanishing Indians as an ideological project, see O'Brien (2010).
11 For a concern about "damage-centered research," see also Tuck (2009).

References

Akers, Donna L. 2004. *Living in the Land of Death: The Choctaw Nation, 1830–1860*. East Lansing: Michigan State University Press.

Anderson, Gary Clayton. 2014. *Ethnic Cleansing: The Crime that Should Haunt America*. Norman: University of Oklahoma Press.

Barta, Tony. 1987. "Relations of genocide: Land and lives in the colonization of Australia". In Isidor Wallimann and Michael N. Dobkowski, eds. *Genocide in the Modern Age: Etiology and Case Studies of Mass Death*. Westport: Greenwood Press, pp. 237–251.

Bauer, Jr., William J. 2009. *We Were All Like Migrant Workers Here: Work, Community, and Memory on California's Round Valley Reservation, 1850–1941*. Chapel Hill: University of North Carolina Press.

Brooks, Lisa. 2008. *The Common Pot: The Recovery of Native Space in the Northeast*. Minneapolis: University of Minnesota Press.

Calloway, Colin G. 1995. *The American Revolution in Indian Country: Crisis and Diversity in Native American Communities*. Cambridge: Cambridge University Press.

Child, Brenda J. 2012. *Holding Our World Together: Ojibwe Women and the Survival of Community*. New York: Viking.

Churchill, Ward. 1997. *A Little Matter of Genocide: Holocaust and Denial in the Americas 1492 to the Present*. San Francisco: City Lights Books.

Deloria, Philip and Neal Salisbury, eds. 2002. *Blackwell Companion to American Indian History*. Malden, MA: Blackwell.

Drinnon, Richard. 1980. *Facing West: The Metaphysics of Indian-Hating and Empire Building*. Minneapolis: University of Minnesota Press.

Ewers, John C. 1997. "The influence of epidemics on the Indian populations and cultures of Texas". In John C. Ewers, ed. *Plains Indian History and Culture: Essays on Continuity and Change*. Norman: University of Oklahoma Press, pp. 82–102.

First International Indian Treaty Council at Standing Rock Indian Country. 1979. "Declaration of Continuing Independence". In United States Commission on Civil Rights, *Hearing Before the United States Commission on Civil Rights: National Indian Civil Rights Issues : Hearing held in Washington, D.C., March 19–20, 1979*. Washington, DC: G.P.O.

Foreman, Grant, ed. 1930. *A Traveler in Indian Territory: The Journal of Ethan Allen Hitchcock, Late Major-General in the United States Army*. Cedar Rapids: Torch Press.

Grenier, John. 2005. *The First Way of War: American War Making on the Frontier, 1607–1814*. Cambridge: Cambridge University Press.

Jacoby, Karl. 2008. "'The broad platform of extermination': Nature and violence in the nineteenth century North American borderlands". *Journal of Genocide Research*, 10: 249–267.

Jones, David S. 2004. *Rationalizing Epidemics: Meanings and Uses of American Indian Mortality since 1600*. Cambridge, MA: Harvard University Press.

Kelton, Paul. 2007. *Epidemics and Enslavement: Biological Catastrophe in the Native Southeast, 1492–1715*. Lincoln: University of Nebraska Press.

Kelton, Paul. 2015. *Cherokee Medicine, Colonial Germs: An Indigenous Nation's Fight against Smallpox, 1518–1824*. Norman: University of Oklahoma Press.

Kiernan, Ben. 2007. *Blood and Soil: A World History of Genocide and Extermination from Sparta to Darfur*. New Haven: Yale University Press.

Kubal, Timothy. 2008. *Cultural Movements and Collective Memory: Christopher Columbus and the Rewriting of the National Origin Myth*. New York: Palgrave Macmillan.

Lemkin, Raphael. 1944. *Axis Rule in Occupied Europe: Laws of Occupation, Analysis of Government, Proposals for Redress*. Washington, DC: Carnegie Endowment for International Peace.

Madley, Benjamin. 2008. "California's Yuki Indians: Defining genocide in Native American history". *Western Historical Quarterly*, 39: 303–332.

Morse, Jedidiah. 1822. *A Report to the Secretary of War of the United States on Indian Affairs*. New Haven: S. Converse.

Moses, A. Dirk. 2004. "Genocide and settler society in Australian history". In A. Dirk Moses, ed. *Genocide and Settler Society: Frontier Violence and Stolen Indigenous Children in Australian History*. New York: Berghahn, pp. 5–58.

Mt. Pleasant, Alyssa. 2007. "After the whirlwind: Maintaining a Haudenosaunee place at Buffalo Creek, 1780–1825". PhD diss., Cornell University.

Norton, Jack. 1979. *When Our Worlds Cried: Genocide in Northwestern California*. San Francisco: The Indian Historian Press.

O'Brien, Jean M. 2010. *Firsting and Lasting: Writing Indians Out of Existence in New England*. Minneapolis: University of Minnesota Press.

Ostler, Jeffrey. 2015. "'To extirpate the Indians': An Indigenous consciousness of genocide in the Ohio Valley and Lower Great Lakes, 1750s–1810". *William and Mary Quarterly*, 3d Ser., 72: 587–622.

Pearson, J. Diane. 2003. "Lewis Cass and the politics of disease: The Indian Vaccination Act of 1832". *Wicazo Sa Review*, 18: 9–35.

Perdue, Theda and Michael D. Green. 2007. *The Cherokee Nation and the Trail of Tears*. New York: Viking.

Rand, Jacki Thompson. 2008. *Kiowa Humanity and the Invasion of the State*. Lincoln: University of Nebraska Press.

Silver, Peter. 2008. *Our Savage Neighbors: How Indian War Transformed Early America*. New York: W.W. Norton.

Slotkin, Richard. 1973. *Regeneration Through Violence: The Mythology of the American Frontier, 1600–1860*. Middletown: Wesleyan University Press.

Smith-Rosenberg, Carroll. 2010. *This Violent Empire: The Birth of an American National Identity*. Chapel Hill: University of North Carolina Press.

Smithers, Gregory D. 2010. "Rethinking genocide in North America". In Donald Bloxham and A. Dirk Moses, eds. *The Oxford Handbook of Genocide Studies*. New York: Oxford University Press, pp. 322–341.

Stannard, David E. 1992. *American Holocaust: The Conquest of the New World*. New York: Oxford University Press.

Straus, Scott. 2001. "Contested meanings and conflicted imperatives: A conceptual analysis of genocide". *Journal of Genocide Research*, 3: 349–375.

Tanner, Helen Hornbeck, ed. 1987. *Atlas of Great Lakes Indian History*. Norman: University of Oklahoma Press.

Thornton, Russell. 1987. *American Indian Holocaust and Survival: A Population History Since 1492*. Norman: University of Oklahoma Press.

Thornton, Russell. 2002. "Health, disease, and demography". In Philip Deloria and Neal Salisbury, eds. *Blackwell Companion to American Indian History*. Malden, MA: Blackwell, pp. 68–70.

Todorov, Tzvetan. 1984. *The Conquest of America: The Question of the Other*, trans. Catherine Porter. New York: Harper & Row.

Tuck, Eve. 2009. "Suspending damage: A letter to communities". *Harvard Educational Review*, 79: 409–427.

Veracini, Lorenzo. 2010. *Settler Colonialism: A Theoretical Overview*. New York: Palgrave Macmillan.

Veracini, Lorenzo. 2013. "'Settler colonialism': Career of a concept". *The Journal of Imperial and Commonwealth History*, 41(2): 313–333.

Vizenor, Gerald. 1994. *Manifest Manners: Post-Indian Warriors of Survivance*. Middletown: Wesleyan University Press.

White, Richard. 1998. "Using the past: History and Native American studies". In Russell Thornton, ed. *Studying Native America: Problems and Prospects*. Madison: University of Wisconsin Press, pp. 217–243.

Wolfe, Patrick. 2006. "Settler colonialism and the elimination of the native". *Journal of Genocide Research*, 8: 387–409.

Revealing, reporting, and reflecting

Indigenous Studies research as praxis in reconciliation projects

Sheryl R. Lightfoot

Throughout the English-speaking settler colonial world, reconciliation has become almost a moral and political imperative. From official apologies to truth commissions to financial and cultural redress, reconciliation projects are charged with improving relationships between Indigenous peoples and the governments that have caused them harm, having spent hundreds of years dispossessing Indigenous peoples of their lands and resources and subjecting them to a variety of forced assimilation programs.

February 13, 2008, Canberra, Australia. In his first act as the incoming Labour government leader, Prime Minister Kevin Rudd rises to the podium and apologizes to the victims of Australia's "Stolen Generations," a term that refers to the multiple generations of Aboriginal children who had been forcibly taken from their homes and placed in residential schools or placed for adoption with white families. Prime Minister Rudd apologizes for the "profound grief, suffering and loss" that past laws and policies of the Australian government had inflicted, and he promises that "such injustices must never, never happen again."[1] The public response to this apology is tremendous. The parliament chamber is packed, and huge crowds have gathered outside Parliament House. Crowds have gathered in public spaces all over the country to watch the apology together on big-screen televisions. Many Aboriginal people wept while the apology was delivered.

December 19, 2009, Washington, DC. President Barack Obama signs a defense appropriations bill into law. Nestled within this bill is an apology "on behalf of *the people* of the United States to all native peoples for the many instances of violence, maltreatment, and neglect inflicted on Native peoples by citizens of the United States."[2] No public mention is made or ceremony held. Most Native Americans are completely unaware that this official apology has even occurred.

December 17, 2010, Waipapa-a-Iwi Marae, near Napier, North Island, Aotearoa-New Zealand. With the sun shining brightly on the *marae* of Ngāti Pāhauwera, and about 1,000 people in attendance, New Zealand's governmental dignitaries approach the *marae* grounds in the *powhiri*, the formal Māori ritual of encounter. The dignitaries are greeted first by the men and boys of the *iwi* followed by the women and girls. Elders are seated at the front, surrounded by proudly displayed photos of the ancestors. Following the *powhiri* and a few welcome remarks by *iwi* dignitaries, Chris Finlayson, Minister of Treaty of Waitangi

Negotiations, stands at the podium. Minister Finlayson reads a full account of historical wrongs committed by the Crown against this particular *iwi*. Specific breaches of the 1840 Treaty of Waitangi are individually acknowledged in intricate detail, a result of years of extensive research by the Waitangi Tribunal, which issued *WAI 199: The Mohaka River Report* in 1992, a report that details the historical Crown violations against this and other *iwi* in the area. Minister Finlayson ends these acknowledgments with an apology on behalf of the Crown. He says the Crown "is deeply sorry for its breaches of Te Tiriti o Waitangi/the Treaty of Waitangi and its principles which left Ngāti Pāhauwera with insufficient landholdings by 1883 ... and unreservedly apologizes for not having honoured its obligations."[3] An *iwi* leader reads the official acceptance of the Crown apology, in both Māori and English, and all parties proceed to formally sign the Deed of Settlement which includes cultural, financial and commercial redress, including return of Crown lands to the *iwi*, in a full settlement package valued at about NZ$70 million.

September 17, 2013, Vancouver, British Columbia. Hundreds of people stand on the shores of False Creek, in front of Science World, watching dozens of canoes of the All Nations Canoe Gathering make their way up from the Salish Sea to be met by the Musquean Tsleil-Waututh and Skwxwú7mesh, the Coast Salish peoples of this territory. Each canoe carries about 12 individuals who paddle together and sing songs to signify their good intentions as they approach. The Coast Salish peoples answer these songs with their own songs indicating their good intentions for the encounter. The All Nations Canoe Gathering is the first official ceremony associated with the West Coast National Event of Canada's Truth and Reconciliation Commission (TRC) which officially opened the next morning at the monstrous Pacific National Exhibition (PNE) building in East Vancouver. Following the lighting of the Sacred Fire, the Coast Salish nations, with drums and songs, lead various dignitaries into the PNE building the next morning, during the official opening ceremony of the West Coast National Event. Coast Salish elders are seated on stage among the commissioners and other leaders, both Indigenous and settler, as opening remarks are made, which begin a difficult three days of truth telling by survivors of Canada's Indian Residential Schools.

As I reflect upon these and numerous other reconciliation events that I have witnessed as an Indigenous scholar, I pause to ask: what is, can be, and should be the role of the researcher in reconciliation projects between Indigenous peoples and the settler states that now surround them? Activism, advocacy and politics are traditionally problematic vantage points for most academics, and yet, this wave of reconciliation is too big and too significant to avoid. Like all Indigenous individuals living in settler colonial states, my ancestors, my family and I have been personally impacted by the historical and ongoing wrongs committed by settler colonial governments. At the same time, I am a scholar, dedicating my career to research of the highest possible academic standard, including adhering to principles of ethical research that meets not only the standards of the profession but also does so by placing responsibility to Indigenous communities at its center.

Given all of these varied and potentially competing obligations, I am forced to ask, and answer, what are the possible and appropriate roles for researchers in such inherently political work as active and ongoing reconciliation projects? Can scholarship and political activism be effectively and ethically bridged through research? I answer in the spirit of McLeod and Thomson, who wrote that researching in an atmosphere of active reconciliation "seeks to capture dynamic processes ... (where) research methods are themselves historically situated techniques producing situated forms of knowledge" (McLeod and Thomson 2009: 7). Researchers can ethically and effectively engage in active reconciliation projects in three "R" ways: Revealing, Reporting and Reflecting – the "past–present–future" concept of researching social change.

Revealing

Researchers play an essential role in investigating historical wrongs in truth telling contexts. Work here can include memory work, oral and life histories, archival work and community-based historical documentary work. Aotearoa/New Zealand's Waitangi Tribunal and Canada's Truth and Reconciliation Commission provide powerful examples.

The Waitangi Tribunal of Aotearoa/New Zealand was established in 1975 as a permanent commission of inquiry under the Treaty of Waitangi Act. Its mandate is twofold: 1) to investigate claims brought by Māori against the Crown relating to either actions or omissions that comprise breaches of the 1840 Treaty of Waitangi, and 2) to make recommendations for settlement of those claims. In short, the Waitangi Tribunal is often, although not always, the important first step in the treaty settlements process, which is research heavy in both documentary and community-based environments.

First, a claim is submitted to the Waitangi Tribunal, and if the claim meets the requirements of the Act, it is registered and assigned a "WAI" number and all interested parties are notified that a claim has been opened so that the research process can begin. Each claim is heavily researched through archival records and tribunal hearings are held. Evidence and submissions are presented first by claimants, and then by the Crown and finally, by anyone else with an interest in the claim. This researching phase is comprehensive, examining all violations of the Treaty of Waitangi against that claimant group, and so the research process can take an extremely long period of time. It is not unheard of for a claim to take as long as 25 years to research. While this is an excruciatingly long period of time, several Māori leaders and academics have reported to me in interviews that this can also be a tremendously healing time for a tribe, or *iwi*. One Māori leader said:

In order to present the claim to the Tribunal, you have to open up the knowledge to that entire *iwi* because you have to piece together all the little bits of history that maybe five individuals know a lot, but they need all the little bits that tie it all together. So when you are going through an actual hearing process, you'll get Auntie so and so whose whole job in life has been to work at the *marae* in the kitchen, but she has a story or she has a photograph or she has a book and it has this really valuable piece of information, just a little piece, but it's really, really important. And so she gets to speak and everyone gets to hear her, and it just changes the way that people feel about each other, and it's a very inclusive process and everyone can participate.[4]

When the research and hearings are complete, the Waitangi Tribunal issues its report on the claims, including its recommendations for settlement of the claim. If both the claimants and the Crown agree to negotiate, they can begin negotiations. If the claimants and the Crown agree on the terms of settlement, then a deed of settlement is signed. The settlement can be implemented and legislation passed if necessary to give effect to the settlement.

The Truth and Reconciliation Commission of Canada came about as part of the 2006 court approved settlement agreement of a class action law suit brought about by groups of survivors of the Indian Residential School (IRS) program which operated in Canada for more than a century – the last school closing its doors in 1996. The mandate of the Truth and Reconciliation Commission was provided for in Schedule N of the Settlement Agreement. The multiple and far-reaching goals of the TRC appear in its mandate:

Produce and submit to the Parties to the Agreement a report including recommendations to the Government of Canada concerning the IRS system and experience including: the history, purpose, operation and supervision of the IRS system, the effect and consequences of IRS (including systemic harms, intergenerational consequences and the impact on human dignity) and the ongoing legacy of the residential schools.[5]

Similar to the Waitangi Tribunal, the first part of the TRC's mandate is to produce a comprehensive report to reveal what happened and what wrongs were committed, which necessarily means locating and compiling all existing school and government records on the Indian Residential Schools. The National Research Centre for Truth and Reconciliation, which opened in 2015, will be the permanent home of all documents, statements and all other materials collected by the Truth and Reconciliation Commission during its mandate. In addition to serving educators, researchers and the public by providing a central place for research on residential schools, it will also serve Indigenous families and communities by preserving the stories of survivors.

Reporting

Researchers can also play an important role in reporting reconciliation, documenting reconciliation events in real time and engaging various communities for their perspectives on the event or the process as it happens. This type of research can include qualitative longitudinal study and ethnography. It can also include active critique of the reconciliation event in process.

At the final Truth and Reconciliation Commission National Event in Edmonton, Alberta in 2014, elder Lorna Standingready was asked to document her perspective on the opening ceremony by Kaitlin Bardswich, a freelance human rights author intent on documenting the personal story of a single survivor of the residential school system and her experience at the TRC National Event. Bardswich asked Lorna Standingready for her thoughts and feelings immediately following the opening ceremony. Standingready said:

> I've been sitting here for a few hours now and I'm feeling really overwhelmed. This is the first Truth and Reconciliation event I've ever been to. ... The thing that stood out for me this morning ... you see, I went to three different residential schools in 10 years, in Saskatchewan and Manitoba ... what stood out for me was when they did an honour song for the survivors. I didn't feel worthy. It's probably because of what happened to me. And then ... I got to thinking ... yes, I should be honoured and everybody should be honoured because we're here and we survived, and we're strong. We are strong people.[6]

At the same time, academic researchers play an important role in helping give voice to critiques of reconciliation projects that may otherwise go unheard or unnoticed by non-Indigenous audiences. As Marc Flisfeder argues, the actual operation of the Canadian Truth and Reconciliation Commission (TRC) is flawed and has not met its multiple and far-reaching goals because in its actual operation, it "focuses too much on truth and not enough on reconciliation" (Flisfeder 2010: 1). As Jennifer Llewellyn notes, reconciliation remains undefined in the mandate or in the operation of the TRC. Neither "the meaning nor the means of reconciliation receive much attention in the mandate despite the hope reflected by its name that this body would be about truth and reconciliation" (Llewellyn 2008: 186). There are several predominant critiques of the Canadian TRC that academic researchers have highlighted.

First, because residential school history is only one cause of Aboriginal communities' problems, other issues must be also identified and addressed. While acknowledging that the TRC, as an alternative dispute mechanism, is preferable to a courtroom-based adjudicative model, Flisfeder also notes the limitations of the TRC's mandate as a weakness. Residential school history is only one problem of Canada's colonial history, and the isolated way the TRC is approaching it, rather than as part of a holistic approach to dealing with a comprehensive colonial history and present, is not only short-sighted but is not in keeping with Indigenous understandings and values that *"everything is related"* (Flisfeder 2010: 2). He claims that the public learns about the mistakes of the past without addressing the ongoing legacy of Indian Residential Schools (IRS). He writes, "these divergent historiographies create a barrier to reconciliation, and non-Aboriginal Canadians would benefit from a greater appreciation of how Aboriginal people and communities view the IRS system" (Flisfeder 2010: 15).

Second, Flisfeder notes that reconciliation must be promoted within the whole society, not only within Aboriginal communities. While truth telling must be largely done by Aboriginal survivors, reconciliation must involve "healing in Aboriginal communities and involve non-Aboriginal communities and the private sector" (Flisfeder 2010: 10). Paulette Regan, director of research for the Canadian TRC and author of *Unsettling the Settler Within: Indian Residential School, Truth Telling and Reconciliation in Canada*, agrees that the reconciliation project must not only involve non-Aboriginal people, but must be equally focused there. She writes:

> To my mind, Canadians are still on a misguided, obsessive, and mythical quest to assuage colonizer guilt by solving the Indian problem. In this way, we avoid looking too closely at ourselves and the collective responsibility we bear for the colonial status quo. The significant challenge that lies before us is to turn the mirror back upon ourselves and to answer the provocative question posed by historian Roger Epp regarding reconciliation in Canada: How do we solve the settler problem?
>
> (Regan 2010: 11)

Regan sees a compelling need to "(reframe) reconciliation as a decolonizing place of encounter between settlers and Indigenous peoples ... by making space for collective critical dialogue—a public remembering embedded in ethical testimonial, ceremonial and commemorative practices" (Regan 2010: 12).

Third, a successful process of reconciliation must involve remembering and change (Lederach 1997) meaning building trust and healing relationships (Snyder and Rice 2008: 45). In other words, reconciliation needs to not focus only on the past but also provide a path forward for the future (Lederach 1997: 46). Flisfeder's fear is that if the truth is told through the TRC and it goes without a response from non-Aboriginal society, "then this might actually further damage the relationships involved" (Flisfeder 2010: 16). Paulette Regan also weighs in on the central goal of reconciliation as change for the future. In a series of "self-reflective critical personal narratives" her book, *Unsettling the Settler Within*, shows how she grapples with the question of how settlers can participate in creating a better future of Indigenous-settler relations by "confront(ing) the Indian residential school narrative as part of a broader decolonization project without falling into the multiple traps that replicate colonizing attitudes and behaviours" (Regan 2010: 13). She calls on settler Canadians to see the TRC and the stories that come out of it as the motivation for changing their ways of interacting with Indigenous peoples, to stay with the discomfort and the dis-quiet in hopes of creating a better future relationship.

Reflecting

Researchers also play a critical role in researching and reflecting on the reconciliation process itself, often in comparative perspective with other reconciliation projects in other countries, in order to understand reconciliation itself, assess its relevance and understand how better to do reconciliation in the future. This role includes revisiting and analysis, and most importantly, learning lessons from other countries and contexts. Jens Meierhenrich notes that "improved conceptual awareness is essential for understanding the *causes* and *consequences* as well as the *courses* of reconciliation" in order to avoid "conceptual confusion" or worse, "conceptual misunderstandings that call into question research findings as well as practical achievements in pursuit of justice in times of transition" (Meierhenrich 2008: 197).

Analyzing the lessons from the South African Truth and Reconciliation experience, James Gibson notes that South Africa ranks high in both political pluralism and rule of law, characteristics that he posits are the "requisite supportive culture and institutions" for a successful truth and reconciliation process (Gibson 2006: 411). By contrast, Adrian Little's assessment of reconciliation in the Northern Ireland context takes a much more critical stance, noting that "reconciliation discourses are embroiled in the framing of Northern Irish politics such that they not only emanate from established senses of identity but also reinforce them" (Little 2012: 95). In the Australian context, Damien Short finds that "restrictive policy framing and lack of political will have ensured that official reconciliation is significantly out of step with indigenous aspirations" (Short 2003: 507). In an attempt to make analytical sense out of a dizzying array of reconciliation projects, Rafi Nets-Zehngut proposed a theoretical taxomony of the reconciliation process of multiple countries, providing an account of various types of activities and the effect of each activity on the process and the parties to reconciliation (Nets-Zehngut 2007). Meanwhile, Shiping Tang notes that much work remains in understanding reconciliation, writing:

> In light of the enormous complexity and challenges posed by reconciliation, much more needs to be done before we can confidently prescribe more extensive and concrete measures for reconciliation. So far, we have only a dim sense about many thorny questions.
>
> (Tang 2011: 744–745)

Research is therefore not only appropriate in active reconciliation projects; it is vital. As John Milloy states:

> everyone who has been involved in this sort of public history—litigation research in general and more particularly, those in Canada who have conducted research into war crimes, the Chinese head tax, Ukrainian prisoners of war, Japanese removal, Aboriginal claims, and various public health and environmental matters, realize that the larger relevant archive is not a site of quiet scholarly activity alone but one of contestation. Political dynamics often determine what is possible and how results will be achieved, indeed, even what those results might be.
>
> (Milloy 2013: 13)

Absent Indigenous studies researchers, reconciliation projects intended to improve relationships between Indigenous peoples and states could easily succumb to political dynamics that trend against the best interests of Indigenous peoples.

Indigenous studies research that engages the three "R"s: Revealing, Reporting and Reflecting upon reconciliation projects helps keep Indigenous voices, perspectives, needs and futures, central to the process.

Notes

1   Apology to Australia's Indigenous Peoples, accessed at www.australia.gov.au/about-australia/our-country/our-people/apology-to-australias-indigenous-peoples.
2   The Senate's "Native American Apology Resolution" S.J. Res. 14. The companion measure in the House of Representatives was H.J. Res. 46.
3   Ngāti Pāhauwera Deed of Settlement, p. 37.
4   Personal interview with author, February 2008, Wellington, Aotearoa/New Zealand.
5   Truth and Reconciliation Commission Mandate: s. 1(f).
6   See http://kaitlinbardswich.ca/2014/04/04/lorna-standingready-a-survivors-story/.

References

Flisfeder, Marc A. 2010. "A bridge to reconciliation: A critique of the Indian Residential School Truth Commission". *The International Indigenous Policy Journal*, 1(1): 1–28.

Gibson, James L. 2006. "The contributions of truth to reconciliation: Lessons from South Africa". *The Journal of Conflict Resolution*, 50(3): 409–432.

Lederach, John Paul. 1997. *Building Peace: Sustainable Reconciliation in Divided Societies*. Washington, DC: United States Institute of Peace.

Little, Adrian. 2012. "Disjunctured narratives: Rethinking reconciliation and conflict transformation". *International Political Science Review*, 33(1): 82–98.

Llewellyn, Jennifer. 2008. "Bridging the gap between truth and reconciliation: Restorative justice and the Indian Residential School Truth and Reconciliation Commission". In M. Brant-Castellano, L. Archibald, and M. DeGagne, eds. *From Truth to Reconciliation: Transforming the Legacy of Residential Schools*. Ottawa: Aboriginal Healing Foundation.

McLeod, Julie and Rachel Thomson, eds. 2009. *Researching Social Change*. London: SAGE Publications.

Meierhenrich, Jens. 2008. "Varieties of reconciliation". *Law & Social Inquiry*, 33(1): 195–231.

Milloy, John. 2013. "Doing public history in Canada's Truth and Reconciliation Commission". *The Public Historian*, 35(4): 10–19.

Nets-Zehngut, Rafi. 2007. "Analyzing the reconciliation process". *International Journal on World Peace*, 24(3): 53–81.

Regan, Paulette. 2010. *Unsettling the Settler Within: Indian Residential School, Truth Telling and Reconciliation in Canada*. Vancouver: UBC Press.

Short, Damien. 2003. "Reconciliation, assimilation, and the Indigenous peoples of Australia". *International Political Science Review*, 24(4): 405–513.

Snyder, Anna and B. Rice. 2008. "Reconciliation in the context of a settler society: Healing the legacy of colonialism in Canada". In M. Brant-Castellano, L. Archibald, and M. DeGagne, eds. *From Truth to Reconciliation: Transforming the Legacy of Residential Schools*. Ottawa: Aboriginal Healing Foundation.

Tang, Shiping. 2011. "Reconciliation and the remaking of anarchy". *World Politics*, 63(4): 711–749.

Index